GREAT SPANISH PLAYS IN ENGLISH TRANSLATION

Edited by
Angel Flores

With a Preface by
John Gassner

DOVER PUBLICATIONS, INC.
New York

Published in Canada by General Publishing Company, Ltd., 30 Lesmill Road, Don Mills, Toronto, Ontario.

Published in the United Kingdom by Constable and Company, Ltd., 3 The Lanchesters, 162–164 Fulham Palace Road, London W6 9ER.

This Dover edition, first published in 1991, is an unabridged and slightly corrected republication of the Bantam World Drama edition (1968) of *Spanish Drama*, originally published by Bantam Books, Inc., New York, in 1962.

Manufactured in the United States of America
Dover Publications, Inc., 31 East 2nd Street, Mineola, N.Y. 11501

Library of Congress Cataloging-in-Publication Data

Spanish drama.
    Great Spanish plays in English translation / edited by Angel Flores ; with a preface by John Gassner.
        p.   cm.
    Reprint. Originally published: Spanish drama. New York : Bantam Books, 1962.
    Includes bibliographical references.
    ISBN 0-486-26898-5 (pbk.)
    1. Spanish drama—Translations into English.   I. Flores, Angel, 1900–   .   II. Title.
PQ6267.E6S64   1991   91-22776
862'.008—dc20   CIP

CONTENTS

PREFACE TO THE
BANTAM WORLD DRAMA EDITION

It is a pleasure to welcome the present volume of Spanish plays, edited by the distinguished scholar-critic Angel Flores, into the Bantam Classics Library of World Drama. The new translations and selections, supplemented with informative introductory material, should help the unspecialized reader to fill a gap in his knowledge of the world's dramatic literature.

Writing shortly before the end of World War I, Barrett Clark noted that "the drama of Spain, early and modern, has in English-speaking countries been sadly neglected." He added that it is a regrettable fact that "one of the most gorgeous and passionate outbursts of national dramatic genius has received but scant attention from English readers," and that "to the majority of English and Americans, Lope de Vega, Tirso de Molina, and Calderón—to mention only the greatest of dozens of dramatists of the time—are a closed book." Two or three Lope de Vega pieces and about fifteen Calderón plays were available; included among the latter were half a dozen free versions of Calderón provided in 1853 by Edward FitzGerald, the translator-adaptor of the *Rubáiyát of Omar Khayyám*. The modern drama in Spain was better represented in English translations, but still inadequately and unattractively.

After 1918, the representation of Spanish drama was only slightly enlarged but mostly with the work of playwrights of secondary significance who were thought to have some popular appeal for American playgoers. Even the literary reputation of Federico García Lorca could not assure his plays a Broadway production, and efforts to give a number of his plays amateur or semiprofessional productions were generally abortive. (It is worth noting, by the way, that the Theatre Guild started its long career in 1919 with a production of Benavente's brilliant comedy *The Bonds of Interest* and nearly died in its infancy with that production.) The need for making the Spanish drama known in the English-speaking world remains as great as before.

1

The actual and potential importance of the Spanish drama in the world's theater can hardly be exaggerated. Lope de Vega and Calderón became world figures inevitably when the Spanish language spread to the Western Hemisphere; and in the present century, the names of Jacinto Benavente and Federico García Lorca won prominence well beyond the Spanish-speaking world. The world-wide diffusion of one dramatic theme, that of Don Juan, first introduced in the seventeenth-century by Tirso de Molina, is of course known even to those who know hardly anything else about the Spanish drama. Among many works, we are indebted to this playwright for Molière's *Don Juan, ou Le Festin de Pierre*, a play that has been called "more daring than *Tartuffe* itself" by one of the playwright's chief critics (Ramon Fernandez), Mozart's imperishable *Don Giovanni*, Rostand's imaginative *Last Night of Don Juan*, and the memorable Don Juan dream interlude of Shaw's *Man and Superman*.

The impact of Calderón's moral-philosophical allegories (his *autos sacramentales*) and other religious plays was bound to be considerable in Catholic countries. Thus, a debt to Calderón was contracted by the gifted Austrian poet-playwright Hugo von Hofmannsthal, especially with his adaptation in 1922 of *El gran teatro del mundo* (*The Great Theatre of the World*), intended for the Salzburg Festival, under the title of *Das Salzburger grosse Welttheater*, which became a noteworthy Max Reinhardt production. And Austria's most distinguished nineteenth-century playwright, Franz Grillparzer (1791-1872), in 1834 based his famous dream play *Der Traum ein Leben* (*The Dream, A Life*) on Calderón's *La vida es sueño*, which Professor Flores has included in the present volume. Grillparzer was anticipated in his enthusiasm for the Spanish playwright by important German romantic writers such as Ludwig Tieck, Clemens Brentano, and the famous critic August Wilhelm Schlegel, who translated a number of Calderón's plays. The great Goethe himself was under obligation to him. Among foreign dramatists only Shakespeare, in fact, had a greater impact on the German-speaking stage than Calderón.

In general, moreover, the contagion of the Spanish theater's theme of honor and punctilio, including the drama of *punto de honor* or "point of honor"—that is, of offended dignity as a motive for dramatic action—was widespread. It reached England in the seventeenth century in the genre of "heroic plays" written by the young John Dryden and other playwrights of the Restoration period. This species of overblown tragedy or near-tragedy was severely taxed for its faults and John Dryden repented of its extravagances later in his career. But what is often forgotten is that the Spanish influence was helpful in counteracting the neoclassic tendency, especially strong in France, to ignore the natural activeness of dramatic art, almost extinguishing overt action and plot in Racine's *Bérénice*, for example. As one theater historian (Donald Clark Stuart) noted, "Because medieval technique had survived to a greater extent in Spain, more of the action was on the stage. There were many incidents which led to extreme complications within the play itself." Seventeenth-century French drama itself was enlivened by Spanish play-writing until the neoclassic rule of the "unities" came to be imposed on the drama strictly enough to discourage plot complications, a restriction that fortunately affected comedy less seriously than it did tragedy. One may well wonder how much less dramatic Corneille's early masterpiece *The Cid* would have been without the influence of Spain on this first of the French master-playwrights. Corneille indeed drew some of his comedies directly from the Spanish of Alarcón and Lope de Vega, and he actually derived *Le Cid*, in part, from the work of another Spanish dramatist, Guillén de Castro.

It may be said that Lope de Vega spoke for most of his fellow playwrights when he wrote the disarming confession, in his "New Art of Writing Comedies in This Time," published in 1609, that no sooner was he tempted to imitate those who followed academic neoclassical principles than the practical showman in him thought better of it. No sooner did he observe the success of other writers' "bizarre" plays, which the multitude gathered to see and women patronized, than he was compelled to alter his course.

Lope's attitude reminds us of Shakespeare's blithe disregard of the restraints with which Renaissance scholars paradoxically proposed to curb the drama in an age of high-spirited adventure. The two great theaters of the Renaissance and the baroque period are indeed those of England and Spain, where the curb of the unities of time, place, and action was adopted only by scholarly playwrights, and at that only half-heartedly; where events were allowed to transpire visibly on the stage instead of being merely narrated; and where a vigorous spirit or, if need be, a world of turbulence and violence escaped suppression by neoclassical "decorum" and logic. Significantly, the popular theaters of both nations remained close to the medieval stage of multiple, simultaneously visible settings and favored the "platform style" of play production. That is, the stage consisted chiefly of a platform extending into the audience, instead of the architectural and painted settings behind a proscenium arch that constituted the so-called picture-frame stage of the courtly theaters of the Renaissance. Just as England had its famous open-air popular theaters such as The Globe occupied by Shakespeare's company, so Spain during approximately the same period had its unroofed *corrales* in the cities of Seville, Valencia, and Madrid; and even after a playhouse acquired a roof after 1580 it retained the traditional features of an open-air theater. The Spanish stage appeared to be as reluctant as the English stage to relinquish its popular characteristics, the chief of which was the free-flowing action of the plays on a platform.

Lope de Vega was indeed a còntemporary of Shakespeare, having been born in 1562, two years before the English playwright (but outliving him by nearly two decades), and many of Lope's contemporaries were also contemporaries of Shakespeare and Ben Jonson. Calderón, the younger man, who was born in 1600, kept the baroque theater of Spain going some thirty years after the Puritans closed the theaters in England, when nothing of significance was being written any longer by British playwrights. It may be said, then, that although neither Lope de Vega nor Calderón can be considered the equal of Shakespeare (and who can?), the baroque theater actually enjoyed a longer span of vitality in Spain than in England.

Like the English-speaking theater, the Spanish can boast of *two* periods of major importance, a Renaissance-baroque age and a modern one, the latter starting during the last decades of the nineteenth century. Without exactly producing playwrights of the stature of Shaw, O'Neill, and O'Casey, the Spanish stage began to acquire world repute again with the production of José Echegaray's The Great Galeoto (*El Gran Galeoto*), in the year 1881. The Spanish theater's modern contribution has been a varied one covering virtually the entire range of modern drama, including psychological and social drama, the thesis play and the Ibsenite "play of ideas," cosmopolitan plays, and regional ones. But without ceasing to follow the contours of the modern drama, the best plays that have come to our attention possess traits uniquely

Spanish. These have appeared conspicuously in regional pieces or dramas of local color, and in poetic drama, whether comic or tragic; especially in the work of Federico García Lorca, who became a major figure in the theater despite his early death in 1936.

Largely through the efforts of this inspired poet, who belonged just about equally to native traditional and cosmopolitan *avant-garde* art, Spain was able to make a special contribution in that department of dramatic art in which modernism has so far proved least effective. I refer, of course, to poetic drama (and its important division, high tragedy), which it may be possible to write with the common man as protagonist but which it is surely impossible to write without poetry. Lorca could supply the poetry that transfigures common people and situations and makes them *uncommon* enough for tragedy. To this rare enterprise, moreover, as well as to the related one of creating comedy of a high order of imaginativeness, Spain itself made a contribution. Spain gave the poet's talent a matrix of life that still possessed the dignity of a people living close to the soil and drawing spiritual nourishment from it. One can almost hear Synge speaking prophetically about Lorca's future work as well as his own plays in the 1907 Preface to *The Playboy of the Western World*: "In countries where the imagination of the people, and the language they use, is rich and living, it is possible for a writer to be rich and copious in his words, and at the same time to give the reality, which is the root of poetry, in a comprehensive and natural form." And an additional contribution not to be slighted was made by the Spanish theater itself with its long-cherished popular traditionalism, which secured for Lorca's dramatic art a characteristic buoyancy and vivid formalism. Lorca's work came to exemplify in Europe a living, folk-rooted *theatricalism* which is the very antithesis of humdrum realism. There may indeed be considerable accuracy in the late Barrett Clark's generalization: "It is a curious fact that Spain is the only country whose drama is fundamentally at its best when it follows the best traditions of its Golden Age."

An approximation of greatness *twice* within four centuries (or, for that matter, within any span of time) has been attained by few nations; and what is particularly noteworthy in this instance is the consistency of the pattern. It may be traced in both the first great period of the Spanish stage and the second, which one hopes did not come to an end with Lorca's untimely death in 1936 during the costly Spanish Civil War. It may be described as a pattern of vivacity and passionateness marked by moments of stabbing immediacy. It is characterized by an intense awareness of self, by a strong sense of what it means to be a human being individually and, at the same time, collectively as part of a family and a people. It is a curious fact indeed that so individualistic a people as the Spaniards should have excelled equally with expressions of extreme individuality and dramas of collective will, producing at about the same time in Spain the dashing "cape-and-sword" adventure plays of Lope de Vega and "group" plays in which injustice is resisted by the common people or by some representative of the people. Lope's celebrated *Fuente Ovejuna* (*The Sheep Well*), in which the peasants of a district turn upon their tyrannical overlord, and Calderón's spirited drama *El alcalde de Zalamea* (*The Mayor of Zalamea*) would be a credit to any "people's theater" or theater of social protest. *Fuente Ovejuna* was indeed staged in Soviet Russia during the nineteen-thirties as a "proletarian" drama.

Still, there is no paradox in the presence of both extreme individualism and strong communal feeling in the Spanish drama. The individual, functioning independently, has a zealous regard for his place in society and its traditions or code, while the communal spirit is manifested through individuals who have a high sense of personal honor, as in the case of Lope's peasants and Calderón's *alcalde*. A theater that could assert both the individual through a community of values and the community through the individuality of its characters could attain vitality of a high order when conditions for the theater were favorable. It also managed to maintain that vitality on a popular level of folk theater even when conditions were unfavorable, as was largely the case during the long interval between the "Golden Age" and the modern period. In introducing us to this theater, Professor Flores has put us under a considerable obligation.

JOHN GASSNER

INTRODUCTION

The earliest manifestations of the theater in Spain are to be found in the medieval church ceremonies and festivities, centering especially on the Nativity, the Epiphany, Easter, and patron saints. The oldest play rescued from oblivion, the *Auto de los Reyes Magos,* belongs to the late twelfth century. In a series of monologues the Magi decide to visit the Messiah whose birth has been announced by a bright star. First they go to Herod who upon hearing of the birth of a new king, "master of the entire World," seems disturbed and summons his rabbis to size up the situation. Unfortunately the 147 verses extant stop at this point, but it may be assumed that the Magi, bearing gifts, went to see the newborn Child. Another specimen of this early theater is the *Misterio de Elche* but there must have been hundreds of such plays—moralities and scenes from the life of Jesus and the saints—all calculated to indoctrinate a public unable to read. Through this medium were depicted vividly the rewards to be derived from virtuous living and the punishments awaiting sinners.

Side by side with this religious drama, and at times merging with it, there developed a popular theater consisting of farces and skits for the entertainment of the populace. These short plays were performed in marketplaces and public squares by *juglares* (juggler-troubadours) who passed their hats around at the end of their performance. Naturally their main concern was to please their audience. To do so they intermingled popular songs with satiric squibs, squeezing as much fun as possible from topical events and, in addition, bringing in all those tricks still in vogue in our circuses and county fairs: sword-swallowing, eating fire or glass, card tricks, and sundry vaudeville acts.

However humble, these beginnings did exert a telling influence upon the development of the Spanish stage. Whereas most European countries, especially France during and after the Renaissance, guided themselves by Horace's *Epistola ad Pisones* and by a misunderstood Aristotle—on the

7

nature of tragedy, the three unities, etc.—neither Spain nor
England took all this seriously, following instead a "romantic" course. No doubt there existed scholars and
rhetoricians who insisted on acclimatizing the Greek tragedy
to Spain but they utterly failed to convince the public. The
popular current was so overwhelming that it entered even
into the works of serious-minded writers: for instance, Juan
de Timoneda (d. 1583), the translator of Plautus, is as
truculently popular in his *Auto de la oveja perdida* (Auto
of the Lost Sheep) as Juan de la Cueva (1550-1610), the
imitator of Greeks and Romans in his *Tragedy of Ajax*
and *Tragedy of the Death of Virginia*.

However, the author most thoroughly saturated with the
folk spirit was the actor and stage director Lope de Rueda
(*ca.* 1510-1565), who wrote one-act farces. These *pasos*, as
he called them, were so deeply set in the Spanish grain,
communicated so readily and attained so huge a success,
that Lope de Rueda has become known as the real founder
of the Spanish theater. In any event, he started a type of
entertainment which has persisted to our own day: the *género
chico* or "lesser genre." Cervantes, Lope de Vega, and in
fact most of the major figures of the Golden Age admired
him and considered him their master.

The broadening of the stage to national theater propor-
tions, its conversion into a social institution inextricably
bound with Spain's ethos and epos, must be assigned to
Lope de Vega (1562-1635). In one of his programmatic
poems he declared:

> And when I have to write a comedy
> I lock up the precepts under six keys
> And I write in the manner of the art invented
> By those who sought popular applause.

In other words, Lope de Vega rejected the Aristotelian as well
as all other precepts, since his only concern was public approval. He draws from the history, lore, and traditions of
Spain for inspiration, or allows his imagination to tangle
up all kinds of far-fetched but pleasing plots and subplots
bursting with action. The unities as well as various stage
conventions go overboard, the tragic is mixed with the comic,
the plebeian with the aristocratic, the lyrical with the
epical. All he wants is an exciting play. Adverse critics
point out that Lope's theater, in fact the Spanish theater

of the Golden Age, failed to produce convincing characters. It is a theater without Hamlets or King Lears. And to a large extent they are right: it is *not* a theater of introspection or psychological soundings. Whatever psychology is to be found in it derives from the action itself—by means of a series of flashes, intuitions, and dynamic projections. Idiosyncrasies, conventions autochthonous to the Spanish ethos serve as barriers to a clear understanding of this theater: not so much the theological problems, so in evidence in the plays of Tirso de Molina and Calderón de la Barca (predestination vs. free will, etc.), but rather the social taboos and essentially Spanish conventions, such as the deeply rooted *punto de honor*, which is an extremely exaggerated conception of man's honor. Spanish pride erected a magnificent myth around the sanctity of woman's virginity, and any transgression of the rigid code (deflowering a virgin, or cuckoldry) required death or at least the shedding of blood. What in the French theater provided humor, in the Spanish provided tragedy.

Stylistically, the Spanish theater developed along free lines, mixing verse and prose. The verse parts followed no rigid pattern of rhyme or meter but were couched in a prosodic mixture, and often songs and sonnets irrelevant to the plot were inserted. Furthermore, Gongorism—the sophisticated style whose loftiest fruition is found in the lyrics of Luis de Góngora—penetrated into the craftsmanship of the playwrights so that the comedies had to bear the overdecorated weight of the Baroque, as may be readily seen in Calderón's *Life Is a Dream*.

After Calderón's death in 1681 the theater in Spain entered a period of decay, suffering from excessive Baroquism, and thereafter from servile imitation of French models. The eighteenth century was totally barren except for the *sainetes* of Ramón de la Cruz (1731-1794), one-act comedies which satirize obsolete social usages and the pretentiousness of the rising bourgeoisie, and for Leandro Fernández de Moratín (1760-1828), who emerged at the end of the century and towered above all his contemporaries. Although a staunch disciple and gifted translator of Molière, and a devoted Francophile who brought the neoclassic to the Spanish stage, Moratín may be considered a precursor of Romanticism. In the plays of this translator of *Hamlet*, the dialogue is sparkling, fluent, and natural, and often the spectator is moved by the spontaneity and humor of the situations. All these

features led the theater historian Angel Valbuena to claim
Moratín as the eighteenth-century writer most deserving
of survival.

The Romantic movement left but little worth mentioning.
A few melodramas are still remembered just because they
found their way into opera librettos: *El Trovador* (1836),
by García Gutiérrez (1813-1884), served Verdi for his
Il Trovatore (1853); *Don Alvaro* (1835), by the Duque de
Rivas (1791-1861), for his *La Forza del Destino* (1862).
But all in all it was a discursive, often hysterical theater of
hot passions, violence, sudden death, and unbearably unreal and pompous afflatus. One piece has survived through
popular acclamation: *Don Juan Tenorio* (1844), by José
Zorrilla (1817-1893). In it once more Don Juan—wicked,
petulant, bold—meets his punishment and redemption. Essentially an allegory, somewhat reminiscent of the rites of
spring, it has become a part of the Spanish tradition:
throughout Spain and Spanish America the play is performed on November 2, the day people visit the cemeteries,
the death background lending poignancy to Don Juan's
overwhelming *élan vital*. Chambermaids, messenger boys,
bootblacks, lottery ticket vendors, all recite copiously the
facile poetry of this, alas, hopelessly corny drama.

As Antoine's Parisian *Théâtre Libre*, with its emphasis
on Naturalism and psycho-biological and social problems
(Ibsen, Strindberg, the early Hauptmann) reached Spain,
the "new spirit" merged with the Romantic hangover. The
plays of the last period of José Echegaray (1832-1916),
obtusely classified as Naturalistic, reek of Romanticism. Even
The Son of Don Juan (1892), dealing with veneral diseases
and modeled after Ibsen's *Ghosts*, is essentially Romantic.
In order to illustrate the Romantic trend in Spain, one is
therefore justified in recurring to such a late play as *El
gran galeoto,* written in 1881. Despite its melodramatic
frenzy and rhetoric, *El gran galeoto* conveys its message
with tremendous force. These strands of a belated Romanticism are discernible even in the first proletarian play of
Spain: *Juan José* (1895), by Joaquín Dicenta (1863-1917).

The "catastrophe," i.e., Spain's defeat by the United States
in 1898, had a sobering effect. The writers endeavored to
discover the cause of Spain's decadence and their realistic
scrutiny filtered through to the stage. Although the so-called
Generation of 1898, which comprised men like Azorín,

Baroja, and Unamuno, were not essentially playwrights, their debates and essays did influence the veteran Benito Pérez Galdós (1863-1920) and younger men such as Jacinto Benavente (1866-1954) and Manuel Linares Rivas (1867-1938).

Pérez Galdós poured into his plays many of the problems which had already been divulged in his enormous series of novels: the evils of abulia, religious fanaticism, beggary, a parasitic military caste, militant clericalism. Linares Rivas incisively commented on Spanish isolationism, on sexual inequities, on the need to institute divorce. Benavente's tone was more glib and sophisticated. His humorous commentary on man's plight was not circumscribed by the immediate Spanish reality. For instance, his allegorical *Bonds of Interest* (1907) scored repeated successes in the theatrical centers of Europe and the Western Hemisphere because his critique of the philistine mentality and the picaresque connivings of his famous hero-ruffian seem as logical to the theatergoers of Copenhagen as to those of Montevideo. For many decades Benavente held full sway over the Spanish stage, and strangely enough the iconoclast was rewarded with a seat in the solemn Spanish Royal Academy, and with a Nobel Prize.

The most remarkable challenge to his monopoly of the theater—he was the author of some 150 plays by the time of his death at the age of eighty-eight—came from a group of young men during the Republic. In the early 1930's the poet Federico García Lorca (1898-1936) organized a company, La Barraca, which, sponsored by the Ministry of Education, traveled from town to town presenting classical and modern plays. It was a most exciting experience for the young man who loved so dearly his people and their folklore. The stimulus led him to write poetical comedies and tragedies, thus opening up new horizons, not only to the Spanish but to the world theater. His *Blood Wedding* (1933) will remain among Spain's loftiest contributions to world literature. After the tragic Civil War, which wrought so much havoc and cut short García Lorca's career, darkness reigned for a decade. Only in recent years has the ferment begun again: within Spain, Antonio Buero Vallejo (b. 1916) and Alfonso Sastre (b. 1926); in exile, Alejandro Casona (b. 1903) and Max Aub (b. 1903). Equally gratifying is the growing interest in the stage shown by gifted writers in Mexico, the

Argentine Republic, and Chile; in fact, Buenos Aires and Mexico City often surpass Madrid in theatrical activity— but to follow these developments further will result, no doubt, in another volume! ...

ANGEL FLORES

THE OLIVES
(El paso de las olivas)

by Lope de Rueda

TRANSLATED BY
Angel Flores

❦

CHARACTERS

TORUBIO, *an old man* · AGUEDA DE TORUEGANO, *his wife*

MENCIGUELA, *his daughter* · ALOJA, *a neighbor*

Lope de Rueda
(*ca.* 1510-1565)

We have scanty information about Lope de Rueda, a Sevillian goldsmith who suddenly took to the stage, and won for himself a reputation as the best impersonator of Negro women, ruffians, and village idiots. Before long he began to direct the plays in the repertory of his strolling company, and then to write one-act farces steeped in popular lore, and more sophisticated full-length comedies. By 1554 he had become so famous that the Count of Benavente entrusted him with the management of the festivities in honor of Philip II, on his way to England. Lope de Rueda's plays were saved for posterity by his literary friend Juan de Timoneda, who collected and published them posthumously. Among these are several comedies (the loveliest, *Eufemia*, resembles Shakespeare's *Cymbeline*), dramatic pastorals, religious pageants, and, above all, some forty one-acters or *pasos* which show him at his best. In these popular skits Lope de Rueda followed neither the allegories of the miracles nor the bombast of the erudite Italian plays, but exploited the popular vein thoroughly. He thus reproduced, though giving to them a genuinely Spanish flavor, the stock characters of the *commedia dell'arte* (the braggart, the pimp, the fool, the pedant), As the characters wag their earthy, slangy tongues, humor flows freely—to the delight of the populace. This truculence is conspicuous in *The Olives*, which derives no doubt from folklore and reappears in different guise and variants in several literatures. With these *pasos* Lope de Rueda created Spain's popular realistic theater, which has persisted through the *entremeses* (interludes) of Cervantes and the playwrights of the Golden Age, and the *sainetes* (comedy of manners) of the eighteenth century, to the *género chico* (lesser genre) of today.

BEST EDITION: J. Moreno Villa (ed.), *Teatro de Lope de Rueda*. Madrid, 1924.

ABOUT: E. Cotarelo Mori, *Lope de Rueda y el teatro español.* Madrid, 1898. E. Salazar, *Lope de Rueda y su teatro.* Santiago de Cuba, 1911.

TORUBIO. Good Lord, the storm certainly has razed the fields! All the way to the mountain clearing yonder! I remember how the bottom simply dropped out of the sky and clouds came crashing down.

Well now, I wonder what that wife of mine has up her sleeve for supper—a pox on her! (*calling*) Agueda, Menciguela, Agueda de Toruegano! (*He bangs furiously at the door.*)

(*Enter* MENCIGUELA.)

MENCIGUELA. Mercy, father! Do you *always* have to smash doors?

TORUBIO. There's a sharp tongue for you! Where's your mother, Miss Chatterbox?

MENCIGUELA. She's next door, helping out with the sewing.

TORUBIO. Blast her sewing and yours! Go call her!

(*Enter* AGUEDA.)

AGUEDA. Well, well! Just look at our lord and master, in one of his nasty moods. What a wretched little bundle of fagots he's loaded on his back!

TORUBIO. Wretched, is it, my fine lady? Why, it took two of us—me and your godson together—to lift it from the ground!

AGUEDA. Hmm—well, maybe! Oh, my, you're soaking wet!

TORUBIO. Drenched to the bone! But for God's sake, bring me something to eat!

AGUEDA. What the devil do you expect? There's not a thing in the house.

MENCIGUELA. How wet this wood is, father!

TORUBIO. Of course it is. But you know your mother; she'll say it's only dew!

AGUEDA. Run, child, go cook your father a couple of eggs, and make his bed.　　(*Exit* MENCIGUELA.)

AGUEDA. I suppose you forgot all about the olive-shoot I asked you to plant?

TORUBIO. If not for that, I'd be home before this.

AGUEDA. You don't say! And where did you plant it?

15

Torubio. Close to the new-bearing figtree; you remember, where I kissed you long, long ago . . .

(*Enter* Menciguela.)

Menciguela. Come, father, everything's ready!

Agueda. Know what I was thinking? In six or seven years we'll have seven or eight bushels of olives, and if we plant a shoot here and a shoot there every now and then we'll have a wonderful grove in another twenty-five years.

Torubio. Right you are, Agueda, a fine-looking grove!

Agueda. And you know what? I'll gather the olives, you'll cart them off on your little donkey, and Menciguela will sell them in the market. (*turning to* Menciguela) But listen to me, Menciguela, don't you dare sell them for less than two Castilian reals a half peck!

Torubio. Good gracious, woman! What are you talking about? Two Castilian reals? Why, such a price would give us nightmares. Besides, the market-inspector would never allow it! Fourteen, or at most fifteen dineros a half peck is quite enough to ask.

Agueda. Bosh, Torubio! You're forgetting that our olives are the finest Cordovans in Spain!

Torubio. Even if they are from Cordova, my price is just right.

Agueda. Bother your prices! Menciguela, don't you sell our olives for less than two Castilian reals a half peck!

Torubio. What do you mean, "Two Castilian reals"? Come here, Menciguela, how much are you going to ask?

Menciguela. Whatever you say, father.

Torubio. Fourteen or fifteen dineros.

Menciguela. So be it, father.

Agueda. What do you mean, "So be it, father"? Come here, Menciguela, how much are you going to ask?

Menciguela. Whatever you say, mother.

Agueda. Two Castilian reals.

Menciguela. Two Castilian reals.

Torubio. What do you mean, "Two Castilian reals"? Let me tell you that if you disobey my orders, you'll surely get two hundred lashes from me. How much are you going to ask, Menciguela?

Menciguela. Whatever you say, father.

Torubio. Fourteen or fifteen dineros.

Menciguela. So be it, father.

Agueda. What do you mean, "So be it, father"? (*striking*

MENCIGUELA) Here, take this "so-be-it" and that "so-be-it," and this, and that—that will teach you!

TORUBIO. Leave the child alone!

MENCIGUELA. Ouch, mamma, stop! Father, she's killing me! . . . Help! Help! . . .

(*Enter* ALOJA.)

ALOJA. What's wrong, neighbors? Why are you beating your daughter?

AGUEDA. Oh, good sir, this awful man is giving things away. He has made up his mind to send his family to the poorhouse. Imagine, olives as big as walnuts!

TORUBIO. I swear by the bones of my ancestors that they're no bigger than pistachio nuts!

AGUEDA. They certainly are!

TORUBIO. They are not!

ALOJA. Very well, my dear lady, please do me the favor of going inside and I'll try to settle the matter.

AGUEDA. You mean muddle it up worse!

(*Exit* AGUEDA.)

ALOJA. Now, dear neighbor, how about the olives? Show them to me and I'll buy them all—up to thirty bushels worth.

TORUBIO. But you don't understand at all! You see, my friend, the olives are not here at home, they're there, out in the fields.

ALOJA. If that's the case, you'll harvest them and I'll give you a fair price for the whole lot of them.

MENCIGUELA. Mother says she must get two Castilian reals a half peck.

ALOJA. My, my, but that's high!

TORUBIO. See what I mean?

MENCIGUELA. My father wants fifteen dineros a half peck.

ALOJA. Show us a sample.

TORUBIO. In God's name, señor, you don't seem to understand! Today I planted the shoot of an olive-tree and my wife claims that in six or seven years she'll gather seven or eight bushels. Then I'll take them to market and our daughter will sell them. She wants her to ask for two Castilian reals per half peck. But I object. My wife insists; so what with one word leading to the next, it turned into a squabble.

ALOJA. A squabble, bah! The trees aren't even planted and you fools beat this poor child for quoting the wrong price!

MENCIGUELA. What shall I do, señor?

TORUBIO. Don't cry, darling! She's pure gold, sir. Run and set the table, and as soon as I make the first sale I'll see to it that you get the prettiest skirt in town.

ALOJA. And you, neighbor, go in and make peace with your wife.

TORUBIO. Goodbye, señor.

(*Exeunt* TORUBIO *and* MENCIGUELA.)

ALOJA. O Lord, what strange things one has to witness in life! The trees haven't even been planted but everyone's up in arms about the olives! A good reason for me to put an end to my mission!

THE VIGILANT SENTINEL
(*La guarda cuidadosa*)

By Miguel de Cervantes

TRANSLATED BY
Angel Flores and Joseph Liss

༄

CHARACTERS

A Soldier, *the vigilant sentinel*
A Wicked Sacristan (*Lorenzo Pasillas*)
A Young Man (*Andres, beggar of alms for Santa Lucia*)
Second Young Man (*Manuel, a peddler of lady's notions*)
A Shoemaker (*Juan Juncos*)

Cristina de Parrazes, *kitchen maid*
The Master *of the house where Cristina works*
The Mistress *of the house where Cristina works*
Second Sacristan (*Grayales*)
Musicians

Scene: *A Street in Madrid.* Time: *May,* 1611.

Miguel de Cervantes

(1547-1616)

Not all readers realize that the author of *Don Quixote*, Spain's most substantial contribution to prose fiction, contributed also to the development of the theater. In 1584 he wrote a historical tragedy of tremendous dramatic intensity, *Numantia*, which has been invariably performed during Spain's various crises. Dealing as it does with the Numantians' heroic defense of their besieged city, the play acquired topicality and poignant meaning when performed in 1808 while the city of Zaragoza was besieged by French invaders, as well as during the Civil War when Nazi and Fascist hordes swarmed over Spain, erasing the Republic.

Cervantes was also the first writer to understand and admire Lope de Rueda, using his *pasos* as models for his *entremeses*. In the racy dialogue of his piquant one-acters, Cervantes mirrored the psychology and manners of the common people. The same realistic vein which flows from his *Novelas ejemplares*, his cautionary tales, and from the lips of Sancho Panza in *Don Quixote*, found on the stage a most adequate means for conveying the flavor and resonance of sixteenth-century Spain. Among the *entremeses*, *El retablo de las maravillas*, *La cueva de Salamanca*, and *La guarda cuidadosa* (*The Vigilant Sentinel*) are best known.

BEST EDITIONS: E. Cotarelo y Mori (ed.), *Entremeses*. Madrid, Nueva Biblioteca de Autores Españoles, Vol. XVII, n.d. A. Valbuena Prat (ed.), *Obras Completas*. Madrid, Aguilar, 1946.

ABOUT: A. F. C. Bell: *Cervantes*. University of Oklahoma, 1947. W. J. Entwistle, *Cervantes*. New York, 1940. J. Fitzmaurice-Kelly, *Miguel de Cervantes*. Oxford, 1913. A. Flores and M. J. Benardete (eds.), *Cervantes Across the Centuries*. New York, 1946. R. L. Grismer, *Cervantes: A Bibliography*. New York, 1946. G. MacEoin, *Cervantes*. Boston, 1950, R. Schevill, *Cervantes*. New York, 1919.

SCENE: *In front of a house in Madrid.*

(*Enter a* SOLDIER, *dressed in tatters, a wretched sash, and a pair of spectacles, brandishing a sword and chasing a* SACRISTAN.)

SOLDIER. Empty shadow! Why do you trail me?

SACRISTAN. I'm no empty shadow but a massive body—flesh and blood!

SOLDIER. Even so—who are you and what are you looking for in this street?

SACRISTAN. I?—I am Lorenzo, sub-sacristan of this parish. I am looking for that which you can't find, although you too are seeking it.

SOLDIER. Are you then—er—perchance looking for Cristina —the kitchen maid—the one from across the street?

SACRISTAN. Right you are!

SOLDIER. So! Come here, you Satan's own sub-sacristan.

SACRISTAN. Why should I, you old war horse?

SOLDIER. Listen here, jackass, do you realize that Cristina is my treasure? *Mine*—you understand!

SACRISTAN. And do you realize, you octopus in men's clothes, that that bit of treasure is *my* very own—mine—that she belongs to me?

SOLDIER. In God's name, don't lie or I'll split you in two (*He brandishes his knife.*) and smash your head into a thousand pieces. Tell me—dog—do you ever speak to Cristina?

SACRISTAN. Sure!—Quite often.

SOLDIER. What presents have you given her?

SACRISTAN. Many.

SOLDIER. How many and what, may I ask?

SACRISTAN. Well, I gave her a big box—one of those which come full of quince marmalade—filled with wafer clippings, white as snow. Also four wax candle ends, as white as ermine.

SOLDIER (*furious*). Yes—and what else?

21

SACRISTAN. A love letter, containing one hundred wishes to serve her.

SOLDIER. And she, how did she return these favors?

SACRISTAN. She assured me that she will presently be my wife.

SOLDIER. But aren't you of the subdeaconry? Aren't you forbidden to marry!

SACRISTAN. It's true that my hair has been clipped as closely as a lay-brother's, but still I haven't a tonsure. I can marry whenever and as often as I damn please—you'll soon see for yourself! (*He is about to go.*)

SOLDIER (*grabbing him*). Come here, you lay-brother of a devil, answer my questions. If this girl has returned so generously—and I don't believe it—your paltry favors, how will she return my splendid ones? Only the other day I sent her a love letter, written on the back-side of a petition intended for His Majesty, in which I pointed out to him the extent and magnitude of my services and my present needs, for a soldier can always say he's poor without falling into disgrace for it. This petition was duly decreed and was doubtless worth four or six reales. Then with incredible liberality and notable ease, I wrote my love letter on the back of it. See!

SACRISTAN. Have you given her anything else?

SOLDIER. Why, certainly!—I gave her sighs, tears, sobs, paroxysms, swoons, with the entire throng of protestations used, at the ripe time, by experienced lovers in order to disclose their passion.

SACRISTAN (*sarcastically*). Have you serenaded her?

SOLDIER. Why, yes—my lamentations, my anguish, my anxiety and grief, are all serenades.

SACRISTAN. And how has Cristina repaid you for the countless services which you have done her?

SOLDIER. Alas, she does not even wish to talk to me—even see me—she curses me whenever she meets me. She soaks me daily with scullery water from her dirty dishes while I stand under her door. I am, as you can see for yourself, a faithful dog, in brief, the farmer's dog, or the dog in the manger, which whether starved or glutted never stops barking—who neither eats the cabbage nor lets others eat it. I may not be able to possess or enjoy her myself, but no one shall as long as I live. (*menacingly*) So!—Señor subsacristan, you better go before I break your head.

SACRISTAN. You say this because I am unknown. There, I'll show you!

SOLDIER. Ha! Ha! What can one expect from a *sub*-sacristan.

SACRISTAN. Wait and see.

(*The* SACRISTAN *dodges and escapes a blow from the* SOLDIER *and runs into* CRISTINA's *house.*)

SOLDIER. O women, women, how fickle and whimsical you are! Cristina, my dove, are you going to leave this budding flower of soldiery out in the cold while you take in that dung-heap of a sub-sacristan? Only a sub-sacristan, mind you—you, who are capable of winning a full-fledged sacristan—aye, even a canon? I am determined to drive away from your door whomever I suspect of being your lover or suitor. I'll win the title of the faithful watch dog. I'll stand firm!—by God—

(*Enter a* YOUNG MAN *with a box with which to beg alms for some saint.*)

YOUNG MAN (*shouting*). In the name of the Lord, give me alms for oil for the lamp of the señora Santa Lucia that she may protect your eyes. (*yelling up to the floor above*) Hey, there? Any alms today?

SOLDIER. Hallo, friend Santa Lucia, come here; what do you want in this house?

YOUNG MAN. Can Your Grace guess? Alms for the oil for the lamp of the Señora Santa Lucia.

SOLDIER. Are you begging alms for the lamp, or for the oil in the lamp?

YOUNG MAN. Every one knows that I ask for the oil of the lamp and not for the lamp of the oil.

SOLDIER. And do they usually give you alms in this house?

YOUNG MAN. Yes, indeed, two maravedies each day.

SOLDIER (*suspicious*). And who comes out to give you the alms, may I ask?

YOUNG MAN. Whoever is nearest the window—usually a young kitchen maid named Cristina—as pretty as glittering gold.

SOLDIER (*tapping his foot knowingly*). So!—the young kitchen maid as pretty as glittering gold, eh?

YOUNG MAN. As pretty as a shining jewel.

SOLDIER. So you think the girl is not bad?

YOUNG MAN (*matter of factly*). Not bad, not bad at all.

SOLDIER. Not bad at all, eh? You numbskull, idiot—oh, whatever is your real name? I don't care to call you Santa Lucia again.

YOUNG MAN. All right, call me Andres.

SOLDIER (*threatening*). All right then, señor Andres, follow my advice; take these eight reales, and consider yourself paid for four days. Then go away, with God's blessings, and don't dare hang around here for the next four days, even if you need oil for your lamp. Otherwise—I'll separate your body from your soul! Understand!

YOUNG MAN (*retreating*). I'll remember that, Your Honor, and I'll not return for a whole month. But, please, take it easy, your excellency. I'm leaving right now.

(*Exit on the run.*)

SOLDIER (*patting himself on the back*). That's the way—keep up your good work, you faithful watch dog.

(*Enter* SECOND YOUNG MAN, *peddling curling irons, Dutch linen, cambric linen, Flemish laces, and Portuguese thread. He yells out, quite vociferously, his wares.*)

SECOND YOUNG MAN. Who buys curling irons, Flemish laces, Dutch linen, cambric linen, Portuguese thread—?

CRISTINA (*from the window*). Hey, there, Manuel, have you any trimming for a pretty chemise?

SECOND YOUNG MAN. Yes, I have, and very good, too.

CRISTINA. Well, then, come in, my lady wants some. (*She retreats within.*)

SOLDIER. Oh, star of my perdition, rather than northern star of hope! (*addressing* YOUNG MAN) Look here—whatever your name is—do you know the maid who called you from the window, eh?

SECOND YOUNG MAN. Indeed, I do—but why does Your Grace ask me?

SOLDIER. She has a pretty face and a lot of charm, eh?

SECOND YOUNG MAN. Aye, sir, I do agree with you!

SOLDIER. Yes, but I have already vowed that you are not going into that house unless you want me to smash every single bone in your body.

SECOND YOUNG MAN. What do you mean? Can't I go where I'm called? I must sell my wares.

SOLDIER (*brandishing his sword*). Shut up! Don't answer back. Now, do what I say and quick, too.

SECOND YOUNG MAN. Easy, señor Soldier, I'm going—I'm going. (*Exit, also on the run.*)

CRISTINA (*at the window*). Are you not coming in, Manuel?

SOLDIER. Manuel is gone away, my love.

CRISTINA. Christ! What a vexatious brute! What do you

want in this street, anyway. Get away from my door. Go away, you fool! (*She goes indoors.*)

SOLDIER. She's gone—left me—and so my sun has hid behind the clouds of my despair.

(*Enter a* SHOEMAKER, *with a pair of new little slippers in his hand. As he tries to go into* CRISTINA'S *house, he is stopped by the* SOLDIER.) My good sir, is Your Grace looking for something in this house?

SHOEMAKER. Yes, I am.

SOLDIER. And whom do you seek, may I ask?

SHOEMAKER. I'm looking for a kitchen-maid who lives in this house to give her a pair of slippers which she ordered me to make for her.

SOLDIER. So, Your Grace is a shoemaker, eh?

SHOEMAKER. I've frequently made shoes for her.

SOLDIER. And do you intend to try these slippers on her now, eh?

SHOEMAKER. That would not be necessary if they were men's slippers; but women's, ah, yes.

SOLDIER. And are these slippers paid for?

SHOEMAKER. Not yet—she intends to pay me for them now.

SOLDIER. Will Your Grace do me a special favor? Trust me with these slippers. As security I'll give you some jewels. Only for two days. After that I expect to receive plenty of money.

SHOEMAKER. It's hard to refuse you! Let's see the jewels. I'm a poor journeyman, mind you, and can't afford to give credit to anyone.

SOLDIER. Look, I'll give Your Grace a toothpick which I hold in great esteem and wouldn't sell for even an escudo. Where is Your Grace's shop whither I may go with money in time to redeem my treasure?

SHOEMAKER. In the Calle Mayor, in one of the stalls. The name is Juan Juncos.

SOLDIER. Well, well, señor Juan Juncos, here's the toothpick, and value it highly, Your Grace, for remember it is mine.

SHOEMAKER (*examining it*). Tut, tut! I expected it to be of gold or silver but this is only a stalk of bishopwood, worth hardly two maravedies—how can Your Grace expect me to consider it worth more?

SOLDIER. Alas, sinner that I am! I only meant it as a reminder—for whenever I dig my hand into my pocket and don't find my toothpick, I'll remember that Your Grace has it and then I shall come for it. Indeed, upon a soldier's word, I give it to you only for that reason. But if you are not pleased with it, I'll throw this sash and these spectacles into the bargain—a good payer never fears to pledge ample security.

SHOEMAKER. Look here, Your Grace, I'm a simple and honest worker. I'd never think of cheating you. You keep your jewelry and valuables and I'll keep my slippers. Simple enough, eh, what!

SOLDIER. How many stitches have they?

SHOEMAKER. Hardly five.

SOLDIER. Alas, slippers of my entrails—I have not six reales to pay for you! Slippers of my entrails! Listen, señor Shoemaker, listen: *Slippers of my entrails*—a most perfect line for a fine poem.

SHOEMAKER. Is Your Grace also a poet?

SOLDIER. Oh, yes—a most famous one, sir. Let me show you; listen to this.

(*He sings the song "Slippers of My Entrails."*)

> *Love is a tyrant, not a dove.*
> *Keep faith in it as heaven above.*
> *But faith in Cristina seems quite in vain;*
> *Dwelling on her may soften the brain.*

> *Little sheaths, your deeds are disdainful*
> *Since softened brains are often painful.*
> *Sole of my head, and heel of my tail*
> *Compose the slippers of my entrail.*

SHOEMAKER. Although I'm not well versed in the art of poetry, these lines sound so good that they seem to have been penned by Lope de Vega himself. They say he's responsible for all the things that are or seem to be good.

SOLDIER. Well, sir, since it can't be helped, and you don't trust me with the slippers—take them back to your shop. I'll call for them in two days. But remember for your own health, Shoemaker, do not dare see or talk to Cristina.

SHOEMAKER. I'll remember—O jealousy, jealousy, thy name is Grief!

(*The* SHOEMAKER *escapes into* CRISTINA'S *house without the* SOLDIER *seeing him.*)

SOLDIER. Unless one becomes a guard, a watchful guard, countless flies will invade the cellar where the wine of felicity is kept. But, hark! Whose voice is that? Cristina's? Indeed, she always sings when she sweeps or scrubs.

(*The high pitched sweet voice* of CRISTINA *is heard off stage amid the clatter of dishes.*)

CRISTINA (*sings*).
My darling sacristan of my life,
I am your own Cristina.
To you I'll e'er be a faithful wife—
We'll live together serene-a.

CHORUS. Sing, hey, sing alleluya!

SOLDIER. God, do I have to listen to all that treachery! That damn sacristan, the darling of her life, eh, I'll kill the scoundrel—the dog—

(*He is about to storm into the house, when he is stopped by the* MASTER *of* CRISTINA's *house who has just entered.*)

MASTER. Young man, what are you doing here? What do you want?

SOLDIER. Who are you to question me?

MASTER. I! I am the master of this house.

SOLDIER. You mean you're Cristina's master?

MASTER. That I am.

SOLDIER (*pulling out many papers*). Tarry a while; glance over these papers. This is my military record—twenty-two honorable mentions certified to by as many generals as I fought under. Further down, thirty-four distinctions certified to by as many Grand-Masters as have immortalized themselves by signing them.

MASTER. But, I dare say, there have not been as many generals and Grand-Masters in the whole Spanish army for the last hundred years.

SOLDIER (*patting the* MASTER *on the back*). Your Grace, you are a peace loving citizen and know nothing of military affairs whatsoever.

MASTER. All right, I believe you—so what?

SOLDIER. I want you to associate me with truth personified so that Your Grace will believe more readily what is to follow: I have been offered one of the three castles and fortresses now vacant in the Kingdom of Naples—namely, Gaeta, Barleta, and Reggio.

MASTER. Even then, what concern is it of mine?

SOLDIER. Indeed, sir, it is.

MASTER. How so?

SOLDIER. Since I'm getting one of these fortresses, I should like to marry Cristina; then, being her husband, I want you to consider me and my huge estates as your own—understand?

MASTER. I believe Your Grace is slightly mad.

SOLDIER. Is that so? Look here! Give her to me or you'll never enter your house alive.

MASTER. You must be completely mad. Who are you to stop me from entering my own house?

(*Enter* SACRISTAN, *armed with a huge lid from huge water jar and a very rusty sword. He is accompanied by* SECOND SACRISTAN *wearing a steel helmet.*)

SACRISTAN. There, friend Grajales, there's the disturber of my peace—the fly in my ointment.

SECOND SACRISTAN. I regret to have brought along such feeble,—aye, tender arms. I need something heavier to dispatch him the quicker to a sweeter and more distant world.

MASTER. Restrain yourselves, gentlemen! What are all these calamities and murders you are planning?

SOLDIER. Scoundrels! You have to organize yourselves into a band in order to face me! And even then you try to strike from behind—you cowards! Mock-sacristans, I'll pound you to death even if you belong to as many orders as the Ceremonial!

(CRISTINA *and her* MISTRESS *appear at the window.*)

CRISTINA. Madam, madam, come quick, they are killing the Master. More than two thousand swords are striking at him! Look how the blades shine—they blind me!

MISTRESS. Is that true, my child? God help him—May Santa Ursula and her eleven thousand virgins protect him! Come Cristina, let us rush to his aid.

(*They leave the window and run downstairs.*)

MASTER. Stop, gentlemen—nothing good will come of this quarrel.

SOLDIER. Drop that sword and that lid—don't you dare awaken my wrath, or I'll cut you into fine chopped hash, eat you up, and then vomit your filthy carcass down the trap door leading to hell.

MASTER (*advances at the* SOLDIER *to stop him*). Hold your tongue, fool, or you'll regret it. I'm getting angry!

(CRISTINA *and* MISTRESS *come running in breathless.*)

MISTRESS. Alas, poor husband, have they wounded you?

CRISTINA. Woe is me! The contestants are my sacristan and my soldier.

SOLDIER. Hurray, she called me *her* soldier—even if she called that dog *her* sacristan.

MASTER. Nothing has happened to me, Madam—but you should know that this feud has been caused by Cristina.

MISTRESS. Alas! What has my poor Cristina to do with all this?

MASTER. As I understand it, these two young men are fighting jealously over her.

MISTRESS. Santa Ursula and the eleven thousand virgins! Is this true, child?

CRISTINA. Yea, Madam, it is, alas!

MISTRESS. Listen to her shameless avowal—you hussy—has any one of them dishonored you?

CRISTINA. Yea, Madam, alas!

MISTRESS. Heaven's above, which one!

CRISTINA. The sacristan. He dishonored me—he did it.

MISTRESS. Didn't I tell you, sir, that this sweet child has blossomed into a juicy wench and should not be allowed out of sight for a second. What shall I tell her father, who brought her to us so clean and so pure? Where did he dishonor you, you shameless wench?

CRISTINA. Nowhere in particular, Madam, just there, in midstreet.

MISTRESS. In midstreet!

CRISTINA. Yes, Ma'am—in the very middle of the Calle de Toledo—in the sight of Almighty God and in front of everybody he called me dishonorable, shameless, lecherous, and all sorts of names—all because he was jealous of the soldier.

MASTER (*with a sigh of relief*). Is that all? Are you sure nothing else took place? That was all the dishonor—in midstreet, too, I mean?

CRISTINA. That was all, my Lord, because after that he quieted down.

MISTRESS (*recovering*). Thank God!

CRISTINA. Then he promised to become my husband—and he wrote it down here, in black and white, on this slip of paper—look.

MASTER. Show it to us.

MISTRESS. Read it aloud, husband.

MASTER. Well, here is what it says: "I, Lorenzo Pasillas, sub-sacristan of this parish, do hereby declare that I love the said Señora Cristina de Parrazes, and in testimony whereof I have issued this document, and signed it with my own hand and seal in the presence of God, in Madrid, St. Andrews' Cemetery, this sixth day of May, in the year of our Lord 1611. Witnessed: my heart, my mind, my will and my memory. Signed, Lorenzo Pasellas." (*He sighs.*) It is indeed a very touching marriage contract.

SACRISTAN. Besides declaring my love for her, I include whatever she may like me to do for her—for he who surrenders his will, surrenders all, you know.

MASTER. So, if it were her desire—you would marry her?

SACRISTAN. Why, certainly.

SOLDIER. If the choice of men depends on her—permit me to say that I am sure—Cristina prefers being the lady of a famous castle than the mistress of a Sacristan—worse—only a sub-sacristan, who needs more than the other half to become a full fledged sacristan.

MASTER. Cristina, do you wish to be married?

CRISTINA. Indeed I do, sir.

MASTER. Well, then, choose—which of these two pretenders do you prefer?

CRISTINA (*with a girlish giggle*). I'm bashful, sir.

MISTRESS. You need not be, darling, for in matters of food and marriage, one should always follow one's own taste rather than obey another's orders.

CRISTINA. Your Graces who brought me up will give me the husband which they consider best—however, I would like to pick one out for myself—if agreeable to Your Graces.

SOLDIER. Sweetheart, take a good look at me—notice my grace and elegance—I am a soldier, but I'll soon be the Lord of a Castle. Courage has been my virtue since cradle days. I am the most gallant of men! From the flash of my eye, you can deduce the sterling qualities of my soul!

SACRISTAN. Cristina, my dove, listen to me. I am a musician, a bellman if you wish, but still, an artist. No sacristan living or dead can surpass me in adorning a grave or in decorating a church for the holidays; and all these duties I can go on fulfilling even after we're married. I'll earn enough so that we can eat bread fit for a prince.

MASTER. So, dear girl, choose your man and thus restore peace between these recalcitrant competitors.

SOLDIER. I'll abide by her decision.

SACRISTAN. And so will I.

CRISTINA (*hesitating coyly*). Well, in that case—I choose —the—the—*Sacristan*.

(MUSICIANS *enter with a guitar, etc.*)

MASTER. Good; now call my neighbor, the barber, and let's celebrate the happy engagement with guitars and songs and dances. And as for you, señor Soldier—you will be our guest of honor?

SOLDIER. I accept, but not too willingly, because it seems to me that

Wherever supernal edicts exist
Reason and taste will ne'er be missed.

MUSICIANS. Good, we're just in time. We even have a chorus for our song. (*They sing.*)

Wherever supernal edicts exist
Reason and taste will ne'er be missed.

SACRISTAN (*sings*).

Good taste in women is very rare,
To gulls and weasels it does compare.
A soldier's courage they ever ravage
For their taste for gold is almost savage.

MUSICIANS AND CHORUS (*sing*).

Wherever supernal edicts exist
Reason and taste will ne'er be missed.

SACRISTAN (*sings*).

A soldier's battles will never cease.
He will never learn to win through peace.
Reason and taste he may conquer and fell
While his hat will burst as his head will swell.

MUSICIANS AND CHORUS (*all exit singing and dancing the chorus*).

Wherever supernal edicts exist
Reason and taste will ne'er be missed.

FUENTE OVEJUNA

by Lope de Vega

TRANSLATED BY
Angel Flores and Muriel Kittel

❧

CHARACTERS

QUEEN ISABELLA OF CASTILE
KING FERDINAND OF ARAGON
RODRIGO TELLEZ GIRON, *Master
of the religious and military
Order of Calatrava*
FERNAN GOMEZ DE GUZMAN,
*Commander of the Order of
Calatrava*
DON MANRIQUE
A JUDGE
TWO COUNCILMEN OF CIUDAD
REAL

ORTUNO   ⎱ *servants of the*
FLORES   ⎰ *Commander*
ESTEBAN   ⎱ *Mayors of Fu-*
ALONZO   ⎰ *ente Ovejuna*

LAURENCIA ⎱
JACINTA   ⎰ *peasant girls*
PASCUALA   ⎰
JUAN ROJO, *Councilman of Fu-
ente Ovejuna, a peasant*
ANOTHER COUNCILMAN OF FU-
ENTE OVEJUNA
FRONDOSO ⎱
MENGO   ⎰ *peasants*
BARRILDO   ⎰
LEONELO, *Licentiate of Law*
CIMBRANOS, *a soldier*
A BOY
PEASANTS, MEN AND WOMEN
MUSICIANS

TIME: 1476.

Lope de Vega
(1562-1635)

No nation, not even the France of Balzac or the Russia of Tolstoy, has produced a writer who can compare in fertility with Lope de Vega. In admiration of the sheer quantity of comedies and perhaps a bit envious of his repeated successes, Cervantes called him the Monster of Nature. Had Lope devoted every single minute of his life to his writings—which include some of the loveliest lyrics in the Spanish language, epic poems, prose fiction, treatises, and so on and on—still it would be diffcult to believe that one single human being could have written those millions of lines, most of them in verse. But what is especially amazing is that Lope did not devote even half of his time to his literary endeavors, for he was extremely fond of the ladies and devoted many hours to them.

Lope de Vega is frequently referred to as the founder of Spain's national theater. The pre-Lopesque period consisted to a large extent of imitations, mainly from the Italians, and some abortive experiments. The most genuinely Spanish utterance derived from Lope de Rueda's and Cervantes' realistic one-acters. But Lope de Vega developed the full-length play, making use of the most varied aspects of Spanish culture: history, traditions, folklore, sociology; and he infused vital breath and dynamic radiance into everything he touched. And so, single-handedly, he established a national theater, peculiarly Spanish, based on plot and action—a good show full of entertainment and highlighting the people's beliefs and moral standards. His works stimulated the luminaries of the Golden Age and this glamorous congeries converted their epoch into one of the climaxes of the world theater. Of special interest to contemporary audiences are the following of his plays: *Fuente Ovejuna, Peribáñez, El Caballero de Olmedo, La dama boba, El perro del hortelano,* and *El mejor alcalde, el rey.*

BEST EDITION: *Obras escogidas.* Madrid, Aguilar, 1946.
ABOUT: L. Astrana Marín, *Vida azarosa de Lope de Vega.* Barcelona, n.d. J. Entrambasaguas, *Lope de Vega.* Barcelona, 1936. A. Flores, *Lope de Vega, Monster of Nature.* New York, 1929. A. Flores, *The Spanish Golden Age.* New York, 1959. H. Rennert, *Life of Lope de Vega.* Glasgow, 1904. H. Rennert and A. Castro, *Vida de Lope de Vega.* Madrid, 1919. A. Valbuena Prat, *De la imaginería de Lope de Vega a la teología sistemática de Calderón.* Murcia, 1943. J. M. Vigil, *Lope de Vega.* Mexico, 1935. K. Vossler, *Lope de Vega y su tiempo.* Madrid, 1935.

ACT I

SCENE 1: *Hall of the* MASTER OF THE ORDER OF CALATRAVA, *in Almagro.*

(*Enter the* COMMANDER *and his servants,* FLORES *and* ORTUNO.)

COMMANDER. Does the Master know that I am here?
FLORES. He does, my lord.
ORTUNO. The Master is becoming more mature.
COMMANDER. Does he know that I am Fernan Gomez de Guzman?
FLORES. He's only a boy—you mustn't be surprised if he doesn't.
COMMANDER. Nevertheless he must know that I am the Comendador.
ORTUNO. There are those who advise him to be discourteous.
COMMANDER. That will win him little love. Courtesy is the key to good will, while thoughtless discourtesy is the way to make enemies.
ORTUNO. If we but realized how it makes us hated and despised by everyone we would rather die than be discourteous.
FLORES. What a nuisance discourtesy is: among equals it's foolish and toward inferiors it's tyrannical. In this case it only means that the boy has not learned what it is to be loved.
COMMANDER. The obligation he took upon himself when he accepted his sword and the Cross of Calatrava was placed on his breast should have been enough to teach him courtesy.
FLORES. If he has been prejudiced against you you'll soon find out.
ORTUNO. Why don't you leave if you're in doubt?
COMMANDER. I wish to see what he is like.

35

(*Enter the* MASTER OF CALATRAVA *and retinue.*)

MASTER. Pardon me, Fernan Gomez de Guzman; I only just heard that you had come. Forgive me if I have kept you waiting.

COMMANDER. I have just cause for complaint. Both my love for you and my rank entitle me to better treatment—for you are the Master of Calatrava and I your Commander and your servant.

MASTER. I did not know of your welcome arrival—let me embrace you again.

COMMANDER. You owe me a great deal; I have risked my life to settle your many difficulties. I even managed to persuade the Pope to increase your age.

MASTER. That is true, and by the holy cross which we both proudly bear on our breasts I shall repay you in love, and honor you as my own father.

COMMANDER. I am satisfied that you will.

MASTER. What news of the war?

COMMANDER. Listen carefully, and I will tell you where your duty lies.

MASTER. I am listening; tell me.

COMMANDER. Master Don Rodrigo Tellez Giron, I need hardly remind you how your brave father resigned his high position as Master to you eight years ago, and appointed Don Juan Pacheco, the Grand Master of Santiago, to be your coadjutor, nor how kings and commanders confirmed and swore to his act, and the Pope* and his successor Paul agreed to it in their bulls; no, what I have come to tell you is this: now that Pacheco is dead and you, in spite of your youth, have sole control of the government, now is the time for you to take up arms for the honor of your family. Since the death of Henry IV your relatives have supported the cause of Don Alonso, King of Portugal, who claims the throne of Castile through his wife Juana. Ferdinand, the great prince of Aragon, makes a similar claim through his wife Isabella. But your relatives do not consider Ferdinand's rights to be as clear as those of Juana—who is now in your cousin's power. So I advise you to rally the knights of Calatrava in Almagro and to capture Ciudad Real, which stands on the frontier between Andalusia and Castile. You will not need many men, because the enemy can count only on their neighbors and a few noblemen who support Isabella

* Pius II.

and consider Ferdinand their legitimate king. It will be wonderful if you, Rodrigo, if you, a youth, can astonish those who say that this cross is too heavy for your young shoulders. Emulate the counts of Uruena from whom you spring, and who from the height of their fame seem to be challenging you with the laurels they have won; emulate the marquises of Villena and those other captains who are so numerous that the wings of fame are not strong enough to bear them. Unsheathe your white sword, dye it red in battle till it matches the cross upon your breast. For I cannot call you the Master of the Red Cross as long as your sword is white: both the sword you bear and the cross you wear must be red. And you, mighty Giron, must add the crowning glory to the immortal fame of your ancestors.

MASTER. Fernan Gomez, you may be sure that I side with my family in this dispute, for I am convinced that they are right. And as I translate my conviction into action at Ciudad Real you will see me tearing the city walls down with the violence of a thunderbolt. I know that I am young—but do not think that my courage died with my uncle's death. I will unsheathe my white sword and its brilliance shall become the color of the cross, bathed in red blood.

But tell me, where do you live, and do you have any soldiers?

COMMANDER. A few—but they are faithful and they will fight like lions. I live in Fuente Ovejuna, where the people are skilled in agriculture and husbandry rather than in the arts of war.

MASTER. And you live there, you say?

COMMANDER. I do. I chose a house on my estate to stay in during these troubled times. Now see that all your people go into action with you—let no man stay behind!

MASTER. You shall see me today on horseback, bearing my lance on high.

(*Exeunt* COMMANDER *and* MASTER.)

SCENE 2: *A public square in Fuente Ovejuna.*

(*Enter* LAURENCIA *and* PASCUALA.)

LAURENCIA. I hoped he would never come back.

PASCUALA. I must say I thought you'd be more distressed at the news.

LAURENCIA. I hoped to God I'd never see him again.

PASCUALA. I have seen women just as adamant as you, Laurencia, if not more so—and yet, underneath, their hearts were as soft as butter.

LAURENCIA. Well, is there an oak tree as hard as I am?

PASCUALA. Be careful. No one should boast that he'll never thirst for water.

LAURENCIA. But I do. And I'll maintain it against the world. What good would it do me to love Fernan? Do you think I would marry him?

PASCUALA. Of course not.

LAURENCIA. Well then, I condemn infamy. Too many girls hereabouts have trusted the Commander only to be ruined by him.

PASCUALA. All the same it will be a miracle if you escape him.

LAURENCIA. You don't understand, Pascuala. He has been after me for a month now, but he has only been wasting his time. His emissary, Flores, and that blustering fool Ortuno have come to show me a blouse, a necklace, a hat, and have told me so many wonderful stories about their lord and master that they have succeeded in frightening me but not in moving my heart.

PASCUALA. Where did they talk to you?

LAURENCIA. Down there by the brook, about six days ago.

PASCUALA. It looks as if they are trying to deceive you, Laurencia.

LAURENCIA. Deceive me?

PASCUALA. If not you, then the priest.

LAURENCIA. I may be a young chicken, but I'm too tough for His Highness. Pascuala, I would far rather put a slice of ham on the fire in the early morning and eat it with my homemade bread and a glass of wine stolen from my mother, and then at noon to smell a piece of beef boiling with cabbage and eat it ravenously, or, if I have had a trying day, marry an eggplant to some bacon; and in the evening, while cooking the supper, go and pick a handful of grapes from the vines (God save them from the hail) and afterwards dine on chopped meat with oil and pepper, and so happily to bed murmuring "Lead us not into temptation"— I would much rather this than all the wiles and tricks of scoundrels. For after all, all they want after giving us so much trouble is their pleasure at night and our sorrow in the morning.

PASCUALA. You are right, Laurencia, for as soon as they tire of love they are more ungrateful than the sparrows are to the peasants. In winter when the fields are frozen hard the sparrows fly down from the roofs, and saying "Sweet Sweet," hop right on to the dining table for crumbs, but as soon as the cold is over and the fields are again in bloom they no longer come down saying "Sweet Sweet," but stay hopping on the roof, mocking us with their calls. Men are the same; when they need us nothing can be sweeter than they—we are their life, their soul, their heart, their all—but as soon as they tire of us their sweetness disappears and their wooing phrases become a mockery.

LAURENCIA. The moral of which is: trust no man, Pascuala.

PASCUALA. That's what I say.

(*Enter* MENGO, BARRILDO, *and* FRONDOSO.)

FRONDOSO. You are wrong, Barrildo, in this argument.

BARRILDO. Well never mind, here's somebody who will settle the matter.

MENGO. Let's have an understanding before we reach them: if I'm right, then each of you gives me a present as a reward.

BARRILDO. All right. But if you lose, what will you give?

MENGO. I'll give my boxwood rebec, which I value more than a barn.

BARRILDO. That's fine.

FRONDOSO. Let's approach them. God bless you, fair ladies.

LAURENCIA. You call us ladies, Frondoso?

FRONDOSO. We want to keep up with the times. In these days all bachelors are licentiates; the blind are one-eyed; the cross-eyed merely squint; and the lame have only a sprained ankle. The unscrupulous are called honest; the ignorant, clever; and the braggart, brave. A large mouth is described as luscious, a small eye as sharp. The pettifogger is called diligent; the busybody, charming; the charlatan, sympathetic; the deadly bore, gallant. The cowardly become valiant; the hard-headed, vivacious; coxcombs are comrades; fools, broad-minded; malcontents, philosophers. Baldness is identified with authority, foolish chatter with wit. People with tumors have only a slight cold, and those who are arrogant are circumspect; the shifty are constant; and the humpbacked, just slightly bent. This, in short—the enumeration could go on indefinitely—was the sort of thing I did in calling you ladies. I merely followed the fashion of the day.

LAURENCIA. In the city, Frondoso, such words are used in courtesy; discourteous tongues use a severer and more acrimonious vocabulary.

FRONDOSO. I should like to hear it.

LAURENCIA. It's the very opposite of yours. The serious-minded are called bores; the unfortunate, lucky; the even-tempered, melancholy; and anyone who expresses disapproval is hateful. Those who offer good advice are importunate; the liberal-minded are dull-witted; the just, unjust; and the pious, weak-kneed. In this language the faithful become inconstant; the courteous, flatterers; the charitable, hypocrites; and the good Christians, frauds. Anyone who has won a well-deserved reward is called fortunate; truth becomes impudence; patience, cowardice; and misfortune, retribution. The modest woman is foolish; the beautiful and chaste, unnatural; and the honorable woman is called . . . But enough! This reply should be sufficient.

MENGO. You little devil!

LAURENCIA. What an elegant expression.

MENGO. I bet the priest poured handfuls of salt on her when he christened her.

LAURENCIA. What was the argument that brought you here, if we may ask?

FRONDOSO. Listen, Laurencia.

LAURENCIA. Speak.

FRONDOSO. Lend me your ear, Laurencia.

LAURENCIA. Lend it to you? Why, I'll give it to you right now.

FRONDOSO. I trust your discretion.

LAURENCIA. Well, what was the wager about?

FRONDOSO. Barrildo and I wagered against Mengo.

LAURENCIA. And what does Mengo claim?

BARRILDO. It is something that he insists on denying, although it is plainly a fact.

MENGO. I deny it because I know better.

LAURENCIA. But what is it?

BARRILDO. He claims that love does not exist.

LAURENCIA. Many people think that.

BARRILDO. Many people do, but it's foolish. Without love not even the world could exist.

MENGO. I don't know how to philosophize; as for reading, I wish I could! But I say that if the elements of Nature live in eternal conflict, then our bodies, which receive from them food, anger, melancholy, phlegm, and blood, must also be at war with each other.

BARRILDO. The world here and beyond, Mengo, is perfect harmony. Harmony is pure love, for love is complete agreement.

MENGO. As far as the natural world goes, I do not deny it. There is love which rules all things through an obligating interrelationship. I have never denied that each person has love proportionate to his humor—my hand will protect me from the blow aimed at my face, my foot will protect me from harm by enabling me to flee danger, my eyelids will protect my eyes from threatening specks—such is love in nature.

PASCUALA. What are you trying to prove, then?

MENGO. That individuals love only themselves.

PASCUALA. Pardon me, Mengo, for telling you that you lie. For it is a lie. The intensity with which a man loves a woman or an animal its mate . . .

MENGO. I call that self-love, not love. What is love?

LAURENCIA. A desire for beauty.

MENGO. And why does love seek beauty?

LAURENCIA. To enjoy it.

MENGO. That's just what I believe. Is not such enjoyment selfish?

LAURENCIA. That's right.

MENGO. Therefore a person seeks that which brings him joy.

LAURENCIA. That is true.

MENGO. Hence there is no love but the kind I speak of, the one I pursue for my personal pleasure, and which I enjoy.

BARRILDO. One day the priest said in a sermon that there was a man named Plato who taught how to love, and that this man loved only the soul and the virtues of the beloved.

PASCUALA. You have raised a question which the wise men in their schools and academies cannot solve.

LAURENCIA. He speaks the truth; do not try to refute his argument. Be thankful, Mengo, that Heaven made you without love.

MENGO. Are you in love?

LAURENCIA. I love my honor.

FRONDOSO. May God punish you with jealousy.

BARRILDO. Who has won the wager then?

PASCUALA. Go to the sacristan with your dispute, for either he or the priest will give you the best answer. Laurencia does not love deeply, and as for me, I have little experience. How are we to pass judgment?

FRONDOSO. What can be a better judgment than her disdain?

(*Enter* FLORES.)

FLORES. God be with you!

PASCUALA. Here is the Commander's servant.

LAURENCIA. His goshawk, you mean. Where do *you* come from, my good friend?

FLORES. Don't you see my soldier's uniform?

LAURENCIA. Is Don Fernan coming back?

FLORES. Yes, the war is over, and though it has cost us some blood and some friends, we are victorious.

FRONDOSO. Tell us what happened.

FLORES. Who could do that better than I? I saw everything. For his campaign against this city, which is now called Ciudad Real,* the valiant Master raised an army of two thousand brave infantry from among his vassals and three hundred cavalry from laymen and friars. For even those who belong to Holy Orders are obliged to fight for their emblem of the red cross—provided, of course, that the war is against the Moors. The high-spirited youth rode out to battle wearing a green coat embroidered with golden scrolls; the sleeves were fastened with six hooks, so that only his gauntlets showed beneath them. His horse was a dappled roan, bred on the banks of the Betis, drinking its waters and grazing on its lush grass. Its tailpiece was decorated with buckskin straps, the curled panache with white knots that matched the snowflakes covering its mane. Our lord, Fernan Gomez, rode at the Master's side on a powerful honey-colored horse with black legs and mane and a white muzzle. Over a Turkish coat of mail he wore a magnificent breast-and-back plate with orange fringes and resplendent with gold and pearls. His white plumes seemed to shower orange blossoms on his bronze helmet. His red and white band flashed on his arm as he brandished an ash tree for a lance, making himself feared even in Granada. The city rushed to arms; the inhabitants apparently did not come out to fight but stayed within the city walls to defend their property. But in spite of the strong resistance the Master

* Royal City.

entered the city. He ordered the rebels and those who had flagrantly dishonored him to be beheaded, and the lower classes were gagged and whipped in public. He remained in the city and is so feared and loved that people prophesy great things for him. They say that a young man who has fought so gloriously and punished so severely all in a short time must one day fall on fertile Africa like a thunderbolt, and bring many blue moons under the red cross. He made so many gifts to the Commander and his followers that he might have been disposing of his own estate rather than despoiling a city. But now the music sounds. The Commander comes. Welcome him with festivity, for good will is one of the most precious of a victor's laurels.

(*Enter the* COMMANDER *and* ORTUNO; MUSICIANS; JUAN ROJO, ESTEBAN, *and* ALONSO, *elders of the town.*)

MUSICIANS (*singing*).

> Welcome, Commander,
> Conqueror of lands and men!
> Long live the Guzmanes!
> Long live the Girones!
> In peacetime gracious,
> Gentle his reasoning,
> When fighting the Moors
> Strong as an oak.
> From Ciudad Real
> He comes victorious,
> Bearing to Fuente Ovejuna
> Its banners in triumph.
> Long live Fernan Gomez,
> Long live the hero!

COMMANDER. Citizens of Fuente Ovejuna, I am most grateful to you for the love you show me.

ALONSO. It is but a small part of the love we feel, and no matter how great our love it is less than you deserve.

ESTEBAN. Fuente Ovejuna and its elders, whom you have honored with your presence, beg you to accept a humble gift. In these carts, sir, we bring you an expression of gratitude rather than a display of wealth. There are two baskets filled with earthenware; a flock of geese that stretch their heads out of their nets to praise your valor in battle; ten salted hogs, prize specimens, more precious than amber; and a hundred pairs of capons and hens, which leave the cocks of the neighboring villages desolate. You will find no arms, no horses, no harnesses studded with pure gold. The only gold is the love your vassals feel towards you. And for purity you could find nothing greater than those twelve skins of wine. That wine could give warmth and courage to your soldiers even unclothed in the dead of winter; it will be as important as steel in the defense of your walls. I leave unmentioned the cheese and other victuals: they are a fitting tribute from our people to you. May you and yours enjoy our gifts.

COMMANDER. I am very grateful to you for all of them. Go now and rest.

ESTEBAN. Feel at home in this town, my lord! I wish the reeds of mace and sedge that we placed on our doors to celebrate your triumphs were oriental pearls. You deserve such tribute and more.

COMMANDER. Thank you, gentlemen. God be with you.

ESTEBAN. Singers, sing again.

MUSICIANS (singing).

> Welcome, Commander,
> Conqueror of lands and men!

(Exeunt ELDERS and MUSICIANS.)

COMMANDER. You two wait.

LAURENCIA. What is Your Lordship's pleasure?

COMMANDER. You scorned me a few days ago, didn't you?

LAURENCIA. Is he speaking to you, Pascuala?

PASCUALA. I should say not—not to me!

COMMANDER. I am talking to you, beautiful wildcat, and to the other girl too. Are you not mine, both of you?

PASCUALA. Yes, sir, to a certain extent.

COMMANDER. Go into the house. There are men inside, so you need not fear.

LAURENCIA. If the elders accompany us—I am the daughter of one of them—it will be all right for us to go in too, but not otherwise.

COMMANDER. Flores!

FLORES. Sir?

COMMANDER. Why do they hesitate to do what I command?

FLORES. Come along, girls, come right in.

LAURENCIA. Let me go!

FLORES. Come in, girl, don't be silly.

PASCUALA. So that you can lock us in? No thank you!

FLORES. Come on. He wants to show you his spoils of war.

COMMANDER (*aside to* ORTUNO). Lock the door after them. (*Exit* COMMANDER.)

LAURENCIA. Flores, let us pass.

ORTUNO. Aren't you part of the gifts of the village?

PASCUALA. That's what you think! Out of my way, fool, before I . . .

FLORES. Leave them alone. They're too unreasonable.

LAURENCIA. Isn't your master satisfied with all the meat given him today?

ORTUNO. He seems to prefer yours.

LAURENCIA. Then he can starve!

(*Exeunt* LAURENCIA *and* PASCUALA.)

FLORES. A fine message for us to bring! He'll swear at us when we appear before him empty-handed.

ORTUNO. That's a risk servants always run. When he realizes the situation he'll either calm down or else leave at once.

SCENE 3: *Chamber of the Catholic Kings, in Medina del Campo.*

(*Enter* KING FERDINAND OF ARAGON, QUEEN ISABELLA, MANRIQUE, *and* ATTENDANTS.)

ISABELLA. I think it would be wise to be prepared, Your Majesty—especially since Don Alfonso of Portugal is encamped there. It is better for us to strike the first blow than to wait for the enemy to attack us.

KING. We can depend on Navarre and Aragon for assistance, and I'm trying to reorganize things in Castile so as to ensure our success there.

ISABELLA. I'm confident your plan will succeed.

MANRIQUE. Two councilmen from Ciudad Real seek audience with Your Majesty.

KING. Let it be granted them.

(*Enter two* COUNCILMEN *of Ciudad Real.*)

1ST COUNCILMAN. Most Catholic King of Aragon, whom God has sent to Castile to protect us, we appear as humble petitioners before you to beg the assistance of your great valor for our city of Ciudad Real. We are proud to consider ourselves your vassals, a privilege granted us by a royal charter but which an unkind fate threatens to take away. Don Rodrigo Tellez Giron, famous for the valiant actions that belie his youth, and ambitious to augment his power, recently laid close siege to our city. We prepared to meet his attack with bravery, and resisted his forces so fiercely that rivers of blood streamed from our innumerable dead. He finally conquered us—but only because of the advice and assistance given him by Fernan Gomez. Giron remains in possession of our city, and unless we can remedy our disaster soon we will have to acknowledge ourselves his vassals against our will.

KING. Where is Fernan Gomez now?

2ND COUNCILMAN. In Fuente Ovejuna, I think. That is his native town and his home is there. But the truth is, his subjects are far from contented.

KING. Do you have a leader?

2ND COUNCILMAN. No, we have none, Your Majesty. Not one nobleman escaped imprisonment, injury, or death.

ISABELLA. This matter requires swift action, for delay will only work to the advantage of the impudent Giron. Furthermore the King of Portugal will soon realize that he can use him to gain entry to Extremadura, and so cause us much damage.

KING. Don Manrique, leave at once with two companies. Be relentless in avenging the wrongs this city has suffered. Let the Count of Cabra go with you. The Cordovan is recognized by everyone as a brave soldier. This is the best plan for the moment.

MANRIQUE. I think the plan is an excellent one. As long as I live, his excesses shall be curbed.

ISABELLA. With your help we are sure to succeed.

SCENE 4: *The countryside near Fuente Ovejuna.*

(*Enter* LAURENCIA *and* FRONDOSO.)

LAURENCIA. You are very stubborn, Frondoso. I left the brook with my washing only half wrung out, so as to give no occasion for gossip—yet you persist in following me. It seems that everyone in town is saying that you are running after me and I after you. And because you are the sort of fellow who struts about and shows off his clothes, which are more fashionable and expensive than other people's, all the

girls and boys in the countryside think there must be something between us. They are all waiting for the day when
Juan Chamorro will put down his flute and lead us to the
altar. I wish they would occupy their minds with things
that are more their business—why don't they imagine that
their granaries are bursting with red wheat, or that their
wine jars are full of dregs? Their gossip annoys me, but
not so much that it keeps me awake at night.

FRONDOSO. Your disdain and beauty are so great, Laurencia, that when I see you and listen to you I fear they
will kill me. You know that my only wish is to become
your husband: is it fair then to reward my love in this way?

LAURENCIA. I know no other way.

FRONDOSO. Can you feel no pity for my troubled mind,
no sympathy for my sad condition when you know I cannot
eat or drink or sleep for thinking of you? Is it possible that
such a gentle face can hide so much unkindness? Heavens!
you'll drive me mad.

LAURENCIA. Why don't you take medicine for your condition, Frondoso?

FRONDOSO. You are the only medicine I need, Laurencia.
Come with me to the altar, and let us live like turtle doves,
billing and cooing, after the church has blessed us.

LAURENCIA. You had better ask my uncle, Juan Rojo.
I'm not passionately in love with you . . . but there is hope
that I might be in time.

FRONDOSO. Oh—here comes the Commander!

LAURENCIA. He must be hunting deer. Hide behind these
bushes.

FRONDOSO. I will. But I'll be full of jealousy.

(*Enter the* COMMANDER.)

COMMANDER. This is good luck. My chase of the timid
fawn has led me to a lovely doe instead.

LAURENCIA. I was resting a bit from my washing. By
Your Lordship's leave I'll return to the brook.

COMMANDER. Such disdain, fair Laurencia, is an insult to
the beauty Heaven gave you; it turns you into a monster.
On other occasions you have succeeded in eluding my desires—but now we are alone in these solitary fields where
no one can help you. Now, with no one to witness, you
cannot be so stubborn and so proud, you cannot turn your
face away without loving me. Did not Salustiana, the wife
of Pedro Redondo, surrender to me—and Martin del Pozo's
wife, too, only two days after her wedding?

LAURENCIA. These women, sir, had had others before you, and knew the road to pleasure only too well. Many men have enjoyed *their* favors. Go, pursue your deer, and God be with you. You persecute me so that were it not for the cross you wear I should think you were the devil.

COMMANDER. You little spitfire! (*aside*) I had better put my bow down and take her by force.

LAURENCIA. What? . . . What are you doing? Are you mad?

(*Enter* FRONDOSO, *who picks up the bow.*)

COMMANDER. Don't struggle. It won't help you.

FRONDOSO (*aside*). I'll pick up his bow, but I hope I don't have to use it.

COMMANDER. Come on, you might as well give in now.

LAURENCIA. Heaven help me now!

COMMANDER. We are alone. Don't be afraid.

FRONDOSO. Generous Commander, leave the girl alone. For much as I respect the cross on your breast, it will not stop me from aiming this bow at you if you do not let her go.

COMMANDER. You dog, you peasant slave!

FRONDOSO. There's no dog here. Laurencia, go quickly now.

LAURENCIA. Take care of yourself, Frondoso.

FRONDOSO. Run . . .   (*Exit* LAURENCIA.)

COMMANDER. What a fool I was to put down my sword so as not to frighten my quarry!

FRONDOSO. Do you realize, sir, that I have only to touch this string to bring you down like a bird?

COMMANDER. She's gone. You damned, treacherous villain. Put that bow down, put it down, I say.

FRONDOSO. Put it down? Why? So that you can shoot me? No, love is deaf, remember, and hears nothing when it comes into its own.

COMMANDER. Do you think a knight surrenders to a peasant? Shoot, you villain, shoot and be damned, or I'll break the laws of chivalry.

FRONDOSO. No, not that. I'm satisfied with my station in life, and since I must preserve my life, I'll take your bow with me.   (*Exit* FRONDOSO.)

COMMANDER. What a strange experience! But I'll avenge this insult and remove this obstacle . . . But to let him go! My God, how humiliating!

ACT II

SCENE 1: *The Plaza of Fuente Ovejuna.*

(*Enter* ESTEBAN *and* 1ST COUNCILMAN.)

ESTEBAN. I don't think any more grain should be taken out of our community granaries, even though they are full right now. It's getting late in the year, and the harvest looks poor. I think it's better to have provisions stored up in case of emergency—though I know some people have other ideas.

1ST COUNCILMAN. I agree with you. And I've always tried to administer the land along such peaceable ways.

ESTEBAN. Well, let's tell Fernan Gomez what we think about it. We shouldn't let those astrologers, who are so ignorant of the future, persuade us that they know all the secrets that are only God's business. They pretend to be as learned as the theologians the way they mix up the past and the future—but if you ask them anything about the immediate present they are completely at a loss. Do they have the clouds and the course of the sun, the moon, and the stars locked up at home that they can tell us what is happening up there and what is going to bring us grief? At seed time they levy tax on us; give us just so much wheat, oats and vegetables, pumpkins, cucumbers, mustard . . . Then they tell us someone has died, and later we discover it happened in Transylvania; they tell us that wine will be scarce and beer plentiful—somewhere in Germany; that cherries will freeze in Gascony, or hordes of tigers will prowl through Hircania. Their final prophecy is that whether we sow or not the year will end in December!

(*Enter the licentiate* LEONELO *and* BARRILDO.)

LEONELO. You won't be awarded the hickory stick to beat the other students with, for it's already been won by somebody else.

BARRILDO. How did you get on at Salamanca?

49

LEONELO. That's a long story.

BARRILDO. You must be a very learned man by now.

LEONELO. No, I'm not even a barber. The things I was telling you about happen all the time in the school I was at.

BARRILDO. At least you are a scholar now.

LEONELO. Well, I've tried to learn things that are important.

BARRILDO. Anyone who has seen so many printed books is bound to think he is wise.

LEONELO. Froth and confusion are the chief results of so much reading matter. Even the most voracious reader gets sick of seeing so many titles. I admit that printing has saved many talented writers from oblivion, and enshrined their works above the ravages of time. Printing circulates their books and makes them known. Gutenberg, a famous German from Mainz, is responsible for this invention. But many men who used to have a high reputation are no longer taken seriously now that their works have been printed. Some people put their ignorance in print, passing it off as wisdom; others inspired by envy write down their crazy ideas and send them into the world under the name of their enemies.

BARRILDO. That's a disgraceful practice.

LEONELO. Well, it's natural for ignorant people to want to discredit scholars.

BARRILDO. But in spite of all this, Leonelo, you must admit that printing is important.

LEONELO. The world got on very well without it for a good many centuries—and no Saint Jerome or Saint Augustine has appeared since we have had it.

BARRILDO. Take it easy, Leonelo. You're getting all worked up about this printing business.

(*Enter* JUAN ROJO *and another* PEASANT.)

JUAN ROJO. Four farms put together would not raise one dowry, if they're all like the one we've just seen. It's obvious that both the land and the people are in a state of chaos.

PEASANT. What's the news of the Commander?—don't get excited now.

JUAN ROJO. How he tried to take advantage of Laurencia in this very field!

PEASANT. That lascivious brute! I'd like to see him hanging from that olive tree! . . .

(*Enter* COMMANDER, ORTUNO, *and* FLORES.)

COMMANDER. Good day to you all!

COUNCILMAN. Your Lordship!

COMMANDER. Please don't get up.

ESTEBAN. You sit down, my lord. We would rather stand.

COMMANDER. Do sit down.

ESTEBAN. Honor can only be rendered by those who have it themselves.

COMMANDER. Sit down, and let us talk things over calmly.

ESTEBAN. Has Your Lordship seen the hound I sent you?

COMMANDER. Mayor, my servants are all amazed by its great speed.

ESTEBAN. It really is a wonderful animal. It can overtake any culprit or coward who is trying to escape.

COMMANDER. I wish you would send it after a hare that keeps eluding me.

ESTEBAN. I'd be glad to. Whereabouts is this hare?

COMMANDER. It's your daughter.

ESTEBAN. My daughter!

COMMANDER. Yes.

ESTEBAN. But is she worth your while?

COMMANDER. Intervene in my favor, Mayor, for God's sake.

ESTEBAN. What has she done?

COMMANDER. She's determined to hurt me—while the wife of a nobleman here in town is dying for an opportunity to see me.

ESTEBAN. Then she would do wrong—and you do yourself no good to talk so flippantly.

COMMANDER. My, my, what a circumspect peasant! Flores, give him a copy of the *Politics* and tell him to read Aristotle.

ESTEBAN. My lord, the town's desire is to live peaceably under you. You must remember that there are many honorable persons living in Fuente Ovejuna.

LEONELO. Did you ever hear such impudence as this Commander's?

COMMANDER. Have I said anything to offend you, Councilman?

COUNCILMAN. Your pronouncements are unjust, my lord, and not worth uttering. It is unfair to try to take away our honor.

COMMANDER. Honor? Do you have honor? Listen to the saintly friars of Calatrava!

COUNCILMAN. Some people may boast of the cross you awarded them, but their blood is not as pure as you may think.

COMMANDER. Do I sully mine by mixing it with yours?

COUNCILMAN. Evil will sully it rather than cleanse it.

COMMANDER. However that may be, your women are honored by it.

ESTEBAN. Such words are dishonorable.

COMMANDER. What boors these peasants are! Ah, give me the cities, where nobody hinders the pleasures of lofty men. Husbands are glad when we make love to their wives.

ESTEBAN. They certainly should not be. Do you expect us to suffer such tribulations as readily? There is a God in the cities too, and punishment falls swiftly.

COMMANDER. Get out of here!

ESTEBAN. Are you talking to us?

COMMANDER. Get off the Plaza immediately. I don't want to see any of you around here.

ESTEBAN. We're going.

COMMANDER. Not in a group like that . . .

FLORES. I beg of you to control yourself.

COMMANDER. These peasants will gossip in groups behind my back.

ORTUÑO. Have a little patience.

COMMANDER. I marvel that I have so much. Let each man go alone to his own house.

LEONELO. Good Heavens! Will the peasants stomach that?

ESTEBAN. I'm going this way.   (*Exeunt* PEASANTS.)

COMMANDER. What do you think of those fellows?

ORTUÑO. You don't seem to be able to hide your emotions, yet you refuse to sense the ill feeling around you.

COMMANDER. But are these fellows my equals?

FLORES. It's not a question of equality.

COMMANDER. Is that peasant to keep my bow unpunished?

FLORES. Last night I thought I saw him by Laurencia's door and I gave him a slash from ear to ear—but it was someone else.

COMMANDER. I wonder where that Frondoso is now?

FLORES. They say he's around.

COMMANDER. So that's it. The villain who tried to murder me is allowed to go about scot-free.

FLORES. Don't worry. Sooner or later he'll fall into the snare like a stray bird, or be caught on the hook like a fish.

COMMANDER. But imagine—a peasant, a boy, to threaten me with my own crossbow, me, a captain whose sword made Cordova and Granada tremble! Flores, the world is coming to an end!

FLORES. Blame it on love.

ORTUNO. I suppose you spared him for friendship's sake.

COMMANDER. I have acted out of friendship, Ortuno, else I should have ransacked the town in a couple of hours. However, I plan to withhold my vengeance until the right moment arrives. And now—what news of Pascuala?

FLORES. She says she's about to get married.

COMMANDER. Is she going to that length?

FLORES. In other words, she's sending you to where you'll be paid in cash.

COMMANDER. What about Olalla?

ORTUNO. Her reply is charming.

COMMANDER. She's a gay young thing. What does she say?

ORTUNO. She says her husband follows her around all the time because he's jealous of my messages and your visits, but as soon as she manages to allay his fears you'll be the first to see her.

COMMANDER. Fine! Keep an eye on the old man.

ORTUNO. You'd better be careful.

COMMANDER. What news from Ines?

FLORES. Which Ines?

COMMANDER. The wife of Anton.

FLORES. She's ready when you are. I spoke to her in her backyard, through which you may go whenever you wish.

COMMANDER. Easy girls I love dearly and repay poorly. Flores, if they only knew their worth! . . .

FLORES. To conquer without a struggle nullifies the joy of victory. A quick surrender impairs the pleasure of love making. But, as the philosophers say, there are women as hungry for men as form is for matter, so you shouldn't be surprised if things are the way they are.

COMMANDER. A man who is maddened by love congratulates himself when girls fall easily to him, but later he regrets it. For however much we desire things we soon forget them, even the most thoughtful of us, if we have gotten them cheaply.

(*Enter* CIMBRANOS, *a soldier.*)

CIMBRANOS. Is the Commander here?

ORTUNO. Don't you see him before you?

CIMBRANOS. Oh, valiant Fernan Gomez! Change your green cap for your shining helmet, and your cloak for a coat of mail! For the Master of Santiago and the Count of Cabra are attacking Rodrigo Giron, and laying siege to Ciudad Real in the name of the Queen of Castile. All that we won at so much cost in blood and men may soon be lost again. Already the banners of Aragon with their castles, lions and bars, can be seen above the high towers of the city. Though the King of Portugal has paid homage to Giron, the Master of Calatrava may have to return to Almagro in defeat. Mount your horse, my lord, your presence alone will force the enemy back to Castile.

COMMANDER. Stop. That's enough. Ortuno, order a trumpet to sound at once in the Plaza. Tell me, how many soldiers do I have?

ORTUNO. Fifty, I believe, sir.

COMMANDER. Order them to horse.

CIMBRANOS. Ciudad Real will fall to the King if you do not hurry.

COMMANDER. Never fear, that shall not happen!

(*Exeunt all.*)

SCENE 2: *Open country near Fuente Ovejuna.*

(*Enter* MENGO, LAURENCIA, *and* PASCUALA, *running.*)

PASCUALA. Please don't leave us.

MENGO. Why? What are you afraid of?

LAURENCIA. Well, Mengo, we prefer to go to the village in groups when we don't have a man to go with us. We're afraid of meeting the Commander.

MENGO. What a cruel and importunate devil that man is.

LAURENCIA. He never stops pestering us.

MENGO. I wish God would strike him with a thunderbolt and put an end to his wickedness.

LAURENCIA. He's a bloodthirsty beast that poisons and infects the whole countryside.

MENGO. I hear that in trying to protect you, here in the meadow, Frondoso aimed his crossbow at the Commander.

LAURENCIA. I used to hate men, Mengo, but since that day I've looked at them with different eyes. Frondoso acted so gallantly! But I'm afraid it may cost him his life.

MENGO. He'll be forced to leave the village.

LAURENCIA. I keep telling him to go away, although I love him dearly now. But he answers all such counsel with anger and contempt—and all the while the Commander threatens to hang him by the feet.

PASCUALA. I'd like to see that Commander carried off by the plague!

MENGO. I'd rather kill him with a mean stone. By God, if I threw a stone at him that I have up at the sheepfold, it would hit him so hard it would crush his skull in. The Commander is more vicious than that old Roman, Sabalus.

LAURENCIA. You mean Heliogabalus, who was more wicked than a beast.

MENGO. Well, Galvan or whoever it was—I don't know too much about history—the Commander surpasses him in wickedness. Can anyone be more despicable than Fernan Gomez?

PASCUALA. No one can compare with him. You'd think he'd sucked his cruelty from a tigress.

(*Enter* JACINTA.)

JACINTA. If friendship means anything, in God's name help me now!

LAURENCIA. What's happened, Jacinta, my friend?

PASCUALA. Both of us are your friends.

JACINTA. Some of the Commander's attendants are trying to take me to him. They're on their way to Ciudad Real, but they're acting more like villains than soldiers.

LAURENCIA. May God protect you, Jacinta! If the Commander is bold with you he'll be cruel to me.

(*Exit* LAURENCIA.)

PASCUALA. Jacinta, I'm not a man, so I can't defend you.

(*Exit* PASCUALA.)

MENGO. But I have both strength and reputation. Stand beside me, Jacinta.

JACINTA. Have you any arms?

MENGO. Yes, those that Nature gave me.

JACINTA. I wish you were armed.

MENGO. Never mind, Jacinta. There are plenty of stones around here.

(*Enter* FLORES *and* ORTUNO.)

FLORES. So you thought you could get away from us, did you?

JACINTA. Mengo, I'm dead with fear.

MENGO. Gentlemen, this is a poor peasant girl . . .

ORTUNO. Oh, have you decided to defend young women?

MENGO. I'm merely asking for mercy. I'm her relative, and I hope to be able to keep her near me.

FLORES. Kill him off!

MENGO. By God, if you make me mad and I take out my sling, your life will be in danger!

(*Enter the* COMMANDER *and* CIMBRANOS.)

COMMANDER. What's all this? Do I have to get off my horse for some petty quarrel?

FLORES. You ought to destroy this miserable village for all the joy it brings you. These wretched peasants have dared to challenge our arms.

MENGO. My lord, if injustice can move you to pity, punish these soldiers who in your name are forcing this girl to leave her husband and honest parents. Grant me permission to take her home.

COMMANDER. I will grant them permission to punish you. Drop that sling!

MENGO. My lord!

COMMANDER. Flores, Ortuno, Cimbranos, tie his hands with it.

MENGO. Is this your justice?

COMMANDER. What do Fuente Ovejuna and its peasants think of me?

MENGO. My lord, how have I or Fuente Ovejuna offended you?

FLORES. Shall I kill him?

COMMANDER. Don't soil your arms with such trash. Keep them for better things.

ORTUNO. What are your orders?

COMMANDER. Flog him. Tie him to that oak tree and beat him with the reins.

MENGO. Pity, my lord, have pity, for you are a nobleman!

COMMANDER. Flog him till the rivets fall from the leather.

MENGO. My God. For such ugly deeds, uglier punishments! (*Exeunt* MENGO, FLORES, *and* ORTUNO.)

COMMANDER. Now my girl, why were you running away? Do you prefer a peasant to a nobleman?

JACINTA. Can you restore the honor which your attendants have taken from me in bringing me to you?

COMMANDER. Do you mean to say your honor has been lost because I wanted to take you away?

JACINTA. Yes. For I have an honest father who, if he does not equal you in birth, surpasses you in virtue.

COMMANDER. All these troubles around this village, where peasants defy their betters, scarcely help to soothe my temper. Come along here now!

JACINTA. With whom?

COMMANDER. With me.

JACINTA. You had better think over what you're doing.

COMMANDER. I have thought it over, and it's so much the worse for you. Instead of keeping you for myself, I shall give you to my whole army.

JACINTA. No power on earth can inflict such an outrage on me while I live.

COMMANDER. Get a move on now, girl.

JACINTA. Sir, have pity!

COMMANDER. There is no pity.

JACINTA. I appeal from your cruelty to divine justice.

(*Exit* COMMANDER, *hauling her out.*)

SCENE 3: ESTEBAN's *house.*

(*Enter* LAURENCIA *and* FRONDOSO.)

LAURENCIA. Are you unaware of your danger, that you dare to come here?

FRONDOSO. My daring is proof of my love for you. From that hill I saw the Commander riding away, and since I have complete confidence in you all my fear left with him. I hope he never comes back!

LAURENCIA. Don't curse him—for the more one wishes a person to die the longer he lives.

FRONDOSO. In that case may he live a thousand years, and so by wishing him well let's hope his end will be certain . . . Tell me, Laurencia, has my fondness for you affected you at all? Is my loyalty safely entrusted? You know that the entire village thinks we are made for each other. Won't you forget your modesty and say definitely yes or no?

LAURENCIA. My answer to you and to the village is—yes!

FRONDOSO. I could kiss your feet for such an answer! You give me new life . . . let me tell you now how much I love you.

LAURENCIA. Save your compliments and speak to my father, Frondoso, for that's the important thing now. Look, there he comes with my uncle. Be calm and confident, Frondoso, for this meeting will determine whether I'm to be your wife or no.

FRONDOSO. I put my trust in God.

(LAURENCIA *hides herself.* Enter ESTEBAN *and the* COUNCILMAN.)

ESTEBAN. The Commander's visit has aroused the whole town. His behavior was most regrettable, to say the least. Everybody was shocked, and poor Jacinta is bearing the brunt of his madness.

COUNCILMAN. Before long Spain will be rendering obedience to the Catholic Kings, as they are called. The Master of Santiago has been appointed Captain General, and is coming on horseback to free Ciudad Real from Giron . . . I'm very sorry about Jacinta, who is an honest girl.

ESTEBAN. The Commander also had Mengo flogged.

COUNCILMAN. Yes. His flesh is darker than ink or a black cloth.

ESTEBAN. Please, no more—it makes my blood boil when I think of his disgusting behavior and reputation. What good is my Mayor's staff against that?

COUNCILMAN. It was his servants who did it. Why should you be so upset?

ESTEBAN. Shall I tell you something else? I have been told that one day Pedro Redondo's wife was found down there in the depth of the valley. He had abused her and then turned her over to his soldiers.

COUNCILMAN. Listen, I hear something . . . Who's there?

FRONDOSO. It is I, Frondoso, waiting for permission to come in.

ESTEBAN. You need no permission, Frondoso, to enter my house. You owe your life to your father, but your upbringing to me. I love you like my own son.

FRONDOSO. Sir, trusting that love, I want to ask a favor. You know whose son I am.

ESTEBAN. Did that crazy Fernan Gomez hurt you?

FRONDOSO. Not a little.

ESTEBAN. My heart told me so.

FRONDOSO. You have shown me so much affection that I feel free to make a confession to you. I love Laurencia, and wish to become her husband. Forgive me if I have been too hasty. I'm afraid I've been very bold.

ESTEBAN. You have come just at the right moment, Frondoso, and you will prolong my life, for this touches the fear nearest my heart. I thank God that you have come to save my honor, and I thank you for your love and the purity of your intentions. But I think it only right to tell your father of this first. As soon as he approves I will give my consent too. How happy I shall be if this marriage takes place.

COUNCILMAN. You should ask the girl about him before you accept him.

ESTEBAN. Don't worry about that. The matter is settled; for they discussed it beforehand, I'm sure. If you like, Frondoso, we might talk about the dowry, for I'm planning to give you some *maravedies*.

FRONDOSO. I'm not concerned about that. I don't need a dowry.

COUNCILMAN. You should be grateful that he doesn't ask you for it in wineskins.

ESTEBAN. I'll ask Laurencia what she would like to do and then let you know.

FRONDOSO. That's fair. It's a good idea to consult everybody concerned.

ESTEBAN. Daughter! . . . Laurencia!

LAURENCIA. Yes, father.

ESTEBAN. You see how quickly she replies. Laurencia, come here a minute. What would you say if your friend Gila were to marry Frondoso, who is as honest a young man as one could find in Fuente Ovejuna?

LAURENCIA. Is Gila thinking of getting married?

ESTEBAN. Why yes, if someone can be found who would be a worthy match for her.

LAURENCIA. My answer is yes.

ESTEBAN. I would say yes too—except that Gila is ugly, and it would be much better if Frondoso became your husband, Laurencia.

LAURENCIA. In spite of your years, you are still a flatterer, father.

ESTEBAN. Do you love him?

LAURENCIA. I am fond of him, and he returns my affection, but you were saying . . .

ESTEBAN. Shall I say yes to him?

LAURENCIA. Yes, say it for me, sir.

ESTEBAN. I? Well, then I have the keys. It's settled then. Let's go to his father.

COUNCILMAN. Yes, let's go.

ESTEBAN. What shall we tell him about the dowry, son? I can afford to give you 4000 *maravedies*.

FRONDOSO. Do you want to offend me, sir?

ESTEBAN. Come, come, my boy, you'll get over that attitude in a day or two. Even if you don't need it now, a dowry will come in handy later on.

(*Exeunt* ESTEBAN *and* COUNCILMAN.)

LAURENCIA. Tell me, Frondoso, are you happy?

FRONDOSO. Happy? I'm afraid I'll go crazy with so much joy and happiness. My heart is so overflowing that my eyes are swimming with joy when I look at you, Laurencia, and realize that you, sweet treasure, will be mine.

(*Exeunt* LAURENCIA *and* FRONDOSO.)

SCENE 4: *Meadow near Ciudad Real.*

(*Enter the* MASTER, *the* COMMANDER, FLORES, *and* ORTUNO.)

COMMANDER. Fly, sir! There's no hope for us.

MASTER. The walls were weak and the enemy strong.

COMMANDER. They have paid dearly for it, though, in blood and lives.

MASTER. And they will not be able to boast that our banner of Calatrava is among their spoils. That alone would have been enough to honor their enterprise.

COMMANDER. Your plans are ruined now, Giron.

MASTER. What can I do if Fate in its blindness raises a man aloft one day only to strike him down the next?

VOICES BACKSTAGE. Victory for the Kings of Castile!

MASTER. They're decorating the battlements with lights now, and hanging out pennants of victory from the windows in the high towers.

COMMANDER. They do that because they have paid heavily in blood—it's really more a sign of tragedy than a celebration.

MASTER. Fernan Gomez, I'm going back to Calatrava.

COMMANDER. And I to Fuente Ovejuna. Now you have to think of either defending your relatives or paying homage to the Catholic King.

MASTER. I'll write to you about my plans.

COMMANDER. Time will tell you what to do.

MASTER. Ah, years full of the bitterness of time's betrayals!   (*Exeunt.*)

SCENE 5: *A meadow near Fuente Ovejuna.*

(*Enter the wedding train:* MUSICIANS, MENGO, FRON-
DOSO, LAURENCIA, PASCUALA, BARRILDO, ESTEBAN, *and*
JUAN ROJO.)

MUSICIANS (*singing*).
Long live the bride and groom!
Many long and happy years to them.
MENGO. It has not been very difficult for you to sing.
BARRILDO. You could have done better yourself, couldn't
you?
FRONDOSO. Mengo knows more about whippings now than
songs.
MENGO. Don't be surprised if I tell you that there's some-
one in the valley to whom the Commander . . .
BARRILDO. Don't say it. That brutal assassin has assailed
everyone's honor.
MENGO. It was bad enough for a hundred soldiers to whip
me that day when all I had was a sling. It must have been
unbearable for that man to whom they gave an enema of
dye and herbs—I won't mention his name, but he was an
honorable man.
BARRILDO. It was done in jest, I suppose . . .
MENGO. This was no joke. Enemas are desirable some-
times, but I would rather die than undergo one like that.
FRONDOSO. Please sing us a song—if you have anything
worth listening to.
MENGO.
God grant the bride and groom long life
Free from envy and jealous strife,
And when their span of years is past,
May they be united at the last.
God grant the bride and groom long life!
FRONDOSO. Heaven curse the poet who conceived such a
poem!
BARRILDO. It was a rather poor job.
MENGO. This makes me think of something about the
whole breed of poets. Have you seen a baker making buns?
He throws the pieces of dough into the boiling oil until the

pot is full. Some buns come out puffed up, others twisted and funnily shaped, some lean to the left, others to the right, some are well fried, others are burnt. Well, I think of a poet composing his verses in much the same way that the baker works on his dough. He hastily throws words into his pot of paper, confident that the honey will conceal what may turn out ridiculous or absurd. But when he tries to sell his poem no one wants it and the confectioner is forced to eat it himself.

BARRILDO. Stop your foolishness now, and let the bride and groom speak.

LAURENCIA. Give us your hands to kiss.

JUAN ROJO. Do you ask to kiss my hand, Laurencia? You and Frondoso had better ask to kiss your father's first.

ESTEBAN. Rojo, I ask Heaven's blessing on her and her husband for ever.

FRONDOSO. Give us your blessing, both of you.

JUAN ROJO. Let the bells ring, and everyone celebrate the union of Laurencia and Frondoso.

MUSICIANS (*singing*).

> To the valley of Fuente Ovejuna
> Came the maid with the flowing hair.
> A knight of Calatrava
> Followed her to the valley here.
> Amid the shrubs she hid herself,
> Disturbed by shame and fear.
> With the branches she covered herself,
> Feigning she had not seen him,
> But the knight of Calatrava drew near:
> "Why are you hiding, fair maiden,
> Know you not that my keen desire
> Can pierce the thickest wall?"
> She made curtains of the branches
> Confused by shame and fear.
> But love passes sea and mountain:
> "Why are you hiding, fair maiden,
> Know you not that my keen desire
> Can pierce the thickest wall?"

(*Enter the* COMMANDER, FLORES, ORTUÑO, *and* CIMBRANOS.)

COMMANDER. Silence! You will all remain quietly where you are.

JUAN ROJO. This is not a game, my lord, and your orders will be obeyed. Won't you join us? Why do you come in

such a bellicose manner? Are you our conqueror? But what
am I saying . . .

FRONDOSO. I'm a dead man. Heaven help me!

LAURENCIA. Quickly, Frondoso, escape this way.

COMMANDER. No. Arrest him, and tie him up.

JUAN ROJO. Yield to them, my boy, and go quietly to
prison.

FRONDOSO. Do you want them to kill me?

JUAN ROJO. Why?

COMMANDER. I am not a man to murder people without
reason. If I were, these soldiers would have run him through
by now. I'm ordering him to be taken to jail where his own
father will pronounce sentence on him.

PASCUALA. Sir, a wedding is in progress here now.

COMMANDER. What is that to me? Is he the only person in
town who counts?

PASCUALA. If he offended you, pardon him, as becomes
your rank.

COMMANDER. Pascuala, it is nothing that concerns me personally. He has offended the Master Tellez Giron, whom
God preserve. He acted counter to his orders and his honor,
and must be punished as an example. Otherwise others
may rebel too. Don't you know that one day this boy aimed
a crossbow at the very heart of the Commander, Mayor?
Loyal vassals you are indeed!

ESTEBAN. As his father-in-law I feel I must come to his
defense. I think it only natural that a man, especially a man
in love, should challenge you for trying to take away his
girl—what else could he do?

COMMANDER. You are a fool, Mayor.

ESTEBAN. In your opinion, my lord!

COMMANDER. I had no intention of taking away his girl—
for she was not his.

ESTEBAN. You had the thought, and that is enough. There
are kings in Castile who are drawing up new rules to prevent disorder. And they will do wrong if, after the wars,
they tolerate in the towns and country districts such powerful
men wearing those huge crosses on their chests. Those
crosses were meant for royal breasts, and only kings should
wear them.

COMMANDER. Wrest the mayor's staff from him!

ESTEBAN. Take it, sir, it is yours to keep.

COMMANDER. I'll strike him with it as if he were an un-
broken horse.

ESTEBAN. You are my lord, and I must bear it: strike, then.

PASCUALA. Shame on you! Striking an old man!

LAURENCIA. You strike him because he is my father—what injury do you avenge in this way?

COMMANDER. Arrest her, and let ten soldiers guard her.

(*Exeunt* COMMANDER *and his men.*)

ESTEBAN. May Heaven visit justice upon him!

(*Exit* ESTEBAN.)

PASCUALA. The wedding has become a mourning.

(*Exit* PASCUALA.)

BARRILDO. Is there not one of us who can speak?

MENGO. I've already had a sound whipping and I'm covered with wales—let someone else anger him this time.

JUAN ROJO. Let us all take counsel.

MENGO. I advise everybody to keep quiet. He made my posterior look like a piece of salmon.   (*Exeunt all.*)

ACT III

SCENE 1: *A room in the Town Hall of Fuente Ovejuna.*

(*Enter* ESTEBAN, ALONSO, *and* BARRILDO.)

ESTEBAN. Has everybody come to the meeting?

BARRILDO. Some people are absent.

ESTEBAN. Then our danger is more serious.

BARRILDO. Nearly all the town has been warned.

ESTEBAN. With Frondoso imprisoned in the tower, and my daughter Laurencia in such peril, if God, in his mercy, does not come to our help . . .

(*Enter* JUAN ROJO *and the* COUNCILMAN.)

JUAN ROJO. What are you shouting about, Esteban? Don't you know secrecy is all important now?

ESTEBAN. I wonder I'm not shouting even louder!

(*Enter* MENGO.)

MENGO. I want to join in this meeting.

ESTEBAN. With tears streaming down my beard, I ask you, honest farmers, what funeral rites can we give to a country without honor—a country that is lost? And if our honor is indeed lost, which of us can perform such rites, when there is not one among us who has not been dishonored? Answer me now, is there anyone here whose life, whose deep life of honor, is still intact? Are we not all of us in mourning for each other now? If all is lost, what is there to wait for? What is this misfortune that has overtaken us?

JUAN ROJO. The blackest ever known . . . But it has just been announced that the Kings of Castile have concluded a victorious peace, and will soon arrive in Cordova. Let us send two councilmen to that city to kneel at their feet and ask their help.

BARRILDO. But King Ferdinand, who has conquered so many enemies, is still busy making war, and will not be able to help us now while he's in the midst of battles. We must find some other way out.

COUNCILMAN. If you want my opinion, I suggest we leave the town.

JUAN ROJO. But how can we do that on such short notice?

MENGO. If I understand the situation at all, this meeting will cost us a good many lives.

COUNCILMAN. The mast of patience has been torn from us, and now we are a ship driven before a storm of fear. They have brutally abducted the daughter of the good man who rules our community, and unjustly broken the staff of office over his head. What slave was ever treated worse?

JUAN ROJO. What do you want the people to do?

COUNCILMAN. Die, or give death to the tyrants, for we are many and they are few.

BARRILDO. What? Raise our weapons against our lord and master!

ESTEBAN. Except for God, the King's our only lord and master, not these inhuman, barbarous men. If God is behind our rightful anger, what have we to lose?

MENGO. Let us be a little more cautious. I'm here to speak for the humblest peasants who always have to bear the brunt of any trouble—and I want to represent their fears prudently.

JUAN ROJO. Our misfortunes have prepared us to sacrifice our lives, so what are we waiting for? Our houses and vineyards have been burned down. They are tyrants and we must have our revenge.

(*Enter* LAURENCIA, *her hair disheveled.*)

LAURENCIA. Let me come in, for I sorely need the advice of men! Do you know me?

ESTEBAN. God in Heaven, is that my daughter?

JUAN ROJO. Don't you recognize your Laurencia?

LAURENCIA. Yes, I am Laurencia, but so changed that looking at me you still doubt it.

ESTEBAN. My daughter!

LAURENCIA. Don't call me your daughter!

ESTEBAN. Why not, my dear? Why not?

LAURENCIA. For many reasons!—chiefly because you let me be carried off by tyrants, by the traitors who rule over us, without attempting to avenge me. I was not yet Frondoso's wife, so you cannot say my husband should have defended me; this was my father's duty as long as the wedding had not been consummated; just as a nobleman about to purchase a jewel need not pay for it if it is lost while still in the merchant's keeping. From under your very eyes, Fernan

Gomez dragged me to his house, and you let the wolf carry the sheep like the cowardly shepherd you are. Can you conceive what I suffered at his hands?—the daggers pointed at my breast, the flatteries, threats, insults, and lies used to make my chastity yield to his fierce desires? Does not my bruised and bleeding face, my disheveled hair tell you anything? Are you not good men?—not fathers and relatives? Do not your hearts sink to see me so grievously betrayed? . . . Oh, you are sheep; how well named the village of Fuente Ovejuna.* Give me weapons and let me fight, since you are but things of stone or metal, since you are but tigers—no, not tigers, for tigers fiercely attack those who steal their offspring, killing the hunters before they can escape. You were born timid rabbits; you are infidels, not Spaniards. Chicken-hearted, you permit other men to abuse your women. Put knitting in your scabbards—what need have you of swords? By the living God, I swear that your women will avenge those tyrants and stone you all, you spinning girls, you sodomites, you effeminate cowards. To-morrow deck yourselves in our bonnets and skirts, and beautify yourselves with our cosmetics. The Commander will hang Frondoso from a merlon of the tower, without let or trial, and presently he will string you all up. And I shall be glad—you race of half-men—that this honorable town will be rid of effeminates, and the age of Amazons will return, to the eternal amazement of the world.

Esteban. Daughter, I will not stay to hear such names. I go now, even if I have to fight the whole world!

Juan Rojo. I'll go with you, in spite of the enemy's power.

Councilman. We shall die together.

Barrildo. Let us hang a cloth from a stick to fly in the wind, and death to the traitors.

Juan Rojo. What are our orders?

Mengo. To kill the Commander without order. To rally the whole town around us: let's all agree to kill the tyrants.

Esteban. Take swords, lances, crossbows, pikes, sticks!

Mengo. Long live the Kings, our only lords and masters!

All. Long live the Kings!

Mengo. Death to the traitor tyrants!

All. Death to the tyrants!   (Exeunt all but Laurencia.)

Laurencia. Go—God will be with you! Come, women of

* I.e., Sheep Well.

the town, your honor will be avenged—rally round me!

(*Enter* PASCUALA, JACINTA, *and* OTHER WOMEN.)

PASCUALA. What's happening? What are you shouting about?

LAURENCIA. Can't you see how they're on their way to kill Fernan Gomez? Every man, boy, and child is rushing furiously to do his duty. Is it fair that the men alone should have the glory of a day like this, when we women have the greater grievances?

JACINTA. Tell us your plans then.

LAURENCIA. I propose that we all band together and perform a deed that will shake the world. Jacinta, your great injury will be our guide.

JACINTA. No more than yours.

LAURENCIA. Pascuala, you be our standard bearer.

PASCUALA. I'll be a good one. I'll put a cloth on a lance and we'll have a flag in the wind.

LAURENCIA. There's no time for that. We'll wave our caps for banners.

PASCUALA. Let's appoint a captain.

LAURENCIA. We don't need one.

PASCUALA. Why not?

LAURENCIA. Because when my courage is up, we don't need any Cids or Rodomontes.*   (*Exeunt all.*)

SCENE 2: *Hall in the castle of the* COMMANDER.

(*Enter* FRONDOSO, *his hands tied,* FLORES, CIMBRANOS, ORTUÑO, *and the* COMMANDER.)

COMMANDER. I want him hung by the cord that binds his wrists, so that his punishment may be the more severe.

FRONDOSO. How this will add to your descendants' honor, my lord!

COMMANDER. Hang him from the highest merlon.

FRONDOSO. It was never my intention to kill you.

FLORES. Do you hear that noise outside? (*Alarum.*)

COMMANDER. What can it be?

FLORES. It looks as if the villagers are planning to stay your sentence, my lord.

ORTUÑO. They are breaking down the doors! (*Alarum.*)

---

* The Cid was the hero of the great Spanish epic; Rodomonte was King of Algiers in the romances of Orlando.

COMMANDER. The door of my house? The seat of the Commandry?

FRONDOSO. The whole town is here!

JUAN ROJO (*within*). Break them down, smash them in, burn, destroy!

ORTUÑO. It's hard to stop a riot once it gets started.

COMMANDER. The town against me!

FLORES. And their fury has driven them to tear down all the doors.

COMMANDER. Untie him. And you, Frondoso, go and calm down the peasant mayor.

FRONDOSO. I'm going, sir—love has spurred them to action.

(*Exit* FRONDOSO.)

MENGO (*within*). Long live Ferdinand and Isabella, and down with the tyrants!

FLORES. In God's name, my lord, don't let them find you here.

COMMANDER. If they persist—why, this room is strong and well protected. They will soon turn back.

FLORES. When villages with a grievance decide to rise against their rulers they never turn back until they have shed blood and taken their revenge.

COMMANDER. We'll face this mob with our weapons, using this door as a portcullis.

FRONDOSO (*within*). Long live Fuente Ovejuna!

COMMANDER. What a leader! I'll take care of his bravery!

FLORES. My lord, I marvel at yours.

(*Enter* ESTEBAN *and the* PEASANTS.)

ESTEBAN. There's the tyrant and his accomplices! Long live Fuente Ovejuna, death to the tyrants!

COMMANDER. Wait, my people!

ALL. Wrongs never wait.

COMMANDER. Tell me your wrongs, and, on a knight's honor, I'll set them right.

ALL. Long live Fuente Ovejuna! Long live King Ferdinand! Death to bad Christians and traitors!

COMMANDER. Will you not hear me? It is I who address you, I, your lord.

ALL. Our lords are the Catholic Kings.

COMMANDER. Wait.

ALL. Long live Fuente Ovejuna, and death to Fernan Gomez!

(*Exeunt all. Enter* LAURENCIA, PASCUALA, JACINTA, *and* OTHER WOMEN, *armed.*)

LAURENCIA. You brave soldiers, no longer women, wait here in this place of vantage.

PASCUALA. Only women know how to take revenge. We shall drink the enemy's blood.

JACINTA. Let us pierce his corpse with our lances.

PASCUALA. Agreed.

ESTEBAN (*within*). Die, treacherous Commander!

COMMANDER. I die. O God, in Thy clemency, have mercy on me!

BARRILDA. (*within*). Here's Flores.

MENGO. Get that scoundrel! He's the one who gave me a thousand whippings.

FRONDOSO (*within*). I won't consider myself avenged until I've pulled out his soul.

LAURENCIA. There's no excuse for not going in.

PASCUALA. Calm yourself. We had better guard the door.

BARRILDO (*within*). I am not moved. Don't come to me with tears now, you fops.

LAURENCIA. Pascuala, I'm going in; I don't care to keep my sword in its scabbard.   (*Exit* LAURENCIA.)

BARRILDO (*within*). Here's Ortuno.

FRONDOSO (*within*). Slash his face!

(*Enter* FLORES, *fleeing, pursued by* MENGO.)

FLORES. Pity, Mengo! I'm not to blame!

MENGO. Oh, no? Not for being a pimp, you scoundrel, not for having whipped me?

PASCUALA. Mengo, give him to us women, we'll . . . Hurry, Mengo!

MENGO. Fine, you can have him—no punishment could be worse!

PASCUALA. We'll avenge the whippings he gave you.

MENGO. That's fine!

JACINTA. Come on, death to the traitor!

FLORES. To die at the hands of women!

JACINTA. Don't you like it?

PASCUALA. Is that why you're weeping?

JACINTA. Die, you panderer to his pleasures!

PASCUALA. Die, you traitor!

FLORES. Pity, women, *pity!*

(*Enter* ORTUNO, *pursued by* LAURENCIA.)

ORTUNO. You know I have had nothing at all to do with it . . .

LAURENCIA. I know you! Come on, women, dye your conquering weapons in their vile blood.

PASCUALA. I'll die killing!
ALL. Long live Fuente Ovejuna! Long live King Ferdinand!   (*Exeunt all.*)

SCENE 3: *Room of the Catholic Kings, at Toro.*

(*Enter* KING FERDINAND, QUEEN ISABELLA, *and the* MASTER DON MANRIQUE.)

MANRIQUE. We planned our attack so well that we carried it out without any setback. There was little resistance —even if they had tried to organize any, it would have been weak. Cabra has remained there to guard the place in case of counterattack.
KING. That was a wise decision, and I am glad that he is in charge of operations. Now we can be sure that Alfonso, who is trying to seize power in Portugal, will not be able to harm us. It is fortunate that Cabra is stationed there and that he is making a good show, for in this way he protects us from any danger and, by acting as a loyal sentinel, works for the good of the kingdom.
(*Enter* FLORES, *wounded.*)
FLORES. Catholic King Ferdinand, upon whom Heaven has bestowed the Crown of Castile, excellent gentleman that you are—listen to the worst cruelty that a man could ever behold from sunrise to sunset.
KING. Calm yourself!
FLORES. Supreme Sovereign, my wounds forbid me to delay in reporting my sad case, for my life is ebbing away. I come from Fuente Ovejuna, where, with ruthless heart, the inhabitants of that village have deprived their lord and master of his life. Fernan Gomez has been murdered by his perfidious subjects, indignant vassals who dared attack him for but a trivial cause. The mob called him tyrant and inflamed by the power of the epithet, committed this despicable crime: they broke into his house and having no faith that he, a perfect gentleman, would right all their wrongs, would not listen to him, but with impatient fury pierced his chest which bore the cross of Calatrava with a thousand cruel wounds and threw him from the lofty windows onto the pikes and lances of the women in the street below. They carried him away, dead, and competed with one another in pulling his beard and hair, and recklessly slashing his face.

In fact their constantly growing fury was so great, that some cuts went from ear to ear. They blotted out his coat-of-arms with their pikes and loudly proclaimed that they wanted to replace it with your royal coat-of-arms since those of the Commander offended them. They sacked his house as if it were the enemy's and joyfully divided the spoils among themselves. All this I witnessed from my hiding place, for my cruel fate did not grant me death at such a time. Thus I remained all day in hiding until nightfall, when I was able to slip away furtively to come to render you this account. Sire, since you are just, see that a just punishment is administered to the brutal culprits who have perpetrated such an outrage.

KING. You may rest assured that the culprits will not go without due punishment. The unfortunate event is of such magnitude that I am astonished; I will send a judge to investigate the case and punish the culprits as an example to all. A captain will accompany him for his protection, for such great offense requires exemplary punishment. In the meantime your wounds will be cared for. (*Exeunt all.*)

SCENE 4: *The countryside.*

(*Enter* PEASANTS, *both men and women, with* FERNAN GOMEZ' *head on a lance.*)

MUSICIANS (*singing*).
> Long live Isabella and Ferdinand
> And death to the tyrants!

BARRILDO. Sing us a song, Frondoso.

FRONDOSO. Here goes, and if it limps let some critic fix it.
> Long live fair Isabella
> And Ferdinand of Aragon.
> He is made for her
> And she is meant for him.
> May St. Michael guide them
> To Heaven by the hand . . .
> Long live Isabella and Ferdinand
> And death to the tyrants!

LAURENCIA. Now it's your turn, Barrildo.

BARRILDO. Listen to this, for I've been working on it.

PASCUALA. If you say it with feeling, it's going to be good.

BARRILDO.

Long live the famous kings
For they are victorious.
They'll be our lords
Happy and glorious.
May they conquer always
All giants and dwarfs . . .
And death to the tyrants!

MUSICIANS (*singing*).
Long live Isabella and Ferdinand
And death to the tyrants!

LAURENCIA. Now it's your turn, Mengo.

FRONDOSO. Yes, Mengo.

MENGO. I'm a most gifted poet, you know.

PASCUALA. You mean a poet with a bruised backside.

MENGO.
I was whipped on a Sunday morning
My back still feels the pain
But the Christian Kings are coming
There'll be no tyrants here again.

MUSICIANS. Long live the Kings!

ESTEBAN. Take away that head!

MENGO. He has the face of one who has been hanged.

(JUAN ROJO *brings in a scutcheon with the royal arms.*)

COUNCILMAN. The scutcheon has arrived.

ESTEBAN. Let's see it.

JUAN ROJO. Where shall we place it?

COUNCILMAN. Here, in the Town Hall.

ESTEBAN. What a beautiful scutcheon!

BARRILDO. What joy!

FRONDOSO. A new day is dawning for us, and that's our sun.

ESTEBAN.
Long live Castile and Leon
And the bars of Aragon.
Down with tyranny!

People of Fuente Ovejuna, listen to the words of an old man whose life has been blameless. The Kings will want to investigate what has happened, and this they will do soon. So agree now among yourselves on what to say.

FRONDOSO. What is your advice?

ESTEBAN. To die saying Fuente Ovejuna and nothing else.

FRONDOSO. That's fine! Fuente Ovejuna did it!

ESTEBAN. Do you want to answer in that way?

ALL. Yes.

ESTEBAN. Well then, I'd like to play the role of questioner
—let's rehearse! Mengo, pretend that you are the one being
grilled.

MENGO. Can't you pick on someone else, someone more
emaciated?

ESTEBAN. But this is all make believe.

MENGO. All right, go ahead!

ESTEBAN. Who killed the Commander?

MENGO. Fuente Ovejuna did it!

ESTEBAN. You dog, I'm going to torture you.

MENGO. I don't care—even if you kill me.

ESTEBAN. Confess, you scoundrel.

MENGO. I am ready to confess.

ESTEBAN. Well, then, who did it?

MENGO. Fuente Ovejuna.

ESTEBAN. Bind him tighter.

MENGO. That will make no difference.

ESTEBAN. To hell with the trial then!

(*Enter the* COUNCILMAN.)

COUNCILMAN. What are you doing here?

FRONDOSO. What has happened, Cuadrado?

COUNCILMAN. The questioner is here.

ESTEBAN. Send him in.

COUNCILMAN. A captain is with him.

ESTEBAN. Who cares? Let the devil himself come in: you
know your answer.

COUNCILMAN. They are going around town arresting people.

ESTEBAN. There's nothing to fear. Who killed the Commander, Mengo?

MENGO. Who? Fuente Ovejuna.   (*Exeunt all.*)

SCENE 5: *Room of the* MASTER OF CALATRAVA, *at Almagro.*

(*Enter the* MASTER *and a* SOLDIER.)

MASTER. What a horrible thing to have happened! Melancholy was his end. I could murder you for bringing me such
news.

SOLDIER. Sir, I'm but a messenger. I did not intend to
annoy you.

MASTER. That a town should become so fierce and wrath-
ful, that it would dare to do such a thing! It's incredible!

I'll go there with a hundred men and raze the town to the ground, blotting out even the memory of its inhabitants.

SOLDIER. Calm yourself, sir. They have given themselves up to the King and the most important thing for you is not to enrage him.

MASTER. How can they give themselves up to the King? Are they not the vassals of the Commander?

SOLDIER. That, sir, you'll have to thrash out with the King.

MASTER. Thrash it out? No, for the King placed the land in his hands and it is the King's. He is the Sovereign Lord and as such I recognize him. The fact that they have given themselves up to the King soothes my anger. My wisest course is to see him, even if I am at fault. He will pardon me on account of my youth. I am ashamed to go—but my honor demands that I do so and I shall not forget my dignity. (*Exeunt the* MASTER *and* SOLDIER.)

SCENE 6: *Public square.*

(*Enter* LAURENCIA.)

LAURENCIA.
    Loving, to suspect one's love will suffer pain
    Becomes an added suffering of love;
    To fear that pain great harm to him may prove
    Brings new torture to the heart again.

    Devotion, watching eagerly, would fain
    Give way to worry, worm of love;
    For the heart is rare that does not bend or move
    When fear his threat on the belov'd has lain.

    I love my husband with a love that does not tire;
    But now I live and move beneath
    The fear that fate may take away his breath.
    His good is all the end of my desire.

    If he is present, certain is my grief;
    If he is absent, certain is my death.
                    (*Enter* FRONDOSO.)

FRONDOSO. Laurencia!

LAURENCIA. My dear husband! How do you dare to come here?

FRONDOSO. Does my loving care for you give you such worries?

LAURENCIA. My love, take care of yourself. I am afraid something may happen to you.

FRONDOSO. It would displease God, Laurencia, if I made you unhappy.

LAURENCIA. You have seen what has happened to your friends and the ferocious rage of that judge. Save yourself, and fly from danger!

FRONDOSO. Would you expect cowardice from me? Do not advise me to escape. It is inconceivable that in order to avoid harm I should forgo seeing you and betray my friends and my own blood at this tragic moment. (*cries within*) I hear cries. If I am not mistaken, they are from someone put to the torture. Listen carefully!

(*The* JUDGE *speaks within, and is answered.*)

JUDGE. Tell me the truth, old man.

FRONDOSO. Laurencia, they are torturing an old man!

LAURENCIA. What cruelty!

ESTEBAN. Let me go a moment.

JUDGE. Let him go. Now, tell me, who murdered Fernan?

ESTEBAN. Fuente Ovejuna killed him.

LAURENCIA. Father, I will make your name immortal!

FRONDOSO. What courage!

JUDGE. Take that boy. Pup, speak up! I know you know. What? You refuse? Tighten the screws.

BOY. Fuente Ovejuna, sir.

JUDGE. By the life of the King, I'll hang the lot of you, you peasants, with my own hands! Who killed the Commander?

FRONDOSO. They're racking the child, and he answers that way . . .

LAURENCIA. What a brave village!

FRONDOSO. Brave and strong.

JUDGE. Put that woman, over there, in the chair. Tighten it up!

LAURENCIA. He's blind with rage.

JUDGE. You see this chair, peasants, this means death to you all! Who killed the Commander?

PASCUALA. Fuente Ovejuna, sir.

JUDGE. Tighter!

FRONDOSO. I hadn't imagined . . .

LAURENCIA. Pascuala will not tell him, Frondoso.

FRONDOSO. Even the children deny it!

JUDGE. They seem to be delighted. Tighter!

PASCUALA. Merciful God!

JUDGE. Tighter, you bastard! Are you deaf?

PASCUALA. Fuente Ovejuna killed him.

JUDGE. Bring me someone a bit bigger—that fat one, half stripped already!

LAURENCIA. Poor Mengo! That must be Mengo!

FRONDOSO. I'm afraid he'll break down.

MENGO. Oh . . . Oh . . .

JUDGE. Give it to him!

MENGO. Oh . . .

JUDGE. Need any help?

MENGO. Oh . . . Oh . . .

JUDGE. Peasant, who killed the Commander?

MENGO. Oh . . . I'll tell, sir . . .

JUDGE. Release him a bit.

FRONDOSO. He's confessing!

JUDGE. Now, hard, on the back!

MENGO. Wait, I'll tell all . . .

JUDGE. Who killed him?

MENGO. Sir, Fuente Ovejuna.

JUDGE. Did you ever see such scoundrels? They make fun of pain. The ones I was surest of lie most emphatically. Dismiss them: I'm exhausted.

FRONDOSO. Oh, Mengo, God bless you! I was stiff with fear—but you have rid me of it.

(Enter MENGO, BARRILDO, and the COUNCILMAN.)

BARRILDO. Long live Mengo!

COUNCILMAN. Well he may . . .

BARRILDO. Mengo, bravo!

FRONDOSO. That's what I say.

MENGO. Oh . . . Oh . . .

BARRILDO. Drink and eat, my friend . . .

MENGO. Oh . . . Oh . . . What's that?

BARRILDO. Sweet cider.

MENGO. Oh . . . Oh . . .

FRONDOSO. Something for him to drink!

BARRILDO. Right away!

FRONDOSO. He quaffs it well! That's better, now.

LAURENCIA. Give him a little more.

MENGO. Oh . . . Oh . . .

BARRILDO. This glass, for me.

LAURENCIA. Solemnly he drinks it!

FRONDOSO. A good denial gets a good drink.

BARRILDO. Want another glass?
MENGO. Oh . . . Oh. . . . Yes, yes.
FRONDOSO. Drink it down; you deserve it.
LAURENCIA. A drink for each turn of the rack.
FRONDOSO. Cover him up, he'll freeze to death.
BARRILDO. Want some more?
MENGO. Three more. Oh . . . Oh . . .
FRONDOSO. He's asking for the wine . . .
BARRILDO. Yes, there's a boy, drink deep. What's the matter now?
MENGO. It's a bit sour. Oh, I'm catching cold.
FRONDOSO. Here, drink this, it's better. Who killed the Commander?
MENGO. Fuente Ovejuna killed him . . .
(*Exeunt* MENGO, BARRILDO, *and the* COUNCILMAN.)
FRONDOSO. He deserves more than they can give him. But tell me, my love, who killed the Commander?
LAURENCIA. Little Fuente Ovejuna, my dear.
FRONDOSO. Who did?
LAURENCIA. You bully, you torturer! I say Fuente Ovejuna did it.
FRONDOSO. What about me? How do *I* kill *you?*
LAURENCIA. With love, sweet love, with lots of love.

SCENE 7: *Room of the Kings, at Tordesillas.*

(*Enter the* KING *and* QUEEN.)

ISABELLA. I did not expect to find you here, but my luck is good.
KING. The pleasure of seeing you lends new glory to my eyes. I was on my way to Portugal and I had to stop here.
ISABELLA. Your Majesty's plans are always wise.
KING. How did you leave Castile?
ISABELLA. Quiet and peaceful.
KING. No wonder, if you were the peacemaker.
(*Enter* DON MANRIQUE.)
MANRIQUE. The Master of Calatrava, who has just arrived, begs audience.
ISABELLA. I wanted very much to see him.
MANRIQUE. I swear, Madame, that although young in years, he is a most valiant soldier.
(*Exit* DON MANRIQUE, *and enter the* MASTER.)

MASTER. Rodrigo Tellez Giron, Master of Calatrava, who never tires of praising you, humbly kneels before you and asks your pardon. I admit that I have been deceived and that, ill-advised, I may have transgressed in my loyalty to you. Fernan's counsel deceived me and for that reason I humbly beg forgiveness. And if I am deserving of this royal favor, I pledge to serve you from now on; in the present campaign which you are undertaking against Granada, where you are now going, I promise to show the valor of my sword. No sooner will I unsheathe it, bringing fierce suffering to the enemy, than I will hoist my red crosses on the loftiest merlon of the battlements. In serving you I will employ five hundred soldiers, and I promise on my honor nevermore to displease you.

KING. Rise, Master. It is enough that you have come for me to welcome you royally.

MASTER. You are a consolation to a troubled soul.

ISABELLA. You speak with the same undaunted courage with which you act.

MASTER. You are a beautiful Esther, and you a divine Xerxes.

(Enter MANRIQUE.)

MANRIQUE. Sire, the judge you sent to Fuente Ovejuna has returned and he asks to see you.

KING (to the MASTER). Be the judge of these aggressors.

MASTER. If I were not in your presence, Sire, I'd certainly teach them how to kill Commanders.

KING. That is no longer necessary.

ISABELLA. God willing, I hope this power lies with you.

(Enter JUDGE.)

JUDGE. I went to Fuente Ovejuna, as you commanded, and carried out my assignment with special care and diligence. After due investigation, I cannot produce a single written page of evidence, for to my question: "Who killed the Commander?" the people answered with one accord: "Fuente Ovejuna did it." Three hundred persons were put to torture, quite ruthlessly, and I assure you, Sire, that I could get no more out of them than this. Even children, only ten years old, were put to the rack, but to no avail—neither did flatteries nor deceits do the least good. And since it is so hopeless to reach any conclusion: either you must pardon them all or kill the entire village. And now the whole town has come to corroborate in person what they have told me. You will be able to find out from them.

KING. Let them come in.

(*Enter the two* MAYORS, ESTEBAN *and* ALONSO, FRONDOSO, *and* PEASANTS, *men and women.*)

LAURENCIA. Are those the rulers?

FRONDOSO. Yes, they are the powerful sovereigns of Castile.

LAURENCIA. Upon my faith, they are beautiful! May Saint Anthony bless them!

ISABELLA. Are these the aggressors?

ESTEBAN. Fuente Ovejuna, Your Majesty, who humbly kneel before you, ready to serve you. We have suffered from the fierce tyranny and cruelty of the dead Commander, who showered insults upon us—and committed untold evil. He was bereft of all mercy, and did not hesitate to steal our property and rape our women.

FRONDOSO. He went so far as to take away from me this girl, whom Heaven has granted to me and who has made me so blissful that no human being can compete with me in joy. He snatched her away to his house on my wedding night, as if she were his property, and if she had not known how to protect herself, she, who is virtue personified, would have paid dearly, as you can well imagine.

MENGO. Is it not my turn to talk? If you grant me permission you will be astonished to learn how he treated me. Because I went to defend a girl whom his insolent servants were about to abuse, that perverse Nero handled me so roughly that he left my posterior like a slice of salmon. Three men beat my buttocks so relentlessly that I believe I still bear some wales. To heal my bruises I have had to use more powders and myrtleberries than my farm is worth.

ESTEBAN. Sire, we want to be your vassals. You are our King and in your defense we have borne arms. We trust in your clemency and hope that you believe in our innocence.

KING. Though the crime is grave, I am forced to pardon it since no indictment is set down. And since I am responsible for you, the village will remain under my jurisdiction until such time as a new Commander appears to inherit it.

FRONDOSO. Your Majesty speaks with great wisdom. And at this point, worthy audience, ends the play *Fuente Ovejuna*.

THE ROGUE OF SEVILLE

(*El burlador de Sevilla*)

by *Tirso de Molina*

TRANSLATED BY
Robert O'Brien

࿇

CHARACTERS

DON DIEGO TENORIO
DON JUAN TENORIO, *his son*
CATALINON, *Don Juan's servant*
THE KING OF NAPLES
DUKE OCTAVIO
DUCHESS ISABELLA

THISBE
ANFRISO
CORIDON   } *fisherfolk*
BELISA

BATRICIO
BASENO
AMINTA   } *peasants*
BELISA

RIPIO   } *servants*
FABIO

SERVANTS, GUARDS, MUSICIANS,
    ETC.

DON PEDRO TENORIO, *Don Juan's uncle and the Spanish Ambassador in Naples*
THE MARQUIS OF LA MOTA
THE KING OF CASTILE
DOÑA ANA, *his daughter*

    SCENE: *Naples, Tarragona, Seville, and Dos Hermanas.*
    TIME: *The fourteenth century.*

Tirso de Molina
(*ca.* 1583?-1648)

"Tirso de Molina" was the pseudonym of the friar Gabriel Téllez, who according to one critic was the illegitimate son of the Duke of Osuna. After completing his studies at the University of Alcalá, he entered the Mercenaries in 1601 and worked for the Order in various cities in Spain and in Santo Domingo, and became Chronicler in 1637 and prior of the monastery in Soria in 1645. During a score of years he wrote over 400 plays of which 86 are extant. When in 1625 the Council of Castile censured him for depicting vice too vividly, he stopped writing altogether.

Tirso subscribed to Lope de Vega's ideas on the theater: he disregarded the unities, mixed the tragic with the comic, and emphasized, above all, a theatrical theater—entertaining and dynamic. His themes ranged from biblical and religious (such as the magnificent *El condenado por desconfiado*, published in 1635), to folk legends (*Los amantes de Teruel*, 1635) and palace plays (*El vergonzoso en palacio*, 1621), in all of which he proved himself to be most convincing in the depiction of female psychology. The play which won him the greatest renown was *El burlador de Sevilla* (*The Rogue of Seville*, 1630), which brought upon the stage for the first time one of the most demonic and ubiquitous characters in world literature: Don Juan.

BEST EDITION: B. de los Ríos (ed.), *Obras dramáticas completas*. Madrid, Aguilar, 1947, 2 vols.

ABOUT: A. H. Bushee, *Three Centuries of Tirso de Molina*. Oxford, 1939. I. L. McClelland, *Tirso de Molina. Studies in Dramatic Realism*. Liverpool, 1948. B. de los Ríos, Study and Notes to her edition of *Obras dramáticas completas*, listed above. Special issue of the magazine *Estudios* (Madrid, 1949) devoted to Tirso de Molina.

ACT I

SCENE 1: *A room in the palace of the* KING OF NAPLES.

(*Enter* DON JUAN *and the* DUCHESS ISABELLA.)

ISABELLA. Duke Octavio, this way! This way is safest.

DON JUAN. My Duchess, again I swear to honor the sweet promise of our troth.

ISABELLA. What glorious hopes! Can they come true? These promises and offerings, your compliments and flatteries, my very dreams and wishes?

DON JUAN. They will, my love.

ISABELLA. Let me find a light.

DON JUAN. Why a light?

ISABELLA. That my eyes may see the splendor of my heart.

DON JUAN. That cannot be.

ISABELLA. It cannot be? Why not? Who are you?

DON JUAN. Who am I? A man without a name.

ISABELLA. Then you are not the Duke?

DON JUAN. No.

ISABELLA. Then what have I done? Oh . . . Guard!

DON JUAN. Wait! Duchess, give me your hand.

ISABELLA. Don't touch me! Help! Guard! Guard!

(*The* KING OF NAPLES *enters with a candle.*)

KING. Who is there?

ISABELLA. It's the King. Everything is lost!

KING. Who are you?

DON JUAN. Can't you see? A man and a woman.

KING (*aside*). This calls for prudence. (*aloud*) Guards! Guards! Arrest this man!

ISABELLA. My honor! Dear God, my honor!

(*Enter* DON PEDRO TENORIO, *the Spanish ambassador, and guards.*)

DON PEDRO. I heard voices, my lord. What is the matter?

83

KING. Don Pedro Tenorio, I charge you to make this arrest. All action in this affair I leave to you. Who these two are and why they are here is yours to know and yours alone. There are some things that a king had best not see.

DON PEDRO. Seize him.

DON JUAN. Who will be the first to dare? It may be that I am marked to die tonight. But I, alone, shall avenge my death on the one who takes my life.

DON PEDRO. Kill him!

DON JUAN. Do not be presumptuous. As a nobleman of the Spanish embassy, I am well prepared to die in my own defense. Therefore let only the one who has the right and rank come forward.

DON PEDRO. Leave us, all of you. And take this woman with you. (*They exeunt.*)

DON PEDRO. Now that we two are alone, let me sample this fire and strength of yours.

DON JUAN. I have ample courage, uncle, but not enough to use against you.

DON PEDRO. Tell me who you are!

DON JUAN. I shall tell you: your nephew!

DON PEDRO (*aside*). Oh, my heart! What kind of treachery is this? (*aloud*) Villain! What have you done? And why are you here in this disguise? Tell me quickly what you've done, rogue. Out with it.

DON JUAN. My lord and uncle, I am a young man as once you were. You, who certainly have known the pull of love, must therefore understand mine. But since you demand the facts of this affair, I shall tell you. Tonight I both deceived and enjoyed the Duchess Isabella.

DON PEDRO. Enough. Hold your peace. Speak softly and tell me how you enjoyed her.

DON JUAN. By pretending to be Duke Octavio . . .

DON PEDRO. That's enough. (*aside*) I am lost if the King should learn of this. What to do? I must use all my ingenuity to negotiate so grave a situation. (*aloud*) Tell me, rogue, was it not enough that you were banished from Spain for similar treachery with another noblewoman, without repeating the act here in Naples, in the royal palace with a woman of even greater rank? May God punish you! Your father sent you from Castille to Naples, whose Italian shores have welcomed you. This warm reception you have repaid by betraying the honor of her most noble lady. But this is a waste of time. Think of what you shall do.

DON JUAN. It would be false of me to beg your pardon for a guilt which I do not feel. My blood, señor, is yours. Shed it and pay this debt of mine. At your feet, señor, I surrender both my blood and sword.

DON PEDRO. Arise and show your courage! For this humility has conquered me. Will you dare to leap this balcony?

DON JUAN. Easily. Your favor gives me wings.

DON PEDRO. Then I will help you. Leave immediately for Sicily or Milan and there hide out.

DON JUAN. Very well.

DON PEDRO. You agree?

DON JUAN. Agreed.

DON PEDRO. My letters will keep you informed of the outcome of this sad affair.

DON JUAN. Though less than sad for me, you must agree.

DON PEDRO. Your youth misleads you. Quick, over the railing!

DON JUAN. So I shall and then to Spain.

(*Exit* DON JUAN *and enter the* KING.)

DON PEDRO. Your commands, great lord, I have done my best to carry out according to the strictest justice. The man . . .

KING. Is dead?

DON PEDRO. Has escaped the vengeance of my sword.

KING. In what way?

DON PEDRO. Like this: No sooner were your orders given, when without warning his sword flashed in his hand. Wrapping his cloak about his arm, he turned upon the soldiers; but seeing no defense from certain death, made a desperate leap from this balcony into the garden. Your men followed quickly and found him writhing like a snake upon the ground. Crying "Kill him!" they rushed upon him. His face smeared with blood, he leaped to his feet, fell upon them, and in this swift confusion made his escape. The woman, you may be surprised to discover, is the Duchess Isabella. She revealed that the man was Duke Octavio who, through deceit and cunning, was able to enjoy her.

KING. What are you saying?

DON PEDRO. I tell you what she herself confessed.

KING. Ah, honor! If you are the very soul of man, why do you entrust yourself to the inconstant hands of woman? Ho there! Guards!

(*Enter a* SERVANT.)

SERVANT. My lord?

KING. Bring the woman into my presence.

DON PEDRO. They are bringing her already, sire.

(*Enter a* GUARD *with* ISABELLA.)

ISABELLA (*aside*). How can I dare to look upon the King?

KING. Leave us and guard the doors. Tell me, woman: What extremities of passion, what angry star has inflamed you to defile the very threshold of my palace with your shameful beauty and arrogance?

ISABELLA. My lord . . .

KING. Silence! Your tongue will never be able to excuse your fault nor ease the offense to me. Was the man Duke Octavio?

ISABELLA. My lord . . .

KING. Are there no fortresses or walls, guards or servants, no moats or battle stations which can keep Love, a mere child, from slipping through our walls? Don Pedro, seize this woman at once and have her taken to some tower. Arrest Duke Octavio as well. He shall complete these vows and promises he made.

ISABELLA. My lord, will you not look at me?

KING. You have taken your advantage when my back was turned. It is only justice that this should continue.

DON PEDRO. Come, Duchess.

ISABELLA. Though my offense can never be erased, the fault will be less if Duke Octavio can amend the shame.

(*They exeunt.*)

SCENE 2: *Naples. The house of* DUKE OCTAVIO.

(*Enter* DUKE OCTAVIO *and* RIPIO, *his servant.*)

RIPIO. You are up so early, sir?

OCTAVIO. Sleep is powerless against the raging flame of my love. For Love is a child and thus he finds no comfort on sheets of Holland linen and no pleasure in a quilt of ermine. He lies down but does not sleep; always longing for the dawn when he can rise and play. And like a child he plays. Thoughts of Isabella surround me, my friend, with a constant torment; for as she lives in my soul, my body watches over her whether she is near or far, constantly guarding the fortress of her honor.

RIPIO. If you'll forgive me, sir, it seems to me that your love is impertinent.

OCTAVIO. What's that, you idiot?

RIPIO. Just this: it is impertinent to love as you do. Do you know why?

OCTAVIO. Go on.

RIPIO. Very well. What makes you think that Isabella loves you?

OCTAVIO. Idiot! Do you doubt it?

RIPIO. Oh no, not at all. But I'd like to ask you: do you really love her?

OCTAVIO. Of course!

RIPIO. Well then, it seems to me that I would be a fool to go out of my senses over a woman I loved if she loved me. On the other hand, if she did *not* love, it would be sensible to plead with her and shower her with gifts and adoration. But I cannot understand these difficulties between two people who adore each other. Why not get married and solve the whole problem?

OCTAVIO. Idiot! You expect me to slip into marriage like some lackey or washerwoman?

RIPIO. I see nothing wrong with a washerwoman who simply washes and cleans, and chats and jokes and spreads her linens out so nicely. Such women are open and giving and nothing can equal that. And if Isabella doesn't know how to give, perhaps she knows how to take.

(*Enter a* SERVANT.)

SERVANT. The Spanish Ambassador has just arrived on horseback. He is already within, demanding to speak to you immediately. I am afraid he means to take you to prison.

OCTAVIO. To prison? On what charge? Go and ask him to come in.

(*Enter* DON PEDRO *with guards.*)

DON PEDRO. To sleep so late one must have a clear conscience.

OCTAVIO. When a man such as your Excellency comes to honor and favor me, it is wrong to sleep at all. My whole life should be an endless vigil. To what do I owe the pleasure of this visit?

DON PEDRO. To the command of the King.

OCTAVIO. If my lord the King keeps me so much in his thoughts at this time, it is only just and reasonable that I should place my very life at his command. Tell me, my lord, what lucky star has decreed that my king should remember me in his thoughts?

DON PEDRO. Less fortunate than you suppose. I am the King's ambassador, entrusted with a most serious matter.

OCTAVIO. Marquis, that does not worry me. Tell me what you must.

DON PEDRO. The King has charged me to arrest you. I ask you not to resist.

OCTAVIO. To arrest me? Upon what charge?

DON PEDRO. This you should know better than I. But since you ask, this is why the King has sent me: When the dark giants of the night were folding their funereal tents and, fleeing from the darkness, stumbling one against another, His Majesty and I were pondering certain affairs of state; for great matters are alien to the sun. Suddenly we heard the cries of a woman echoing through silent halls. Again we heard her cries for help and, rushing to her aid, found Isabella enveloped in the arms of a man whose gigantic monstrosity defied the very heavens. At the King's command that they be seized, I grappled with the man who, I believe, must have been the Demon in human shape. Wrapped in mist and smoke, he threw himself from the balcony to the feet of the mighty elms whose branches form a crown of spires above the palace. We turned to the Duchess who declared, in the presence of all, that this man, the Duke Octavio, had enjoyed her as a husband does his wife.

OCTAVIO. What are you saying?

DON PEDRO. I say only what the whole world knows, only what is clear to all; that Isabella in a thousand ways . . .

OCTAVIO. Spare me! Do not say these things and use the name of Isabella. But if her love makes her use deception as a substitute for silence . . . Continue, sir. Touch my heart with the full measure of this poison that my firm love may prove its strength against those scandalmongers who conceive in the ear so that their mouths may give birth. Could it be that Isabella has so forgotten my love that she should wish my death? For it appears that beautiful dreams are but a prelude to the evils of awakening. Yet my heart rejects these thoughts. They are but whims which, to increase my passion, have entered my understanding, that what my ears have heard may temper the visions of my eyes. Marquis, is it possible that Isabella has deceived me and made a mockery of my love? But this is impossible! Oh, woman! What horrible law is at the core of honor? And

who is responsible for my terrible instruction? Tonight in
the palace Isabella was found in the arms of a man! I must
be mad!

DON PEDRO. Is it true? Are there birds upon the wind?
Fish within the sea? Are the four elements shared by all?
Are the blessed in glory? Does loyalty become the friend
and treachery mark the enemy? If night breeds no shadows
and light does not become the day, then there is no truth
in what I say.

OCTAVIO. Marquis, I must believe you. Henceforth, nothing
will astonish me. For I have found that the most constant
of women was, after all, only a woman. Knowing that, I
wish to know no more.

DON PEDRO. You seem both wise and prudent. If I were
to give you the chance . . .

OCTAVIO. I would leave immediately.

DON PEDRO. Then go quickly, Duke Octavio.

OCTAVIO. I will sail for Spain and, there, live out my miserable life.

DON PEDRO. Quickly now, through the garden!

OCTAVIO. Ah, Isabella! A weathervane would have been
more firm, a reed less quick to bend. And now, because of
this, I must scramble to safety in a foreign land. Goodbye,
my country! Tonight in the palace Isabella was found in the
arms of a man! I must be mad!

SCENE 3: *Seashore near Tarragona.*

(*Enter* TISBEA *alone with a fishing rod in her hands.*)

TISBEA. I alone of those beside the sea, whose waters kiss
their feet of jasmine and rose, am free of Love. I alone
wander free of the prison he has filled with madmen. Here
beneath the lazy sun where the sapphire waves frighten off
the shadows; here upon the white sands glistening like drops
of dew or atoms of the sun; here beside the waters beneath
the calling and pleading of birds and the sweet attack of
the water upon the stones, I make my humble home. With
this rod that bends of its own weight I catch the little,
eager fish upon the waters of the sea or with my net dip
down among their world of shells for those that live below.
And this my freedom is my delight. For I have never been

attacked by the adder of Love. Among the thousand love-torn hearts I walk untouched, scornful of their plight. So my blessings are numbered in the thousands for Love has left my home unharmed nor disturbed me in my bed. My hut is just a house of straw with neither cicadas nor turtledoves. My virtue is thus wrapped in straw like packing around a glass that's sent to market. My fellow fishermen in Tarragona do commend my virtue. But I am deaf to their entreaties and stand their waves of pleas like stone.

Anfriso is a man endowed with all the graces, generous, well-spoken and brave who loves to haunt my hut and wear out the night with waiting. He cuts green boughs to crown my home and beneath the stars at midnight pleads his suit with guitar and tambourine. But this is nothing to me for I am ruler of the land of love. Others sigh for him whom I disdain. For this is love . . . to die for those who cause you pain. And so I spend my young years untrapped by others' madness. My one pleasure and desire is to cast my line to the wind and waves. But look: two men have jumped from that boat which flounders in the sea. Now it seems to be upon the reef and now it starts to sink, flinging its topsail like a kite to the wind . . .

VOICE (*off*). Help, I'm drowning!

TISBEA. A man swept fighting through the waves, carrying his friend upon his back as once Aeneas did Anchises. Now he cuts the waves. But who will help him when he reaches shore and pull him from the foam? Anfriso, shipwrecks are coming. Tirseo, Alfredo! Will no one hear? But by some miracle they've come stepping through the booming surf. Although the man who swam is being carried by the one he bore.

(*Enter* CATALINON *carrying* DON JUAN.)

CATALINON. Oh, for a drop of Cana's wine; the sea is much too salty. True, it's free enough for those who have to swim for their lives, but it is strange that God should have created so much water and forgotten to mix in some wine.

Master!—He seems to be cold and stiff. Are you dead? Although the sea caused it, suppose they put the blame on me? Curses on the one who first placed pine trees upon the sea and tried to contain its limits with boards of wood. Curses on Jason and Theseus. He's dead and no one will believe that I am innocent. Ah, Catalinon, what can I do?

TISBEA. Such great troubles, my man?

CATALINON. Ah, girl, I am all trouble and no luck. I see

my master has freed me from his service by dying. See if that isn't true.

TISBEA. No, he's breathing.

CATALINON. How could that be?

TISBEA. It's true though. Go call those fishermen in that hut over there.

CATALINON. Will they come?

TISBEA. At once. Who is this gentleman?

CATALINON. The son of the chamberlain of the King who will probably be made a count within the next six days in Seville. That is if the King and I agree.

TISBEA. His name?

CATALINON. Don Juan Tenorio.

TISBEA. Go call my people.

CATALINON. Right away.

(*Exit* CATALINON. TISBEA *places* DON JUAN's *head in her lap.*)

TISBEA. Excellent young man, come back to the living.

DON JUAN. Where am I?

TISBEA. As you can see: in the arms of a woman.

DON JUAN. I live in you, one who died in the sea. I will never doubt that I am in the bosom of heaven as I was once in the hell of the sea. We were wrecked by a storm which has swept me at last to safety at your feet.

TISBEA. You have a great deal of breath for one who almost had none at all, since you seem to be able to raise so much voice. They must be strange storms indeed which can toss you all about and still leave you free to talk like this. I almost believe that you were feigning death upon this beach. Perhaps you are my Trojan horse come to wreak revenge. If you can so touch me with fire when you are damp, what will you do when you are dry again? You promise much fire! Please God may it be true.

DON JUAN. My country girl, I wish that God had drowned me in the waves that I might have been spared the madness of my love for you. The sea is wild for one can drown in it; but here I may be burned to death. You are like the sun which burns while it appears like snow.

TISBEA. Though you seem cold, the flames within me seem to grow. May God grant that you do not lie!

(*Enter* CATALINON, ANFRISO, CORIDON *and others.*)

CATALINON. They have come.

TISBEA. Your master's alive.

CORIDON. What is your wish?

TISBEA. Anfriso, Coridon and friends . . .

CORIDON. Whatever your wishes or your commands, you have only to tell us, Tisbea. For words which fall from your pink lips must guide those of us who adore and watch over you. For you we would dig the ground or plow the sea; crush the wind or air or fire.

TISBEA (*aside*). How ridiculous their vows once seemed to me. But now I understand that they do not lie. (*aloud*) Friends, as I sat here fishing, I saw a ship sink beneath the waves and these two swimming clear. I called for help but no one seemed to hear. One of them, a nobleman, lay as if dead upon the sands where he was placed by his friend. So I sent the other to find and bring you here.

ANFRISO. We are at your command, which now seems kinder than what we've known.

TISBEA. Let us take him to my hut where, with gratitude, we'll mend his clothes and put them right. This breath of kindness will please my father.

CATALINON (*aside*). She is a beauty!

DON JUAN. Come here a moment.

CATALINON. I'm listening.

DON JUAN. If they ask who I am, you do not know.

CATALINON. Ah, me . . . Don't you think I know anything?

DON JUAN. I am dying with love for her. This very night I must enjoy her.

CATALINON. How will you . . . ?

DON JUAN. Be quiet and follow me.

CORIDON. Anfriso, within the hour all the fishermen will be singing and dancing.

ANFRISO. Come, tonight we must mend these clothes.

DON JUAN. I am dying, Tisbea.

TISBEA. And still you talk.

DON JUAN. I can scarcely move as you can see.

TISBEA. You talk too much.

DON JUAN. But you understand.

TISBEA. God grant that he does not lie.

SCENE 4: *Seville. The Alcazar.*

(*Enter the* KING *with* DON GONZALO DE ULLOA.)

KING. Was your embassy successful, Don Gonzalo?

Don Gonzalo. I found your cousin, King Don Juan,* there in Lisbon preparing a fleet of thirty men-of-war.

King. Where were they bound?

Don Gonzalo. They told me Goa but I believe they had some nearer destination such as Ceuta or Tangiers which they may besiege this summer.

King. God aid him and heaven reward this tribute to its glory. Did you come to any agreement?

Don Gonzalo. My lord, in return for Serpa, Olivenza, Mora, and Toro he will give you Villaverde, Mertola, and Herrera which lie between Castile and Portugal.

King. Seal the agreement, Don Gonzalo. But tell me of your journey. I suppose you found it both expensive and fatiguing.

Don Gonzalo. Nothing is too difficult when one serves you, my lord.

King. What sort of place is Lisbon?

Don Gonzalo. The largest city in all of Spain. If my lord wishes, I would be happy to describe it to him.

King. I would like to hear it. Bring me a chair.

Don Gonzalo. Lisbon is the eighth wonder of the world. In the land of Cuenca rises the magnificent Tagus to cross the breadth of Spain and enter the ocean between the sacred banks of this city. But before it loses both itself and its name, it creates a harbor among the mountains where ships, boats, galleys, caravels, and schooners from all corners of the globe come to anchor, creating near the shore another great city where Neptune is king.

At its western end, the city is guarded by two fortresses, Cascaes and San Juan. Slightly more than half a league from these is the convent of Belen, known by its stone and guarded by a lion, where Catholic kings and Christians find eternal homes. Beyond this complex, a mighty league from Alcantara, lies the convent of Jabregas in a beautiful valley crowned with three peaks, which would have tempted the famous painter Apelles. For it appears as a cluster of pearls suspended from the heavens in whose vastness are contained ten Romes, encrusted with convents and churches, buildings, and streets, in lands and mansions, letters, arms and precise justice. And the Misericordia, a most amazing edifice even to its roof from which one can see sixty towns scattered seven leagues on every side, each of them touched

---

* John I, King of Portugal.

by the sea. One of these is the convent of Olivelas where my eyes beheld six hundred and thirty cells and twelve hundred nuns. In this part of Lisbon there are fifteen hundred country homes much like the ones that we in Andalusia call "*sortijos,*" each surrounded by poplars and gardens. In the center of the city is the square called Rucio, large, beautiful and well paved; where a hundred years ago there was only sea, now thirty thousand homes are standing, extending from the city to the shore. Here there is a street called the Rua Nova where the grandeur and riches of the Orient are concentrated. Here there is a merchant who counts his wealth, not in coins but in bushels. Terrero, where the royal family lives, is alive with ships filled with wheat and barley from France and England. The Royal Palace which is kissed by the Tagus is the House of Ulysses. For in Latin times Lisbon was called Ulissibona. The arms of the city are a great globe depicting the wounds the King Don Alfonso Enriquez received in the service of Our Great King and Father. In the arsenal of Tarazana there are many ships, among them the great vessels of the conquest, whose masts seem to scrape against the sky.

Most excellent it is that citizens, while at their tables, are able to buy from a copious supply of fish. Some can even catch as many as they need from the doors of their own homes. Above all, each afternoon a thousand cargo-laden ships unload at their docks varieties of merchandise and common goods—bread, oil, wine, and wood, fruit in infinite variety and ice from the Sierra de Estrella—which are hawked through the streets by women with baskets on their heads. But enough. To recount but a fraction of the marvels of this opulent city would be to count the stars. For the city numbers a hundred and thirty thousand souls, my lord, and among them, a king who would kiss your hands.

KING. Excellent, Don Gonzalo. I felt from your vivid description that I had seen the place myself. Tell me, have you any children?

DON GONZALO. My great lord, I have a beautiful daughter in whose face nature sees itself in admiration.

KING. Then I wish to give her myself in marriage.

DON GONZALO. Your wishes on her behalf are mine, my lord. But who is to be her husband?

KING. Although he is not in the country, he is from Seville. His name is Don Juan Tenorio.

DON GONZALO. I shall go and inform Doña Ana.

KING. Go at your leisure, Don Gonzalo, and return soon with your reply.

SCENE 5: *Near Tarragona.*

(*Enter* DON JUAN *and* CATALINON.)

DON JUAN. Since we have the time, go saddle the mares.

CATALINON. Maybe I'm just Catalinon but still, you must confess, señor, that, in spite of all, I am a man of sorts. No one can call me coward; in fact, you might say the exact reverse is true . . .

DON JUAN (*brusquely*). The fishermen are lost in their fiesta; quick, saddle the mares. Few friends are as trustworthy as the galloping hoof.

CATALINON. You mean you'll even trick Tisbea?

DON JUAN. Why not? You expect a change? You know me better.

CATALINON. I know you are the scourge of women.

DON JUAN. I am dying for Tisbea. A delicious girl!

CATALINON. What a wonderful guest you are!

DON JUAN. Fool. Aeneas did no less to the Queen of Carthage.

CATALINON. Oh, master. Those who cheat and toy with women will surely have their reward . . . after death.

DON JUAN. Death cannot frighten or restrain me. Not all of us are in such fear of death.

CATALINON. I'd rather be a little respectful of death than run all over women like you do. Look, here she comes!

DON JUAN. Quick, go saddle the horses.

CATALINON. Poor girl! You'll soon find out how some people pay for the comfort of a warm bed.

(*Exit* CATALINON *and enter* TISBEA.)

TISBEA. When you are not beside me, part of me is gone.

DON JUAN. A beautiful thought . . . If I could believe it.

TISBEA. But why not?

DON JUAN. If you loved me, you would comfort me.

TISBEA. But I'm yours.

DON JUAN. How can I believe you when you withhold what love must give?

TISBEA. It must be Love's punishment for what I've done that makes me hold back from you.

DON JUAN. In you alone, my beloved, do I live. My one brief life is yours until I lose it in your service. I can promise no more, except to be your loving husband.

TISBEA. But you are a gentleman.

DON JUAN. Love is a king whose just laws can bind the homespun with the silk.

TISBEA. If I could believe you . . . If I did not know the ways of men.

DON JUAN. Perhaps you are offended by my fumbling attempts at love? But my heart and mind and tongue are bound in the richness of your hair.

TISBEA. And I am held by the word and hand of husband.

DON JUAN. By these eyes, in which I see my certain death, I swear to be your husband!

TISBEA. Remember, darling; remember God and death.

DON JUAN. Death cannot frighten me! And God has given me life to be your slave. Will you take my hand and my undying loyalty?

TISBEA. I can no longer refuse what you desire.

DON JUAN. And I . . . tremble with love.

TISBEA. Come, my love, and see the hut of love which shall house our bridal bed. Hide yourself among these reeds until our special hour.

DON JUAN. But how shall I come?

TISBEA. Come and I will show you.

DON JUAN. You have opened my soul to light.

TISBEA. May my love bind yours, if not, I leave you to God and death.

DON JUAN. Death cannot frighten me!

(*Exeunt* DON JUAN *and* TISBEA; *enter* CORIDON, ANFRISO, BELISA, *and musicians.*)

CORIDON. Call Tisbea and the rest so that the guest can see our retinue.

ANFRISO. Tisbea, Lucinda, Atandra! Nothing can be more cruel than the sight of her who lives salamander-like within our fire of love. Before we dance let's call her.

BELISA. Yes, let's.

CORIDON. Come.

BELISA. This is her hut.

CORIDON. Wait! For she has other guests, whose presence would fill a thousand hearts with envy.

ANFRISO. She is always envied.

BELISA. Let's sing while we wait for her to come and join our dance.

ANFRISO (*aside*). How can one sing in the constant shadow of jealousy?

ALL SING. A maid there was who used to cast
Her shining nets in the rolling waves
And when she pulled them in at last
They were filled with the hearts of loving slaves.
(*Enter* TISBEA, *distraught.*)

TISBEA. Fire! Fire! I'm burning! How my hut burns and flames! Sound the alarm, my friends, while my eyes bring water. Here is another Troy in flames. For since the Trojans were destroyed, love has brought its fire to simple huts. And if love can turn stones to flame, what chance has a little wisp of straw? Fire, my friends! I beg you for water! May love have pity on a soul in flames! And you, my little house, vile scene of my dishonor and my infamy; den of thieves and shelter of my woes! The rays of burning stars have enflamed these tresses and they have been brushed by an evil wind. Ah, false guest, how could you so dishonor a woman? You are a cloud come from the sea to flood my soul. Fire, my friends! I beg you for water! May love have pity on a soul in flames! For I am the one who once made fun of men; but she who makes sport of others comes at last to be another's sport. This cavalier deceived me with his pledge of marriage and soiled both my honor and my bed. Not only has he enjoyed me, but I myself have foolishly supplied the mares on which he has escaped. Follow him, all of you! Follow him! No, wait; I shall take my grievance to the king and beg him to take my vengeance for me. Fire, my friends! I beg you for water! May Love have pity on a soul in flames. (*Exit* TISBEA.)

CORIDON. Follow the traitorous cavalier.

ANFRISO. I must bear my sadness in silence until the time comes for vengeance on this ingrate. Come, let's follow her. For, in her despair, she may do herself even greater harm.

CORIDON. So much for pride. Here ends its madness and bold confidence.

TISBEA (*within*). Fire! Fire!

ANFRISO. She has thrown herself into the sea.

CORIDON. Wait, Tisbea. Stop!

TISBEA (*within*). Fire, my friends! I beg you for water! May Love have pity on a soul in flames!

ACT II

SCENE 1: *The Alcazar.*

(*Enter the* KING *and* DON DIEGO TENORIO.)

KING. What are you saying?

DON DIEGO. It's true, my lord. I have just received this letter from my brother, your ambassador. He was caught in the King's apartments with a beautiful lady from the palace.

KING. A lady of rank?

DON DIEGO. Señor, she was the Duchess Isabella.

KING. Isabella?

DON DIEGO. The very same.

KING. What gall! Where is he now?

DON DIEGO. I cannot hide the truth from you, my lord. He just arrived in Seville with his servant.

KING. Tenorio, you know the esteem in which I hold you. I shall find out more of this from the King of Naples. Then we'll marry the boy to Isabella and relieve the innocent Duke Octavio of his problems. But from this moment, Don Juan is banished from Seville.

DON DIEGO. Where to, my lord?

KING. Tonight he must leave Seville for Lebrija. He should thank your great merit that the punishment is not greater. At the same time consider what should be said to Don Gonzalo de Ulloa. Under the present circumstances Don Juan's marriage to his daughter is out of the question.

DON DIEGO. I hope, my lord, I hope that you find some way to honor the lady as befits the daughter of such a man.

KING. I have a way to assuage Don Gonzalo's wrath: he shall be major-domo of the palace.

(*Enter a* SERVANT *and then* DUKE OCTAVIO.)

SERVANT. My lord, there is a gentleman here from abroad. He claims to be the Duke Octavio.

KING. The Duke Octavio?

SERVANT. Yes, my lord.

KING. Undoubtedly he suspects Don Juan and has come, eager for vengeance, to engage him in a duel.

DON DIEGO. My lord, my life is in your hands; for my real life is the life of my disobedient son who, as a mere child, was a brave and gallant boy whom all the other boys called the Hector of Seville because of his many wonderful deeds. I beg of you, my lord, prevent this duel if possible.

KING. Enough. Your plea has been heard, Tenorio.

DON DIEGO. Señor, grant this favor and I will never ask another.

(*Enter* DUKE OCTAVIO.)

OCTAVIO. Great king, I throw myself at your feet, an unhappy wanderer and exile and, in your presence, completely forgetting all the dangers of my journeys.

KING. Duke Octavio.

OCTAVIO. I come here a fugitive from the madness of a woman and the heedless act of some cavalier to seek refuge at your feet.

KING. Duke, I already know of your innocence and have dispatched letters to the King my vassal restoring your possessions and any damages you may have suffered in your absence. I shall marry you in Seville, if you agree and the lady is willing, to a lady whose beauty far outshines that of Isabella, even though she were an angel. Don Gonzalo de Ulloa, the grand commander of Calatrava, whom the Moors honor in their fear (for flattery and cowardice are twins), has a daughter whose virtue, which I rank second only to her beauty, would in itself be dowry enough. Among all the stars of Seville, she ranks as the sun. She is the one I wish you to marry.

OCTAVIO. Then I count my journey worthwhile, my lord, if I may have the chance to do your bidding and give you pleasure.

KING. See that the Duke is lodged and served to the limits of our hospitality.

OCTAVIO. My lord, he who puts his trust in you wins every prize. Although the eleventh of the Alfonsos, you rank as the first.

(*Exeunt the* KING *and* DON DIEGO. *Enter* RIPIO.)

RIPIO. What happened?

OCTAVIO. My labors are rewarded. I placed my plea before the King and he honored me. Caesar was with Caesar. As you can see, I came, I saw, I conquered. Besides, he has found a wife for me and commanded the King of Naples to repeal the edicts made against me.

RIPIO. He is well named the Generous! And he has offered you a wife?

OCTAVIO. Yes, my friend, and not only a wife but one from Seville. For not only does Seville produce strong and gallant men but magnificent women as well. With their graceful airs and the mantles and veils which cover such magnificent treasures. Where can you find these, if not in Seville? I am content; it is worth all the trouble.

(*Enter* DON JUAN *and* CATALINON.)

CATALINON. Wait, master, there is the Duke, the innocent Sagittarius of Isabella. Or perhaps I should say her Capricorn.*

DON JUAN. Dissimulate.

CATALINON. Those he sells he flatters.

DON JUAN. My friend, pardon me. I was forced to leave Naples so quickly on business for the King that I was unable to pay my proper respects before leaving.

OCTAVIO. My friend, Don Juan, this needs no pardon from me. For I see we have met again today in Seville.

DON JUAN. Who would have thought that I would see you in Seville and have the opportunity of serving you? Although it is true that Naples is an excellent town, I think you'll find Seville a worthy match.

OCTAVIO. Before I came this way I would have laughed at what you've said. But having seen Seville, I find your praises very faint. But who is this gentleman coming toward us?

DON JUAN. The Marquis de la Mota. If you will pardon my discourtesy . . .

OCTAVIO. If ever you should need my arm and sword, they are at your command.

CATALINON (*aside*). Or better still, an offer to lend his name to trick a lady.

DON JUAN. I am delighted to have met you.

(*Exeunt* OCTAVIO *and* RIPIO. *Enter the* MARQUIS DE LA MOTA.)

MARQUIS. I have been following you all day without success. Don Juan, how could you return and force your oldest friend to track you down?

DON JUAN. By God, my friend, you'd think I'd really wronged you. Tell me, how is Seville?

---

* These are both signs of the zodiac: Sagittarius is the archer; Capricorn is the goat. Perhaps the goat's horns are meant to imply cuckoldry.

MARQUIS. The court is completely different.

DON JUAN. And the women?

MARQUIS. Judge for yourself.

DON JUAN. Ines?

MARQUIS. Gone to Vejel. To pass the time.

DON JUAN. Perhaps to die. And Constanza?

MARQUIS. Ah, poor Constanza. I'm afraid her hair and eyebrows are going. A Portuguese once remarked that she was getting along and she thought he said she was beautiful.

DON JUAN. Of course, since the Portuguese word for "old" sounds like the Castilian for "beautiful." What about Theodora?

MARQUIS. This summer she managed to slake the French disease in a veritable river of sweat. She's grown so docile that she even pulled a tooth for me and showered me with flowers.

DON JUAN. And Julia of the Lamplight?

MARQUIS. Now she lightens herself with paint.

DON JUAN. Is she still selling herself for trout?

MARQUIS. These days she has slipped to cod.

DON JUAN. What about Catarranas. Is it still loaded with the same old people?

MARQUIS. Loaded with gibbering idiots.

DON JUAN. What about those two sisters?

MARQUIS. And their mother, that monkey-woman Celestina who pumped them full of her scriptures.

DON JUAN. The old wife of Beelzebub! Tell me, what's happened to the older daughter?

MARQUIS. These days she's whiter than white. She's found herself a saint to fast for.

DON JUAN. And she always keeps the same vigil?

MARQUIS. Absolutely strict and saintly in the observance.

DON JUAN. And the younger one?

MARQUIS. Much better. She doesn't mind the rubble.

DON JUAN. Perhaps I should have been a bricklayer. Tell me, Marquis, have you laid any dead dogs to rest lately?

MARQUIS. Last night Don Pedro de Esquivel pulled a really mean trick. And tonight should be even better.

DON JUAN. I'll join you and perhaps add a few touches of my own. Tell me, my friend, any news from lovers' lane?

MARQUIS. Don't even mention it. I'm in danger on that score.

DON JUAN. How so?

MARQUIS. I'm in a hopeless affair.

DON JUAN. She doesn't return it?

MARQUIS. No, she loves me well enough.

DON JUAN. Who is she?

MARQUIS. My cousin, Doña Ana, who has just arrived in town.

DON JUAN. Where has she been?

MARQUIS. In Lisbon with her father the ambassador.

DON JUAN. Beautiful?

MARQUIS. Marvelous. Doña Ana de Ulloa is nature's masterpiece.

DON JUAN. As beautiful as that? By God, I'd love to see her!

MARQUIS. Truly she is the most beautiful thing under the eyes of the sun!

DON JUAN. Then marry this paragon of nature.

MARQUIS. The King wants to marry her to God knows who.

DON JUAN. But she loves you?

MARQUIS. So she writes me every day.

CATALINON (aside). The idiot must babble everything to the greatest rogue in Spain.

DON JUAN. Then you should be very satisfied in your love. Draw her out, plead with her, write her, and enjoy her.

MARQUIS. I'm on my way now to see if there have been any changes in plans.

DON JUAN. I wouldn't think of detaining you. I'll be here when you return.

MARQUIS. I'll be back.

CATALINON (to the SERVANT). Señor Cuadrado, so very round to be so square, goodbye.

SERVANT. Goodbye.

(Exeunt MARQUIS DE LA MOTA and his SERVANT.)

DON JUAN. Listen, my friend, now that we are alone. Follow the Marquis and find out where he goes.

(Exit CATALINON. A woman speaks at the window.)

WOMAN. Who am I speaking to?

DON JUAN. What's that?

WOMAN. Since you seem noble and prudent and are a friend of the Marquis, give him this letter. The honor of a lady depends upon it.

DON JUAN. As I am his friend and a gentleman, I will.

WOMAN. Thank you, stranger. Goodbye. (She disappears.)

DON JUAN. The voice has disappeared. This stroke of fortune is magic itself; as if the wind brought all lucky mail to me. This must be a letter from the lady whom the Marquis described so exquisitely. In Seville I am called the Rogue and my greatest delights are at the expense of the honor of women. Once out of sight I shall read the letter. When I think of her careful precautions I have to laugh. Ah, the letter's already open. And there's the signature: Doña Ana. It says: "My unkind father has betrothed me in secret. I cannot resist. I do not see how I can go on living since he has robbed me of life itself. If you respect me and my love for you, show it this one time. To show you my love for you, come to me this evening at eleven; the door will be open and I waiting. And we shall enjoy our love together. So that my servants may know you, wear a crimson cape. I send you all my love. Farewell." The poor deceived lovers! Could anything be easier? I cannot keep from laughing. This will be as easy as the affair in Naples with Isabella.

(*Enter* CATALINON.)

CATALINON. Here comes the Marquis.

DON JUAN. The two of us are going to have a busy night.

CATALINON. Some new trick?

DON JUAN. My greatest.

CATALINON. Master, I cannot approve of this. We cannot keep on like this time after time. Sooner or later we'll be caught. He that lives by tricks will be tricked by tricks.

DON JUAN. Has the impertinent fool started preaching again?

CATALINON. The truth of what I say gives me the courage to speak out.

DON JUAN. Just as fear makes you a coward. When a man is a servant he does not need to be bothered by decisions and matters of the will. He does all things and speaks of nothing. He who wishes to be always employed finds it most expedient to be always active. The one who does the most, gains the most.

CATALINON. And those who are most active, are most often liable to meet with disaster.

DON JUAN. This time I'm warning you. I won't do it again.

CATALINON. Whatever you say or command I'll do just as if I were caught between a tiger and an elephant.

DON JUAN. Quiet, here comes the Marquis.

CATALINON. Is he the next victim?

(*Enter the* MARQUIS DE LA MOTA.)

DON JUAN. While you were gone, Marquis, I received a message from this window very pleasing to you. I was unable to see the person but she had a woman's voice. She said that you should come in secret to the door on the stroke of midnight wearing a crimson cape so that you will be recognized by the maids.

MARQUIS. What did you say?

DON JUAN. This was the message I received although I could not see who spoke.

MARQUIS. This message is the breath of life to me. Ah my friend, I could kiss your feet.

DON JUAN. My friend, since I am not your cousin, why should you waste your kisses on me? Particularly, since you will soon be sharing embraces with her.

MARQUIS. Your wonderful message has made me wild. Oh sun, you must go down!

DON JUAN. It seems to be going in that direction.

MARQUIS. Come on, my friends, we shall wait for the night which must come quickly. My joy has made me mad!

DON JUAN (aside). That's not hard to see. I think it should reach its crest at about midnight.

MARQUIS. Ah, cousin of my soul. How wonderfully you have repaid my loyal love.

CATALINON (aside). Christ, right now I wouldn't give a penny for his cousin's chances.

(Exit the MARQUIS and enter DON DIEGO.)

DON DIEGO. Don Juan?

CATALINON. It's your father.

DON JUAN. Yes, father?

DON DIEGO. I wish I might see a son with a better reputation. Do you wish me to die of shame at your affairs?

DON JUAN. Why are you so upset?

DON DIEGO. Because of your mad behavior, the King has commanded your exile from the city. He is angry about a crime which though unknown to me was known to him—one which is so vile that I can scarcely bring myself to speak of it. Such a treacherous betrayal of your friend and in the royal palace, too! May God call you to answer for your crimes. For although he now seems to condone your actions and give them license by withholding his hand, your punishment is sure. What an awful doom awaits those who profane his name, and mighty judgment after death.

DON JUAN. After death? So long a time? Then I have ample leisure in which to seek repentance.

DON DIEGO. When the time comes it will seem all too short.

DON JUAN. As to His Highness' punishment? Will it too be for long?

DON DIEGO. Until the grave injury done to Duke Octavio has been mended and the wrongs to Isabella have been set to right. You will live in exile in Lebrija. You will leave immediately and thank his mercy for so light a sentence.

CATALINON (aside). If he knew about the fishergirl the old man would take the lightness of the sentence even more heavily.

DON DIEGO. Since you are oblivious to my entreaties and the seriousness of earthly punishment, I leave you in the hands of God. (Exit DON DIEGO.)

CATALINON. I think he was a little upset.

DON JUAN. That's his age. Come, nightfall is on its way, it's time to attend to the Marquis.

CATALINON. And to his lady.

DON JUAN. Which should be a fine exploit.

CATALINON. If nothing happens.

DON JUAN. Enough, Catalinon.

CATALINON. Master, as far as women are concerned, you are like a plague of locusts. To give them a fair chance, just before you arrive in a town, a proclamation should be posted: "Beware of the man whom all women should fear, the Rogue of Spain."

DON JUAN. What an excellent title!

(It is now night. The MARQUIS enters with musicians who flank the stage.)

MUSICIANS.   He who pines for his delight
                Anxiously awaits the night.

MARQUIS. Ah night, wonderful and cold, herald of my joy. Run clocks to the midnight hour and protect me from the vengeance of the dawn.

DON JUAN. What's this?

CATALINON. Music.

MARQUIS. I feel the touch of the poet. Who's there?

DON JUAN. A friend.

MARQUIS. Don Juan?

DON JUAN. Marquis?

MARQUIS. Who else?

DON JUAN. I recognized you by your cape.

MARQUIS (to the MUSICIANS). Sing, for Don Juan is here.

MUSICIANS.   He who pines for his delight
Anxiously awaits the night.

DON JUAN. Whose house is that that you seem to admire so much?

MARQUIS. The house of Don Gonzalo de Ulloa.

DON JUAN. Where are we off to?

MARQUIS. To the street of the Portuguese.

DON JUAN. In Seville?

MARQUIS. Aren't you aware that the very best (or worst) of Portugal lives right here with us in Spain?

DON JUAN. Do they? Where?

MARQUIS. In the Street of the Serpent where the Portuguese Adam insists that a thousand Eves consume a bit of his pockets. And the hungry wenches take quite a bite in dorados and doubloons.

DON JUAN. I will join you there. But first I have a bit of business.

MARQUIS. There is a man who has followed me . . .

DON JUAN. If he comes this way, he will not leave alive.

MARQUIS. I will go; take this cape for your protection.

DON JUAN. Good; now show me the house.

MARQUIS. Now, while you are doing this, change your voice and way of speaking. Do you see that lattice?

DON JUAN. I see it.

MARQUIS. Then move quite close and whisper: "Beatrice." Then slip in.

DON JUAN. And the woman?

MARQUIS. Cool but firm and round.

CATALINON. Sounds like a water jar.

MARQUIS. I'll meet you on the cathedral steps.

DON JUAN. Goodbye, Marquis.

CATALINON. Where to now?

DON JUAN. Quiet, fool. We're off to my appointment.

CATALINON. Can nothing escape you?

DON JUAN. I love these little exchanges.

CATALINON. Will you throw the cape at the bull?

DON JUAN. No need, for the bull has lent his cape to me. And she will think that I am he.

MUSICIANS. How cleverly it's done.

DON JUAN. And error shall be king.

MUSICIANS. All the world is error-ridden!
He who pines for his delight
Anxiously awaits the night.

SCENE 2: *The house of* DON GONZALO.

DOÑA ANA (*within*). Traitor, you have deceived me. You are not the Marquis.

DON JUAN (*within*). I tell you I am.

DOÑA ANA (*within*). Traitor! You lie, you lie!

(*Enter* DON GONZALO *with drawn sword.*)

DON GONZALO. This is Doña Ana's voice.

DOÑA ANA (*within*). Is there no one to kill this traitor who has destroyed my honor?

DON GONZALO. Can this be? Her honor destroyed? And her tongue like a bell proclaims it for all to hear.

DOÑA ANA (*within*). Kill him.

(*Enter* DON JUAN *and* CATALINON *with drawn swords.*)

DON JUAN. Who is this?

DON GONZALO. The barbican of the tower of my honor has been toppled, traitor. Though my life stood guard there.

DON JUAN. Let me pass.

DON GONZALO. Pass? Over the point of my sword.

DON JUAN. You shall die.

DON GONZALO. No matter.

DON JUAN. Do you realize that I must kill you?

DON GONZALO. Die yourself, traitor!

DON JUAN. This is how I die. (*Stabs* DON GONZALO.)

CATALINON. If I escape, I swear I shall take part in no more tricks and no more feasts.

DON GONZALO. You have killed me.

DON JUAN. You have killed yourself.

DON GONZALO. What reason did I have to live?

DON JUAN. Let's be off.

(*Exeunt* DON JUAN *and* CATALINON.)

DON GONZALO. You have filled my chilly blood with fury. I am dead. No better fate awaits me. My fury will follow you, traitor. For a traitor is a traitor because he is a coward.

(DON GONZALO *dies. Enter the* MARQUIS DE LA MOTA *with the* MUSICIANS.)

MARQUIS. Midnight will be striking soon. Don Juan's late. How difficult it is to wait.

(*Enter* DON JUAN *and* CATALINON.)

DON JUAN. Is it the Marquis?

MARQUIS. Don Juan?

DON JUAN. Yes. Here's your cape.

MARQUIS. And your joke . . .

DON JUAN. I'm afraid it ended in death.

CATALINON. Master, flee from the dead man.

MARQUIS. Did you trick her?

DON JUAN. I did.

CATALINON (*aside*). And you too, quite handsomely.

DON JUAN. But the joke spilt blood.

MARQUIS. Don Juan, I'll pay it all, for the girl will blame me.

DON JUAN. Goodbye, Marquis.

MARQUIS. May this joyful night last forever.

DON JUAN. Let's go.

CATALINON. I think I could outrace an eagle.

(*They exeunt.*)

MARQUIS. You may all go home; I'll go on from here alone.

SERVANTS. God made the night for sleep.

(*They exeunt.*)

VOICES (*within*). Have you ever seen a greater tragedy or disgrace?

MARQUIS. God protect me! These voices seem to come from the plaza of the Alcazar. What could be happening at such an hour? My breast is frozen. I seem to see Troy afire again, for there are torches flashing giant flames like comets streaming their fiery trains. Why are there these squadrons of fire like stars dividing into squads? I will find out.

(*Enter* DON DIEGO *and* GUARDS *with torches.*)

DON DIEGO. Who's there?

MARQUIS. One who comes to find the reason for all this clamor.

DON DIEGO (*to guards*). Arrest him!

MARQUIS. Arrest me?

DON DIEGO. Return your sword to its sheath. There is greater courage in not resorting to arms.

MARQUIS. Do you know that you are speaking to the Marquis de la Mota?

DON DIEGO. Give me your sword. The king has ordered your arrest.

MARQUIS. My God!

(*Enter the* KING *and attendants.*)

KING. See that he does not escape in Spain or in Italy if he should go there.

DON DIEGO. My lord, here is the Marquis.

MARQUIS. Is it true that Your Highness ordered my arrest?

KING. Take him, and place his head upon a stake. Remove him from my presence.

MARQUIS. Ah, how quickly the glories of love can turn into disaster. "There is many a slip between the cup and the lip." But what can be the reason for the King's actions? I do not know why I have been arrested.

DON DIEGO. Who can know better than you?

MARQUIS. Me?

DON DIEGO. Come.

MARQUIS. Fantastic!

KING. Try him tonight and cut off his head in the morning. As for the commander, with much solemnity and majesty, as is given to royalty, conduct him to his grave. His tomb shall be a monument of bronze and many types of stone, engraved with gothic letters announcing his vengeance. His statue shall adorn the tomb. Where is Doña Ana?

DON DIEGO. She has fled to sanctuary with the Queen.

KING. Castille has suffered a great loss; have each captain of the realm weep for Calatrava.

SCENE 3: *Near Dos Hermanas.*

(*Enter* BATRICIO *and his betrothed* AMINTA, *the elderly* GASENO, BELISA, *and* MUSICAL PEASANTS.)

MUSICIANS (*singing*).
The handsome April sun glides on above
With bloom and clover and with love;
Our star on earth thus serves the skies;
His beauty multiplies in Aminta's eyes.

BATRICIO. On this carpet of flowers strewn upon the frost-like earth, the dying sun loses its light and hastens on to its own rebirth. Let us sit and enjoy the beauties of this place.

AMINTA. Fill the ears of my Batricio with a thousand charming melodies.

MUSICIANS (*singing*).
The handsome April sun glides on above
With bloom and clover and with love;
Our star on earth thus serves the skies;
His beauty multiplies in Aminta's eyes.

GASENO. Beautifully sung. Even the Kyries * do not have a finer sound.

BATRICIO. When the April sun sees your crimson lips and shining teeth, it hides its face in shame.

AMINTA. Batricio, in spite of the outrageous flattery in your words, I thank you. But from this time on I shall be the moon and take my light from you, my all-commanding sun. And may the dawning ever touch us with its gentle light.

MUSICIANS (singing).
The handsome April sun glides on above
With bloom and clover and with love;
Our star on earth thus serves the skies;
His beauty multiplies in Aminta's eyes.

(Enter CATALINON in traveling attire.)

CATALINON. Señores, two more guests have come to join your wedding feast.

GASENO. Let the whole world come; we will welcome them all. Who is with you?

CATALINON. Don Juan Tenorio.

GASENO. The old man?

CATALINON. No, Don Juan, the son.

BELISA. He must be a fine figure of a man.

BATRICIO (aside). This is an evil omen. This dashing gentleman will stir up jealousy and cast a shadow over the affair. How did he hear of our wedding feast?

CATALINON. On the road to Lebrija.

BATRICIO (aside). The devil must have sent him. But why do I brood? Let everyone join hands and enjoy the wedding feast. But still, a gentleman at my wedding . . . an evil sign.

GASENO. Let them all come, the Colossus of Rhodes, the Pope and Prester John, Don Alfonso the Eleventh, his court and all his followers too. For we have mountains of bread, Guadalquivirs of wine, Babylons of bacon, and larders full of birds and doves and basted hens. You are welcome to Dos Hermanas; bring in your noble gentleman who does such honor to this old head.

BELISA. He is the son of the chancellor.

BATRICIO. An evil omen, for they must seat him by the bride. I have no appetite for this affair. I am condemned to jealousy, to love, to suffer and be silent.

(Enter DON JUAN.)

DON JUAN. As I was passing on the road, I heard that

* A part of the Mass which follows the Introit; music accompanies it.

there was a wedding celebration here. So I have come to share your joy.

GASENO. Your very presence does us honor.

BATRICIO (*aside*). And I, the host, say to myself that the hour of your arrival is an evil one.

GASENO. Find a place for the gentleman.

DON JUAN. With your kind permission I'll sit here. (*He sits next to the bride.*)

BATRICIO. Señor, if you sit down before me, you'll be in the place of the bridegroom.

DON JUAN. I could not object to that.

GASENO. But this is the bridegroom.

DON JUAN. You must pardon me for my error and ignorance.

CATALINON (*aside*). Pity the poor bridegroom.

DON JUAN. I believe he is angry.

CATALINON. I can see that. But if he is to be the bull then it seems to be quite natural. I would not give one toss of his horns for his honor or his wife. Poor fellow, he's in the hands of Lucifer.

DON JUAN. I cannot believe my good fortune. I almost envy your husband.

AMINTA. You're flattering me.

BATRICIO. It is true that noblemen are bad luck at weddings.

GASENO. Let us eat and drink so that our great señor may have a chance to rest.

(DON JUAN *takes* AMINTA'S *hand.*)

DON JUAN. Why do you hide your hand?

AMINTA. It's mine.

GASENO. Come.

BELISA. Let's have a song.

DON JUAN. What do you think?

CATALINON. Me? I think we are going to die a wretched death at the hands of these peasants.

DON JUAN. Those eyes and the whiteness of those hands. They burn me with their nearness.

CATALINON. And so it's time to brand another lamb. This makes four.

DON JUAN. Come, they're watching me.

BATRICIO. An evil omen: a noble at my wedding.

GASENO. Sing.

BATRICIO. I'm dying.

CATALINON. They'll sing now and cry later.

ACT III

SCENE 1: *Dos Hermanas.*

(*Enter* BATRICIO, *deep in thought.*)

BATRICIO. Jealousy, clock of fear, that at all hours strikes torment, kills with each disjunct blow. Jealousy, with its ignorance, contempt for life, turns all it touches from delight to foolishness. Stop your torments! When love has brought me life, why do you seek my death? And you, cavalier, what do you want from me that you should bring this torment? For, just as I said when he came to share the wedding celebration, "his arrival is an evil one." How well he feasted, sitting by my bride, dipping his fingers into my plate while I was brushed aside. Then, each time I tried to share the nuptial plate, he pushed my hand away and, while he drank, exclaimed, "What rude and rustic manners!" And then when I appealed to the others, they just smiled and said, "You have no reason to object. This is nothing. What have you to fear? Be quiet for this is the way such things are done at Court." A fine custom this is! Even in Sodom such things were not done. Another man eating with the bride in front of the hungry groom! Then this rascal, at every bite, would ask, "Not eating that?" and then declare, "My friend you have no taste for the finer things." And that was when I ran off and left them. For this was an evil joke and not a marriage. Now no one will suffer my presence, and I cannot walk among honest Christians. Since he has shared the marriage feast, he will, I suppose, if he wishes, follow us to bed; and when I take my wife will say: "What rude and rustic manners!" But here he comes; there's nothing I can do. For he has seen me, and now I cannot hide.

(*Enter* DON JUAN.)

DON JUAN. Batricio.

BATRICIO. Yes, my lord? What do you want?

112

DON JUAN. I thought you should know . . .

BATRICIO (*aside*). It can only be more misfortune.

DON JUAN. . . . some time ago, Batricio, I gave my heart to Aminta and, in return, enjoyed . . .

BATRICIO. Her honor?

DON JUAN. Yes.

BATRICIO (*aside*). This confirms what I have seen. He would never have come if she had not wanted it. (*aloud*) So after all, she is only a woman.

DON JUAN. And, after all, being only a woman she grew jealous of my absence; she married another man. In short, she wrote begging me to come and I promised to enjoy what our hearts had pledged before. Briefly, that is the reason why I am here. Now that you know my intentions, I suggest that you take heed for your own life. If you try to stop me, I'll kill you without a scruple.

BATRICIO. I will not stand in your way. For both honor and women are stained by gossip and, under the force of rumor, a woman will always lose more than she gains. For she is like a bell, respected for her sound. And when that sound betrays a crack, it is well known that rumor sweeps in to destroy. Since you have wrecked for me the beauties that love invites, I no longer want a woman caught between bad and good, like a coin seen in conflicting lights. Enjoy her, señor, for a thousand years. I would rather die undeceived than live a cuckold. (*Exit* BATRICIO.)

DON JUAN. Through his honor I conquered him. For these peasants carry their honor in their hands so that they may constantly consult it; this same honor that once felt so much at home in the city but now has taken refuge in a more rural setting. Before I continue my hoax I must pretend to give satisfaction. I will talk to her father and receive his permission to marry and so lend his parental authority to my evening's entertainment. Tonight I must enjoy her and night is coming on. You stars which light my way, give me luck in this adventure. And keep the payment, which death must exact, due for many years to come.

(*Exit* DON JUAN.)

(*Enter* AMINTA *and* BELISA.)

BELISA. Look, Aminta, here comes your bridegroom. Quick, go prepare to receive him in your bed.

AMINTA. Belisa, I don't know what to think of this unhappy wedding. All day my Batricio has been bathed in melancholy. Confusion and jealousy are everywhere. Nothing but misfortune! Tell me, who is this nobleman who keeps me from my husband? It seems that impudence has become the mark of Spanish nobility. Please leave me, I have lost all sense and am ashamed. May evil destroy this nobleman who has robbed me of my pleasure!

BELISA. Quiet! I think I hear him coming. May no one dare to disturb the house of such a vigorous bridegroom.

AMINTA. Goodbye, my dear Belisa.

BELISA. Comfort him in your arms.

AMINTA. May the heavens turn my sighs into words of love and my tears into words of love.

(*Exeunt* AMINTA *and* BELISA. *Enter* DON JUAN, CATALINON *and* GASENO.)

DON JUAN. Goodbye, Gaseno.

GASENO. Let me come with you so that I may inform my daughter of her good fortune.

DON JUAN. Tomorrow will be soon enough for that.

GASENO. Very well. And may I say that I am proud to offer my own soul along with the girl.   (*Exit.*)

DON JUAN. He should have said "the bride." Saddle the mares, Catalinon.

CATALINON. When do we leave?

DON JUAN. At dawn when, almost dead with laughter, the morning comes to witness this splendid joke.

CATALINON. I hope you haven't forgotten that you have another wedding in Lebrija. You'd better take care of this one as fast as possible.

DON JUAN. This will be the most brilliant and exciting of my accomplishments.

CATALINON. If we come out of it alive.

DON JUAN. Isn't my father chief justice of the realm and one of the closest to the King? Then what can you be afraid of?

CATALINON. God takes his vengeance on despoilers and sometimes the spectators suffer as much as those who act. Since I have been the spectator to most of your adventures, I fear that I too will be caught by the thunderbolt which destroys you.

DON JUAN. Go, saddle the mares. Tomorrow night we'll sleep in Seville.

CATALINON. In Seville?

DON JUAN. Yes.

CATALINON. What are you saying? Look what you have done, master, and see how quickly death comes to cut off even the longest life. I tell you it's coming: punishment and pain and death.

DON JUAN. Death and vengeance hold no terrors for me!

CATALINON. But master . . .

DON JUAN. Go! Spare me your petty fears.

CATALINON. All power to the Turk and the Scythian, to the Persian and the Libyan, to the Galician, to the Torglocyte, to the German and the Japanese, to the tailor with his needle of gold in his hand, continuously imitating the white girl.   (*Exit.*)

DON JUAN. Night envelops us in black silence and the Pleiades in clusters of stars climb high above the Pole. Now is the time for adventure. Love, whom no man can resist, will guide my inclination. For I must reach her bed. (*calls*) Aminta!

(AMINTA *appears from within, dressed for bed.*)

AMINTA. Who is calling me? Is it you, Batricio?

DON JUAN. No, I am not Batricio.

AMINTA. Then who are you?

DON JUAN. Look carefully, Aminta, and you will know me.

AMINTA. Oh, I am lost! If we were found together at this hour.

DON JUAN. These precious hours are mine.

AMINTA. Go away or I will call for help. Don't try to presume on the courtesy which Batricio has shown to you. In Dos Hermanas we have Emilias and avenging Lucretias.

DON JUAN. Allow me just two words and keep the crimson blush of your cheeks hidden in your rich and precious heart.

AMINTA. Go, my husband is coming.

DON JUAN. Have no fear; I am your husband.

AMINTA. Since when?

DON JUAN. From now on.

AMINTA. Who arranged this?

DON JUAN. My desire.

AMINTA. And who married us.

DON JUAN. Your eyes.

AMINTA. On what authority?

DON JUAN. The authority of sight.

AMINTA. Does Batricio know of this?

DON JUAN. Yes, he has forgotten you.

AMINTA. Forgotten me?

DON JUAN. Yes, that I may adore you.

AMINTA. How?

Don Juan. In these two arms.

Aminta. Leave me!

Don Juan. How can I? If I were to leave you I would die.

Aminta. What a lie!

Don Juan. Aminta, listen and understand and you will know that I tell the truth; for women are the friends of truth. I am a nobleman, heir to the ancient family of the Tenorios, the conquerors of Seville. My father, after the King, is the most revered and esteemed in all the court; his lips hold the power of life or death. Traveling this way I happened to see you. For love guides these coincidences and then forgets, himself, that they were not merely chance. I saw you, adored you; I was consumed with the presence of you and determined to marry you. This I shall do though the King should roar and forbid it, though my father should rage and raise innumerable threats. I must be your husband. What have you to say?

Aminta. I don't know; for your truths are weighted down with lying rhetoric. I am a bride, this is certain; I am married to Batricio even though he deserts me.

Don Juan. An unconsummated marriage, whether through malice or trickery, can be annulled.

Aminta. In Batricio all was simple truth.

Don Juan. Enough of that; give me your hand and with it confirm our oaths.

Aminta. You're not deceiving me?

Don Juan. It is I who would be deceived.

Aminta. Then swear that you will fulfill your promises.

Don Juan. I swear by this hand, sweet lady, this winter of snowy white, to honor my promises.

Aminta. Swear to God that you will be damned if you fail.

Don Juan. If I default in either word or faith, I pray that God will deliver my life by perfidious treachery into the hands of a man. (aside) A dead man, of course. God forbid that he should be alive!

Aminta. With this vow I become your wife.

Don Juan. My soul is yours, here in my outstretched arms.

Aminta. To you I give my life and soul.

Don Juan. Ah, Aminta, wonder of my eyes! Tomorrow, your beautiful feet will walk in polished silver slippers, embellished with buttons of purest gold, your alabaster throat imprisoned in necklaces, and your fingers within their rings will seem to be fine transparent pearls.

AMINTA. From this day forward, my husband, my wish shall bend as yours, for I am yours.

DON JUAN (*aside*). How little you know the Rogue of Seville!   (*They exeunt.*)

SCENE 2: *Near Tarragona.*

(*Enter* ISABELLA *and* FABIO *in traveling clothes.*)

ISABELLA. How treacherously he robbed me of my rightful master, who both respected and admired me! What a fatal blow to truth fell on that horrid night . . . that cloak of day, the Antipodes of the sun, the bride of dreams.

FABIO. What is the good of this sadness, Isabella, which fills your heart and eyes, if love is but a crafty art, the spoils of which is sadness? If he who laughs today must cry tomorrow? The sea, disturbed by this towering storm, runs with danger. The galleys have already sought shelter, Duchess, beneath the towers that crown this beach.

ISABELLA. Where are we now?

FABIO. At Tarragona. In a little while we shall be in the beautiful city of Valencia, the very palace of the sun. Then, after several days of rest and pleasure, you will sail to Seville, the eighth wonder of the world. Why weep over the loss of Octavio? For Don Juan is more noble and his fame shines like the sun itself. Then why be sad? They say that Don Juan Tenorio is now a count and the king himself has arranged this match. And Don Juan's father is second only to the King.

ISABELLA. I am not sad at marrying Don Juan, whose nobility is known throughout the world. I weep because my lost honor must rattle back and forth on the tongue of the world for the rest of my life.

FABIO. Look, here comes a fishergirl, tenderly sighing and lamenting, her face sweet with tears. No doubt she has come to find you. While I go find the rest of your escort, you two may console yourselves in sweet laments together.

(*Exit* FABIO *and enter* TISBEA.)

TISBEA. Rough Spanish sea with billows of fire and flying waves; Troy of my poor home; in whose abysmal depths this fire was forged which the sea belched forth and which now burns my eyes with tears. Damned be that wooden hulk that, through your crystal, brought grief to Medea; damned be the first hemp, and the first cloth sails nailed to a cross in the wind—deceitful instruments!

ISABELLA. Beautiful fishergirl, why do you complain so tenderly of the sea?

TISBEA. I have made a thousand lamentations. Be happy that you can laugh at this.

ISABELLA. I, too, weep because of the sea. Where are you from?

TISBEA. From those huts which the wind has blasted and the storms so overrun that birds come to nest among the shattered pilings. Are you the beautiful Europa which the bulls are drawing here?

ISABELLA. Against my wishes, they are taking me to Seville to be married.

TISBEA. If you can pity my sad plight—for you too have been injured by the sea, take me with you as your humble slave. For I must see the King and beg his just reparation for an evil deed which a nobleman has played upon us. For I found Don Juan Tenorio upon the shore, half-drowned. I nursed him back to health; then, when his life was out of danger, like a snake in the grass he turned my head with promises of marriage and used my body for his pleasure. Evil comes to the woman who listens to the words of a man! For then he ran away. Now tell me if I have a right to vengeance.

ISABELLA. Silence, woman. Begone before you kill me. But if your words are wrung from you by grief, then you are not at fault. Continue! But are you speaking the truth?

TISBEA. If only it were false.

ISABELLA. Evil comes to the woman who believes the words of a man! But who is this with you?

TISBEA. A fisherman whose name is Anfriso. My poor father who can testify to the wrongs I have received.

ISABELLA. Although no vengeance can wipe out the enormity of such a crime, you are both welcome to join my escort.

TISBEA. Evil comes to the woman who believes the words of a man.   (*They exeunt.*)

SCENE 3: *A church in Seville.*

(*Enter* DON JUAN *and* CATALINON.)

CATALINON. Things have gone from bad to worse.
DON JUAN. How's that?
CATALINON. Octavio has found out about the affair in
Italy. The Marquis has discovered that the message you
gave him was a fake. Isabella has come to Spain to be your
wife and . . .
DON JUAN. Enough! (*hits him*)
CATALINON. You've broken a tooth!
DON JUAN. Tell me, where did you hear all this nonsense?
CATALINON. Nonsense! What nonsense? This is the truth.
DON JUAN. No matter. Let Octavio come. Am I not alive
with hands to help me? Where are our rooms?
CATALINON. In a very secret street.
DON JUAN. Good.
CATALINON. And the church is sacred ground.
DON JUAN. I don't think it's likely that they'll try to kill
me here in broad daylight. Did you see that peasant bride-
groom from Dos Hermanas?
CATALINON. Yes, he seemed both anxious and sad.
DON JUAN. It's been two weeks now, and Aminta has still
not discovered the hoax.
CATALINON. She's been so completely deceived that she
goes around calling herself Doña Aminta.
DON JUAN. What a beautiful joke!
CATALINON. A beautiful joke. And one she'll cry over for-
ever.
(*They see the Sepulchre of* DON GONZALO DE ULLOA.)
DON JUAN. Whose tomb is this?
CATALINON. This is where they buried Don Gonzalo.
DON JUAN. The man I killed? They seem to have done
quite admirably by him.
CATALINON. The King ordered it. What does that writing
say?
DON JUAN (*reading*). "Here the most loyal of knights
waits for God's vengeance on a traitor." Hilarious! And how
do you plan to take this vengeance, old man with your
stony beard?

CATALINON. Don't do it, master! There are some beards that are dangerous to pluck.

DON JUAN (*to the statue of* DON GONZALO). Tonight you must be my guest for dinner in my quarters. Then, if you are still bent on vengeance, we will fight. Although I'm afraid you'll have some difficulty with that sword of stone.

CATALINON. Master, it's getting very dark. We should be going.

DON JUAN (*to the statue*). This vengeance seems somewhat slow in coming; particularly if it depends on you. You must wake up! If you plan to wait for death to take revenge, you'll lose so many beautiful chances. There will be time enough till then. (*They exeunt.*)

SCENE 4: *The quarters of* DON JUAN.

(*Enter two* SERVANTS *who begin to lay the table.*)

FIRST SERVANT. We must prepare for dinner, for Don Juan is coming.

SECOND SERVANT. The tables are ready. There's nothing to do but wait. He's already late but what can I do? The wine will get warm and the food will get cold. Can you expect order from Don Juan, the king of disorder?

(*Enter* DON JUAN *and* CATALINON.)

DON JUAN. You locked the doors?

CATALINON. Just as you ordered.

DON JUAN. Quickly! Bring me my dinner.

SECOND SERVANT. It's here, sir.

DON JUAN. Sit down, Catalinon.

CATALINON. I'd rather not eat so fast.

DON JUAN. I said: Sit down!

CATALINON. If you say so.

FIRST SERVANT (*aside*). He must think he's on the road, to eat with his servant.

DON JUAN. Sit down.

(*A knock on the door.*)

CATALINON. Now that's what I call a knock!

DON JUAN. We seem to have a caller. Go see who it is.

FIRST SERVANT. Right away.

CATALINON. Perhaps it's—Justice, master.

DON JUAN. Perhaps it is. I'm not worried.

(*The* First Servant *returns, horrified.*)

Don Juan. Who is it? Why are you shaking?

Catalinon. Oh, he has seen something evil!

Don Juan. Don't make me angry. Tell me what you've seen. Is it some demon? (*to* Catalinon) Go see who it is. Quick!

Catalinon. Me?

Don Juan. Yes, you. On your feet, quick!

Catalinon. But, you see, they found my grandmother swinging back and forth like a bunch of grapes and ever since then, they say, she has walked the earth, a soul eternally damned. I don't much like the sound of this knock.

Don Juan. The door, Catalinon.

Catalinon. But master, you said yourself that I was a coward . . .

Don Juan. The door!

Catalinon. What a mess!

Don Juan. Are you going?

Catalinon. Who has the keys?

Second Servant. The door's just bolted, that's all.

Don Juan. Are you going or not?

Catalinon. Today Catalinon is finished! But suppose the outraged women have come for their revenge?

(Catalinon *goes to the door and rushes back, falls and jumps up.*)

Don Juan. What is it?

Catalinon. God protect me! They're killing me, they've got me!

Don Juan. Who's got you and killing you? What did you see?

Catalinon. Master, I went . . . I saw . . . When I was . . . What is it? What's happened to me? I opened it . . . and went blind . . . And then. . . . I swear to God . . . I spoke and I said, "Who are you?" And he said, he said . . . I ran into and I saw . . .

Don Juan. Who?

Catalinon. I don't know.

Don Juan. This is what comes of too much wine. Give me the candle, chicken-heart, I'll go myself.

(Don Juan *takes the candle and moves toward the door. Suddenly, he stops, confronted by* Don Gonzalo *in the shape of the statue at the tomb.* Don Juan *falls back, amazed, his hand on his sword, the other holding the candle. Slowly, ponderously,* Don Gon-*

ZALO *moves toward* DON JUAN *who retreats until they are standing in the center of the stage.*)

DON JUAN. Who is it?

DON GONZALO. It is I.

DON JUAN. But who are you?

DON GONZALO. The honorable knight whom you invited to dine.

DON JUAN. There's enough for two. In fact, if you've brought anyone with you, they are welcome to join us. Everything is ready. Sit down.

CATALINON. May God preserve me . . . And Saint Panuncio and Saint Anton! Tell me, is it possible for the dead to eat? He's nodding yes.

DON JUAN. Join us, Catalinon.

CATALINON. No thank you, master, I've had all I want.

DON JUAN. What's the matter? Are you afraid of a dead man? Suppose he were alive? You and your peasant superstitions!

CATALINON. You and your guest enjoy yourselves. I'm really quite full.

DON JUAN. Do you want to make me angry?

CATALINON. Spare yourself, master. I stink to high heaven.

DON JUAN. I am waiting for you to sit down!

CATALINON. I must be dead; I feel as if I were dead.

(*The* SERVANTS *are trembling.*)

DON JUAN. And you two. What is it? Tell me: Why are you trembling?

CATALINON. You know how it upsets me to have to eat with foreigners. And then you force me to sit down with a guest of stone . . .

DON JUAN. What idiotic fear! if he is stone, then why are you worried?

CATALINON. It just makes me nervous.

DON JUAN. Talk with him . . . courteously.

CATALINON. How are you? This other life, do you like it? Is it flat there or, maybe, mountainous? Uh, I suppose they have many prizes for poetry there?

FIRST SERVANT. He has nodded "Yes" to everything.

CATALINON. I suppose you have lots of taverns? Of course you do if Noah* is there with you.

DON JUAN. Quick, bring us some wine!

CATALINON. Señor . . . Señor Dead Man, in this coun-

---

* The incident of Noah's drunkenness is recorded in the Bible.

try of yours do they drink the wine plain or with ice? (DON
GONZALO *nods.*) With ice? Sounds like a fine place.
DON JUAN. If you would like some music, I'll have them
sing.
(DON GONZALO *nods.*)
FIRST SERVANT. He says "Yes."
DON JUAN. Let's have some music.
CATALINON. This is a fine dead man. He has wonderful
taste.
FIRST SERVANT. Of course. He's a nobleman and appre-
ciates the finer things.
(*They sing within.*)
SERVANTS.
If you, dear lady, await the day
When my reward shall come in death,
Be advised I still have breath
And many years before I pay.
CATALINON. He certainly isn't eating very much, this
Señor Dead Man. Perhaps, it's the summer weather, or
maybe he just doesn't eat very much. Funny, I just don't
seem to be able to keep my hands from trembling. He
seems to be a light drinker, too. I guess I can drink for
both of us. (*He drinks.*) A toast of stone. By God, I feel
better already.
(*The song continues.*)
SERVANTS.
For this delay I give my thanks
And for your patience through the years.
I'll mix my pleasure with your tears
For many more shall join your ranks.
CATALINON. Of all the women you have cheated, master,
tell me which one they were singing about.
DON JUAN. Tonight I laugh at them all, my friend. Isabella back in Naples . . .
CATALINON. But, master, she hasn't really been cheated,
since you are going to have to marry her . . . as of course
you should. But how about that fishergirl who saved your
life when you were drowning? She certainly received her
reward. And how about Doña Ana . . . ?
DON JUAN. Idiot! Must you insult my guest by bringing
up the very thing for which he waits to be revenged.
CATALINON. And there's no doubt but he's a man of
courage. Besides, he's made of stone and you're only flesh
and blood. This doesn't look good.

(DON GONZALO *signals that he wishes to be alone with* DON JUAN.)

DON JUAN. Here, clear the table! He wishes the rest of you to go and leave us alone.

CATALINON. This looks bad. For the love of God, don't do it, master! This dead stone man could kill a giant with one blow.

DON JUAN. Out, all of you. Luckily, I'm not Catalinon. Go on, before he becomes impatient. (*They leave.*) Now, the door is shut and we are quite alone; I am at your command. Tell me what you wish, whether you are spirit, phantom, or vision. If you live in agony or are waiting for some satisfaction to cure you, then tell me. I give my word that I will do what you command. Are you in God's grace or did I kill you before you could purge some mortal sin? Speak, I am waiting.

DON GONZALO (*speaking slowly as if from another world*). You swear to keep your word as a gentleman?

DON JUAN. Upon my honor I will keep it. I am a gentleman.

DON GONZALO. Then give me your hand. You hesitate.

DON JUAN. What? I afraid? Were you Hell itself, I'd give you my hand. (*He does.*)

DON GONZALO. You have given both your word and your hand. Tomorrow at ten you will be my guest at supper. Will you come?

DON JUAN. I expected something greater than that. Tomorrow I shall be your guest. But where?

DON GONZALO. At my tomb.

DON JUAN. Shall I come alone?

DON GONZALO. No, the two of you. I expect you to keep your word as I have kept mine.

DON JUAN. I shall keep it. I am a Tenorio.

DON GONZALO. And I an Ulloa.

DON JUAN. I'll be there without fail.

DON GONZALO. I believe you. Goodbye. (*He moves toward the door.*)

DON JUAN. Goodbye. Wait, I'll give you a man with a light.

DON GONZALO. I need no light. I am in a state of grace. (*He leaves very slowly, watching* DON JUAN. *When he has gone* DON JUAN *reveals his nervousness.*)

DON JUAN. God help me! My body is soaked with sweat.

And my heart is frozen in my entrails. When he took my hand I could feel the blistering fires of Hell. And yet when he spoke, I was chilled by the frost of his infernal breath. But this is my imagination. Fear, particularly the fear of the dead, is villainous. Why should I, who am not afraid of the noblest of men, alive with strength of mind and courage, tremble before a cold dead one? Tomorrow I shall be his guest in the chapel and all Seville will marvel at my courage.

SCENE 5: *The Alcazar.*

(*Enter the* KING *and* DON DIEGO TENORIO.)

KING. And Isabella has come at last?

DON DIEGO. But not eagerly, my lord.

KING. She is not happy with this marriage?

DON DIEGO. She has lost her good name, my lord.

KING. Her torment comes from something else. Where is she?

DON DIEGO. She is staying at the Convent of the Barefooted Nuns.

KING. Then send to the convent for her; for it is my wish that she wait upon the Queen.

DON DIEGO. If she is to be married to Don Juan, my lord should command his presence here at court.

KING. Send for him. I shall make this marriage famous throughout the world. From this day forth he shall be Don Juan Tenorio, Count of Lebrija, to rule and possess it. For though Isabella may have lost a Duke, she has gained a Count.

DON DIEGO. I kiss your feet for these gracious favors.

KING. They are no less than you deserve. This present favor is but partial payment for the many debts of service that I owe you. It also seems that today should witness also the wedding of Doña Ana.

DON DIEGO. With the Duke Octavio?

KING. Would it not be well for Octavio to save her from her grief? Doña Ana and the Queen have petitioned me to pardon the Marquis. And now that her father is dead, she wants a husband. Since she has lost one, I shall provide her with another. I wish you to go, with few men and as quietly as possible, to the fort at Triana and inform the Marquis that because of the petitions of his injured cousin I pardon him.

DON DIEGO. Now I have seen my greatest wish fulfilled.

KING. I have decided that the weddings will be performed this very evening.

DON DIEGO. Thus all things are resolved for the best. It should not be difficult to persuade the Marquis of the love his cousin bears him.

KING. And warn Octavio to caution. With women the Duke seems to be most unfortunate. For him they seem to be all appearance and opinion. I have also heard that he bears a grudge against Don Juan.

DON DIEGO. It does not surprise me since he knows the trick that Don Juan played which has brought so much pain to so many. Here comes the Duke.

KING. Stay with me for you, too, are implicated in this affair.

(*Enter* DUKE OCTAVIO.)

OCTAVIO. Unconquerable King, I beg permission to kiss your feet.

KING. Rise, Duke, and put on your hat. What is your problem?

OCTAVIO. I come to prostrate myself before you and beg of you a favor that I may restore my honor and my dignity.

KING. I am aware of your misfortune. What is your petition?

OCTAVIO. You know, my lord, by letters from your ambassador what the world knows from the tongue of rumor, how Don Juan, with Spanish arrogance, one night in Naples, a night most evil for me, with my name did profane the honor of a lady.

KING. Enough. All this I know. What precisely do you want?

OCTAVIO. Your permission to meet this traitor in open combat.

DON DIEGO. It cannot be. His blood is too noble . . .

KING. Don Diego!

DON DIEGO. My lord!

OCTAVIO. Who is this who dares speak like this before the King?

DON DIEGO. One who is silent at the King's command. If this were not the case, I would answer with my sword.

OCTAVIO. You are old.

DON DIEGO. When I was a young man in Italy, your countrymen, to their despair, knew my sword from Naples to Milan.

OCTAVIO. But now your blood is cold. What once was no longer is.

DON DIEGO. I was and I am. (*draws his sword*)

KING. Hold, enough! Be silent, Don Diego. You show little respect for my person. And you, Duke: after the marriages are celebrated we shall pursue this subject in a quieter vein. Don Juan is a gentleman of my court, a part of me and a member of my ancient line. You would do well to remember this in your dealings with him.

OCTAVIO. My lord, if this is your command, I will obey.

KING. Come with me, Don Diego.

DON DIEGO (*aside*). My son, what evil payment you have made for the love I bear you!

KING. Duke!

OCTAVIO. My lord!

KING. Tomorrow you shall be married.

OCTAVIO. If it is my lord's command.

(*Exeunt the* KING *and* DON DIEGO. *Enter* GASENO *and* AMINTA.)

GASENO. Perhaps this gentleman can tell us. Señor, could you tell us where to find Don Juan Tenorio? That is, if there is a famous Don Juan here at court of that name?

OCTAVIO. You said Don Juan Tenorio?

AMINTA. Yes, señor. That's the Don Juan we mean.

OCTAVIO. He's here. Why do you wish to see him?

AMINTA. Well, this gentleman is my husband.

OCTAVIO. How's that?

AMINTA. You mean you live at the palace and haven't heard?

OCTAVIO. Don Juan said nothing to me about it.

GASENO. Can that be possible?

OCTAVIO. That's the way it is.

GASENO. You see Doña Aminta here is a very honorable woman. When they are married she will bring to him an ancient Christian lineage. On top of that, she is sole heir of the hacienda we run in Dos Hermanas as if we were Counts or Marquis or something. You see, Don Juan took her from Batricio, the man she was engaged to marry.

AMINTA. Tell him I was a virgin before Don Juan came.

GASENO. Don't you think we have a just complaint?

OCTAVIO. This is another of Don Juan's tricks. These people are just in time to serve my vengeance well. What do you want?

GASENO. Since time is running on, I want this marriage settled. Otherwise I'll take this matter to the King himself.

OCTAVIO. That's fair enough.

GASENO. All I want is what is right and just.

OCTAVIO (aside). This comes just as I would have wished. (aloud) We are having a wedding in the palace.

AMINTA. I knew it! It's mine.

OCTAVIO. That is what we shall find out. Señora, come with me. You shall dress as befits a lady of the court and then you will be presented to the King.

AMINTA. Here is my hand; take me to Don Juan.

OCTAVIO. This, I assure you, is the best way.

GASENO. So it seems to me.

OCTAVIO (aside). These people will be the instruments of my revenge upon Don Juan for the outrage upon Isabella.

SCENE 6: *A street. On one side is the church where the* COMMANDER *is buried.*

CATALINON. How did the King receive you?

DON JUAN. More lovingly than my father.

CATALINON. Did you see Isabella?

DON JUAN. I did.

CATALINON. How was she?

DON JUAN. Like an angel.

CATALINON. Did she receive you well?

DON JUAN. Her face was bathed in rose and white, like a rose bursting its green prison at dawn.

CATALINON. So the wedding is tonight?

DON JUAN. Without fail.

CATALINON. Perhaps if you'd had a taste of marriage before, you wouldn't have had to taste so many women. Well, now you will have a wife and all the heavy responsibilities.

DON JUAN. Are you still playing the fool?

CATALINON. I just can't see why you had to get married today when you could have waited until tomorrow.

DON JUAN. What's wrong with today?

CATALINON. It's Tuesday. "For that Tuesday will be evil when you take a wife or travel."

DON JUAN. Nonsense! This is the combined idiocy of a thousand fools. I will call the day evil and unlucky when I run short of funds. Till then I am content.

CATALINON. Come. You must get dressed. It's late; they'll be waiting for you.

DON JUAN. First we have another appointment. Until it is over, they must wait.

CATALINON. What appointment?

DON JUAN. I am having supper with the dead man.

CATALINON. Do you have to?

DON JUAN. You know I gave my word.

CATALINON. And if you took it back what difference would it make? I don't see why stone people should expect live ones to keep their word.

DON JUAN. Because the dead man could denounce me as dishonorable.

CATALINON. Well, the church is locked anyhow.

DON JUAN. Well, knock then.

CATALINON. Why should I knock? Who'll open it? All the sacristans are asleep.

DON JUAN. Knock!

CATALINON. It's open!

DON JUAN. Then go in.

CATALINON. Let the friars go in with their stoles and hyssops.

DON JUAN. Then follow me and be quiet.

CATALINON. Quiet?

DON JUAN. Yes.

CATALINON. I'll be quiet. Oh God, please let me come out of here alive. Oh my, but this is a dark church.

(*They go in one door and out another.*)

CATALINON. Master, do you really . . . Oh me! Help me, master, they've got hold of my cape!

(DON GONZALO *enters as before and confronts them.*)

DON JUAN. Who is it?

DON GONZALO. It is I.

CATALINON. I am dead . . . I am petrified with fear.

DON GONZALO. I am the dead one. Do not worry. I did not believe that you would keep your word since you treat everything as a joke.

DON JUAN. You think me a coward?

DON GONZALO. Yes, because you fled just after killing me.

DON JUAN. I didn't want to be recognized. But I am here now. What do you want of me?

Don Gonzalo. I wish you to be my guest for supper.

Catalinon. You must excuse us. You see we are not accustomed to the food . . .

Don Juan. We shall stay.

Don Gonzalo. In that case, you must lift the top from this tomb.

Don Juan. The pillars too, if you like.

Don Gonzalo. Your courage and eagerness do you honor.

Don Juan. I don't lack for energy and courage.

Catalinon. What kind of African table is this? Don't you have anyone to wash it?

Don Gonzalo. Be seated.

Don Juan. Where?

Catalinon. Look, here come two black servants with stools. (*Two figures in black enter with stools.*) Well, I see dead people also use Flanders cloth.*

Don Gonzalo. Be seated.

Catalinon. You see, señor, I had an early dinner . . .

Don Gonzalo. I asked you to sit.

Catalinon. I'm sitting. God protect me. What do you call this dish?

Don Gonzalo. Tarantulas and vipers.

Catalinon. Oh, I see. Wonderful!

Don Gonzalo. This is what we eat here. You don't like it?

Don Juan. I would eat it, were it all the snakes in Hell itself.

Don Gonzalo. Now I shall have them sing for you.

Catalinon. What sort of wine is this?

Don Gonzalo. Try it.

Catalinon. Frost and vinegar!

Don Gonzalo. This is the wine that comes from our presses. (*They sing within.*)

> Mark those well whom God has judged
> And punished for their crimes.
> The day of reckoning arrives
> When this world's debts are paid.

Catalinon. God protect me from this song. I know it but it has never been sung for me before.

Don Juan. I feel a dagger of ice in my heart. (*They sing within.*)

> Meanwhile in the living world
> Let no shameless man declare

---

* Flanders was noted for fine weaving.

That death is many years away.
There'll come a time when he must pay.

CATALINON. What's in this little casserole?

DON GONZALO. Fingernails.

CATALINON. Then they must be the claws of a tailor.

DON JUAN. I have finished. Have them clear the table.

DON GONZALO. Give me your hand, if you are not afraid to give me your hand.

DON JUAN. What? I afraid? (*He grasps* DON GONZALO'S *hand.*) I'm on fire. Don't burn me so with your fire!

DON GONZALO. This is but a taste of the fire which you deserve. Wondrous are the ways of God, Don Juan. He has delivered you into the hands of the dead. This is God's justice. You pay for what you have done.

DON JUAN. I'm burning! Let me go! I'll kill you with this dagger! But the blows are lost in the thin air! Señor, your daughter was not harmed. She discovered the plot in time.

DON GONZALO. That matters little. The intent was there.

DON JUAN. Then let me call a priest so that I may confess and receive absolution.

DON GONZALO. You should have thought of that before. It's too late now.

DON JUAN. I am alive with fire! I'm burning! It's killing me! (*He falls dead.*)

CATALINON. There's no escape. And I must die for being your companion.

DON GONZALO. This is the justice of God. You pay for what you have done.

(*The tomb disappears with* DON JUAN *and* DON GONZALO *in a clap of thunder, leaving* CATALINON *alone.*)

CATALINON. God help me! What is this? The whole chapel is on fire with light and I am left to guard the dead. I'll slip out of here and tell his father. Saint George and the Holy Lamb of God protect me at least as far as the street. (*Exit.*)

SCENE 7: *The Alcazar.*

(*Enter the* KING, DON DIEGO, *and company.*)

DON DIEGO. The Marquis is here. He wishes to kiss your royal feet.

KING. Send him in and advise the Count so that he will not be kept waiting.

(*Enter* BATRICIO *and* GASENO.)

BATRICIO. My lord, do you permit impudence to go so far that even your own servants may abuse poor and humble people?

KING. What do you mean?

BATRICIO. The treacherous and detestable Don Juan Tenorio, on the night of my wedding before the nuptials, stole my wife. I have witnesses to prove it.

(*Enter* TISBEA *and* ISABELLA *and their train.*)

TISBEA. Señor, if Your Highness will not bring Don Juan Tenorio to justice, for the rest of my life I will proclaim my injury to God and man. When he was thrown half-drowned upon my shore I gave him life and comfort. He, in turn, repaid me with deceit and lust and promises of marriage.

KING. What are you saying?

ISABELLA. She speaks the truth.

(*Enter* AMINTA *and* DUKE OCTAVIO.)

AMINTA. Where is my husband?

KING. Who is he?

AMINTA. Don't you know? I have come to marry Don Juan Tenorio, a man of honor who will not break his promise of marriage.

(*Enter the* MARQUIS DE LA MOTA.)

MOTA. Great lord, the time has come to bring truth into the light. You should know that Don Juan Tenorio is guilty of the very crime for which you punished me. Not only is he guilty of the offense but he has cruelly tricked his best friend. These witnesses can testify to what I say.

KING. Could anything be worse than this? He must be seized and put to death.

DON DIEGO. If I have served you well, let this be my reward: arrest and destroy him lest the heavens strike me down for having cursed the world with a son so evil.

KING. So this is how my favorites act!

(*Enter* CATALINON.)

CATALINON. My lords, listen to the strangest story the world has ever heard and if you believe I lie, then kill me. One afternoon Don Juan came upon the statue of the Commander whom he had deprived of life and all its ornaments; he pulled his granite beard and mockingly invited him to dine. If only he had not done it! The statue came to dine and invited him in return. To keep the story short, after dinner, amid a thousand evil omens, he took Don Juan by the hand and crushing the life from him said: "God has ordered me to kill you in this fashion as punishment for your many crimes. You pay for what you have done."

KING. What is this?

CATALINON. I swear it's the truth. Just before he died, Don Juan swore that Doña Ana had not lost her honor but had discovered the trick in time.

MOTA. For this one bit of news you shall have a thousand gifts.

KING. God has delivered his just punishment! Let those who were supposed to wed be married, since the cause of all their grief is dead.

OCTAVIO. Since Isabella is now a widow, I shall marry her.

MOTA. And I my cousin Ana.

BATRICIO. And we shall join with ours for here ends *The Guest of Stone*.

KING. The tomb shall be carried to the church of San Francisco in Madrid so that the memory of these events shall be preserved in years to come.

THE TRUTH SUSPECTED
(*La verdad sospechosa*)

by Juan Ruiz de Alarcón

TRANSLATED BY
Robert C. Ryan

⬥

CHARACTERS

DON BELTRAN, *father to Don Garcia*

TRISTAN, *servant to Don Garcia*

DON GARCIA, *young gallant*

SEÑOR LICENCIADO, *lawyer and tutor to Don Garcia*

SEÑORITA JACINTA, *young lady*

SEÑORITA LUCRECIA DE LUNA, *young lady, friend of Jacinta*

ISABEL, *maid to Jacinta*

DON JUAN, *suitor of Jacinta*

DON FELIX, *friend of Don Juan*

DON SANCHO, *uncle to Jacinta*

CAMINO, *servant to Lucrecia*

PAGE, *servant to Don Juan*

DON LUIS DE LUNA, *father to Lucrecia*

Juan Ruiz de Alarcón

(1581-1639)

Born of aristocratic Spanish parents in Mexico City, Ruiz de
Alarcón went to Spain when scarcely twenty to study law and
theology at the University of Salamanca. Returning in 1607, he
pursued advanced studies at the University of Mexico. Finally in
1614 he settled in Spain for good. Sensitive and perceptive, he
tried his hand at playwriting, and wrote the best of his twenty
plays between 1615 and 1625. If he was one of the least prolific
writers of the Golden Age, he was also the most critical and one
of the most consummate craftsmen. He believed that the theater
should combine entertainment with social edification, and his
characters often become types representing vices or moral truths.
The fact that he was a foreigner in Spain and a scarecrow to
boot—a bowlegged little man, red-bearded, hunchbacked—made
him an easy target for his many jealous rivals. To some extent he
was to blame, due to his excessive pride, his pedantry, and ironically enough, his Don Juanism: he insisted on being a ladykiller!
However this may be, his well-contrived plays, admirably versi-
fied and deeply concerned with motivation and characterization,
did immortalize his name. Such plays as *La verdad sospechosa*
(*The Truth Suspected,* 1619), *Las paredes oyen* (1617), *Mudarse
por mejorarse* (1618), and *El tejedor de Segovia* (1622), not only
succeeded in Spain but found imitators in other countries, such
as Corneille, Molière, Goldoni, Schiller, and Victor Hugo.

BEST EDITIONS: A. Millares Carlo (ed.), *Obras completas.*
Mexico, Fondo de Cultura Económica, Vol. I, 1957; Vol. II,
1959; Vol. III, forthcoming.

ABOUT: A. Castro Leal, *Juan Ruiz de Alarcón su vida y su
obra.* Mexico, 1943. P. Henríquez Ureña, *Juan Ruiz de
Alarcón.* Havana, 1915. J. Jiménez Rueda, *Juan Ruiz de
Alarcón y su tiempo.* Mexico, 1939.

ACT I

SCENE 1: *A room in* DON BELTRAN'S *house.*

(DON GARCIA *and an old lawyer dressed as students, and in traveling costume, walk in through one door;* DON BELTRAN *and* TRISTAN *come in through another.*)

BELTRAN. Welcome home, my son. The trip must have been tiring.

GARCIA. Give me your hand, father. It's good to see you.

BELTRAN. How are you?

GARCIA. Tired, but happy to be home. The trip is a hard one. The only thing that kept me going was the thought of seeing you again.

BELTRAN. Well, now that you're here, you can start taking it easy. My, you look older! Tristan . . .

TRISTAN. Sir?

BELTRAN. You have a new master to take care of. From now on, you will serve my son, Garcia; you are wise in the ways of Madrid, and he will need you.

TRISTAN. I shall do my best to serve his every need. My knowledge shall be his knowledge.

BELTRAN. Tristan is no common servant, Garcia; he is a counsellor and a valued friend.

GARCIA. I'm sure that his counsel will prove valuable.
(Exits.)

BELTRAN. Now, Tristan, why don't you go help Garcia unpack?

TRISTAN. Certainly, sir. *(Exits.)*

BELTRAN. Well, old friend, how have things been going?

LAWYER. As a student, your son has made excellent progress. I shall miss his company greatly.

BELTRAN. May God be with you, señor Licenciado. You have always been grateful and discreet. I am pleased that Garcia has gained so much of your affection and confidence.

I assure you that I am so grateful that as well as obtaining for you, as I have, a position as magistrate, I would have— if I but could have—secured you a place on the highest court in the land, the Royal Council.

LAWYER. You are very good to me, señor.

BELTRAN. Yes, I have been. But I know that if I have helped you start up the ladder of success, you will now be able to climb, without my aid, to the very topmost rung— the Royal Council itself!

LAWYER. I am your servant, anytime, any place.

BELTRAN. Well, now, señor Licenciado, before you leave the helm of Garcia's ship and before I take on the responsibility of steering it on a straight course, I would like you to do one more thing for me and for him.

LAWYER. Señor, I am at your service.

BELTRAN. First, you must give me your word that you will do what I would have you do.

LAWYER. As God is my witness, señor, I swear that I will comply with your wishes.

BELTRAN. All that I wish to ask is that you tell me one thing. You know that it was my intention that Don Garcia should pursue a liberal arts course and finally become a lawyer. I knew that for him, as a second son, law provided the best door to the honors of the world. Then, as it pleased God to take away Don Gabriel, my older son, who originally was destined to carry on the family name and to assume the family responsibilities, I decided that Don Garcia should leave his law studies and come here to Madrid. Here, in the court of the King, he can mingle with the well-born gentlemen of Spain and, in my opinion, it is good that the noble houses should thus give their heirs to the service of the King. Well, Don Garcia is now a grown man who no longer needs a tutor and who must now be under my direction. My paternal love with just reason desires that, even if he is not better than everyone else, at least he shall not be called the worst. I want you, señor Licenciado, to tell me clearly, without flattery, what you think, inasmuch as you have trained him, what you think about his character and natural disposition, about his behavior and the way he spends his time, and what bad habits he has, if any. If he has any habit that I must take care to correct, don't think that you will anger or displease me by telling me about it. That he has bad habits is almost—almost—inevitable. Although this possibility grieves me, knowing what they are will be useful to me, even if the knowledge isn't pleasant. In no other way, by my faith, can you make me happier, or better show what affection you have for Garcia, than by giving me this information now, since I must have it before some harm or wrong results.

LAWYER. Such a strict admonition, señor, was not necessary to induce me to do what I have an obligation to do. It goes without saying that if a horse is delivered to a man, and if the horse-breaker does not inform the new owner of the good and bad habits of the horse, the horse will suffer and so will the new owner. It is right that I should tell you the truth. But please bear in mind that truth is a medicine which often tastes bad and does good. All of Don Garcia's actions have a certain quality; they are all quite fitting to his high birth. He is magnanimous and valiant, he is wise and he is ingenious, he is liberal, pious, and kindly, although at times he is hasty and impatient. I won't speak of the passions common to youth because with age conditions change. Just one fault—no more—have I found in him, and in spite of my scolding him about it, he has never corrected it.

BELTRAN. A thing that will jeopardize his position in Madrid?

LAWYER. Perhaps.

BELTRAN. What is it? Speak!

LAWYER. He doesn't always tell the truth.

BELTRAN. *He lies?* What an ugly trait in a man of obligation, in a man whose noble birth obliges him to act honorably!

LAWYER. I think that, whether it be his nature or just a bad habit, the vice will vanish. After all, you have a great deal of influence with him and his judgment is getting better with age.

BELTRAN. If the twig has not straightened itself while it was young and flexible, what will it be now that it is a sturdy tree?

LAWYER. In Salamanca, señor, the young men give rein to their high spirits. Each one follows his own pleasure. They make vice into a grace and an accomplishment, mischief into a gay celebration; in short, youth exercises its prerogative of turning the world and its values upside down. But here in Madrid, where we can see so many respected and accepted standards of honor, we can better hope for his reform.

BELTRAN. It almost makes me laugh to see how uninformed you are about Madrid. Do you think there is no one here who will teach him to lie? Even if Don Garcia were an expert liar, in Madrid, there are those to be found every day who could give him a handicap of a thousand lies and beat him before lunch. Let's drop this subject. As the bull who is goaded by a skilled hand attacks the nearest person, without looking for the one who has wounded him, so I, because of the sadness this news of my son has caused me, vented my anger on the first person I encountered. Believe me, if Garcia were to dissipate my fortune in blind love affairs, or if he were to consume it in gambling day and night; if he were of a reckless nature and inclined to quarreling and brawling; if he were to make a bad marriage, even if—yes, even if he were to die, I would be better able to stand all of these things than face the fact of his being a liar. What an ugly and horrible thing lying is! How opposed to my nature! Well now: I know what I must do—get him married before this defect comes to be generally known. I remain very satisfied with your devotion and care to Garcia, and I confess myself obligated to you for the good deed you have done me. When do you have to leave?

LAWYER. I would like to leave immediately.

BELTRAN. Won't you rest here for a while and enjoy Madrid?

LAWYER. I assure you that I would like to remain here with you, but my judicial duties await me.

BELTRAN. I understand. You're anxious to get started in your new job. Goodbye.   (Exits.)

LAWYER. Goodbye. My news seems to have disturbed Don Beltran. When all is said and done, even the wisest of men take disillusionment bitterly.   (Exits.)

SCENE 2: *Las Platerias—a section of the Calle Mayor where there are many silversmith's shops. It is a day later.*

(*Enter* DON GARCIA, *dressed as a gallant, and* TRISTAN.)

GARCIA. Does this outfit look good on me?

TRISTAN. It looks fine.

GARCIA. Good! Now, how's the woman situation?

TRISTAN. You're in town one day and already you begin looking for a woman?

GARCIA. Or women.

TRISTAN. Ha, ha. Are you an amorous young man?

GARCIA. Let us just say that I am a young man.

TRISTAN. Well, today you come to a place where love does not live idly. Beautiful women glitter in Madrid in the same way that bright stars glitter in the sky. In vice, in virtue, and in the state they have, as their influence varies, differences of splendor and magnitude. I don't intend that the noble ladies should be included in this group, for they are angels about whom no one dares have a bad thought. I will tell you only about those with "lusty" spirits who, though being divine, are still human; though being stars, may still be brought to earth. You will see beautiful married women, approachable yet discreet, that I will call "planets" because they shine very brightly. These, in conjunction with good-natured husbands, inspire generous natures in strangers. There are others, whose husbands are gone on missions, or are employed in the Indies or in Italy. Not all of them tell the truth in this, for there are a thousand sly ones who pretend to be married so that they may live in liberty. You will see wise and unscrupulous old women who have just "adopted" beautiful daughters to sell to the highest bidder. The daughters, if I may call them that, are fixed stars, and their recently acquired mothers are wandering stars. There is a great multitude of higher-class courtesans who, among courtesans, are of the first magnitude. Following these, there are others who wish to be like them, and although they aren't so good, they are better than streetwalkers. These are stars that give off less illumination; but if necessity arises, you will have to use them for lighting. I don't count the streetwalker as a star, for she is a comet; neither is her light perfect, nor is her exact position known. In the morning she demands her money, and as soon as she secures it she promptly disappears. Then, you can always find girls who are only out for pleasure. These are meteors who only last as long as they burn. But it would be well for you to keep in mind, if you plan on reaching for some of these stars, that very few of them are stable, even if you were to give them a fortune. Keep in mind, as I always do, that there is only one sign of the Virgin in the zodiac, and that there are three with horns: the Ram, the Goat, and the Bull. And so, without trusting them, remember this: money is the axis around which all of these stars revolve.

GARCIA. Are you an astrologer?

TRISTAN. I studied astrology while I was seeking a government post.

GARCIA. Then you have been an office-seeker?

TRISTAN. I was an office-seeker, to my sorrow.

GARCIA. Why didn't you get a position, then?

TRISTAN. Because, señor, I lacked the fortune and the means—although he who serves you could not hope for better luck.

GARCIA. Forget that flattery and look at that marble-white hand, at those eyes that are shooting arrows of death and love at the same moment.

TRISTAN. Are you talking about that señorita going by in the carriage?

GARCIA. Indeed, what else merits such praise? The first woman that I see in Madrid enchants me.

TRISTAN. The first one you've ever seen on earth?

GARCIA. No. The first one in heaven, yes; for this woman is divine.

TRISTAN. You will be continually finding so many beautiful ones that you won't be able to be content with one who only resembles the others. I have never had a constant love or desire here; whenever I see a new beauty, I immediately forget the one I have just seen.

GARCIA. Where is there brightness that could outshine the brilliance of those eyes?

TRISTAN. When one looks at things through the spectacles of desire, those things generally look better.

GARCIA. Do you know her, Tristan?

TRISTAN. Don't bring down to earth that which you adore as divine. Such noble señoritas don't have any contact with Tristans.

GARCIA. Well, anyway, whoever she may be, I love her and I must find out who she is. Tristan, follow her.

TRISTAN. Wait. She is getting out at the shop.

GARCIA. I want to approach her. Is this acceptable in Madrid?

TRISTAN. Yes, provided that you remember the rule I told you about money being the axis.

GARCIA. Tristan, my fortune.

TRISTAN. Go ahead! And may you carry Caesar with you. But watch out that what I say doesn't lead you astray as to my thought. Consider, señor, that the other lady who is now following her out of the coach might just as well be a heaven worth attaining.

GARCIA. She is beautiful also.

TRISTAN. Be sure to see if her maid is ugly.

GARCIA. The carriage is a bow of love, and they are arrows which it shoots forth. I shall approach them.

TRISTAN. I would tell you a proverb first which should be useful when approaching such a divine woman.

GARCIA. And what is it?

TRISTAN. She repays him who pays—himself.

GARCIA. May I have such luck!

TRISTAN. Well then, while you are talking, I will go and strike up a conversation with the coachman to find out who they are.

GARCIA. Will he tell you?

TRISTAN. Why not? He's a coachman, isn't he?   (*Exit.*)
(*Enter* JACINTA, LUCRECIA *and* ISABEL *with mantillas;* JACINTA *falls down and* GARCIA *comes up and gives her his hand.*)

JACINTA. Heaven help me!

GARCIA. Pray allow this hand to raise you, if I deserve to be an Atlas to such a splendid heaven.

JACINTA. You must be Atlas, because you come to lift it up.

GARCIA. It is one thing to touch and another thing to deserve. What victory is there in touching beauty, if I may do so only because it is necessary, and not because the beauty wishes it. With my own hand I touch the sky; but of what significance is this touching if I may do so only because it has fallen and not because I have risen?

JACINTA. What is your wish, then?

GARCIA. To attain—and obtain.

JACINTA. But to arrive at the goal without first going through the intermediate steps—wouldn't this be luck?

GARCIA. It would, indeed, my lady.

JACINTA. Then why do you complain? If you didn't deserve your good luck, aren't you all the luckier?

GARCIA. Kind and unkind actions take their meaning from the way they were intended. I am not favored by touching you if you do not desire me to be. And so, allow me to regret gaining such good fortune, if I gain your hand without your heart.

JACINTA. How can you judge my heart when you have seen me just this once?
(*Enter* TRISTAN.)

TRISTAN (*aside*). The coachman told me what I wanted to know. I know who they are.

GARCIA. You mean that you have not noticed me until now?

JACINTA. How could I, when I have never seen you before?

GARCIA. Oh, to be so ignored! Haven't you seen that for more than one whole year I have adored you from afar?

TRISTAN (*aside*). A year? He only arrived in Madrid yesterday!

JACINTA. More than a year? I swear that I have never seen you before in my life.

GARCIA. When I arrived here from the Indies, the first woman that I saw was heavenly. And although I immediately gave up my heart and soul to you, you have not known it because I have not had the occasion to tell you how I feel.

JACINTA. You're from the Indies?

GARCIA. And, since I saw you, my riches are greater than those of all my gold mines in Peru.

TRISTAN (*aside*). Indies? Gold mines?

JACINTA. And are you as stingy as rich men are reported to be?

GARCIA. Love makes even the worst miser generous.

JACINTA. Well then, if you are telling the truth, may I expect precious gifts?

GARCIA. If my money may give credit to my heart—gold is but a small investment to show you how much I adore you—I will give you worlds of gold for just one world of love. But insofar as I neither merit your divine beauty, nor can I balance the power of it with just the greatness of my adoration, may I ask that, as a small sign of my love, you allow me to buy you anything and everything you desire from this jewel shop.

JACINTA (*aside*). I have never seen such a man in Madrid. (*to* LUCRECIA) Lucrecia, what do you think of this generous stranger?

LUCRECIA. That you don't think badly of him, and that if you don't think badly of him, he is deserving.

GARCIA. The jewels that you like I will give you. Take anything you want from those showcases.

TRISTAN (*aside to* GARCIA). You're being very rash, señor.

GARCIA. I am lost, Tristan.

ISABEL (*aside to the women*). Don Juan approaches.

JACINTA. I am pleased, señor, with what you offer me.

GARCIA. You will offend me if you don't take advantage of my offer.

JACINTA. You are mistaken, señor, in presuming that I can receive more than just the offer.

GARCIA. Then what have I received in exchange for the heart I have given you?

JACINTA. My interest in what you have said.

GARCIA. I place a great value on that.

JACINTA. Goodbye.

GARCIA. Goodbye, and give me permission to love you.

JACINTA. The heart needs no permission to love.

(*The women exeunt.*)

GARCIA. Follow them.

TRISTAN. If you want me to follow them in order to find out where your beautiful lady lives, I already know.

GARCIA. Well then, don't follow them; for such ill-timed diligence might prove annoying to her.

TRISTAN. The coachman said, "Doña Lucrecia de Luna, who is my mistress, is the name of the most beautiful one; and the other woman who accompanies her, I know where her house is, but I don't know her name."

GARCIA. Doña Lucrecia de Luna—what a beautiful name! Well, if the most beautiful one is named Lucrecia, there is no question about it; it is to her that I spoke, and her whom I love. For just as the rising sun makes the stars vanish, she shone so much brighter than the others that they disappeared in her brilliance.

TRISTAN. Well, as far as I'm concerned, the one who didn't talk very much was the most beautiful.

GARCIA. What good taste you have!

TRISTAN. It's certain that I have no say in this. But I am attracted to any woman who keeps her mouth shut; it is enough reason for me to judge the other woman more beautiful by the very fact that she kept silent. But supposing you're wrong, señor, I can quickly find out from the coachman which one is which.

GARCIA. And Lucrecia, where is her house?

TRISTAN. If I remember correctly, he said it was near the convent of La Victoria.

GARCIA. Ah! Such a fashionable part of the city is an appropriate universe for my lady of the moon!

(*Enter* DON JUAN *and* DON FELIX *from another direction.*)

JUAN. Dinner with music? Ah, what luck!

GARCIA. Isn't that Don Juan de Sosa?

TRISTAN. The same.

JUAN. Who could the fortunate lover be who has me so jealous?

FELIX. I am confident you will soon find out.

JUAN. To think that another lover has taken her who called herself mine to dinner—with music—by the river!

GARCIA. Don Juan de Sosa!

JUAN. Who is it?

GARCIA. Have you already forgotten Don Garcia?

JUAN. I never expected to see you in Madrid. That and your new clothing made me forget momentarily.

GARCIA. I must look a lot different from the way I looked in Salamanca, eh?

JUAN. You were dressed like all of the rest of the students in Salamanca. Now you look more like a gallant than a student.

GARCIA. Yes.

JUAN. Welcome to Madrid.

GARCIA. You, Don Felix, how are you?

FELIX. I'm really quite happy. Welcome to Madrid, and I hope you are well.

GARCIA. At your service. What are you doing here? What did I just hear you talking about?

JUAN. Well, just now the conversation was about a dinner with music given by a gallant to a certain señorita by the river last night.

GARCIA. Dinner with music, Don Juan? And last night?

JUAN. Yes.

GARCIA. Something extraordinary? A big celebration?

JUAN. So rumor has it.

GARCIA. And was the lady very beautiful?

JUAN. They tell me she is very beautiful.

GARCIA. Well!

JUAN. Why are you so mysterious?

GARCIA. Because I'm wondering if, in praising that lady and that dinner, you are also praising my celebration and my lady.

JUAN. Then you also had a celebration by the river last night?—with music?

GARCIA. All night long.

TRISTAN (aside). What celebration and what lady is he talking about if he only arrived in the capital yesterday?

JUAN. Even though you've just recently arrived, you already have someone to give a party for? You come upon love rapidly, señor.

GARCIA. I've already been in Madrid for a month, but I've been resting in my house for almost all of the time.

TRISTAN (*aside*). I swear he arrived only yesterday! He has some sort of motive in saying this.

JUAN. I didn't know. I would have come to pay my respects the moment I heard about your arrival.

GARCIA. I have been here secretly.

JUAN. That must be the reason. But was this celebration a big affair?

GARCIA. The river has probably never seen a bigger and better one.

JUAN (*aside*). Oh, how insanely jealous I am! Who can doubt that it was last night in the grove by the river that . . . ? (*Here he stops, and cannot go on.*)

GARCIA. Your actions seem to indicate that you know the lady as well as I.

JUAN. I'm not totally uninformed, although I don't know everything. I mean to say, my information is just slightly confused; enough to make me want to hear the truth from you. Curiosity is inevitable in an idle courtier . . .

TRISTAN (*aside*). Or in a jealous lover.

FELIX (*to* JUAN, *aside*). Notice how unexpectedly the heavens have come to show you your rival.

GARCIA. Well, listen carefully then, and I'll tell you all about the celebration. I can see that you're already burning with desire to hear about it.

JUAN. You will be doing us a great favor.

GARCIA. Among the dark, thick shadows that in the elm grove were caused by the trees, and in the night by darkness itself, was hidden a clean, square, fragrant table, to the Italian elegant, to the Spaniard opulent. On the tablecloth and napkins there were embroidered birds and animals that seemed ready to fly or run away into the forest at any moment. Four side tables there were nearby on which were displayed silver and gold table utensils, crystal goblets, and porcelain dishes. There was hardly an elm tree standing in that grove out of which six houses could not have been built. Four different groups of musicians were concealed in four different pavilions; in another there were hors-d'oeuvres and desserts; and in yet another there were the main dishes. My lady arrived in her carriage giving envy to the stars, sweetness and gentleness to the breezes, and happiness to the banks of the river. Hardly had her adorable foot touched the ground, making the grass into emeralds, the river water into crystal, and the sand into pearls, when a great quantity of rockets, fire-bombs, and pin-wheels were shot off into the sky bringing to that one piece of earth the whole fabled region of fire. Then, even before the fireworks had stopped, twenty-four huge torches were lit which rivaled the stars in their brilliance. First the choirs of oboes played; after them, in the second pavilion, the group of guitar players; from the third pavilion came the sweetness of flutes; and from the fourth, four voices with small guitars and harps were heard. Meanwhile, thirty-two courses were served, not counting appetizer and dessert courses, which were almost as numerous. The chilled fruits and drinks were so covered with snow to keep them cold that as the river passed through the elm grove, it thought that it was going through the mountains. The sense of smell was not idle while the sense of taste thus enjoyed itself, for gentle essences of perfume, of myrrh, flowers, and herbs turned that elm grove into a fragrant heaven. Even the toothpick holder was exquisitely out of the ordinary. It was a diamond-studded man thrust through with delicate arrows of gold for toothpicks. "After all," I said to my lady, "the toothpicks must be gold when the teeth are pearls." Meanwhile, the musicians began to play music more beautiful than the music of the heavenly spheres, until Apollo, becoming envious, hurried along in his path. And thus, the dawn of the new day put an end to the celebration.

JUAN. I swear that you have painted it in such perfect colors that hearing about it is just the same as having been there.

TRISTAN. (aside). The devil must protect such a man! He can so glibly describe, on the spur of the moment, a festivity that never took place that the description begins to sound like the truth!

JUAN (to FELIX, aside). I'm insane with jealousy.

FELIX. The others didn't tell us such things about that celebration.

JUAN. What difference does it make, if the essentials, the time, and the place agree?

GARCIA. What did you say?

JUAN. That this celebration was grander than Alexander the Great could have given.

GARCIA. Oh, this was a trifling affair arranged on the spur of the moment. Give me one day in which to prepare and I'll show you a party that will make the Roman and Greek celebrations, which the world now stands in awe of, look like petty luncheons for small children. (*He looks away.*)

FELIX (*to* JUAN, *aside*). Jacinta is sitting in the middle seat in Lucrecia's carriage.

JUAN (*to* FELIX, *aside*). I would swear that Don Garcia's eyes are following her.

FELIX. You're uneasy and inattentive.

JUAN. Now my suspicions are confirmed.

JUAN AND GARCIA. Goodbye.

FELIX. Both of you take leave of each other at the same time. (*Exeunt* JUAN *and* FELIX.)

TRISTAN (*aside*). I've never seen such a simultaneous and abrupt leave-taking.

GARCIA. That heavenly creature, the prime mover of my actions, draws me irresistibly to her.

TRISTAN. Have patience, for to show yourself the impatient lover can do you more harm than good; and I have always noticed that cool-headed people are luckier. Women and devils walk down the same path, neither following nor tempting the souls who are already lost and ruined; as soon as they have these souls securely in hand, they forget them. They only pursue those who might be able to escape.

GARCIA. That's true; but I'm not master of myself.

TRISTAN. Until you are sure what her social position is, don't surrender yourself so quickly. Many a man has walked into a swamp and rashly acted upon his belief that anything green was grass.

GARCIA. Then find out everything about her, today.

TRISTAN. Don't worry. It's in my hands. But now, before you burst, tell me, in the name of God, what you hope to accomplish with the stories that I have just heard you tell? Even though I would like to help you, if we get caught lying, it will mean instant dishonor. You pretended to be as rich as a Peruvian gold miner with those ladies.

GARCIA. It's certain, Tristan, that foreigners are more attractive to women, and especially if these foreigners are from Peru—a sure indication of wealth.

TRISTAN. I know what you are trying to do, but you're going about it in the wrong way. They're finally going to find out who you are.

GARCIA. When they find out, I will have already gained

entry into their houses or their hearts. Afterward, I will be able to handle them.

TRISTAN. You've convinced me, señor; but now explain that business of your having been in the capital for a month. What intention did you have in that—having arrived just yesterday?

GARCIA. Now you know that it is an indication of greatness when one remains concealed or retired in his village, or resting in his house.

TRISTAN. My congratulations. But now what about the imaginary celebration?

GARCIA. You don't know what a pleasure it is, when a proud tale-bearer comes to tell about some deed or celebration, to shut his mouth myself with such another one that he returns to his home fairly bursting, with his own news still in him, and with my news piled on top of his.

TRISTAN. But this is foolish and dangerous. You'll be the gossip of Madrid if you're caught in these stories.

GARCIA. So what? To be talked about is an accomplishment—even if what is said is spiteful gossip. He who lives without thinking and feeling and perceiving, he who just adds himself to the numbers of the world, and does what everyone else does, how is he different from the beasts? To be famous is a great thing, whatever the means may be. In ancient times, a shepherd burned down the temple of Diana at Ephesus just to gain a name for himself. And, finally, I enjoy myself and the way I live—which is the best reason.

TRISTAN. Your ideas are somewhat childish; you will be better off in Madrid if you start acting more sensibly.

(*Exeunt.*)

SCENE 3: *A room in* DON SANCHO'S *house.*

(*Enter* JACINTA *and* ISABEL, *with mantillas,* DON BELTRAN *and* DON SANCHO.)

JACINTA. Such a great honor?

BELTRAN. You know that the friendship between this house and mine has not been of just one day's duration; so you should not be surprised at my visit.

JACINTA. If I am surprised, señor, it is because it has been such a long time since you have done us the honor of visiting us. Please excuse me; for, not knowing that you were here, I delayed in the Street of the Silversmiths, bargaining for certain jewels.

BELTRAN. Ah, señorita, I too have been bargaining for a certain jewel. I have been discussing, with Don Sancho, your uncle, the matter of changing our already close relationship into a yet closer one. He says, and I agree with him, for it is proper, that this change should take place only with your permission. I speak, of course, of your marriage with my son, Don Garcia. Since you already know of the wealth and nobility of my family you have only to judge the appearance of Garcia himself. And although he just arrived in Madrid yesterday from Salamanca, and received a good sunburn on the way—Apollo was jealous of him!—I am willing to put him before your eyes, confident that he will please you completely, if you will give him permission to swear his love to you in person.

JACINTA. It is useless to exaggerate what I would gain in accepting your offer. I am flattered that you should want me to be your daughter-in-law; but to give my consent now, even though I gained much by giving it, would seem to me to be both ill-considered and frivolous in an honorable woman. If one makes up one's mind rapidly in things of such importance, either one has very few brains, or a great desire to get married. And as for my seeing him, it seems to me, if it pleases you, that, in order to avoid mutual embarrassment, he might first pass by in the street so that I could see him. For if the marriage were called off, as frequently happens, what reputation would I gain from the visits of a gallant with the privileges of a husband?

BELTRAN. I shall hold my son lucky if he becomes your husband, as much because of your good judgment as because of your beauty.

SANCHO. She could be a mirror held up to prudence.

BELTRAN. Not without cause, Don Sancho, do I agree with your opinion. This afternoon I shall pass by in your street with Garcia.

JACINTA. I shall be at the window.

BELTRAN. I beg you to take a good look at him, for tonight I must return, beautiful Jacinta, to find out what you think of him.

JACINTA. So soon?

BELTRAN. Don't be offended if I seem anxious. My haste is a tribute to your virtues. Goodbye.

JACINTA. Goodbye.

BELTRAN. Where are you going?

SANCHO. To accompany you.

BELTRAN. Oh, you don't have to.

SANCHO. I'll go to the corridor with you, if you don't mind.   (*Exeunt* BELTRAN *and* SANCHO.)

ISABEL. The old man is really rushing you.

JACINTA. I would be in a still greater rush, for the marriage would do me great honor, if my love did not already lie elsewhere. For, although the obstacles in the way of Don Juan's obtaining a military commission—which would enable us to marry—constitute a logical reason for my accepting other suitors, I love him so much that I cannot throw away his love. He is the master of my thoughts, he has a permanent place in my soul, and I tremble, Isabel, when I think that another must be my husband.

ISABEL. I thought that you had already forgotten about Don Juan, seeing that you were accepting other suitors.

JACINTA. Don't deceive yourself, Isabel; I have my motives. For, insofar as Don Juan's commission in one of the King's military orders has very little chance of becoming a reality, and he can't become my husband unless he does get a commission, I have given the whole matter up as a lost cause. So in order to keep from dying I wish to talk and have a good time rather than torment myself in vain; for I don't approve of persisting until death in an impossible course of action. Perhaps I shall meet someone else who will deserve my hand and heart.

ISABEL. I don't doubt that time will offer someone worthy of your love; and if I'm not mistaken, that gallant from the Indies didn't exactly displease you.

JACINTA. My friend, would you like to have me tell you the truth? He pleased me very much. And so much that I promise you that if Don Beltran's son were so discreet, so gallant, and such a gentleman, the marriage would be just as good as made.

ISABEL. This afternoon you will see him in the street with his father.

JACINTA. I will see only his face and his form; his spirit and his soul, which are more important, I would have to see in talking with him.

ISABEL. Talk with him, then.

JACINTA. Don Juan will be offended if he finds out about

it; and I don't want to decide to lose him until I know that I must have another husband.

ISABEL. Well, make some resolution. Remember, time is passing and you must make up your mind; for Don Juan is, as far as this matter is concerned, the dog in the manger who wouldn't eat the cabbages and wouldn't let anyone else eat them. You can, if you wish, talk with Don Beltran's son without Don Juan's knowing anything about it; for the plots of women are always proper in matters like this.

JACINTA. I can think of one such scheme that would be fitting in this case: Lucrecia is my friend; she could send for Don Garcia in her own name; and I could get to talk to him if I hid myself next to Lucrecia in her window.

ISABEL. Such a splendid scheme could proceed only from your imagination.

JACINTA. Now go, Isabel, and tell my plan to Lucrecia. Tell her that a moment's delay is the same as a century in carrying out my plan.

ISABEL. Don Garcia's practically on his way!

(DON JUAN *enters and meets* ISABEL *going out.*)

JUAN. May I speak with your mistress?

ISABEL. Only for a moment, for Don Sancho will be coming any minute now to take her in to dinner. (*Exit.*)

JUAN. Now, Jacinta, that I lose you, now that I lose myself, now . . .

JACINTA. Are you insane?

JUAN. Who could be sane, with the things you do?

JACINTA. Restrain yourself and speak softly; my uncle is in the next room.

JUAN. How can you be so indifferent when it is you who went to eat by the river?

JACINTA. I . . . ?

JUAN. What music!

JACINTA. What are you saying? Are you in your right mind?

JUAN. When in order to stay up all night you make an engagement with someone else . . . (JACINTA *makes a hushing motion, indicating that her uncle is in the other room*) Why do you pretend with me that your uncle is in the next room?!

JACINTA. Stay up all night with another? Be warned that even if this were true, you would be taking a great deal of liberty in speaking to me in this way; and what is more, this madness is all a product of your insane imagination.

JUAN. I now know that it was Don Garcia at that celebration on the river. I now know about the fireworks salute when your carriage arrived. I now know about the twenty-four giant torches that made daylight in the elm grove at midnight. I now know about the four side tables with different kinds of table-service and about the four pavilions filled with instrumentalists and singers, and about the thirty-two different courses, not counting appetizers and desserts, and about the little man set with diamonds in which were set little golden arrows for toothpicks. Oh, I know all; and I know that you unwillingly watched the envious sun come up over the river. Say now that this is madness and a product of my insane imagination. Say now that I take a great deal of liberty in speaking to you in this way, when there are two things you should be ashamed of—the injury you have done me, and your own fickleness.

JACINTA. God give me strength!

JUAN. Quit making up stories; be quiet; don't say anything to me, for in a proven offense apologies and excuses will not do. Now, false one, now I know what danger I'm in; don't deny that I have lost you; your fickleness has offended me, the disillusionment doesn't offend me. And although you deny what I heard, you will confess that I saw, for today I saw that which you are denying mirrored in Garcia's own eyes. And his father? What did he want here now? What did he tell you? Are you with the son at night, and with the father during the day? I saw it. Your plans to deceive me are in vain; I now know that your delays are gross examples of your fickleness. But, cruel one, by the skies above, may you not live content! Would that the volcano of my jealousy would burst open and consume you in its fire! May Garcia lose you, just as I lose you!

JACINTA. Are you sane?

JUAN. How can one be sane, and, at the same time, in love and despairing?

JACINTA. Come now, listen; for if the truth is worth anything, you will soon see how badly informed you are.

JUAN. I must leave; for your uncle is coming.

JACINTA. He's not coming. Listen, for I am sure that I can convince you.

JUAN. All your talk is in vain unless you promise me your hand in marriage right here and now.

JACINTA. My hand? Here and now? My uncle is coming.

ACT II

SCENE 1: *A room in* DON BELTRAN'S *house.*

(*Enter* DON GARCIA, *in a dressing gown, reading from a note;* TRISTAN *and* CAMINO *attend him.*)

GARCIA (*reading*). "The exigency of the occasion makes me depart from the decorum of my rank. You will know what I speak of if you come tonight to my balcony. There the bearer of this note will tell you the rest which cannot be written. May our Lord protect you . . ." Who wrote this note to me?

CAMINO. Doña Lucrecia de Luna.

GARCIA. My lady of the moon! Isn't she the beautiful lady who was in the Street of the Silversmiths this morning?

CAMINO. Yes, señor.

GARCIA. What luck! Tell me—quickly—all about this lady.

CAMINO. I'm very surprised that you don't already know of her. Because you have seen her, I needn't tell you that she is beautiful, but she is likewise discreet and virtuous. Also, her father is a widower and very old, and she will inherit an annual income of fully two thousand ducats when he dies.

GARCIA. Do you hear that, Tristan?

TRISTAN. I hear, and I'm not unhappy.

CAMINO. And there is no question of her nobility; her father's last name is Luna, and her mother's was Mendoza, both very distinguished names. In short, Doña Lucrecia deserves a king for a husband.

GARCIA. Love, I pray for your wings to carry me up to such an elevated lady! Where does she live!

GARCIA. My good fortune is certain. It says here that you
CAMINO. Near the convent of La Victoria.
are the one who will guide me to this glorious heaven.

CAMINO. My guidance will insure your good fortune.

GARCIA. And I shall be very grateful.

CAMINO. I shall come for you tonight when the clock is striking ten o'clock.

GARCIA. I'll be waiting. Here—for you.

CAMINO. May God be with you.   (*Exit.*)

GARCIA. Ah, what happiness! Love, what good fortune is this? Remember Tristan, how the coachman called Lucrecia, the lady to whom I spoke, the most beautiful? I am certain that the one who talked to me is the one who sent me this note.

TRISTAN. You're presuming a lot.

GARCIA. Who else would have a reason for writing to me?

TRISTAN. Well, at the very worst, all doubt will be removed soon, for in your conversation tonight you will be able to tell if you are, indeed, speaking to your lady.

GARCIA. And it's certain that I won't be deceived, because the sweet sound of her voice has left a definite impression on my consciousness.

(*Enter a* PAGE, *with a note; he gives it to* DON GARCIA.)

PAGE. This is for you, Don Garcia.

GARCIA. You don't have to take your hat off.

PAGE. I am a servant, sir.

GARCIA. Put it back on, I beg you. "I wish to see you alone to verify a certain important matter. I will be waiting for you near the hermitage of San Blas at the top of the hill of Antocha at seven o'clock. —Don Juan de Sosa." (*aside*) My God! San Blas is where they hold duels! What grievance can Don Juan have if I just arrived yesterday and he is such a good friend of mine? Tell Don Juan that I will meet him at the appointed place and time.

(*Exit* PAGE.)

TRISTAN. Señor, you're pale. What's happened?

GARCIA. Nothing, Tristan.

TRISTAN. I can't know what's wrong?

GARCIA. No.

TRISTAN. It is certainly a serious matter.

GARCIA. Get my cloak and sword.   (*Exit* TRISTAN.)

GARCIA. What grievance have I given him?

(*Enter* DON BELTRAN.)

BELTRAN. Garcia?

GARCIA. Señor?

BELTRAN. We have to take a horseback ride today, for I have some things I must talk over with you.

GARCIA. You want me to do something else?

(*Enter* TRISTAN; *he starts to put* DON GARCIA'S *sword and cloak on.*)

BELTRAN. Where were you going when the sun is so oppressively hot?

GARCIA. I'm going to play billiards with our neighbor, the Count.

BELTRAN. Since you have only been here since yesterday, I don't approve of your hurrying to make the acquaintance of a thousand people you don't know, unless you observe very carefully two conditions. And these are: don't incur gambling debts and utter only moderate judgments. As long as you keep these things in mind you can't go wrong.

GARCIA. It is always right to follow your counsels.

BELTRAN. Make sure that a horse is bridled and saddled for you.

GARCIA. I'll go to arrange for one now. (*Exits.*)

BELTRAN. Goodbye. (*aside*) It pains me to think of Garcia's behavior in Salamanca. Still, he may have mended his ways. Have you been with Garcia, Tristan?

TRISTAN. All day, señor.

BELTRAN. Now, Tristan, forget for a moment that he is my son. Remember only your faithfulness to me. What do you think of him?

TRISTAN. What opinion could I have formed of him in such a short time?

BELTRAN. Your tongue isn't very daring; for there has been enough time, and especially for your quick and perceptive understanding. By my life, tell me, without flattery, what you think of him.

TRISTAN. To tell you what I think about Don Garcia, for I must tell you the truth, and since you have sworn by your life . . .

BELTRAN. In this way you have always won my regard.

TRISTAN. He has an excellent imagination full of many subtle thoughts; but he also has juvenile caprices and imprudent arrogance. The ink is still wet on his diploma from the university, and he still has the contagious bad habits of that crowd of irresponsible boys. He talks at a gallop, he lies recklessly and extemporaneously, he brags incessantly, and he is extreme and extravagant in everything. Today, in the space of one hour, he told five or six lies.

BELTRAN. God help me!

TRISTAN. You're astonished? The worst is yet to come, for these are such lies that he can be caught in any one of them.

BELTRAN. Oh, God!

TRISTAN. I would not tell you that which gives you so much pain, if you did not compel me.

BELTRAN. I know your faith and love well.

TRISTAN. I trust in your prudence, señor. I know that it is unnecessary to mention what risk I run if Don Garcia finds out that I have told you this.

BELTRAN. I give you my word, Tristan. Don't fear anything. Go now and have the horses saddled.   (*Exit* TRISTAN.)

BELTRAN. God, since you permitted this to be, it must be right. But how can heaven have so counterbalanced the joy I should have in my old age with my only remaining son? Well, enough of that. Fathers always have had such disappointments. And old men always see many bad things. Patience! Today I must complete the arrangements for his marriage, if I can. Thus, this danger can be avoided before his fault of lying becomes known in the capital and his chances of making a good marriage are destroyed. Perhaps marriage will straighten him out and his ugly habit will be corrected. For it is vain to think that scolding and giving advice are enough to correct such a hateful fault.

(*Enter* TRISTAN.)

TRISTAN. The horses are waiting, señor.

BELTRAN. Then tell Garcia that I'm ready.

TRISTAN. He is already waiting for you, dressed so gallantly that the capital will think that the sun is rising in the middle of the afternoon.   (*Exeunt.*)

SCENE 2: *A room in* DON SANCHO'S *house.*

(*Enter* ISABEL *and* JACINTA.)

ISABEL. Lucrecia immediately wrote the note you desired her to write to Don Garcia, telling him that she would speak with him tonight if he would come to her balcony. Camino, her servant, a man who can undoubtedly be trusted, carried the note to Don Garcia.

JACINTA. I owe Lucrecia a great deal.

ISABEL. She shows that she is your true friend on any occasion.

JACINTA. Is it late?

ISABEL. It's five o'clock.

JACINTA. Even while sleeping I was bothered with the memory of Don Juan, for during my nap I dreamed that he was jealous of another gallant.

(*Enter* DON BELTRAN *and* GARCIA.)

ISABEL. Oh, señorita. Don Beltran and the rich Peruvian at his side!

JACINTA. What are you saying?

ISABEL. The man you talked with this morning is coming down the street with Don Beltran.

JACINTA. By my life, you're telling the truth. It is he.

BELTRAN. Wait here, son, I have just a short errand.

GARCIA. Yes, father. (BELTRAN *exits*.)

JACINTA. Can this be? Why did the impostor pretend to be a rich Peruvian, if he is Don Beltran's son?

ISABEL. Those who go courting always place a lot of value on money. And with this device he hoped to gain your heart. He felt that here he would be better off being rich than being handsome.

JACINTA. He lied also in saying that he had been watching me for a year, because Don Beltran told me that his son just arrived from Salamanca yesterday.

ISABEL. If you look at it carefully, señorita, it is perhaps all truth. He could have seen you, could have left Madrid, and then have come back from Salamanca. And if not, does it surprise you that an aspiring lover, in order to raise himself in his loved one's eyes, should tell a lie? It happens all the time. Moreover, I think it is evident, if my suspicions are not wrong, that he is not urging his love in vain, for he undoubtedly sent his father here today to talk to you. It was no accident, my lady, that the same day that he saw you and showed that he loved you, his father should come to offer him to you as your husband.

JACINTA. Well said; but it seems to me that the time that passed between the son's speaking to me in the Street of the Silversmiths and his father's coming to see me was very brief.

ISABEL. Don Garcia knew who you were; he met his father in the Street of the Silversmiths; he talked to him; and since Don Beltran was not ignorant of your qualities, and since he very justly adores Don Garcia, he immediately came to speak to you about the marriage.

(*Enter* DON BELTRAN.)

JACINTA. Well then, let things be as they should be. I am satisfied with him; the father desires it; the son loves me; consider the marriage made.   (*Exeunt.*)

SCENE 3: *A path on the hill of Antocha.*

(*Enter* DON BELTRAN *and* DON GARCIA.)

BELTRAN. What are you thinking about now?

GARCIA. That I have never seen a better animal in my life.

BELTRAN. A beautiful beast!

GARCIA. Trained, and with a rational disposition. What a good disposition, and yet what spirit!

BELTRAN. Your brother, Don Gabriel, may God rest his soul, considered him his best horse.

GARCIA. Now that we have reached the solitude of the hermitage tell me what it is you want me to do.

BELTRAN. You should say, what you have done to me. Are you a gentleman, Garcia?

GARCIA. I'm your son.

BELTRAN. And to be a gentleman it's enough to be my son?

GARCIA. I think so, señor.

BELTRAN. What an erroneous idea! A gentleman must act like a gentleman in order to be one. What started the noble houses? The illustrious deeds of their founders. The deeds of these humble men are honored by their descendants who do not look at the mere circumstances of their birth. Then doing good or doing bad is the same as being good or being bad. Isn't that right?

GARCIA. I don't deny that deeds grant nobility; but neither do I deny that without them birth can also grant it.

BELTRAN. Then if he who was born without honor can gain it, isn't it certain, on the other hand, that he who was born with it can lose it?

GARCIA. That's true.

BELTRAN. Then if you did disgraceful things, even though you were my son you would cease to be a gentleman; then if your actions defamed you in society, coats of arms and noble ancestors would do you no good. What then do you say to what I hear—that in Salamanca your lies and deceits were a constant source of amazement? A gentleman? Nothing! Bah! Is it possible that a man could have such low thoughts that he could live subject to a vice which yields neither pleasure nor profit? The lascivious have carnal pleasures; the miserly have the power that money gives; the glutton has the joy of eating; the gambler has the incentive of winning and a way to pass his time; the killer has his vengeance; the robber his loot. All vices, in short, either give pleasure or profit, except lying. And what can be gained from lying, except infamy and scorn?

GARCIA. Whoever says I lie, lies himself.

BELTRAN. That is also a lie. You don't even know how to contradict, except by lying some more.

GARCIA. Well if you insist on not believing me . . .

BELTRAN. Wouldn't I be silly if I believed that only you told the truth, and that everyone else lied? The important thing is to contradict what is being said about you with deeds; to start over again speaking little and truthfully; to be aware that here you are dealing with great and titled gentlemen who, if they discover your weakness, will lose all respect for you; to remember, in short, that you are now a man, that you wear a sword at your side, that you were born nobly, and that I am your father. I don't have to tell you more; this reprimand should be enough for one of quality and understanding. And now, so that you shall understand that I am concerned for your welfare, know, Garcia, that I have arranged an excellent marriage for you.

GARCIA (aside). Oh, my Lucrecia!

BELTRAN. Never, my son, have the heavens granted so many divine qualities to a mortal woman, as they have to Jacinta, the daughter of Don Fernando Pacheco, from whom I hope to have, in my old age, delightful grandchildren.

GARCIA (aside). Oh, Lucrecia! If it is possible, only you must be my wife.

BELTRAN. What's this? No answer?

GARCIA (aside). By the heavens above, I must be yours alone.

BELTRAN. What saddens you? Speak; don't keep me in suspense.

GARCIA. I am saddened because it is impossible to obey you.

BELTRAN. Why?

GARCIA. Because I'm already married.

BELTRAN. Married? Heavens! What is this? How could you be without my knowing about it?

GARCIA. It was necessary that I get married, and the marriage is a secret.

BELTRAN. Could there be a more disgraced father?

GARCIA. Don't be distressed, for upon learning the cause you will consider the effect a fortunate one.

BELTRAN. Get on with it, then; and make it fast, for my life hangs upon a hair.

GARCIA (aside). Now I really need some cunning subtleties from my imagination. (aloud) In Salamanca, señor, there is a noble gentleman whose name is Don Pedro de Herrera. To this gentleman heaven gave another heaven for a daughter whose ruddy cheeks make bright horizons for her sunlike eyes. In short, to get to the point, all the qualities that nature could give to a young girl, she had. But bad fortune, being opposed to such an excess of merits, made her poor. For, in addition to the fact that her family is not so rich as it is noble, there were also two male children born before her to inherit the family fortune. I saw her, then, one afternoon, going to the river in her carriage. I would have thought that hers was the carriage of Phaeton, son of Apollo, who was thrown into the Po River by Zeus because he was about to set the universe on fire—except that it was the Tormes River she was approaching. I don't know who can say that Cupid shoots fiery arrows, for a sudden chill came over me then. What does fire have to do with the anxieties and ardors that filled my soul and my rigid body? It was inevitable that I should see her again; seeing her, be blinded with love; then, burning with love, follow her everywhere. Let the hardest-hearted judge it as they please. I walked back and forth in front of her house in the daytime; I haunted her door at night; with messengers and messages I told her of my love, until—at last—sympathetic and in love—she responded. Love also has jurisdiction with the gods. I kept increasing my attentions, and she her favors, until one night I ascended to the heaven of her room. And while my ardent proposals, conquering all scruples, were seeking an end to the enormous pain in my heart, I heard her father coming to her room; my bad fortune must have called him that night, for he never came to her room ordinarily. She, alarmed, but courageous—a woman after all!—began to hide my almost dead body by pushing me behind her bed. Don Pedro came

in, and his daughter, pretending pleasure, embraced him so
that he couldn't see her face until she got some color back
into it. The two of them sat down, and he with prudent reasons proposed to her a marriage with one of the Monroyes.
She, honest as well as cautious, replied to him in such a
way that neither did she resist him, nor did she anger me.
With that, they said good night to each other; and the old
man was just about to go out the door when—cursed be the
inventor of chiming watches!—my watch began to strike
twelve. Don Pedro heard it and, returning to his daughter,
he said, "Where did that watch come from?" She replied,
"My cousin, Don Diego Ponce, sent it to me to have it
fixed, because there is no watch-maker where he lives."
"Give it to me," said her father, "and I'll take the responsibility of sending it back to him." Well then, Doña Sancha,
for that is the name of the lady, ran to take the watch from
me before her father could take a notion to get it himself. I
took it out of my pocket, and just as I was about to hand it
to her luck made the watch-chain tangle itself with the trig-
ger of a pistol I had in my hand. The hammer fell, the pistol went off; Doña Sancha fainted at the explosion; the old
man grew excited and began to shout for help. I, seeing my
heaven on the floor, with her sun-like eyes in eclipse, judged
that she was undoubtedly dead; I thought that the small,
swift balls of lead from my pistol had committed such a horrible sacrilege. Desperate, then, with this thought, I furiously took out my sword; a thousand men, on that occasion,
would have been but a handful for me. To prevent my escape, her two brothers, like two brave lions, and her servants,
opposed me with their weapons; but, although my sword
and my fury could have easily destroyed them all, there is
no human force that can impede the decrees of fate. For
just then, just as I was going out the half-opened door, I was
seized by the hook of the door-knocker right in the straps
that held up my sword belt! Imagine my predicament! There
I was with a wall of swords in front of me, and in order to
free myself from the door-knocker I would have to turn my
back to them. At this moment Sancha recovered consciousness, and in order to prevent the sad end to which these
horrible events were leading, she courageously closed the
door of the room, leaving me and her inside, away from my
attackers. We piled trunks, chests, and boxes against the
door, hoping that delay would calm the fiery wrath of my
attackers. We wished to secure ourselves even more strongly,

but my ferocious opponents tore down the wall and broke through the door. I, seeing that were I to delay longer, it would be impossible to resist forever the attack of such offended and noble enemies, seeing at my side the beautiful partner in my misfortunes, from whose cheeks fear had robbed all color; seeing, without its being her fault, how her fortunes ran with mine, and how she fought so bravely against misfortune; to reward her loyalty, to put an end to her fears, to put an end to further sufferings, and to keep from being killed, I had to yield, and to ask that these bloody differences be resolved by union in marriage of the bloods of our two families. They, who saw the danger, and who knew my quality and nobility, accepted the offer, after a short period of disagreement among themselves. Her father left to tell the Bishop, and soon returned with an order that any priest could officiate at the wedding. It was done, and the mortal battle was changed into a sweet peace, giving you the best daughter-in-law in the whole world. But we were agreed that you should not know, both because we didn't know what you would think, and because my wife is so poor. But now that you know it was necessary that I get married, consider whether you would rather have me dead—or alive with a noble lady.

BELTRAN. The circumstances of this case are such that one can see that fortune destined this woman for you; and so, I don't hold you guilty for more than not telling me about the marriage.

GARCIA. I was afraid of grieving you, señor.

BELTRAN. If she is so noble, what difference does it make if she is poor? The worst thing is that now I must return with this news to Doña Jacinta, to whom I gave my word that you would be her husband! Look what a predicament you put me in! Take your horse and get home soon; tonight we will talk over your problems at greater length.

GARCIA. I will meet you there when the Angelus bell rings. (DON BELTRAM leaves) Fortunately it worked. The old man is convinced; now he won't say that there is no pleasure or profit in lying. It's such an obvious pleasure to see that he has believed me, and profitable in that I have escaped an unpleasant marriage. How wonderful that one minute he should be rebuking me for lying, and in the next believing as many lies as I could tell him! How easy it is to persuade someone who always wants to believe the best of everybody! And how easy is believing for the man who doesn't know how to lie! But now I wait for Don Juan. (*He turns.*) Hello! I hear a horse. I find such terrible things happening to me that this must be madness; I arrived yesterday and practically in the same moment I find love, a marriage, and cause for a duel.

(*Enter* DON JUAN.)

JUAN. You have acted bravely and honorably in presenting yourself for this duel, Don Garcia.

GARCIA. Who could think less, knowing the noble blood that flows in my veins? But let's get to the cause of your calling me here, Don Juan. Tell me, what reason do you have for this duel?

JUAN. That lady you told me you gave a celebration for last night by the river is the cause of my suffering, and it is to her that I have been engaged for two years, although the marriage has been unavoidably delayed. You have been here a month, and from that I infer that you could not have been ignorant of the situation, my attentions having been such public ones, and thus you have offended me. And now that I have said this, I say what I must say; and that is, either you must desist paying your attentions to my fiancée or, if you consider my request unreasonable, you must agree to refer the matter to the sword, with the victor winning the lady.

GARCIA. It saddens me that, without being fully informed on the matter, you have brought me to this place. The lady at my celebration, Don Juan de Sosa, as God is my witness, is a lady you have never seen, nor could she be your fiancée. This woman is married, and she arrived in Madrid such a short time ago that I know that I am the only one who has seen her.

JUAN. With this you have quieted my suspicions, and I am satisfied.

GARCIA. But now I must be satisfied, for you have challenged me to a duel, and my dignity cannot be soothed with words. It was easy enough to call me out here, but having come, I am obliged, and it is necessary—since I must act as an honorable gentleman—to return dead or victorious.

JUAN. Understand then that, although you have calmed my anxieties, the memory of my jealousy still leaves me angry. (*They take out their swords and fight.*)

(*Enter* DON FELIX.)

FELIX. Stop, gentlemen, for I am here.

GARCIA. Let him come who thinks he can stop me!

FELIX. Put your swords away, for the cause of your quarrel was false.

JUAN. Don Garcia has already told me, but because of the obligation placed upon him by my challenge, he must fight.

FELIX. He has acted as a very valorous and spirited gentleman; and so, since you should be satisfied with that, grant me that you give your pardon and your hand to him who was mistaken out of jealousy. (*They shake hands.*)

GARCIA. That is just and I commend it. But consider carefully from now on, Don Juan, before you rush into such an important matter. You should try every solution you can before you decide on a duel, for it is madness to start a duel, because of the way it must end. (*Exits.*)

FELIX. It is a good thing I arrived on time.

JUAN. Then I really was wrong?

FELIX. Yes.

JUAN. Who did you find out from?

FELIX. I found out from one of Lucrecia's pages.

JUAN. Tell me, then. What did he tell you?

FELIX. The truth is that Doña Jacinta's coach and coachman went last night to the elm-grove of Sotillo, and that once there those who went in the coach had a wonderful time at the celebration—but the coach had been borrowed. And the case was that at the time that Jacinta went to visit Lucrecia; those two women-friends of Lucrecia, the ones with the bewitching eyes, were already there.

JUAN. The two that live on Carmen Street?

FELIX. Yes. Well, they borrowed the coach from Doña Jacinta, and in it they both rode to the elm-grove, under the cover of the moonless night. Then your page, whom you left to follow the coach, having seen two women enter it as night was falling, and not seeing any indication of any other passengers, believed that these two were Jacinta and Lucrecia.

JUAN. And with reason.

FELIX. He followed the coach diligently and when it came to the elm-grove where the celebration was being held he left it and returned to Madrid to look for you. If it hadn't been for that you would never have had occasion for such grief, because, if you had gone to the elm-grove yourself, you would have found out the truth.

JUAN. That's where my error was. But finding out that I

was wrong makes me so happy that I consider the grief I have passed through to have been well worth while.

FELIX. I found out another thing that is very amusing.

JUAN. Tell on.

FELIX. Our friend Don Garcia arrived only yesterday from Salamanca, and upon arriving he went to bed and slept all night, and the celebration he told us about was all a fraud.

JUAN. What are you saying?

FELIX. It's the truth.

JUAN. Don Garcia is a liar?

FELIX. A blind man could see that. So many different kinds of pavilions, sidetables, gold and silver dishes, so much silver, so many groups of instrumentalists and singers—doesn't that sound like an obvious lie?

JUAN. What makes me doubtful is wondering how such a valiant man could be a liar. For his sword would frighten Hercules.

FELIX. He is a liar by habit; he is valiant by inheritance.

JUAN. Let's go. I must go ask for forgiveness from Jacinta, and tell her how this impostor brought about my suspicions.

FELIX. From now on, Don Juan, don't believe a thing he says.

JUAN. And even if he tells the truth, I will consider it a fable. (*Exeunt.*)

SCENE 4: *A street.*

(*Enter* TRISTAN, DON GARCIA, *and* CAMINO, *in night cloaks.*)

GARCIA. May my father pardon me, for it was necessary to deceive him.

TRISTAN. It was an ingenious excuse; but tell me, what trick are you going to use now to keep him from finding out that the story of your marriage is all a hoax?

GARCIA. I will just have to intercept the letters he writes to Salamanca, and make up some replies myself. Thus, I can stick with the story as long as I want to.

(*Enter* JACINTA, LUCRECIA, *and* ISABEL, *at the window.*)

JACINTA. Don Beltran returned with this displeasing news when I had already become content with the marriage.

LUCRECIA. Then Don Beltran's son is the would-be Peruvian?

JACINTA. Yes, my friend.

LUCRECIA. Who told you that he lied about the banquet in the elm-grove?

JACINTA. Don Juan.

LUCRECIA. When did you see him?

JACINTA. Earlier this evening. He spent all the time that he could be with me telling me about Don Garcia's fantastic stories.

LUCRECIA. What gigantic lies Don Garcia tells! He deserves a good, hard punishment from you!

JACINTA. It appears that those three men are nearing our balcony.

LUCRECIA. It must be Don Garcia, for in my note this is the time I told him to come.

JACINTA. Isabel, while we speak with him, you go spy on the old men.

LUCRECIA. My father is slowly telling your uncle a great long story.

ISABEL. I'll let you know what's happening when I get back.   (Exit.)

CAMINO. This is the balcony where you await such happiness.   (Exit.)

LUCRECIA. You know the story; answer him in my name pretending that you are me.

GARCIA. Is that you, Lucrecia?

JACINTA. Is that you, Don Garcia?

GARCIA. It is he who today discovered, in the Street of the Silversmiths, the most precious jewel heaven ever made; it is he who, upon seeing her, thought so highly of her value that he, consumed with love, gave his life and soul to her. I am, in short, he who would take pride in being hers, and I am he who today begins to be hers, because I am the slave of Lucrecia.

JACINTA (aside to LUCRECIA). Friend, this gentleman loves everyone.

LUCRECIA. The man is a charlatan.

JACINTA. He is a big impostor.

GARCIA. My lady, I now await your commands.

JACINTA. That which you wish to talk about cannot now take place . . .

TRISTAN (into his master's ear). Is that your Lucrecia?

GARCIA. Yes.

JACINTA. I intended to talk to you about a very important marriage, but now I know that it is impossible to marry you.

GARCIA. Why?

JACINTA. Because you're already married.

GARCIA. I'm married?

JACINTA. You.

GARCIA. I am single, I swear to God! Whoever told you that has deceived you.

JACINTA (*aside to* LUCRECIA). Have you ever seen a better liar?

LUCRECIA. He doesn't know how to do anything but lie.

JACINTA. You wish to persuade me so much?

GARCIA. I swear to God that I'm single!

JACINTA (*aside to* LUCRECIA). And he swears on his lies.

LUCRECIA. It has always been the custom of liars to swear on the doubtful things they say, in order that they may be believed.

GARCIA. I hope that I will not offend you by being able to prove this accusation false so easily.

JACINTA (*aside*). With what confidence he lies! Doesn't it almost seem like the truth?

GARCIA. I will give you my hand, my lady, and with that you will believe me.

JACINTA. I do believe you would give your hand—to three hundred women within one hour!

GARCIA. I am discredited with you.

JACINTA. Then the punishment is just; for the things you have said have been counterfeit, and it is only right that your credit should be destroyed. He does not deserve to be trusted who, having been born here in Madrid, today declared that he was a rich Peruvian; who, having arrived in the capital just yesterday, affirmed today that he had been here for a whole year; who, having passed the whole night in his bed, told that he had spent it giving a party for a lady; who, finally, having confessed this afternoon that he had been married in Salamanca, is now denying it as fast and as vehemently as he can.

TRISTAN. Everything is known.

GARCIA. My heaven, listen to me and I will tell you the pure truth; for I know now where the error is in the story. I pass by the other things, for they are of little moment, to speak of the marriage matter, which is the important thing. If you, Lucrecia, were the reason why I had to say I was married, would I be guilty of having lied?

JACINTA. I the cause?

GARCIA. Yes, my lady.

JACINTA. How?

GARCIA. I want to tell you about it.

JACINTA (*aside to* LUCRECIA). Listen, for the prevaricator will tell some lovely lies now.

GARCIA. My father came to engage me to another woman today; but I, who am yours, tried to avoid this by telling him that I was already married. For, insofar as I wish to take only your hand in marriage, I am married for everyone else, and only for you am I single. Since your note came to give strength to my desires, I prevented this undesired engagement the only way I could. This is my case; if my well-intended lie surprises you, consider, Lucrecia, that the truth of my love for you told the lie.

LUCRECIA (*aside*). Oh, if it were only so!

JACINTA (*aside*). How well he invents a story on the spur of the moment! Well then, how can I give you such pangs of love in such a short time? You have hardly seen me, and already you are so lost with love? You have hardly known me, and you want me to be your wife?

GARCIA. I saw your great beauty for the first time today, señorita; love obliges me to tell you the truth now. But if the cause of my love is divine, the effect is a miracle, for Cupid does not travel on feet, but on wings. To say that more time is needed for you to inspire love in me is to deny your divine power, Lucrecia. You say that because I hardly know you I cannot be lost with love. Would to God that I didn't know you at all!—so that I should be doing even more by loving you! I know you well: I know well the qualities that Fortune gave you; that you are a Luna without eclipse, that you are a Mendoza without blemish, that your mother is deceased, that you are alone in your house, that your father's income exceeds a thousand doubloons. See if I am badly informed. I hope, my love, that you will understand and be sympathetic toward the things I have said.

LUCRECIA (*aside*). He almost makes me love . . .

JACINTA. Well, how about Jacinta? Isn't she beautiful, isn't she discreet, rich and such a one that the most famous noble would wish her to be his wife?

GARCIA. She is beautiful, discreet, and rich, but she doesn't suit me.

JACINTA. Then tell me, what defect does she have?

GARCIA. The biggest one. I don't love her.

JACINTA. Well, I would have you married to her; that is the only reason I asked you to come here.

GARCIA. Well, it will be vain stubbornness to recommend it, for when my father intended the same thing, today, I told him that I was married elsewhere. And if you, my lady, intend to talk me into the same thing, pardon me, for to avoid this marriage with Jacinta I will be married in Turkey. This is the truth, as God is my witness, because my love abhors everything else, my Lucrecia, that is not you.

LUCRECIA (aside). Would that it were so!

JACINTA. That you should regale me with such infamous falsehoods! Tell me: Don't you have any memory? Don't you have any shame? Why, if today I heard you tell Jacinta that you loved her, why do you deny it now?

GARCIA. I love Jacinta? As God is my witness, you're the only woman I have talked to since I arrived in this city.

JACINTA. You could tell your shameless lies up to now. But if you dare to lie to me about what I have heard with my own ears, can you tell me any truth? Leave! And if I should ever grant you another opportunity to speak with me, you should know that it will only be to amuse myself— as when, to avoid the annoying weariness of weighty business matters, one spends some spare time reading the fables of Ovid. (Exit.)

GARCIA. Listen to me, my beautiful Lucrecia.

LUCRECIA (aside). I'm still confused. (Exit.)

GARCIA. I'm insane! Are truths valued so little?

TRISTAN. In a lying mouth.

GARCIA. What reason could I have given her for not believing what I said?

TRISTAN. Why are you surprised, if she has definitely caught you in five or six lies? From now on, if you should happen to think about it, you will see clearly that he who lies in little matters is not believed in the big ones.

ACT III

SCENE 1: *A room in* DON SANCHO's *house*.

(*Enter* CAMINO, *with a note; he gives it to* LUCRECIA.)

CAMINO. I was given this note for you by Tristan, whom Don Garcia rightly trusts just as much as you trust me. For, although he has not been very successful and he remains a servant, he is very well-born. And he has said so much emphasis on the importance of your reply that he swears that Don Garcia is insane with love for you.

LUCRECIA. What a strange situation! Is it possible that a man who is so persistent is deceiving me? The most devoted lover gives up if he is not loved in return. Can it be that Don Garcia, being so scorned, is pretending to be so faithful?

CAMINO. I, at least, if I know the signs of love, will swear, from the symptoms I have observed in him, that his illness is love. He who paces up and down in your street night and day; he who so attentively waits at your window; he who sees you leave your balcony when he is arriving; who neither sees you, nor is seen by you, and still remains firm in his love for you; he who cries, he who despairs, he who, because I am with you, gives me money which in these days is the truest sign—he is one whose character is being assassinated by those who say he lies!

LUCRECIA. It is evident, Camino, that you have never heard him lie. Would to God that his love were certain! For, to tell the truth, if his love were real, his desires would not be long in finding a door to my heart. For his exaggerations, although I didn't believe them, have at least awakened my thoughts. For, granted that it is foolish to believe a liar, hope and self-esteem oblige me to believe that with me he could change his habits. And so, in order to protect

172

my honor I wish to proceed bearing equally in mind the good things and the possible dangers, neither accepting his falsehoods, nor dismissing his true statements.

CAMINO. I agree with you.

LUCRECIA. Then tell him that I cruelly tore up his note without looking at it, and that this is the reply I give him. Then tell him later, as if on your own account, not to despair; and that if he would like to see me, he should go to the religious festival at the convent of Magdalena this afternoon.

CAMINO. I go.

LUCRECIA. My hopes are built on you.

CAMINO. They won't be lost on me, for I am Camino.

(*Exeunt.*)

SCENE 2: *A room in* DON BELTRAN'S *house.*

(*Enter* DON BELTRAN, DON GARCIA, *and* TRISTAN. DON BELTRAN *takes out an open letter; he gives it to* DON GARCIA.)

BELTRAN. Have you written to your wife, Garcia?

GARCIA. I will write tonight.

BELTRAN. Well then, I give you my letter unsealed, so that after reading it you may conform with what I have said when you write to your father-in-law; for I am determined, as is reasonable, that you should go in person to bring your wife here. It would be in poor taste to send for her, insofar as you are able to bring her here yourself.

GARCIA. That's true; but my journey would be useless.

BELTRAN. Why?

GARCIA. Because she is with child; and until she gives you a happy grandchild, it isn't wise to risk her traveling so far.

BELTRAN. Of course not! It would be madness for her to travel in her condition. But tell me, Garcia, why haven't you told me about this before?

GARCIA. Because I didn't know it myself. In the letter I received from Doña Sancha just yesterday, she tells me that it is certain that she is now with child.

BELTRAN. If she gives me a grandson, my old age will be

happy. Give me the letter. (*He takes it from* DON GARCIA.)
I must add how happy this news makes me. But, say, what
is the first name of your father-in-law?

GARCIA. Of whom?

BELTRAN. Of your father-in-law.

GARCIA (*aside*). I'm done for now. Don Diego.

BELTRAN. Either I am mistaken, or on another occasion
you called him Don Pedro.

GARCIA. I also remember the same thing myself; but both
of the names are his, señor.

BELTRAN. Diego and Pedro both?

GARCIA. Don't be startled, for as a condition of inheritance, the successor to his family name and possessions
must be called Don Diego. They called him Don Pedro
before he inherited the family name and possessions; and as
he afterward became Don Diego because he had inherited
them, he is therefore now called Don Pedro and Don Diego
both.

BELTRAN. This condition of inheritance is not a new thing
in many Spanish families. I'm going to write to him.

(*Exit.*)

TRISTAN. Your confusion was remarkable this time.

GARCIA. Did you understand the story?

TRISTAN. And there was plenty to understand. He who
lies has need of a great imagination and a greater memory.

GARCIA. I thought I was done for.

TRISTAN. You'll come to that in the end, señor.

GARCIA. Meanwhile, I will see the good or bad outcome of
my love. What news is there from Lucrecia?

TRISTAN. I imagine that even though she boasts of being
so hard and unyielding, you will have to use some other
method than force to conquer Lucrecia.

GARCIA. She received the note?

TRISTAN. Yes; although she told Camino to tell you that
she had torn it up; and he told me. And since she accepted
it, your courtship doesn't go badly, if we can believe that
epigram that I believe Martial, the Roman, wrote to his
sweetheart, Naevia: "I wrote, Naevia didn't answer; now
she is hard; but she will soften, since what I wrote, she
read."

GARCIA. I doubt that he is telling the truth.

TRISTAN. Camino is on your side, and he promises to reveal his secrets; and I expect that he will keep his promises,
if you keep him generously supplied with money—for there

is no better instrument of torture for getting confessions than money. And it would be well, señor, if you were to conquer your ungrateful lady with gifts; love gives mortal wounds with golden arrows.

GARCIA. I have never seen you be vulgar except in these opinions you have just now expressed. Is this woman one of those who surrender themselves for money?

TRISTAN. Virgil says that Dido was consumed with love for Aeneas as much because of the gifts he had given her as because of Cupid who had been sent by Venus to bewitch her. And Dido was a queen! Don't be horrified by my crude opinions, for money overcomes family pride just as diamonds can cut other diamonds.

GARCIA. Didn't you see that my offer of jewels offended her when I talked to her in the Street of the Silversmiths?

TRISTAN. Your offer would offend her, señor, but not your jewels. Be guided by custom, for no one here has ever been broken on the wheel because he was over-bold in giving.

GARCIA. Grant me that she would wish it, and I would give her a whole world.

TRISTAN. Camino will show the way, for he is the guiding star of Lucrecia. And so that you will know that your love affairs are in good order, señor, she commanded Camino to tell you as if it were on his own account that today she goes to the festival at the convent of Magdalena.

GARCIA. Sweet release from my agony! So slowly do you tell me news that drives me crazy with joy?

TRISTAN. I give it to you little by little, because that way the pleasure lasts longer. (*Exeunt.*)

SCENE 3: *Cloister of the convent of Magdalena, with a door to the church.*

(*Enter* JACINTA *and* LUCRECIA, *with mantillas.*)

JACINTA. What? Don Garcia still persists?

LUCRECIA. In such a way that, although I know his deceiving behavior, he is so stubborn that he almost makes me doubt myself.

JACINTA. Perhaps you aren't deceived; for the truth is not prohibited in the lying mouth. Perhaps it is true that he loves you, and especially since your beauty is so great that any man cannot help but love you.

LUCRECIA. You always flatter me; but I would better believe it were so if he had not seen you, for you yourself dim the light of the sun.

JACINTA. You well know your worth; and that in this competition there has never been a verdict, because we both receive the same number of votes. And it is not only beauty that causes amorous ardor, for there is always a bit of luck involved in love. I am very happy that you, my dear, could take my place, and that you could attain that which I didn't deserve; for neither is it your fault, nor does he have any obligations to me. But understand that you will have no excuse if you rush madly into loving someone whom you have been warned knows only how to deceive—and end up being deceived.

LUCRECIA. Thank you, Jacinta, but I would like to correct your suspicions; I said that I am inclined to believe him, not that I am inclined to love him.

JACINTA. He will oblige you to believe, and you will love without obligation; it is a short journey from believing to loving.

LUCRECIA. Then, what would you say if you knew that I had received a note?

JACINTA. I would say that you already believe him. I would even say that you already love him.

LUCRECIA. You would be wrong, and you might consider that sometimes one does things out of curiosity that one would not do out of love. Didn't you enjoy talking to him in the Street of the Silversmiths?

JACINTA. Yes.

LUCRECIA. And were you, in listening to him there, in love or curious?

JACINTA. Curious.

LUCRECIA. Well then, just as you were curious in listening to him, so, too, have I been curious about his note.

JACINTA. You will see your evident error if you realize that listening is just courtesy, and that accepting a note is an obvious encouragement.

LUCRECIA. That would be so if he knew that I had accepted his note, but he thinks that I tore it up, without reading it.

JACINTA. Then in that case it is certain that you were only curious.

LUCRECIA. In my life, it has been worth a great deal of pleasure to be curious. And insofar as you know his ability for lying, listen, and consider whether the lie that seems more like the truth itself, is a lie. (*She takes out a note, opens it, and reads secretly.*)

(*Enter* CAMINO, DON GARCIA, *and* TRISTAN *from another direction.*)

CAMINO. Do you see the one who has a note in her hand?

GARCIA. Yes.

CAMINO. Well, that one is Lucrecia.

GARCIA (*aside*). Oh beautiful cause of such inhuman grief! I'm burning with jealousy. Oh, Camino, how much I owe you!

TRISTAN (*to* CAMINO). Tomorrow—a new suit.

CAMINO. I'm very happy on your account. (*Exit.*)

GARCIA. Tristan, if possible, I want to get close enough to her so that I can read the note she's looking at, without her seeing me.

TRISTAN. That's not difficult; for if you go that way, keeping close to this chapel, you can come out over there, and come up right behind them. (*Exit.*)

GARCIA. Good idea. They're looking over here. (*Exit.*)

JACINTA. Read it aloud softly. You're being discourteous.

LUCRECIA. You won't hear me. Take it and read it for yourself. (*She gives the note to* JACINTA.)

JACINTA. That's better.

(*Enter* TRISTAN *and* GARCIA, *by another door; they come up in back of the women.*)

TRISTAN. We got here in good shape.

GARCIA. You try to read the note, Tristan; you can see better than I can.

JACINTA (*reading*). "Since you disbelieve my heart-felt words, tell me if my deeds will be believed—for they never lie. For if being your husband, señorita, depends on being believed, and if being believed must furnish the motive for favoring me; by way of this note, my Lucrecia, which I give you signed as an assurance of my integrity, I say that I am already your husband, Don Garcia."

GARCIA (*aside to* TRISTAN). My God, that's my note!

TRISTAN. Then, what is it doing here? Didn't she look at it at home?

GARCIA. Perhaps she is rereading it to entertain herself.

TRISTAN. Whatever the case may be, things are going well for you.

GARCIA. Whatever the case may be, I am happy.

JACINTA. It is brief and concise; either he is sincere, or a good liar.

GARCIA (*to* JACINTA). Señorita, turn away those eyes whose beams I cannot resist.

JACINTA (*aside to* LUCRECIA). Put your veil over your face—he hasn't seen you yet—and be disillusioned now.

(LUCRECIA *and* JACINTA *cover themselves.*)

LUCRECIA (*aside to* JACINTA). Don't let him know who you are and don't call me by name.

GARCIA. Take away the delicate veil from that wonder of the heavens, from that heaven of men. Is it possible that I really see you, murderer of my life? But it must be you, because as you are my murderer you would be taking sanctuary in the church to escape prosecution. But if you feel that you must grant me a reprieve, you should not be afraid, because the laws of love are so confused that they send the killed to prison and let the killer go free. I may now hope that you are so touched by my grief, my dear, that being repentant has brought you to the convent of Magdalena. See how love ordains recompense for the sadness I feel; for because I have borne the torment of your cruelty, señorita, I now have this happiness at your repentance. You don't speak to me, loved one? Doesn't my sadness compel you to sympathy? Do you perhaps repent of having repented? Beware, I beg of you, señorita, if you are planning to kill me again. If you are considering running me through with the sword points of your eyes, remember that you will not be able to take shelter here, for sanctuary in the church is not extended to those who have committed crimes in the church itself.

JACINTA. Do you know me? (*unveiling*)

GARCIA. And well, as God is my witness! So much so that since that day that I spoke with you in the Street of the Silversmiths I can't tell myself from you; to such a point that of the two I live more in you than in myself; so much so that since the first moment I saw you I was transformed into you, for neither do I know who I am, not do I remember who I was.

JACINTA. It is evident that you are the one you have forgotten about, since without considering that you are married, you are seeking a new love.

GARCIA. I married? Do you still persist in that idea?

JACINTA. Then you aren't married?

GARCIA. What silly madness! As God is my witness, that was a story I made up in order to be yours.

JACINTA. Or in order to not be; and if they begin to talk to you again about being married to Jacinta, you will be married in Turkey.

GARCIA. And I swear again, as God is my witness, that as far as anyone else is concerned I am married, and that I am unmarried for you alone.

JACINTA (*to* LUCRECIA). Are you disillusioned?

LUCRECIA (*aside*). Oh, how is it possible? Hardly a spark of love felt, and volcanoes of jealousy born from it now?

GARCIA. Didn't I tell you the whole situation that night I spoke to you at your balcony?

JACINTA. To me at my balcony?

LUCRECIA (*aside*). Oh, traitress!

JACINTA. You're deceived, señor. You talked to me?

GARCIA. Well, as God is my witness!

LUCRECIA (*aside*). You yourself talk to him at night and you give me advice?

GARCIA. And the note that you received. Will you deny that?

JACINTA. I, a note?

LUCRECIA (*aside*). What a faithful friend!

GARCIA. And I know that you read it.

JACINTA. Lying can pass as an accomplishment when it is not dangerous; but it cannot be tolerated when it goes beyond that boundary.

GARCIA. I didn't speak with you three nights ago at your balcony, Lucrecia?

JACINTA (*aside*). I Lucrecia? That's good. A new bull enters the ring, and the bullfighter must make up new tricks. He has recognized Lucrecia, and it's very certain that he adores her, so he pretends, so as not to anger her, that he has mistaken me for her.

LUCRECIA (*aside*). Now I understand everything. Oh, traitress! She undoubtedly let him know somehow that the veiled woman was me, and he wants to patch things up now by pretending that the reason for his speaking to her was that he mistook her for me.

TRISTAN (*to* GARCIA). She has to deny being Lucrecia because of the other woman sitting beside her.

GARCIA. I understand; since if she were denying it because of me she would have covered her face. But not knowing each other, would they talk to each other?

TRISTAN. It frequently happens that in the churches people talk to each other without knowing each other, just because they happen to be together.

GARCIA. You're probably right.

TRISTAN. You can patch things up now by pretending that your eyes deceived you.

GARCIA. The fancies of an ardent love, señorita, have so dazzled me that I have mistaken you for another. Pardon me, for the error was caused by that veil. For, as desire easily deceives the imagination, I think that every lady I see is my own.

JACINTA (*aside*). I knew that was his intention.

LUCRECIA (*aside*). I knew that sly witch had let him know.

JACINTA. According to what you have just said, then Lucrecia is your adored one.

GARCIA. My heart made her the mistress of my love, from the very first time I saw her.

JACINTA (*aside to* LUCRECIA). This is good!

LUCRECIA (*aside*). That this one should be making fun of me! I won't even show that I heard her, in order to avoid making a scene here.

JACINTA. Well, I think that if she were sure of that, Lucrecia would be very happy.

GARCIA. Do you know her?

JACINTA. I know her, and she is a friend of mine; so great a friend that I would dare say that in me and in her lives one heart only.

GARCIA (*aside*). Since you are she, this is very certain. How well you make clear to me your caution and your meaning! Since my good fortune arranges such a wonderful occasion, and since you are an angel, be the messenger of my sorrow now. Tell her of my firmness, and pardon me for giving you this duty.

TRISTAN (*aside*). By nightfall it will be the duty of all the women in Madrid.

GARCIA. Persuade her that she may not be ungrateful to such a great love.

JACINTA. Make her believe it, and I will make sure that she softens.

GARCIA. Why will she not believe that I die for love of her, since I have seen her beauty?

JACINTA. Because, if I may tell you the truth, she doesn't think you are truthful.

GARCIA. It is the truth, as God lives!

JACINTA. Make her believe it. What difference does it make if it be the truth, if he who tells it is you? For the lying mouth falls into such infamous disgrace, that only on its tongue does the truth become suspected.

GARCIA. Señorita . . .

JACINTA. Enough; you're attracting attention.

GARCIA. I obey.

JACINTA. Are you satisfied? (*Exit.*)

LUCRECIA. I am thankful for your good will, Jacinta.
(*Exit.*)

GARCIA. Wasn't Lucrecia clever? With what astuteness she made it understood that she didn't want to be known as Lucrecia!

TRISTAN. She's not foolish in love.

GARCIA. Undoubtedly she wouldn't want that woman she was talking with to know who she was.

TRISTAN. There certainly couldn't have been another reason for her denying such an obvious thing, because she didn't deny that she talked to you at her balcony, and she herself touched on the same points that you touched on when you talked with her there.

GARCIA. And another thing, she didn't conceal her face from me.

TRISTAN. And for that reason she said: "And if they begin to talk to you again about marrying Jacinta, you will be married in Turkey." And this conjecture is made more certain by her denying that she was Lucrecia, and by her speaking later of her own thoughts as if they were someone else's, telling you that she knew that Lucrecia would require your amorous intentions, if you could make her believe that they were sincere.

GARCIA. Ah, Tristan! What can I do to prove my love?

TRISTAN. You want to get married?

GARCIA. Yes.

TRISTAN. Then ask her.

GARCIA. And if she resists?

TRISTAN. It seems that you didn't hear what she just now said: "Make her believe it, and I will make sure that she softens." What better indication do you need that she wants to be yours? She who accepts your notes, who speaks to you at her window, has fully shown the affection she has for you. The thought that you are married is the only thing that holds her back; and this obstacle can be removed by marrying her; since the very fact of your planning to be married, being a great gentleman, is proof that you are a bachelor. And when she would oblige you to substantiate your claim, for fear of being deceived, Salamanca isn't so far away that you can't bring proof from there that you aren't married; Salamanca isn't in Japan.

GARCIA. Yes it is, for he who desires; and my desires are now so strong that seconds are like centuries for me.

TRISTAN. Isn't there anyone here who can be a witness?

GARCIA. Perhaps.

TRISTAN. It's an easy thing to find one.

GARCIA. I will look for some at once.

TRISTAN. I will give you one.

GARCIA. And who is it?

TRISTAN. Don Juan de Sosa.

GARCIA. Who? Don Juan de Sosa?

TRISTAN. Yes.

GARCIA. He knows it well.

TRISTAN. Since the day that he talked to you in the Street of the Silversmiths, I haven't seen him, nor has he seen you. And although I have always wanted to learn what distressed you in the note he wrote to you, I have never asked you about it, seeing that when I asked you about it then, you turned pale and angrily denied that there was anything that was bothering you. But now that such an appropriate time has come, I would like to think that I can ask you now, señor, since you have made me the secretary of the archives of your thoughts, and since that furor has passed.

GARCIA. I want to tell you about it; for, since I know by experience your ability to keep a secret and your prudence, I can trust you well. Don Juan de Sosa wrote me that at seven P.M. he would be waiting for me at the hermitage of San Blas to speak with me about a very important matter. I remained silent on the matter, because I knew this meant a duel; and he who is not silent at such a time hopes either that he will be prevented from going to the duel, or that he will be aided, both of which are cowardly solutions. I arrived at the assigned place, where I found Don Juan waiting for me with his sword and his jealousy, weapons which immediately gave him the advantage. He set forth his grievance; I agreed to his demands; and, finally, in order to do things properly, we unsheathed our swords. I immediately chose my distance, and advancing rapidly and to one side of the line of engagement so as to attack him from the side, I gave him a strong thrust. His life was saved by a medallion of the lamb of Christ which he was wearing; and, furthermore, when the point hit this medallion, my sword broke into two pieces. He fell back from this great blow; but with fierce rage he returned, delivering a thrust; but I caught the thin part of his sword with mine, forming a guard. But then, since I had so little steel left to contain his movements—for two thirds of my sword was gone—he quickly freed his sword, thus . . . and as he had me in close, because I, being handicapped with my broken sword, had gotten as near to him as I could, he aimed a furious slash at my head. I received it on my crippled weapon almost before it began to descend, and my sword being under his stopped all movement. So it was at Troy! Then came the crisis! I gave him a backhand blow with such force—the weakness of my sword made very little difference then— that a slash as wide as my hand was opened up in his head, and he fell to the ground senseless, and I even suspect lifeless. I left him as he was, and secretly returned to Madrid. That's what happened; and that's the reason you haven't seen him around recently, Tristan.

TRISTAN. What a remarkable outcome! And you think he died?

GARCIA. It's a certainty, because even his brains were scattered out on the battlefield.

TRISTAN. Poor Don Juan!

(*Enter* DON JUAN *and* DON BELTRAN *from another direction.*)

TRISTAN. But isn't this he who is coming?

GARCIA. What a remarkable thing!

TRISTAN. You try to deceive me, too? Deceive the secretary of your thoughts! (*aside*) That I believed what he said, even though I knew his tricks! But who wouldn't be deceived by such perfectly concocted lies?

GARCIA. They have undoubtedly cured him with a spell.

TRISTAN. A slash as wide as your hand that tore up his brains, healed in such a short time?

GARCIA. Is this so inconceivable? I know of a man in Salamanca whose arm was amputated, and who stuck it back on again with the aid of a spell, and in less than one week he was as healthy and well as he had been at the beginning.

TRISTAN. You're raving mad!

GARCIA. This wasn't told to me; I saw it myself.

TRISTAN. That's enough.

GARCIA. I swear on my life that I will not take one word away from the truth.

TRISTAN (aside). Is it possible that you can never really know anyone? Señor, you can pay for my services by teaching me this spell.

GARCIA. It is in Hebrew, and if you don't know the language you wouldn't know how to pronounce the words.

TRISTAN. And you, you know Hebrew?

GARCIA. That's a good one! Better than Spanish; I speak ten languages.

TRISTAN (aside). And all of them together don't have enough words for your lies. With reason do they call your body, "the body full of truths," since not one truth comes out of it, nor is there a lie in it that doesn't get out.

BELTRAN (to DON JUAN). What did you say?

JUAN. It's the truth; in Salamanca neither gentleman nor lady has those names you have asked me about, if I'm not mistaken.

BELTRAN (aside). It's certain that this was another of Garcia's stories. May you enjoy for many years the large income which will now be yours, since you have been awarded the order of the Cross of Calatrava.

JUAN. I am always your servant no matter how rich I become. And now please excuse me; for in order that I may go give my thanks to those who have conferred this honor on me, I will let you go on to your house by yourself. (Exit.)

BELTRAN (aside). May God protect me! Is it possible that I should not be spared from this boy's vice? That he should lie to my face at the same time that I was reproving him for lying? And that I, in such an important matter, should so readily believe him, having already heard of his reputation for falsehoods? But who would believe that he would lie to me when I was censuring him for that very same thing? And what judge would suspect that the same thief whose punishment he was determining would rob him?

TRISTAN (to GARCIA). You're determined to approach him?

GARCIA. Yes, Tristan.

TRISTAN. Then may God protect you.

GARCIA. Father . . .

BELTRAN. Don't call me father, base one; call me enemy; since he who does not resemble me in anything, doesn't have any blood of mine in his veins. Get out of my sight,

for as God is my witness, if I didn't see that you were my
son . . .

TRISTAN (*to* GARCIA). A big storm is threatening; wait
for a better occasion.

BELTRAN. Heavens! What punishment is this? Is it possible that to one who loves the truth as I do, you could give
a son of such a contrary nature? Is it possible that one who
guards his honor as much as I do, could engender a son of
such base inclinations? And that you could take away Gabriel, my oldest son, in the flower of youth, who gave honor
and life to my blood. These are things which, if I did not
view them in a Christian spirit . . .

GARCIA (*aside*). What is this?

TRISTAN (*aside to* DON GARCIA). Get out of here. What
are you waiting for?

BELTRAN. Leave us here alone, Tristan. No, on second
thought, come back; don't go; perhaps the shame of your
knowing of his infamy will effect in him that which respect
for my age could not. And if this shame doesn't make him
mend his faults, the public recounting of them will at least
humiliate him. Speak, wicked one: What are your intentions? Insane one, speak: What pleasure do you get from
lying so recklessly? And even if you follow your lying inclination with everyone else, couldn't you at least refrain
from it with me? With what intent did you pretend the marriage in Salamanca, in order to discredit my words also?
With what countenance will I speak to those whom I told
that you were married to Doña Sancha de Herrera? With
what countenance, when, learning that Doña Sancha is non-
existent, they defame my noble gray head as an accomplice
of a liar? How can I erase this stain, since the best I can do,
if I wish to remove the stain from myself, is put it on my
son; and saying that you were the cause, I must myself be
the herald of your infamy? If you had some problem of love,
why didn't you come to me, your father? Just the name "father" is enough for you to know how your desires would
move me to compassion. An old man who was once a young
one, and who knows well the force with which the calls of
love take hold in young hearts.

GARCIA. Well, if you know this force, and it would have
sufficed to excuse me; I will avail myself of it in order that
you may pardon me. It was an error, it wasn't a crime; it
wasn't a fault, it was ignorance. The cause: love. You, my
father, you say that this is enough. And now that I have

learned of the offense, hear the beautiful cause, because the offender herself should make you be satisfied with the offense. Doña Lucrecia, the daughter of Don Luis de Luna, is the soul of my life; she is the head and heiress of her family; and in order to make myself happy with her beautiful hand, the only thing lacking is that you should consent to it, and declare that the story of my being married had this cause, and that the story is false.

BELTRAN. No, no! Be quiet. Must you get me involved in another lie? Enough. If you tell me now that this is the truth, I must think that you deceive me.

GARCIA. No, señor; that which is proven by deeds is certainly the truth; and Tristan, in whom you trust, is a witness to my desires. Tell him, Tristan.

TRISTAN. Yes, señor; he's telling the truth.

BELTRAN. Aren't you ashamed of this? Speak, aren't you ashamed that it is necessary for your servant to vouch for what you say? Well now: I want to speak with Don Luis, and heaven grant that he give you to Lucrecia; for you are such that she is the deceived one. But first I must find out about this matter of Salamanca; since I'm now afraid that in telling me that you deceived me, you deceive me. For, although I knew before I came to speak to you that what you have told me is true, you have made this truth unbelievable just by confessing it.   (*Exit.*)

GARCIA. It turned out well!

TRISTAN. And how well! So much so, that I thought you were testing on yourself that Hebrew spell that heals up severed arms.   (*Exeunt.*)

SCENE 4: *A room with a view of a garden, in* DON LUIS DE LUNA's *house.*

(*Enter* DON LUIS DE LUNA *and* DON SANCHO.)

LUIS DE LUNA. It seems that the night has cooled off.

SANCHO. Don Luis, at my age it is too cool to go to eat by the river.

LUIS DE LUNA. It will be better that we eat here in my garden.

SANCHO. That would seem to be wiser. We will be able to

go to the river on a warmer night; these extremes endanger the health.

LUIS DE LUNA (*turning himself toward the inside of the house*). Entertain your beautiful companion in the garden tonight, Lucrecia.

SANCHO. If God be willing, you will see her well married; she is an angel.

LUIS DE LUNA. Besides not being foolish, and being, as you can see, so beautiful, she values virtue more than life.

(*Enter a* SERVANT.)

SERVANT (*to* DON SANCHO). Don Juan de Sosa just came to the door asking permission to speak with you.

SANCHO. At such an hour?

LUIS DE LUNA. It must be an important matter.

SANCHO. Tell Don Juan to come in. (SERVANT *exits.*)

(*Enter* DON JUAN, *with a paper.*)

JUAN (*to* DON SANCHO). I would never have come here without this paper that you see in my hand; but now that I have it, I lacked the patience to stay away; for my love didn't wish to delay the news one moment, if attaining the heaven of my loved one's countenance consists in having this paper. I have received my commission as commander of the military Order of Calatrava; if you remember that promise you made me that you would give me your daughter's hand in marriage if I obtained such a commission, you will now keep your word by acknowledging my victory.

SANCHO. You have rewarded my faith in you, señor Don Juan, by not delaying for one moment such happy news. I'll go now and tell it to my beautiful Jacinta: and please excuse me for not asking her to come out, for she isn't dressed.

LUIS DE LUNA. I always knew you would win out; for heaven always aids the most hidden and oppressed truth; there could be delay, but never doubt.

(*Enter* DON GARCIA, DON BELTRAN, *and* TRISTAN *from another direction.*)

BELTRAN. This is not an appropriate occasion on which to speak to him; this is a very serious matter which must be treated in private.

GARCIA. Don Juan de Sosa will serve before us as a witness in the matter of Salamanca.

BELTRAN. That it should be necessary! What a disgraceful thing! Until I tell Don Luis de Luna of our intentions, you will, I hope, be able to delay this matter.

LUIS DE LUNA. My friend, Don Beltran!

BELTRAN. Don Luis, my friend!

LUIS DE LUNA. Such an excess of courtesy at such an hour?

BELTRAN. In this courtesy you will recognize my great love.

LUIS DE LUNA. How fortunate is he who could deserve it!

BELTRAN. You must excuse me. I found your door open, and the friendship I have for you gave me the permission I lacked to enter.

LUIS DE LUNA. I am anxious to know the reason for this visit.

BELTRAN. I want to tell you, then, what I come for.

GARCIA (to DON JUAN DE SOSA). I've heard about your obtaining the commandership. You can believe, as God is my witness, that your victory has made me happy.

JUAN. Insofar as this comes from you, I believe it.

GARCIA. May you enjoy the commandership, as you deserve it, and I wish it.

LUIS DE LUNA. Lucrecia is so fortunate in this, that I think that this good I see is the product of a dream. With the permission of Don Juan, I would have a word with Don Garcia; Don Beltran has told me that you wish Lucrecia to be your wife.

GARCIA. My soul, happiness, honor and life are in her hands.

LUIS DE LUNA. I, henceforth, give you my hand as a pledge for hers (They shake hands.) since just as I know what I gain in this, she knows also, for I have heard her speak of you.

GARCIA. I am deeply grateful to you for your supreme good will, Don Luis.

(Enter DON SANCHO, JACINTA, and LUCRECIA.)

LUCRECIA. At last, after such troubles, you realize your fondest hopes.

JACINTA. With the realization of yours, I will be happy about everything.

LUIS DE LUNA. She enters with Jacinta, unaware of her own approaching wedding. Wait until I ask her for the reward due to a bearer of such happy news.

BELTRAN (aside to DON GARCIA). Here is Don Sancho. Consider what I am going to look like now!

GARCIA. He who is wise pardons errors caused by love.

LUCRECIA. He wasn't married in Salamanca?

LUIS DE LUNA. It was a story he made up, so that his father wouldn't marry him to another.

LUCRECIA. Being so, my will is yours, and I am happy.

SANCHO. Go, illustrious young men to your happy sweethearts, for they say that they are happy and that they await you with love.

GARCIA. Now my actions will give proof to my truths.

(DON GARCIA *and* DON JUAN *go to* JACINTA.)

JUAN. Where are you going, Don Garcia? You see beautiful Lucrecia, there.

GARCIA. How Lucrecia?

BELTRAN. What is this?

GARCIA (*to* JACINTA). You are my lady, señorita.

BELTRAN. Do we have another lie?

GARCIA. If I was wrong about the name, I am not wrong about the person. You are the one I asked for, and the one that my soul adores.

LUCRECIA. And this note, deceiver (*She takes out a note.*) that is in your own handwriting, do you now contradict what it says?

BELTRAN. What dishonor you put me in!

JUAN. Give me your hand, Jacinta, and put an end to these things.

SANCHO. Give Don Juan your hand.

JACINTA (*to* DON JUAN). I am yours.

GARCIA. I have lost my glorious heaven.

BELTRAN. As God lives, if you don't take Lucrecia as your wife, I will take away your life.

LUIS DE LUNA. By giving you my hand in Lucrecia's name, I definitely pledge her to marry you; if your insane inconstancy has changed you so quickly, I will wash away my dishonor with blood from your veins.

TRISTAN. The guilt is all yours; if you had told the truth at the beginning, you would now have Jacinta. There's nothing that can be done. Ask Lucrecia's pardon and give her your hand, for she is also a beautiful girl.

GARCIA. I give you my hand.

TRISTAN. And now you will see how dangerous lying is; and the audience will see that in the mouth of him who usually lies, the truth is suspected.

LIFE IS A DREAM
(*La vida es sueño*)

by Pedro Calderón de la Barca

TRANSLATED BY
Edward and Elizabeth Huberman

ᗌᗂᗌ

CHARACTERS

BASILIO, *King of Poland*
SEGISMUNDO, *the Prince*
ASTOLFO, *Duke of Muscovy*
CLOTALDO, *an old man, tutor*
of Segismundo
CLARIN, *a talkative clown*

ESTRELLA, *a princess*
ROSAURA, *a lady*
SOLDIERS, GUARDS, MUSICIANS,
ATTENDANTS, SERVANTS, AND
LADIES

SCENE: *In the Polish court, in a fortress a short
distance away, and in the country.*

Pedro Calderón de la Barca

(1600-1681)

With Lope de Vega, Calderón towers above all the other playwrights of the Golden Age. Calderón derived from the lower aristocracy and attended the Colegio Imperial of the Jesuits and both the Universities of Alcalá and Salamanca. His work deals with philosophy or theology and there is little that can be called extemporaneous in his plays: everything is well contrived and minutely calculated, and his style is cluttered with figures of speech, and metaphysical conceits—an outstanding example, indeed, of the Baroque.

Calderón began to write in his early youth, when he participated in contests connected with the religious festivals. By 1623 he was finishing his first play, *Amor, honor y poder*, but he interrupted everything to join the military expedition against Breda. Back home two years later, he set down to work in earnest. Recognition did not delay in coming. After the success of *La vida es sueño* (*Life Is a Dream*, 1635), the Count of Olivares invited him to produce plays on the lagoon of his new palace and it was in the magnificent gardens of the Buen Retiro that Calderón presented his mythological play *El mayor encanto amor*. So lavish in pageantry, so elaborate in stage machinery was the performance that Philip IV conferred upon him the Order of Santiago, and after Lope's death (1635) appointed him court dramatist. Calderón wrote over one hundred comedies as well as some seventy religious pageants, mostly dealing with the Eucharist and called *auto sacramentales*. Among his outstanding later achievements were *El gran teatro del mundo* (*The Great Theater of the World*, for which see a new English version in my anthology *Masterpieces of the Spanish Golden Age*), *El mágico prodigioso*, *El príncipe constante*, *El médico de su honra*, *El condenado por desconfiado*, and *El Alcalde de Zalamea*.

BEST EDITION: A. Valbuena Prat (ed.), *Obras completas*. Madrid, Aguilar, 1945.

ABOUT: M. A. Buchanan, "Segismundo's Soliloquy on Libreta in Calderón's *La Vida es sueño*," *PMLA*, XXIII (1908), 240-253; "Calderón's *Life Is a Dream*," *PMLA*, XLVIII (1932), 1303-1321. E. Frutos, *Calderón de la Barca*. Barcelona, 1949. A. A. Parker, *The Allegorical Dramas of Calderón*. Oxford, 1943. A. Valbuena Prat, *Calderón*. Barcelona, 1941. W. W. Whitby, "Rosaura's Role in the Structure of *La vida es sueño*," *Hispanic Review*, XXVIII (1960), 16-27.

ACT I

SCENE 1: *On one side a craggy mountain; on the other a tower whose lower section serves as a prison for* SEGISMUNDO. *The door facing the audience is half open. The action begins at nightfall.*

(ROSAURA, *in man's clothing, appears high up on the rocks, and comes down to the plain.* CLARIN *follows her.*)

ROSAURA. Wild hippogriff,* running swift as the wind, flash without flame, bird without color, fish without scales, unnatural beast, where are you wildly rushing in the intricate labyrinth of these bare rocks? Stay here on this mountain, so that the beasts may have their Phaëthon. For I, taking the only path the laws of destiny allow me, blind and hopeless descend through the jagged tangles of this high hill, which wrinkles its frowning forehead at the sun.

Unkindly, O Poland, do you receive a stranger; for you inscribe her arrival in your land with blood; and hardly does she arrive, but she comes to grief. My fate will testify to this; but where did an unhappy person ever find pity?

CLARIN. Make it two unhappy people, and don't forget me when you complain. It was two of us who left our country to seek adventures, two of us who passed through misfortunes and madness to reach this place, and again two of us who have fallen down the mountain; shouldn't I grieve if I shared in the trouble, but not in the telling of it?

ROSAURA. I do not share my complaints with you, Clarin, because I do not wish to deprive you of your right to be consoled by weeping about your own problems. For there's so much pleasure in complaining, some philosopher once said, that troubles should be sought just for the sake of complaining about them.

* A mythological creature, half-horse, half-griffin.

CLARIN. That philosopher was a wretched drunkard. Oh, if someone had only punched him a thousand times or more! Then he would have something to complain of! But what are we to do, señora, on foot, alone, and lost on a deserted mountain at this hour when the sun is leaving for another horizon?

ROSAURA. Whoever has seen such strange events? If my sight is not suffering the deceptions of fancy, it seems to me that in what remains of twilight I can see a building.

CLARIN. Either my desire is lying to me, or I can make out the signs myself.

ROSAURA. Here amid bare rocks rises a rustic palace, so small it scarcely dares to look at the sun. It's built with such crude skill that, at the base of so many sun-touching rocks and crags, it seems itself like some huge rock that must have tumbled from the summit.

CLARIN. Let's go nearer. While this is fine to see, señora, it would be finer if the people who live here would be kind enough to let us in.

ROSAURA. The door, or rather, the dismal mouth, is open, and from its center the night itself is born, engendered in that darkness.

(*The noise of chains is heard within.*)

CLARIN. Heavens, what do I hear?

ROSAURA. I can't move! I'm fire and ice!

CLARIN. Is a chain making that noise? May they kill me, if that isn't a galley slave being punished. My fear tells me that it is.

SEGISMUNDO (*within the tower*). Alas, wretched me! How unhappy I am!

ROSAURA. What sad voice do I hear? Now I must face new pains and anguish.

CLARIN. And I new fears . . .

ROSAURA. Clarin . . .

CLARIN. Señora . . .

ROSAURA. Let us run away from the dangers of this enchanted tower.

CLARIN. When it comes to that, I have no mind to flee.

ROSAURA. Isn't that faint exhalation, that pallid star, a sort of light? It trembles, fades, flares, and flashes, and makes this dim room even darker with its doubtful glow. Yes, it is! For by its beams I can make out, even from afar, a gloomy prison room, the grave of a living corpse. Stranger still, dressed in the skins of beasts, and loaded with chains, a man lies on the floor, with no company but this light. Since we can't run away, let's listen from here to his complaints; let's learn what he says.

(*The doors swing open, and* SEGISMUNDO *is seen, chained and clad in skins. There is a light in the tower.*)

SEGISMUNDO. Oh, wretch that I am! Oh, unfortunate! I try, oh heavens, to understand, since you treat me so, what crime I committed against you when I was born . . . but, since I *was* born, I understand my crime. Your cruel justice has had sufficient cause. For man's greatest crime is to have been born at all.

Still, I should like to know, to ease my anxiety—leaving aside, ye gods, the sin of being born—in what way I could offend you more, to deserve more punishment? Were not all other men born too? If so, why do they have blessings that I never enjoyed?

The bird is born, with the gaudy plumage that gives it unrivalled beauty; and scarcely is it formed, like a flower of feathers or a winged branch, when it swiftly cuts the vaulted air, refusing the calm shelter of its nest. But I, with more soul, have less liberty!

The beast is born, too, with skin beautifully marked, like a cluster of stars—thanks to Nature's skilled brush; then stern necessity, cruel and savage, teaches it to be cruel also, and it reigns a monster in its labyrinth. Yet I, with better instincts, have less liberty!

The fish is born, unbreathing, a creature of spawn and seaweed, and scarcely is it seen—a scaly vessel in the waves—when it darts in all directions, measuring the vastness of the cold and deep. And I, with more free will, I have less liberty!

The stream is born, a snake uncoiling among the flowers, and scarcely does this serpent of silver break through the blossoms, when it celebrates their grace with music, and with music takes its passage through the majesty of the open plain. Yet I, who have more life, have less liberty!

As I reach this pitch of anger, like a volcano, an Aetna, I could tear pieces of my heart from my own breast. What law, justice, or reason, can deny to man so sweet a privilege, so elementary a freedom, as God has given to a brook, a fish, a beast, and a bird?

ROSAURA. His words make me feel pity and fear.

SEGISMUNDO. Who's been listening to me? Clotaldo?

CLARÍN (*aside, to* ROSAURA). Say yes!

ROSAURA. It's only a sad wanderer—alas!—who heard your moans in these cold vaults.

SEGISMUNDO. Then I shall kill you here (*He seizes her.*), so that you may not know my weakness. My strong arms seize you, to tear you to pieces, only because you have heard me.

CLARÍN. I'm deaf; I couldn't hear you.

ROSAURA. If you were born a human being, throwing myself at your feet should be enough to make you let me go.

SEGISMUNDO. Your voice calms me, your presence stops me, and your look disturbs me. Who are you? For even though I know so little of the world, inasmuch as this tower has been cradle and tomb for me; and even though, since I was born—if this is to be born—I have seen only this wilderness where I live in misery, a living skeleton, a moving corpse; and even though I have seen and talked to only one man here who pities my distress, and who has taught me all I know of earth and heaven; and although here—to astonish you more, and make you call me a human monster—here among terrors and fearful fancies, I am a man among wild beasts, and a beast among men; and although in my grave misfortunes I have studied politics, been instructed by the beasts and advised by the birds, and have measured the circles of the smooth-slipping stars, you only, only you have calmed my anger, brought wonder to my eyes, and astonishment to my ears.

Each time I look at you, I feel new admiration; the more I look at you, the more I want to look. My eyes must have the dropsy, I believe, for though it's death to drink, they drink even more. And thus, although I see that seeing brings me death, I still must see. But let me look at you, and die. For if seeing you kills me, I do not know, your victim that I am, what not seeing you will do to me. It would be worse than fierce death, worse than rage, madness, and terrible grief. It would be life. And of this fate I have taken the measure, for to grant life to an unhappy man is the same as to slay a happy one.

ROSAURA. Amazed to look at you, and filled with wonder to hear you, I do not know what to tell you, nor what to ask. I can only say that heaven has guided me here today to console me, if it can be the consolation of one unlucky being to see another more unlucky still.

They tell the story of a wise man who was so poor and

wretched that he survived only by eating the herbs he gathered. "Can there be anyone else," he said to himself, "poorer and sadder than I?" And when he turned his head, he found the answer, for he saw another wise man gathering the leaves which he had thrown away.

I lived in this world complaining of my fortune, and when I asked myself: "Can there be some other person plagued by worse luck than I?" mercifully, you answered me. For when I think things over, I find that you have gathered my pains, and made joys of them.

If then, by chance, my troubles can in any way relieve you, listen to them carefully, and take what I have left over. I am . . .

CLOTALDO (*within*). Guards of the tower! Afraid or asleep, you let two people break into the prison . . .

ROSAURA. Still more trouble!

SEGISMUNDO. That's Clotaldo, my warden. My misfortunes are not over yet!

CLOTALDO (*within*). Come here, be careful! Capture them or kill them, before they can defend themselves!

VOICES (*within*). Treason!

CLARIN. Guards of the tower, who let us enter here, since you give us a choice, capturing us is easier.

(CLOTALDO *and soldiers enter, the former with a pistol and all with faces covered.*)

CLOTALDO (*aside to the soldiers, as they enter*). All of you cover your faces. It is important, while we are here, to be careful no one recognizes us.

CLARIN. Is this a masquerade?

CLOTALDO. You there! You who in ignorance passed the limits and boundary of this forbidden place, contrary to the decree of the King, who commands that no one dare look upon the prodigy hidden among these crags, surrender your arms and yourselves, or this pistol, this metal asp, will spit out the penetrating poison of its two bullets, with a blast that will shock the air.

SEGISMUNDO. Before you hurt them, oh tyrant master, my life will be the spoil of these miserable chains, for, God help me, I would sooner tear myself to pieces, with my hands, with my teeth, among these rocks, than permit any misfortune to occur to them or have to lament an outrage done to them.

CLOTALDO. Since you know, Segismundo, that your misfortunes are so enormous that before birth you died by heaven's law; since you know that these prison walls are a rein to check your proud fury, and a bridle to halt it, why talk like such a braggart? (*to the soldiers*) Shut the door of this narrow cell! Hide him in it!

SEGISMUNDO. O heavens! How well you do to take away my freedom! For I would assault you like a giant, piling mountains of jasper on foundations of stone to break the glassy crystals of the sun!

CLOTALDO. Perhaps the punishment you suffer today will prevent you from building such piles!

(*Several soldiers take* SEGISMUNDO *away, and shut him in his prison.*)

ROSAURA. Now that I have seen you so much offended by pride, it would be stupid of me not to be humble, and fall at your feet to beg my life. May you be moved by pity toward me, for it would be extraordinary harshness, indeed, if neither pride nor humility found favor with you.

CLARIN. And if you can be influenced by neither Humility nor Pride, characters which a thousand morality plays have set in motion and shifted about, then I, neither humble nor proud, but a mixture of half and half, I beg that you help and succor us.

CLOTALDO. Ho there!

SOLDIERS. Sir?

CLOTALDO. Disarm both of them, and bind their eyes, so that they may not see how or where they leave.

ROSAURA. Here is my sword, which must be yielded to you only, because you are the chief of all here; it cannot be given to any lesser person.

CLARIN (*to a soldier*). Mine is the sort that can be given to the meanest; here, you, take it!

ROSAURA. And if I must die, I wish to leave you, in consideration of your pity, a pledge that could be truly valued by its owner, who one day girded it on. Guard it, I charge you, for although I do not know of what secret it may hint, I do know that this golden sword is the key to great mysteries. Trusting only in it, I have come to Poland to revenge an injury.

CLOTALDO (*aside*). Blessed heavens! What is this? Now my worries and bewilderment, my anxiety and my griefs, are all compounded. Who gave this to you?

ROSAURA. A woman.

CLOTALDO. What is her name?

ROSAURA. It is forbidden me to tell it.

CLOTALDO. What were you implying just now, or how do you know there is a secret in this sword?

ROSAURA. She who gave it to me said: "Go to Poland, and by trick or art or study, arrange for the leaders and nobles to see this sword in your possession, for I know that some one of them will favor and protect you." But who that was she did not wish to say, in case he might be dead.

CLOTALDO (aside). Heaven preserve me! What do I hear? I still cannot determine if these happenings are illusion or reality. This is the sword I left with the beautiful Violante as a pledge that I would treat him who wore it girded on his belt as if he were my son; and as a father, I would help him. But what must I do—alas!—in such a quandary, if he who carries it to gain my favor, carries it for his own death, since sentenced to death he comes to my feet? What a strange confusion! What an unhappy destiny! What inconstant luck! This is my son; the signs agree with the signals of my heart which calls from my breast when it sees him, and beats its wings. And because it cannot break the locks, it does what a man would do who was shut in and heard a noise in the street—he looks out the window; likewise my heart, since it knows not what goes on, and hears the noise, comes to my eyes, which are the windows of the heart, to look out. And from thence it flows out in tears.

What must I do? Heaven help me! What am I to do? To take him to the King is to take him—too sad to think of—to his death. Yet hide him from the King I cannot, because of my oath of allegiance. On one side love for my own, and loyalty on the other; I am torn apart. But why do I hesitate? Does not loyalty to the King come before life and honor? Then let the King prevail, and life yield place.

Besides, now I remember, he said he comes here to avenge an insult. A man who has been insulted is infamous. He is not my son, not my son, he does not bear my noble blood. But what if some danger, some accident occurred, from which no one escaped—for honor is such a fragile substance that a single touch may break it, or the very breeze injure it—what more, then, can he who is noble do in his own behalf than to come, at great risk, to seek his honor again? He is my son; his blood is mine, since he has such valor. And thus, between one doubt and another, the most important step is to go to the King and tell him that this is my son, and that he must kill him. Perhaps the very concern I have for my honor may move the King in my behalf; and if my merit wins my son's life, I'll help him to avenge that insult. But if the King, unbending in his harshness, condemns him to death, he will die without knowing I am his father.

(*To* ROSAURA *and* CLARIN) Come with me, strangers. Do not fear that you lack company in your misfortunes, for in this doubt of life or death, I know not whose misery is greatest. (*Exeunt.*)

SCENE 2: *Hall of the royal palace in the Court.*

(*Enter* ASTOLFO *and soldiers on one side, and on the other, the* INFANTA ESTRELLA *and her Ladies. Military music within, and salvos.*)

ASTOLFO. At the sight of your bright and peerless eyes, flashing like comets, the drums and trumpets, birds and fountains mingle their varied salutes; marveling at your heavenly appearance, they blend in similar music, as trumpets made of feathers, or as birds of metal. And thus, señora, the guns salute you as their queen; the birds greet you as Aurora; the trumpets, as Pallas; and the flowers, as Flora. For you mock the day, now exiled by night, and appear like Aurora in joy, Flora in peace, Pallas in war, and sovereign in my heart.

ESTRELLA. If words are to be measured by actions, you have done ill in speaking such elegant niceties when all that martial display against which I boldly fight may prove you a liar; for the flatteries I hear from you do not agree, I fear, with the terrors that I see. Mark well: it is an ignoble act, fitting only for a wild beast, the source of deceit and treachery, to flatter with the tongue while planning to kill.

ASTOLFO. You are badly informed, Estrella, to doubt the faith of my tender words; and I beg you to hear my cause, to see if I can tell it correctly. When Eustorgio the Third, King of Poland, died, he left Basilio as his heir, and two daughters, from whom you and I were born. I do not wish to tire you with what has no place here. Clorilene, your mother and my aunt, who now, beneath a canopy of stars, rules in a better kingdom, was the elder. You are her daughter. The younger, my mother and your aunt, was the graceful Recisunda, whom God preserve for a thousand years. She married in Muscovy, and of her I was born.

Now let us return to the beginning: Basilio, who now, señora, yields to the common scorn of time, is more inclined to studies than to women, and is a childless widower. You and I aspire to his throne. You argue that you are the elder sister's daughter; I, that I was born a man, and though a child of the younger sister, I ought to be preferred to you. We have related your aim and mine to our uncle. He has answered that he wishes to reconcile us, and with that in mind we appointed this place and this day. With this purpose I left Muscovy and my native land; for this reason I came here, not to make war on you, but for you to war on me. Oh, may Love, wise God, be willing that the people, sure astrologers, today conclude this agreement for us, that you may be queen, but queen by my free will. And for greater honor, our uncle will give you his crown, your own valor will give you triumphs, and your empire will be my love.

ESTRELLA. To such gracious gallantry my heart replies in kind, for I should be glad if the imperial throne were mine, only to make it yours. Still my love is not quite satisfied that you are to be trusted, for I suspect that portrait hanging at your breast gives the lie to all you say to me.

ASTOLFO. I shall try to satisfy you about that . . . But no occasion is left us. (*Drums sound.*) That sonorous instrument informs us that king and parliament now approach.

(KING BASILIO *enters with his following.*)

ESTRELLA. Wise Thales . . .

ASTOLFO. Learned Euclid . . .

ESTRELLA. Who among signs . . .

ASTOLFO. Who among stars . . .

ESTRELLA. Today rules . . .

ASTOLFO. Today dwells . . .

ESTRELLA. And their paths . . .

ASTOLFO. And footsteps . . .

ESTRELLA. Describes . . .

ASTOLFO. Measures and marks . . .

ESTRELLA. Permit me, humbly twining . . .

ASTOLFO. Allow me, with tender embraces . . .

ESTRELLA. Like ivy to surround this trunk.

ASTOLFO. To sink in supplication at your feet.

BASILIO. My nephew and my niece, embrace me. Believe me, since you come with such affection, obedient to my loving command, neither of you will have cause to complain; both shall be treated equally. And thus, when I confess myself overcome by the tedious weight of years, I ask only for your silence; the event itself will strike you with amazement.

You already know—attend me well, my beloved niece and nephew, illustrious court of Poland, vassals, kinsmen, friends—you already know that because of my learning I have won in the world the title of Learned; for, despite time and forgetfulness, Thimantes' brushes and Lysippus' marbles proclaim me throughout the globe, Basilio the Great. You know too that the science I most study and esteem is subtle mathematics, by which I steal from Time, by which I tear from fame the province and the office of revealing what each day shall be. For when, in my calculations, I behold the events of coming centuries as if they were present, I win Time's thanks, who then has only to tell what I have told already.

These circles of snow, these canopies of glass, lighted by the sun's rays and divided by the circuits of the moon; these diamond orbs, these crystal globes which the stars adorn, and where the signs of the Zodiac are set, these are the major study of my years. These are the books where, on diamond pages, in sapphire notebooks, and in golden lines of clearest letters, heaven writes our fates, whether adverse or benign. These I read so swiftly that with my spirit I follow their rapid movements, their roads and courses. Would it had pleased heaven, before my skill became a marginal commentary and an index of these pages, that my life had been first destroyed by their rages, and that therein had been all my tragedy! For to the unfortunate, even merit is a knife; he whom knowledge harms, murders himself! This I tell you now, even though my history will say it better; and to wonder at this, once more I ask your silence.

By Clorilene, my wife, I was given an unhappy son, at whose birth the heavens were consumed by prodigies. Before the living sepulchre of her womb—for birth and death are much alike—delivered him to the light of the sun, his mother numberless times, half in fancy, half in the visions of dreams, saw a rude monster in man's form tear through her entrails. Stained with her blood, he took her life, thus becoming at birth the human viper of the century. The day of birth arrived, the omens were fulfilled (for seldom or never do those that presage evil err). He was born with such a horoscope that the sun, dyed with blood, dueled furiously with the moon. With the earth as battleground, the two divine lamps struggled, not arm to arm, but light to light. This was the greatest, the most terrifying eclipse the sun has suffered since with its blood it wept the death of Christ. For the orb, flooded with living fire, seemed to be sustaining its final paroxysm; the heavens darkened; buildings shook; the clouds rained stones; the rivers ran blood. And in that frenzy, that delirium of the sun, was Segismundo born, indicating his nature at once by killing his mother. With that cruel act he seemed to say: "I am a man, since I now begin to repay kindnesses with evil."

Turning to my studies, I saw in them and in everything that Segismundo would be the most insolent man, the cruelest prince, the most impious monarch, by whose hand the kingdom would be shattered and divided, a school for treason, an academy for vice. And he, borne on by his fury, among crimes and terrors, was to set his feet upon me; and I, to see myself a suppliant before him (with what shame I speak it!) the white hairs of my head a rug beneath his heel. Who does not easily believe evil, particularly the evil he has seen in his own study, where self-love fortifies the argument? So I believed the fates that with foreknowledge prophesied danger in their fatal oracles, and I determined to lock up the wild beast that had been born, to see if the sage could hold mastery over the stars. It was announced that the infant was born dead, and, forewarned, I ordered a tower, its entrance guarded by rough obelisks, to be built among the rocks and crags of those mountains, where the light scarcely finds its way. Severe penalties and laws, publicly proclaimed, declaring that no one might enter the forbidden area of the mountain, grew out of the reasons I have told you.

There lives Segismundo, wretched, poor and captive, where only Clotaldo has talked with him, dealt with him, and seen him. Clotaldo has taught him the sciences, has instructed him in the law of the church, has been the sole witness of his misery.

Here now are three considerations: first, that I love thee, Poland, so much that I desire to free thee from oppression and servitude under a tyrant king. For he would not be a kind lord who would put his country and his realm in such danger. Second: if I deprive my own child of the right accorded by law, both human and divine, it is not Christian charity, since no law states that because I keep another from being an insolent tyrant, I may myself become one; nor that, if my son is a tyrant, I may commit crimes to prevent him from committing them. The last and third consideration is this: to see how great an error it is to believe too easily in predictions. For although his inclination may dictate rash acts, perhaps they will not overcome him; because the sternest fate, the most violent inclination, the most nefarious planet, merely influence the free will; they do not force it. And so, vacillating and thinking of one argument and another, I hit upon such a remedy as will astound your senses. Tomorrow I intend to place Segismundo—for that is his name—without his knowing that he is my son and your king, under my canopy, on my throne, and indeed, in my place where he may govern and command you, and where all of you as subjects will swear him obedience. For with this act I achieve three results with which I answer the three considerations of which I told you. First is this: if he is prudent, discreet, and benevolent, giving the lie in every way to what fate predicted for him, you will enjoy your natural prince, who has been a courtier of the mountains, and a neighbor of wild beasts. The second is this: that if, arrogant, high-mettled, insolent, and cruel, he runs unchecked the field of his vices, then will I piously have complied with my duty; and then, in dispossessing him, I shall act as king infallible, since returning him to prison will not be cruelty but punishment. And the third result is this: should the prince prove as I describe him, I shall give you, because I love you, rulers more worthy of the crown and scepter. They will be my niece and nephew, who, with their rights joined in one and cemented by a pledge of marriage, will have what they deserve. This as king I command you; this as a father I beg you; this as a sage I urge you; this as an old man I tell you; and if, as Spanish Seneca said, a king is the humble slave of his republic, then as a slave I beseech you.

ASTOLFO. If it is my place to respond, as he whose interests are most concerned here, in the name of all I say, let Segismundo appear. It is enough that he is your son.

ALL. Give us our prince, whom now we ask for king.

BASILIO. Vassals, that courtesy I value and I thank you for it. Conduct my niece and nephew, my two supporting pillars, to their rooms. Tomorrow you shall see the prince.

ALL. Long live great King Basilio!

(*Exeunt all, accompanying* ESTRELLA *and* ASTOLFO;
the KING *remains.*)

(CLOTALDO *enters with* ROSAURA *and* CLARIN.)

CLOTALDO (*to the* KING). May I speak to you?

BASILIO. Ah, Clotaldo, you are very welcome!

CLOTALDO. Although I ought to be welcome when I fall
at your feet, my lord, this time harsh, sad fate breaks the
privilege of the law and the pattern of custom.

BASILIO. What's the matter?

CLOTALDO. A misfortune, sire, has descended upon me;
in other circumstances I should consider it the greatest joy.

BASILIO. Continue . . .

CLOTALDO. This handsome youth, daring or careless, entered the tower, Sire, where he saw the prince. And he is . . .

BASILIO. Do not worry, Clotaldo. If this had happened at
another time, I confess I should have been incensed. But
now I have told the secret, and it does not matter that he
knows it. Attend me later, because I have many things to
tell you, and many tasks that you must do for me. For you
must be, I warn you, the instrument of the most tremendous event the world has seen. As for these prisoners, so
that you will not think I am punishing your carelessness,
I pardon them.   (*Exit.*)

CLOTALDO. May you live, great Sire, a thousand centuries! (*aside*) Heaven has changed our luck for the better.
I shall not say now that he is my son, since I can avoid it.
(*aloud*) Wandering strangers, you are free.

ROSAURA. I kiss your feet a thousand times.

CLARIN. And I *miss* them. —Two friends don't worry about
one letter more or less.

ROSAURA. Since you have given me my life, señor, I
live because of you. Eternally I shall be your slave.

CLOTALDO. It is not life I have given you, because a man
well born does not live if his honor has been stained. Since
you have come to avenge yourself for an insult, as you yourself have told me, I have not given you life, because you
have not brought it with you. A dishonorable life is no life
at all. (*aside*) Those words will spur him on!

ROSAURA. I confess I do not possess it, even though I receive it from you. But by vengeance I shall leave my honor
so clean that then my life, overcoming all dangers, can well
appear your gift.

CLOTALDO. Take the burnished steel you brought. I know

that it will be enough, dyed in the blood of your enemy, to avenge you. For steel that was mine (I refer to the little while I held the sword in my possession) will know how to take vengeance.

ROSAURA. In your name, a second time I gird it on, and on it I swear my vengeance, however powerful my enemy.

CLOTALDO. Is he so powerful?

ROSAURA. So much so that I shall not tell you of it. Not because I do not trust your prudence in greater things, but so that the wondrous favor of your mercy will not turn against me.

CLOTALDO. First you should gain my help by telling me, for that would prevent me from aiding your enemy. (*aside*) Oh, if I only knew who he is!

ROSAURA. So that you will not think I hold your trust in low esteem, know that my adversary is no less than Astolfo, Duke of Muscovy.

CLOTALDO (*aside*). Ill can I withstand this sorrow, for it is graver when known than I had imagined. (*aloud*) Let us clarify the matter further. If you were born a Muscovite, he who is your natural lord can hardly have been able to insult you. Return, then, to your fatherland, and leave the burning valor that drives you.

ROSAURA. I know that although he was my prince, he was able to injure me.

CLOTALDO. He could not, even though he rudely struck your cheek with his hand.

ROSAURA. Oh heaven, my injury was greater!

CLOTALDO. Tell me now, since you cannot say more than I imagine.

ROSAURA. Yes, I shall tell you; but I do not know, with such respect I regard you, with such affection I venerate you, with such esteem I look upon you, how I shall dare to tell you that this outward clothing is a riddle, since it is not whose it appears. Judge wisely, if I am not what I seem, and if Astolfo has come to marry Estrella, whether he may injure me. I have said enough.

(*Exeunt* ROSAURA *and* CLARIN.)

CLOTALDO. Listen! Beware! Wait! What a confused labyrinth is this, where reason cannot find the thread. It is my honor that is smirched. The enemy is powerful, I a vassal, she a woman. Reveal the way, oh heaven; but I know not if heaven can. In such a confused hell, the whole sky's a dreadful omen, and the whole world a prodigy.

ACT II

SCENE 1: *The palace.*

(*Enter* BASILIO, CLOTALDO.)

CLOTALDO. Everything has been done, just as you ordered.

BASILIO. Tell me, Clotaldo, how it happened.

CLOTALDO. Thus, Sire: with the tranquilizing drink you ordered prepared, full of ingredients combining the virtues of certain herbs, the sovereign force and secret power of which suspend, steal, and alienate the human reason and leave a man a living corpse; the violence of which takes from him, while he sleeps, his senses and his powers. We need not argue if this be possible, since experience has so often told us, Sire, that it is. For it is certain that medicine is full of natural secrets, and there is neither animal, plant, nor stone which does not have its distinct property. Moreover, if our human malice can find a thousand poisons which bring death, how much more likely is it that, once the violence of these fatal poisons be tempered, they should bring sleep? Let us leave aside, then, the question of whether this could possibly happen, since evidence and reason have already proved it. Well, with that drink, composed of opium, henbane, and the drowsy poppy, I went down to Segismundo's narrow cell. I talked with him a while of the humanities, wherein mute Nature, with her hills and heavens, has instructed him. In her divine school he learned the rhetoric of birds and beasts. To raise his spirit further toward the enterprise you desire, I took as subject the speed of a mighty eagle, which, scorning the sphere of the wind, passed on to soar in the supreme regions of fire, like a feathered flame or a strayed comet. I acclaimed its lofty flight, saying: "You, Eagle, are King of the Birds, and thus it is right that you excel them all." Further urging was not necessary. Eagerly, proudly, he explained his views on royalty, for, in fact, his blood incites him, stirs and moves him toward great deeds. "So," said he, "even in the noisy commonwealth of the birds there is one who makes them swear obedience! While I reason thus, my misfortunes console me, for if I am subdued, at least it is only by force. Voluntarily I would submit to no man."

Seeing him now enraged by this, which has been the theme of all his suffering, I offered him the potion. Scarcely had the liquid passed to his throat from the cup, when sleep overcame him. A cold sweat ran through all his limbs and veins, so that, if I had not known his death was feigned, I should have doubted of his life. Just then the people to whom you trusted the outcome of this experiment arrived. Putting him into a carriage, they brought him to his room, which had been prepared with all the majesty and elegance worthy of his person. On your bed they laid him, and when the lethargy has spent its force, they will serve him as they would you. For so, Sire, you commanded. And if having obeyed you merits a reward, I would only ask (pardon the liberty I take) that you tell me what your purpose is in bringing Segismundo in this way to the palace?

BASILIO. Clotaldo, the doubt you have is very reasonable, and I wish to satisfy you concerning it. The influence of the stars (well do you know this) threatens my son Segismundo with a thousand misfortunes and tragedies. I wish to test whether heaven, which cannot lie and which has given us so many proofs of harshness in his cruel nature, still may not mitigate, or at least temper, its decrees, and, won over by valor and prudence, retract its doom. For man is master of the stars. This I wish to put to trial by bringing him where he may know he is my son, and where he may make proof of his nature. If magnanimity prevails in him, he shall reign; but if he shows himself cruel and tyrannical, I shall return him to his chains. Now you will ask why, for this test, was it necessary to have him carried here asleep in this way? I want to satisfy you, to give a reply to every question. If he knew today that he is my son, and tomorrow saw himself a second time reduced to miserable captivity, it is certain he would despair of his condition. For knowing who he is, what consolation can he have? Therefore I have intended to leave a way out of this danger: to tell him he only dreamed what he saw. Thus two things may be tried out: first, his nature, for when he wakens, he will act as thought and imagination dictate; and second, a means of consolation; for even though he now may be master and later is returned to his prison, he will be able to believe he dreamed. And he will be right in so believing, Clotaldo, for all of us who live in the world are dreaming.

CLOTALDO. I should not lack reasons to prove your course in error, but now it's too late for that. By all signs, it seems he has awakened and approaches us.

BASILIO. I wish to withdraw. You, as his tutor, remain, and by telling him the truth relieve him of the confusion that surrounds him.

CLOTALDO. You mean, you give me license to tell him his history?

BASILIO. Yes, for it may be, if he knows the truth, that the danger, once recognized, may more easily be overcome. (*Exit* BASILIO.)

CLARIN (*entering, aside*). Since getting here cost me four blows from a redheaded guard, who grew a beard to match his livery, I have to see what's happening. Well, there's no window better than what a man carries with him, without appealing to a ticket agent, since, stripped or strapped, one can always get a peep at a show by pure effrontery.

CLOTALDO (*aside*). This is Clarin, the servant of that girl (oh, heavens!) that dealer in misfortune who has brought to Poland an insult for me. (*aloud*) Clarin, what news?

CLARIN. Why, the news is, my lord, that your great mercy, disposed to avenge Rosaura's wrongs, counsels her to put on her proper dress.

CLOTALDO. And that is well, to keep her from appearing improper.

CLARIN. More news is this: by changing her name and discreetly taking that of your niece, she now grows so rapidly in honor that she lives in the palace as lady-in-waiting to the one and only Estrella.

CLOTALDO. It is well, too, that for once she should gain honor through me.

CLARIN. More news yet: she is hoping the time and occasion will arrive for you to defend her honor.

CLOTALDO. This is a sure forecast: that in the end time will take care of these problems.

CLARIN. And here's a final bulletin: while she is regaled and served like a queen, as your niece, here am I, who came with her, dying of hunger, and nobody notices me. But after all, I am Clarin, and if this clarion sounds off, it may

tell what's going on to the King, to Astolfo and Estrella.
For a clarion and a servant are two things which keep a
secret very ill. And perhaps, if the silence her hand has im-
posed on me were lifted, I might be singing these words:
    The Clarion that at daybreak blows
    Loud shall tell what Clarin knows.
CLOTALDO. Your complaint is justified, and I'll satisfy it.
Meanwhile, be my servant.
CLARIN. Here comes Segismundo!
    (*Enter* MUSICIANS, *singing, and* SERVANTS *attiring*
    SEGISMUNDO, *who seems dumbfounded.*)
SEGISMUNDO. Heaven help me, what do I see! Heaven
help me, what do I gaze upon! I wonder at it with some
fear; I believe it, yet with much doubt. I, in a sumptuous
palace? I, among silks and brocades? I, surrounded by servants so brave and splendid? I, awakened from sleep in so
excellent a bed? I, in the midst of so many people who help
me to dress? To say I am dreaming is not true; I know well
that I am awake. Am I not Segismundo? Grant, oh heavens,
that I may be freed from illusion! Tell me, what could
have happened in my fancy while I slept that I now see
myself here? But be that as it may, who will make me argue
about it? I wish to continue being served, and let come
what will come.
FIRST SERVANT (*aside to second servant and to* CLARIN).
How melancholy he is!
SECOND SERVANT. Who wouldn't be if such a thing happened to him?
CLARIN. I.
SECOND SERVANT. Now he's going to speak to him.
FIRST SERVANT (*to* SEGISMUNDO). Shall they sing again?
SEGISMUNDO. No, I don't want them to sing any more.
SECOND SERVANT. Since you are so filled with amazement, I
wanted to amuse you.
SEGISMUNDO. I have no need to soothe my sorrows with
their voices; martial music alone has pleased my ear.
CLOTALDO. Your highness, great Sire, give me your hand
to kiss, for I must be the first to give you this token of
allegiance.
SEGISMUNDO (*aside*). It's Clotaldo; how can he who
treated me so badly in prison now address me with such
respect? What is happening to me?
CLOTALDO. In the great confusion which your new estate
causes you, your mind and reason must suffer a thousand

doubts. But now I want to free you of all these, if possible, because you must know, Sire, that you are the Crown Prince of Poland. If you have been withdrawn and hidden, it has been in obedience to the cruelty of fate, which promises a thousand tragedies to this kingdom when its sovereign laurel crowns your august head. But in the trust that your good will may overcome the stars—for it is possible that a noble man may triumph over them—you have been brought, while overcome by sleep, to this palace from the tower where you lived. Your father, the King, my lord, will come to see you, and from him, Segismundo, you will learn the rest.

SEGISMUNDO. You vile and infamous traitor, what more do I have to know, now that I know who I am, to show from this day on my pride and power? How have you committed such treason against your country, that against right and reason you hid me and denied me this estate?

CLOTALDO. Ah, woe is me!

SEGISMUNDO. You were a traitor to the law, a flatterer to the King, and cruel to me. And thus the King, the law, and I, all victims of these wicked misdeeds, condemn you to death at my hands.

SECOND SERVANT. Sire . . .

SEGISMUNDO. Let no one interfere; it is useless to try. By the living God, if you put yourselves in the way, I'll throw you out the window!

SECOND SERVANT. Flee, Clotaldo!

CLOTALDO. Alas for you! What arrogance you display, not knowing that you are only dreaming!

(*Exit* CLOTALDO.)

SECOND SERVANT. Remember . . .

SEGISMUNDO. Get out of here!

SECOND SERVANT. . . . that he obeyed his king.

SEGISMUNDO. Inasmuch as the law was not just, he was not bound to obey the King; and I was his prince.

SECOND SERVANT. He had no right to question whether the law was good or bad.

SEGISMUNDO. I suspect you don't care about your life, since you persist in answering me back.

CLARIN. What the prince says is right, and you are wrong.

SECOND SERVANT. Who gave you leave to talk?

CLARIN. I took it.

SEGISMUNDO. Who are you, pray tell?

CLARIN. A meddler, and the chief of that calling, for I'm the greatest busybody ever known.

SEGISMUNDO. In these new worlds where I move, only you have pleased me.

CLARIN. Sire, I make a habit of pleasing all the Segismundos.

ASTOLFO (entering). Happy a thousand times, O Prince, the day when you, the sun of Poland, show yourself and fill the sky, from horizon to horizon, with a divinely crimson flush of joy and splendor. For you come to us like the sun, from the bosom of the mountains! Rise, then, and although the laurel wreath that crowns your brow has come so late, long may it remain, and late wither.

SEGISMUNDO. May God keep you.

ASTOLFO. Only because you did not know me I forgive you for paying me no further honor. I am Astolfo, born Duke of Muscovy, and your cousin. We are peers.

SEGISMUNDO. If I say, "May God keep you," do I not show you sufficient courtesy? But since you complain of this, and because you boast of who you are, the next time you see me I shall say, "May God not keep you."

SECOND SERVANT (to ASTOLFO). Your highness must consider that since he was born in the mountains he behaves this way with everyone. (to SEGISMUNDO) Astolfo, Sire, prefers . . .

SEGISMUNDO. He tired me, the way he came to speak to me so solemnly. And the first thing he did was put on his hat.

SECOND SERVANT. He is a grandee.*

SEGISMUNDO. I am even grander.

SECOND SERVANT. Yet it is fitting that there should be more respect between you two than among others.

SEGISMUNDO. And who set you onto me?

ESTRELLA (entering). Many times welcome, Sire, to this canopied throne, which gratefully receives and desires you! And may you reign, august and lofty, despite deceit, not for years but for centuries!

SEGISMUNDO (to CLARIN). You, tell me now, who is this sovereign beauty? Who is this human goddess, at whose divine feet heaven's radiance lies prostrate? Who is this lovely woman?

CLARIN. She is, Sire, your cousin Estrella.

SEGISMUNDO. Estrella—that means star. Better you should say "the sun." (to ESTRELLA) Although it is well that you

---

* Only a grandee could wear a hat in the presence of royalty.

congratulate me on my good fortune, only because I have seen you today will I accept your compliment. So, since I find myself with a blessing I don't deserve, I thank you for your courtesy, Estrella, that you could dawn and give the light of gladness to the brightest star. When you rise with the day, my lady, what is left for the sun to do? Give me your hand to kiss, from whose snowy cup the breeze drinks purity.

ESTRELLA. You are gallant, but be more restained.

ASTOLFO. If he takes her hand, I am lost.

SECOND SERVANT (aside). I understand Astolfo's grief, and I'll interrupt. (to SEGISMUNDO) Remember, Sire, it is not right to be so insolent. And since Astolfo . . .

SEGISMUNDO. Didn't I tell you not to meddle with me?

SECOND SERVANT. I say only what is right.

SEGISMUNDO. All that annoys me. Nothing seems right to me which isn't to my taste.

SECOND SERVANT. Well, Sire, I've heard from you yourself that it is proper to obey and serve what is right.

SEGISMUNDO. You have also heard me say that I would throw anyone who crossed me off the balcony.

SECOND SERVANT. With men like me, that can't be done.

SEGISMUNDO. No? By God! Then I'll have to prove it! *(Seizes him in his arms and exits. All follow and enter again immediately.)*

ASTOLFO. What is this I've just seen?

ESTRELLA. Go all of you to hold him back! *(Exit.)*

SEGISMUNDO (returning). He fell from the balcony into the water! By the living God, it could be done!

ASTOLFO. Measure more wisely, then, your violent actions, for the difference between men and beasts is equal to that between a mountain and a palace.

SEGISMUNDO. If you go on talking so much, you may be left without a head to put your hat on! *(Exit ASTOLFO.)*

BASILIO (entering). What has happened?

SEGISMUNDO. Nothing has happened. I tossed a man who tired me from the balcony.

CLARIN (to SEGISMUNDO). Be careful: that's the King!

BASILIO. Your coming cost a life so quickly, the very first day?

SEGISMUNDO. He told me it couldn't be done, and I won the wager.

BASILIO. It grieves me much, Prince that, when hoping foreknowledge would enable you to triumph over stars and fates, I come at last to see you, I find you so pitiless, so cruel. Yes, your very first deed has been a foul murder. With what love can I now offer you my arms if I know that your haughty embrace gives death? Who would not fear, that saw the naked dagger which dealt a mortal wound? Who would not feel it, that saw the bloody place where another man was slaughtered? In the strongest, this would be a natural response. So I, who behold in your arms the instrument of this death and see before me the bloody spot, I withdraw from your arms. And although I hoped to encircle your neck with loving embraces, I shall retire without them, for I am afraid of your arms.

SEGISMUNDO. I can do without them, as I have done without them until now. For it's of little importance that such a father should not embrace me—a father who could use such harshness against me, whose cruelty kept me from his side and brought me up like a beast; yea, who treated me like a monster, sought my death, and robbed me of the very nature of a man.

BASILIO. Would to heaven and God that I had never given you that nature! Then I never would have heard your voice, nor seen your insolence.

SEGISMUNDO. If you had never given it to me, I would not reproach you. But once you gave it, yes, I do reproach you for taking it away. For even though to give is the most noble and distinguished action, to give and then take away is the lowest.

BASILIO. This is fine thanks for my changing you from a poor, humble prisoner into a prince!

SEGISMUNDO. Why should I thank you for that? You have been a tyrant over my will, and now that you are old and weak and dying, what do you give me? Do you give me more than is mine? You are my father and my king; therefore nature gives me all this grandeur by right of law. And therefore, too, although my state be great, I'm not beholden to you, and I can call you to account for the time you've robbed me of liberty, life, and honor. Therefore you should thank me, that I do not claim my due from you, for you are my debtor.

BASILIO. Barbarous, rash man! Heaven has fulfilled its word; and to that very Heaven I appeal, that it may see your pride and vanity. And although you may know who you are, free at last of all deceptions; although you may see yourself in a place where all defer to you, still take heed

of my warning: Be gentle and humble, for perhaps you are
dreaming, although you seem to be awake.   (*Exit.*)

SEGISMUNDO. Perhaps I'm dreaming, although I seem
awake? I do not dream, for I touch, I feel, and I believe
what I have been and what I am. Now you may repent,
but you have little remedy. I know who I am, and you
cannot, with all your sighs and regrets, annul the fact that
I was born heir to this crown. If at first I was bound in
prison, that was because I did not know who I was. But
now I have been taught who I am, and I know that I'm a
mixture of man and beast.

(*Enter* ROSAURA, *dressed as a woman.*)

ROSAURA (*aside*). I come to find Estrella, but I am most
fearful of finding Astolfo. For Clotaldo wishes him not to
know who I am, nor to see me, because, so Clotaldo says,
it is important to my honor. I trust Clotaldo's intent, for to
him I owe, most gratefully, the protection I have found here
for my life and honor.

CLARIN (*to* SEGISMUNDO). What has pleased you most of
all you have seen and admired here?

SEGISMUNDO. Nothing has astonished me; everything has
been as I expected; but if I had to admire something in
the world, it would be woman's beauty. I read once, in the
books I had, that the creation to which God gave his greatest art was man, because man is a whole world in small
compass. But now I suspect that artful creation was rather
woman, since she is a whole heaven, and is as far superior
to man in beauty as heaven is to earth. And farther still
if she be this one whom I see.

ROSAURA (*aside*). The prince is here; I'll withdraw.

SEGISMUNDO. Wait, woman! Wait and listen! Do not make
the sun set just as it rises, by fleeing at your first step hither:
for if dawn and sunset, light and cold shade, should merge,
the very day would be cut short. But what is this I see?

ROSAURA. I doubt I've seen the same before; yet I believe
I have.

SEGISMUNDO (*aside*). I have seen this beauty before.

ROSAURA (*aside*). And I have seen this pomp and grandeur held fast in a narrow prison cell!

SEGISMUNDO (*aside*). Here I have found my life! (*to*
ROSAURA) Woman, for that name is the tenderest endear-
ment man can use: who are you? For even without my
having seen you, you owe me worship, and luckily I have a
faith which binds you closer yet, for I am sure that I have

seen you somewhere else! Who are you, lovely woman?

ROSAURA (*aside*). I must pretend. (*to* SEGISMUNDO) I am an unlucky lady in Estrella's train.

SEGISMUNDO. Do not say that. Say you are the sun, in whose flame that star, Estrella, lives, since from your rays she receives splendor. I saw a kingdom all of colors, where, among troops of flowers, the divine rose reigned; and she owed her empire to her loveliness. Among precious gems, in the deep academy of the mines, I saw the diamond preferred, and hailed as emperor for its brilliance. In these beautiful courts of the restless republic of the stars, I have seen the morning star take first place, as the king. And, in the perfect spheres, where the sun calls the planet to his parliament, I have seen that he is sovereign, as the chief oracle of day. How then, if among flowers, stars, stones, signs, and planets the most beautiful take precedence, how have you served one of less beauty, you who have been, for loveliness and grace, the sun, the morning star, the diamond, the planet, and the rose?

CLOTALDO (*entering, aside*). I'd like to be the one to cut this Segismundo down to size, for after all, I brought him up. But what do I see?

ROSAURA. I respect your favor. For me, the rhetoric of silence must answer. When reason itself stumbles, Sire, he speaks best who is most quiet.

SEGISMUNDO. Wait, you need not leave. Why do you wish to leave my meaning in the dark?

ROSAURA. I beg this liberty of your highness.

SEGISMUNDO. To run away so impetuously is not to beg liberty, but to seize it.

ROSAURA. But if you won't give it to me, I'll have to take it.

SEGISMUNDO. You will change my courtesy to rudeness, because resistance is a poison that kills my patience.

ROSAURA. Although that poison, full of fury, rage, and harshness, conquers your patience, it still would not dare, nor could it conquer your respect for me.

SEGISMUNDO. You'll make me, just to see if I could, lose that fear I have of your beauty. For I am much inclined to risk the impossible. Today I threw from this balcony a man who said I couldn't do it. In the same way, to see if I could do it, it would be very easy for me to throw your honor out the window!

CLOTALDO (*aside*). He is growing most insistent! Heavens, what can I do, when, because of an insane lust, I see my honor risked a second time?

ROSAURA. Not false, surely, was the prophecy which foretold the crimes, the treachery, the wrath, the murders, which your tyranny would bring to this unhappy kingdom. But what else could be expected of a man who had no human quality except the name? A man ruthless, inhuman, cruel, proud, and barbarous, born among beasts?

SEGISMUNDO. So that you would not heap insults on me, I showed myself so courteous to you in the hope that this would win you. But if, in speaking courteously, I am all the things you say I am, then by God! you shall have good cause to call me those names. You there! Leave us alone! Close that door and let no one enter!

(CLARIN *and* SERVANTS *leave.*)

ROSAURA. I am lost! Take care! . . .

SEGISMUNDO. I am a tyrant, and now in vain will you try to overthrow me!

CLOTALDO (*aside*). Oh, what a terrible predicament! I'll intervene, even though he kills me for it! Sire! (*He appears.*) Wait! Look here!

SEGISMUNDO. A second time you provoke me to anger, you feeble, foolish old man. Do you set so little value on my rage and fury? How did you get here?

CLOTALDO. Summoned by the accents of that voice, I came to warn you to calm your violence if you wish to reign here as king. Do not be cruel, just because you seem to be master of everything, for perhaps it is all a dream.

SEGISMUNDO. You drive me to madness, when you talk of illusions. I'll see, by killing you, whether this is dream or reality!

(*As he pulls out his dagger,* CLOTALDO *seizes it and kneels before him.*)

CLOTALDO. In this way, I hope to save my life.

SEGISMUNDO. Take your rash hand from the blade!

CLOTALDO. Until someone comes to check your wrath and rashness, I'll not let go.

ROSAURA. Oh, God!

SEGISMUNDO. Let go, I say, you weak and foolish, old and barbarous enemy, or you'll be crushed dead between my two arms! (*They struggle.*)

ROSAURA. Come, everyone, quickly! Clotaldo is being

murdered!   (*Exit* ROSAURA.)

(ASTOLFO *enters,* CLOTALDO *falls at his feet, and* ASTOLFO *steps between him and* SEGISMUNDO.)

ASTOLFO. Why, what goes on here, noble prince? Is such bright steel to be stained in an old man's frozen blood? Return that shining blade into its shealth.

SEGISMUNDO. When I see it colored with that vile blood.

ASTOLFO. His life has taken refuge now at my feet; that he has reached sanctuary should be of some profit to him.

SEGISMUNDO. May death be your profit, for in this way I shall also be able to take vengeance, by your death, for that annoyance you caused me before.

ASTOLFO. I fight in self-defense; in this there lies no offense to your majesty.

(ASTOLFO *draws his sword, and they fight.*)

CLOTALDO. Do not harm him, my lord.

(BASILIO *enters with* ESTRELLA, *and* ATTENDANTS.)

BASILIO. What, swords here?

ESTRELLA (*aside*). Alas! It is Astolfo, in a furious rage!

BASILIO. What has happened?

ASTOLFO. Nothing, Sire, since you have arrived.*

(*They sheath their swords.*)

SEGISMUNDO. Much, Sire, although you have come. I tried to kill that old man.

BASILIO. Have you no respect for these white hairs?

CLOTALDO. Sire, behold, the hairs are mine; the matter is not important, you will see.

SEGISMUNDO. It's vain to expect *me* to respect white hairs! For even yours (*to the* KING) may some day be seen at my very feet. I have not yet taken vengeance for your injustice in the way you brought me up.   (*Exit* SEGISMUNDO.)

BASILIO. Before you see that happen, you will return to sleep where you will believe that all that has happened to you, however real it was, was only dreaming.

(*The* KING, CLOTALDO, *and* ATTENDANTS *leave.*)

ASTOLFO. How seldom fate lies when it foretells misfortunes! Predicting evil is as certain as predicting good is doubtful! What an excellent astrologer he would be who foresaw only unhappy events, for there's no doubt but that they'd always prove true! This may be proved by me and Segismundo, Estrella, for both of us bear different signs. For him the signs prophesied harshness, arrogance, misfor-

---

* Dueling had to cease when a king entered, and the affair was considered to be honorably ended.

tune, death; and in all this they told the truth, because all
this is happening. But for me, when I saw, señora, those
surpassing eyes, of which the sun was only a shadow and
the sky an intimation, the fates were foretelling happiness,
trophies, wealth, applause; and then they spoke both truth
and falsehood. For the fact is that the stars are right only
when they promise favors and perform misfortunes.

ESTRELLA. I have no doubt that those fine words are
meant sincerely, but meant for another woman—her whose
portrait you wore hanging at your neck, Astolfo, when you
first came here to see me. Since this is so, those endear-
ments belong only to her. Run to her to receive payment
for them, for neither courtesy nor faith owed to other ladies
and other kings is good currency in the court of love.

ROSAURA (entering, aside). Thank God, that now my
cruel misfortunes have come to an end, for whoever sees this
fears nothing more!

ASTOLFO. I shall tear that picture from my breast to make
way for the image of your beauty. Where Estrella enters,
shadow has no place, nor a star where the sun shines. I'll
go get that portrait. (aside) Pardon, lovely Rosaura, for
this injury; when absent from each other, men and women
never keep better faith than this.   (Exit ASTOLFO.)

ROSAURA (aside). For fear of being seen, I couldn't hear
a word.

ESTRELLA. Astrea!

ROSAURA. My lady.

ESTRELLA. I'm so pleased it's you who came, for to you
only would I entrust a secret.

ROSAURA. You honor, señora, one who obeys you.

ESTRELLA. In the short time that I have known you, Astrea, you have gained the keys of my heart. For that reason,
and for your own sake, I dare to tell you what I have often
hidden from myself.

ROSAURA. I am your slave.

ESTRELLA. To make it brief, then, my cousin Astolfo
(calling him cousin is enough, for there are things that are
spoken just by thinking them) is to marry me if fortune
pleases to cancel so many misfortunes with one great happiness. It bothered me that the first day I saw him he had a
portrait of a lady hung 'round his neck. I spoke about it
courteously; he is gallant and loves me well, and he has
gone to get it, and will bring it here. I should be embar-
rassed if he gave it to me. Therefore you stay here, and

when he comes, tell him to give it to you. I shall say no
more. You are discreet and beautiful, and you know well
what love is.   (*Exit* ESTRELLA.)

ROSAURA. Would that I did not know! Heaven help me!
Who could be wise enough to know what to do now, in such
a difficulty? Can there be anyone else in the world whom
merciless heaven surrounds with more sorrows, attacks with
more misfortunes? What shall I do, confused as I am, when
it seems impossible to find a means of help, nor any help
that could comfort me? From my first misfortune, I've experienced nothing except further misfortunes; each succeeds
the other, and inherits its qualities. Like the Phoenix, each
is born from the other; each lives from that which dies, and
becomes the warm, live tomb of its own ashes. Once a wise
man said that cares were cowards, for it seemed that they
never came singly. But I say they are brave, for they always advance and never turn their backs. He with whom
they travel may dare everything, for never is there danger
that they will leave him. I can well say this, for so many
troubles have come to me in my life, I've never found myself
without them, nor will they tire of me until they see me,
mortally wounded by my fortune, in the arms of death.

Ah me! What must I do now? If I tell who I am, Clotaldo, to whom I owe my life's honor and protection, may
be offended with me; for he tells me that by keeping silent
I may expect both honor and reparation. If I don't tell
Astolfo who I am, and he sees me, how shall I dissimulate?
For even though my voice, my tongue, and my eyes may
seek to deceive him, my heart will tell him they are lying.
What shall I do? But why do I worry about what to do,
since it's clear that however much one worries, thinks, and
prepares, when the time comes there's nothing to do except
what pain demands? For no one has power over his sorrows.
And since my soul dare not determine what's to be done, let
grief today come to its end, and pain to its extremity, and
let me escape at last from doubts and deceptions. But until
then, help me, Heaven, help me!

(ASTOLFO *enters carrying the portrait.*)

ASTOLFO. This, señora, is the portrait; but . . . God!

ROSAURA. Why is your highness amazed? . . . At what do
you wonder?

ASTOLFO. To hear you, Rosaura, and to see you.

ROSAURA. I, Rosaura? Your highness must be deceived, if
you take me for another lady. I am Astrea, and my humble

station does not deserve the good fortune to cause you that agitation.

ASTOLFO. Enough, Rosaura, that's enough pretending. For the soul never lies, and although I look at you as Astrea, I love you as Rosaura.

ROSAURA. I have not understood your highness, and therefore I do not know how to answer you. All I shall say is that Estrella (who might be the star of Venus, since Estrella means star) commanded me to wait for you here, and to tell you in her behalf to give me that portrait—a very reasonable request—and I shall take it to her. So Estrella desires, and even her least commands, though they may be hard for me, must be complied with if she so wishes.

ASTOLFO. Oh Rosaura, how ill you deceive, however hard you try! Tell your eyes to tune their music with your voice, because it's necessary to gainsay and give the lie to such a jarring instrument, which seeks to adjust and measure the lies you speak with the truth you feel.

ROSAURA. I tell you, I am waiting only for the portrait.

ASTOLFO. Since you wish to carry on the deception, I'll answer in deception's terms: Say, Astrea, to the Princess, that I esteem her so that when she seeks a portrait of me, it seems a small favor to send it to her. And therefore, because I esteem and prize her, I am sending her the original; and you may take it to her, since you carry it with you as you carry yourself.

ROSAURA. When a bold man, proud and brave, resolves to carry out an enterprise, even though he may by agreement be offered something worth much more, he still feels foolish and slighted if he doesn't attain his goal. I come for a portrait, and although I might own the more valuable original, without the copy I shall feel slighted. Therefore give me that portrait, your highness, since without it I shall not return.

ASTOLFO. How are you going to take it if I don't give it to you?

ROSAURA. This way. Let it go, you ingrate! (*She tries to seize it from him.*)

ASTOLFO. It's no use.

ROSAURA. As God lives, this isn't going to fall into another woman's hands!

ASTOLFO. You are a fury!

ROSAURA. And you are unfaithful!

ASTOLFO. That's enough, my Rosaura!

ROSAURA. I, yours? You lie, villain!

(*Both are grasping the portrait.*)

ESTRELLA (*entering*). Astrea, Astolfo, what is this?

ASTOLFO (*aside*). There's Estrella.

ROSAURA (*aside*). Let love give me skill to recover my portrait! (*to* ESTRELLA) If you wish to know what has happened, señora, I'll tell you.

ASTOLFO (*aside to* ROSAURA). What are you trying to do?

ROSAURA. You commanded me to wait here for Astolfo, and on your behalf to ask him for a portrait. I remained alone, and as one's thoughts travel easily from one subject to another, since you had spoken of portraits, the memory of that reminded me that I had one of my own in my sleeve. I wished to see it, for someone all alone amuses herself with foolish things. It fell from my hand to the floor. Astolfo, who came to give you the portrait of another woman, picked it up, and so unwilling is he to give you what you ask, that instead of giving one, he wishes to take another; for even with pleas and persuasion I still could not regain my own. Then, angry and impatient, I tried to take it from him. That one he has in his hand is mine, you will see, for you can see it looks like me.

ESTRELLA. Astolfo, let go of the picture.

(*She takes it from his hand.*)

ASTOLFO. Señora . . .

ESTRELLA. The colors, in truth, are not unflattering.

ROSAURA. Is it not mine?

ESTRELLA. What doubt is there?

ROSAURA. Now tell him to give you the other one.

ESTRELLA. Take your picture, and go.

ROSAURA (*aside*). I have my portrait; now let come what will! (*Exit.*)

ESTRELLA. Now give me that portrait of yours which I asked for. Although I do not intend to see or talk to you again, I do not want you to retain it, no, if only because I so foolishly desired it of you.

ASTOLFO (*aside*). How can I get out of such a predicament? Although I wish, beauteous Estrella, to serve and obey you, I cannot give you the portrait you seek, because . . .

ESTRELLA. You are a coarse and clownish lover. I don't want you to give it to me; for neither do I want, by taking it, to make you remember that I asked for it! (*Exit.*)

ASTOLFO. Hear me! Listen! Look! I'll explain! Oh, curses on you, Rosaura! Whence, how, by what fortune did you come to Poland today, to destroy me and to destroy yourself?

SCENE 2: *The* PRINCE'S *prison in the tower.*

(SEGISMUNDO, *as in the beginning, wearing skins and chains, lying on the ground;* CLOTALDO, *two* SERVANTS, *and* CLARIN.)

CLOTALDO. Here you must leave him, for today his pride ends just where it began.

SERVANT. Just as it was, I shall fasten the chain once more.

CLARIN. Don't wake too soon, Segismundo, for you will find yourself lost, your luck completely changed, and your glory only imaginary—a shadow of life, a flame of death.

CLOTALDO. For one who talks so much, it would be wise to prepare a place where he may have plenty of room to argue. (*to the* SERVANTS) This is the man you are to seize, and that's the cell in which to lock him up. (*pointing to the next room*)

CLARIN. Why me?

CLOTALDO. Because a noisy clarion like you, who knows secrets, needs to be locked up tight in prison, where he can't sound off.

CLARIN. Did I by chance try to kill my father? No. Did I throw a lesser Icarus off the balcony? Am I dreaming, or am I sleeping? Why do they lock me up?

CLOTALDO. Because you are Clarin, a noisy trumpet.

CLARIN. Well now I say I shall be a cornet, which is a vile instrument, and so I shall remain silent.

(*They take him away, and* CLOTALDO *remains alone. Enter* BASILIO, *masked.*)

BASILIO. Clotaldo.

CLOTALDO. Sire! Your Majesty comes here in disguise?

BASILIO. A foolish curiosity, alas! to see what's happening to Segismundo has brought me here in this condition.

CLOTALDO. Look at him there, reduced again to misery.

BASILIO. Alas, unhappy prince, born at a sad conjunction of the stars. Come, wake him up, for the opium he drank has robbed him of his strength and vigor.

CLOTALDO. Sire, he is restless, and he mutters.

BASILIO. What is he dreaming now? Let's listen!

SEGISMUNDO (*talking in his sleep*). A merciful prince is one who punishes tyrants. May Clotaldo die at my hands! May my father kiss my feet!

CLOTALDO. He's threatening me with death!

BASILIO. And me with harshness and insult!

CLOTALDO. He intends to take my life.

BASILIO. And to humiliate me.

SEGISMUNDO (*in his sleep*). Let my peerless valor enter on the wide stage of the great theater of the world. So that my vengeance may be fitting, let all see Prince Segismundo triumph over his father. (*He awakes.*) But alas! Where am I?

BASILIO (*to* CLOTALDO). He must not see me. You know what you are to do. I'll listen from over there. (*withdraws*)

SEGISMUNDO. Can this be me? Do I, captive and in chains, see myself in such a state? Oh tower, are you not still my tomb? Yes! Oh God, how many things I've dreamed!

CLOTALDO (*aside*). Now it is my turn to come in and to pretend.

SEGISMUNDO. Isn't it time to wake up?

CLOTALDO. Yes, it is time. Will you spend the whole day sleeping? Since I followed that eagle which flew by on slow wings, and you stayed here, have you not wakened once?

SEGISMUNDO. No, nor have I now awakened. For, as I understand, Clotaldo, I'm still sleeping. And I am not deceived, because if I dreamed what I really saw and felt, then what I see now must be unreal. I see, being asleep, that when awake one dreams.

CLOTALDO. Tell me what you dreamed.

SEGISMUNDO. Supposing that it *was* a dream. No, I shall not tell you what I dreamed, but what I *saw*, Clotaldo. I awoke and found myself in a bed which might have been, such were its hues and colors, the cradle of the flowers woven by Spring. Here a thousand bowing nobles called me their prince, and bestowed on me finery, jewels, and rich robes. Then you yourself whirled me into rapture when you told me my good fortune: that, regardless of my present state, I was Prince in Poland.

CLOTALDO. For bringing you that news I must have had a good reward!

SEGISMUNDO. Not very. Twice, boldly and bravely, I tried to kill you, because you were a traitor.

CLOTALDO. Such harsh treatment for me?

SEGISMUNDO. I was lord of all, and on all I took my vengeance. Only one I loved, one woman . . . That, I believe, was true. For all the rest has vanished away, and this alone remains.   (*Exit the* KING.)

CLOTALDO (*aside*). What the King has heard has moved him. (*to* SEGISMUNDO) Because we were talking of that eagle, while you slept your dream was one of empire. But in your dreams it might be well to give honor to the one who cared for you so faithfully; for even in dreams, Segismundo, one should not cease to do good.   (*Exit.*)

SEGISMUNDO. That's true. Then let us restrain this fierceness, this fury, this ambition, in case some time we dream again. And dream we will, for we are in so odd a world that just to live is to dream. Experience teaches me that each man who lives dreams what he is, untill he wakes. The king dreams he is a king, and in this deception spends his days, commanding, governing, disposing. But this renown he receives is written on the wind. At the touch of death—oh dread misfortune—it turns to ashes. Can there be any who would want to reign, seeing that each king must wake in the dream of death?

The rich man dreams of his riches, which only bring him greater care. The poor man dreams that he suffers misery and want. He who is beginning to prosper dreams it; he who pushes and presses ahead dreams it; he who commits injuries and offenses dreams it. And to conclude, through the whole world, though no man knows it, all men dream the lives they lead.

I dream that I am here, weighed down with chains, and I dreamed that I was in another, happier state. What is life? A madness. What is life? An illusion, a shadow, a story. And the greatest good is little enough: for all life is a dream, and dreams themselves are only dreams.

ACT III

SCENE 1: *The tower.*

CLARIN. Well here I am, it seems, a prisoner in an enchanted tower. What can they do to me for what I don't know, if they've killed me for what I do? O, that so hungry a man should have to die this living death! I pity myself. Everyone will say "I certainly believe it"; and well may it be believed, since this silence does not at all agree with my name, Clarin, and I cannot keep quiet. My companions here, if I guess right, are mice and spiders. What sweet songbirds they are! My last night's dreams have made my poor head ring with a thousand clarinets, trumpets, and delusions; with processions, crosses, and flagellants; some of them rise, others descend. Some faint when they see the blood that smears the others. But as for me, the truth is that I faint because I haven't eaten. I see that I am in a jail where daily I read the philosophy of no meals, and nightly, that of no suppers. If they call silence saintly, as in the new calendar, Saint Secret is for me, because I fast for him, and never feast. Still, the punishment I suffer is well deserved, since, although I am a servant, I held my tongue, and that, for a servant, is a major sacrilege.
(*Drums and bugles sound. Voices offstage.*)
FIRST SOLDIER (*offstage*). This is the tower he's in. Smash the door to the ground! Everybody rush inside!
CLARIN. God does live! They must be looking for me, since they say I'm here! What can they want of me?
FIRST SOLDIER (*offstage*). Everybody go inside.
(*Enter several soldiers.*)
SECOND SOLDIER. Here he is.
CLARIN. He's not.
SOLDIERS (*all together*). Sire . . .
CLARIN (*aside*). Surely they're drunk!
FIRST SOLDIER. You are our prince. We neither desire nor

226

will we tolerate any but our native lord; we want no foreign prince. Give us your feet to kiss.

SOLDIERS. Long live our great prince!

CLARIN (*aside*). Surely they're drunk! Good God, they really mean it! Is it the custom in this kingdom to take somebody every day, make him a prince, and then send him back to the tower? Yes, since I see it happen every day. Now I must play my rôle.

SOLDIERS. Give us your feet.

CLARIN. I cannot, because I need them for myself. A prince without feet would be pretty funny.

SECOND SOLDIER. We all told your father himself that we recognized only you as prince, and not that fellow from Muscovy.

CLARIN. Have you lost all respect for my father? You are worthless fellows.

SECOND SOLDIER. It was our heartfelt loyalty.

CLARIN. If it was loyalty, I pardon you.

SECOND SOLDIER. Come out and regain your empire. Viva Segismundo!

ALL. Viva!

CLARIN (*aside*). Is it Segismundo they say? Good: they call all counterfeit princes Segismundos.

SEGISMUNDO (*entering*). Who here calls Segismundo?

CLARIN (*aside*). Now I'm certainly a hollow prince!

FIRST SOLDIER. Which one is Segismundo?

SEGISMUNDO. I am he.

SECOND SOLDIER (*to* CLARIN). You insolent, foolish fellow, how dare you pose as Segismundo?

CLARIN. I Segismundo? I deny that. You were the ones who turned me into Segismundo; yours was the only insolence, the only foolishness.

FIRST SOLDIER. Great Prince Segismundo (for yours is the bearing of the prince we seek, and now by faith we hail you as our lord), your father, great King Basilio, fearful that heaven may fulfill a prophecy which says he is to see himself prostrate at your feet, conquered by you, is trying to rob you of your claim and title, and give them to Astolfo, Duke of Muscovy. To accomplish this he convened his Court, but the people, knowing that they have a native king, want no foreigner to come and rule over them. And thus, nobly scorning that harsh prophecy, they have sought you out where you live imprisoned, so that, helped by their arms, you may leave this tower, regain your imperial crown and scepter, and wrest them from the tyrant. Come out, then; for in this waste-land a large army of outlaws and commoners acclaims you. Liberty awaits you; hearken to its voice.

VOICES (*offstage*). Hail, all hail Segismundo!

SEGISMUNDO. What is this, O heavens? Again do you want me to dream of greatness which time must destroy? Do you wish me again to see, through uncertain shadows, that majesty and pomp which must disappear in the wind? Do you wish me once more to feel disillusion, once more to undertake the risk to which all human power lives exposed? It must not be! I must not see myself again subjected to my fate. And since I know that this whole life is a dream, go, you shadows which feign body and voice to my numbed senses while the truth is that you have neither voice nor body. For I want no pretended majesty, no fantastic pomp, illusions which at the slightest gust of air must disappear, just as the flowering almond tree which blossoms too early, without warning, wilts at the first breath. At the first breath, the rosy buds fade and lose the splendor of their light and beauty. Oh, I know you, indeed I know you, and I know you play the same cheat with anyone who sleeps. For me there's no more pretending. I've learned my lesson, and I know well that life is a dream.

SECOND SOLDIER. If you think we are deceiving you, turn your eyes toward those proud mountains where you may see the people waiting to obey you.

SEGISMUNDO. Once before, I saw the same, as clearly and distinctly as I see it now, and it was all a dream.

SECOND SOLDIER. Great events, great lord, always bring their omens; and this would be an omen, if you dreamt it first.

SEGISMUNDO. You say well, it was an omen; and in case it be true, since life is so short, let us dream, my soul, let us dream again; but it must be with prudence and the knowledge that we must awaken from this pleasure when the pleasure's greatest. Knowing disillusionment must come, we'll be less disillusioned when it does come. For to anticipate the remedy is to make mock of the hurt. With this forewarning, then, that even when it's most assured, all power is borrowed and must return to its owner, let us dare all. Vassals, I thank you for your loyalty. In me you have a leader who with daring and skill will free you from foreign slavery. Sound the call to arms, so that you may soon see **my** great valor! I shall endeavor to take arms against my father and confirm the prediction of the stars. Soon I shall see him at my feet . . . (*aside*) But if I awake before then, will it not be better to say nothing of it, especially if I am not to accomplish it?

ALL. Hail, all hail Segismundo!

CLOTALDO (*entering*). Heavens, what is this uproar?

SEGISMUNDO. Clotaldo.

CLOTALDO. My lord . . . (*aside*) He's trying his harshness out on me.

CLARIN (*aside*). I'll bet he throws him down the mountain. (*Exit* CLARIN.)

CLOTALDO. I come, I know, to die at your royal feet.

SEGISMUNDO. Rise, father, rise from the ground; for you must be polestar and guide in whom I may entrust my better deeds. I know I owe my upbringing to your great loyalty. Come, embrace me!

CLOTALDO. What are you saying?

SEGISMUNDO. That I am dreaming, and that I wish to do well, since good deeds are not lost, even in dreams.

CLOTALDO. Well, my lord, if doing good is now your motto, then I am sure it won't offend you that I attempt today to do the same. Must you make war on your father? I can neither advise you nor be of use to you against my king. Here I am at your feet. Kill me!

SEGISMUNDO. Worthless fellow! Traitor! Ingrate! (*aside*) Oh heavens, I should control myself, for I still do not know if I am waking. Clotaldo, I envy you your courage and I thank you for it. Go serve the King, and let us meet on the field. You there, sound to arms!

CLOTALDO. A thousand times I kiss your feet.

(*Exit* CLOTALDO.)

SEGISMUNDO. O fortune, we are going to reign. If I am sleeping, do not wake me; and if this is true, do not put me to sleep. But whether it be dream or truth, to do well is what matters. If it be truth, for truth's sake. If not, then to gain friends for the time when we awaken.

(*Exeunt. Drums beat.*)

SCENE 2: *Hall in the royal palace.*

(BASILIO *and* ASTOLFO.)

BASILIO. Who, Astolfo, has the skill to check a wild stallion's fury? Who can hold back the current of a river, as it races proud and headlong to the sea? Who can boldly stop a great boulder as it falls, torn from a mountaintop? Yet all these seem easier to tame than the angry passion of a mob. Proclaim to them some partisan rumor, and at once from the depths of the mountains the repeated echo resounds: "Astolfo!" some shout, and others, "Segismundo!" The royal throne, reduced to a different function, to a horror, has become a bloody stage where troublesome Fortune acts out tragedies.

ASTOLFO. Sire, let all joy today be held in check. Cancel the praise and the soft pleasure promised me by your great hand. For if Poland (which I aspire to rule) today resists me, it is so that I may first earn her allegiance. Give me a horse, and as my shield boasts thunder, so may I proudly strike like lightning.   (*Exit.*)

BASILIO. Against the inevitable there's small protection, and great danger lies in what has been foretold. If it must happen, defense is impossible; and he who most avoids it only brings it closer. Harsh law! Remorseless fate! Oh horror, horror! to meet the peril, when one intends to flee it! Because of what I have kept in hiding, I have lost myself, and I, I myself, have brought my country to destruction.

ESTRELLA (*entering*). O great king, if by your presence you do not try to check the tumult spreading from one faction to another through all the streets and public squares, you'll see your kingdom bathed in waves of scarlet, dyed in the purple of its own blood. For now, alas! all is misfortune, all is tragedy.

So great is the ruin of your empire, and so fierce the power of rough and bloody violence, that to see it causes wonder, to hear it, terror. The sun darkens and the wind's obstructed. Each stone becomes a pyramid, and each flower a monument. Each building is a living sepulcher, and each soldier, though alive, a skeleton.

CLOTALDO (*entering*). Thank God that I have reached your feet alive!

BASILIO. Clotaldo, how is it with Segismundo?

CLOTALDO. The mob, a blind, headlong monster, broke into the tower, and from its depths set free the Prince. When he saw his grandeur restored to him a second time, he showed himself valiant, crying fiercely that he would draw the truth from heaven.

BASILIO. Give me a horse! I must in person boldly subdue that ingrate son. And in defense of my crown, may steel succeed where knowledge failed!   (*Exit.*)

ESTRELLA. Then I, beside the Sun, shall be Bellona, and next to his I hope to place my name; for I must fly on wide extended wings, if I would rival Pallas' deity.

(*Exit; a call to arms is sounded.*)

(*Enter* ROSAURA, *who detains* CLOTALDO.)

ROSAURA. Even though the valor in your breast calls you to battle, listen awhile to me, for war, I know, is everywhere. And you well know that when I came to Poland poor, humble, and unhappy, I was protected by your valor; in you I found pity. You ordered me (ah heavens!) to live disguised in the palace and to try, hiding my jealousy, to conceal myself from Astolfo. Finally he did see me, and so much does he still tread upon my honor that, even though he recognized me, he continues to talk by night to Estrella in the garden. I have the key to it, and I can provide an opportunity for you to enter and put an end to my care. Thus, daring, strong, and haughty, you can defend my honor, since you are resolved to avenge me with his death.

CLOTALDO. It is true, Rosaura, that from the moment I saw you, I was inclined to do for you all that I could. Your tears were witness. First I besought you to discard the man's clothing you were wearing, so that if by chance Astolfo saw you, it might be in your own proper dress; nor would he judge as lightness a mad rashness which abuses honor. At the same time I planned what might be done to regain your lost honor, even (so much that honor swayed me) if it had to be by killing Astolfo. What senile madness! Yet since he's not my king, this deed's not one to amaze me, nor dismay me. I had thought then of killing him. But when Segismundo tried to murder me, Astolfo came to my defense. He ignored his own danger and showed a good will and a rashness surpassing courage. Now how can I, whose soul is grateful to him, kill this man who saved my life? And thus, with my affection and care divided between the two of you, since I have given life to you and received it from him, I do not know which of you to help; I do not know which of you to support. If I am bound to you because of what I gave you, I am likewise bound to him for what I have received from him. In this action, hence, there's nothing that satisfies my love because I must both do the deed, and suffer for it.

ROSAURA. It is not for me to tell so great a man that to give is noble, while to receive is base. Once you accept this principle, you need not be grateful to him. For if it is he who has given life to you, and you to me, it's clear that he forced your nobleness to commit a mean act, while I prompted you to a generous one. Therefore you are offended by him, and obliged to me, since you have given to me what you received from him. And thus you should defend my honor in so great a peril, for my case is stronger than his, by so much as giving is better than receiving.

CLOTALDO. Although nobility comes with giving, gratitude comes with receiving. And since I have known how to give, I have the name of a generous man as well as an honorable one. Leave me the name of a grateful man too, then, since to attain it I need only be grateful as well as generous; for there is as much honor in giving as in receiving.

ROSAURA. From you I received life, and you yourself told me, when you gave it to me, that a life with injured honor was no life at all. Then I have received nothing from you, since the life your hand gave me has not been a life. And if you'd rather be a creditor than a debtor (as I have heard from you yourself), I hope you will bestow that life on me, which you have not yet given. And because to give is more ennobling, if you are generous first, you will be grateful afterward.

CLOTALDO. Convinced by your argument, I shall first of all be liberal. Rosaura, I shall give you my fortune, and you must enter a convent. The proposal I offer is well thought out: in fleeing from a crime you will find yourself a sanctuary. And I, of noble birth, shall not be the one to intensify the misfortunes of our divided kingdom. When I choose this remedy, I am loyal to the kingdom, generous with you, and grateful to Astolfo. Take this course, then, which best suits you, and let the matter rest between us two. Heaven knows I could not do more if I were your father.

ROSAURA. If you were my father, I would endure this injury. But since you are not, I will not suffer it.

CLOTALDO. Then what do you intend to do?

ROSAURA. Kill the Duke.

CLOTALDO. A woman who never knew her father has so much courage?

ROSAURA. Yes.

CLOTALDO. What's driving you on?

ROSAURA. My reputation.

CLOTALDO. Observe that you must see in Astolfo . . .

ROSAURA. He who tramples all my honor underfoot!

CLOTALDO. Your king, the husband of Estrella.

ROSAURA. By the living God, he will not be that!

CLOTALDO. It's madness.

ROSAURA. So I see.

CLOTALDO. Then conquer it.

ROSAURA. I cannot.

CLOTALDO. Then you will lose . . .

ROSAURA. I know it.

CLOTALDO. Life and honor.

ROSAURA. Well do I believe it!

CLOTALDO. What are you after?

ROSAURA. My death.

CLOTALDO. That's merely spite.

ROSAURA. It's honor.

CLOTALDO. It's madness.

ROSAURA. No. It's courage.

CLOTALDO. Call it frenzy.

ROSAURA. It's rage and wrath.

CLOTALDO. Is there no way to restrain your blind passion?

ROSAURA. No.

CLOTALDO. Who will help you?

ROSAURA. I myself.

CLOTALDO. Is there no remedy?

ROSAURA. None.

CLOTALDO. Just think. Is there some other way?

ROSAURA. Only some other way to be lost.   (*Exit.*)

CLOTALDO. Then if you must be lost, my daughter, wait, and let us both be lost together.   (*Exit.*)

SCENE 3: *A field.*

(SEGISMUNDO, *clothed in skins. Soldiers marching.*
CLARIN. *Drums are beating.*)

SEGISMUNDO. If Rome in the triumphs of her golden age
could see me this day, how she would rejoice to behold so
strange a sight—armies led by a wild animal, for whose high
vigor heaven itself would be a minor conquest! But oh my
soul, let us beat back that flight. Not in that way do we
make light of this unstable applause, which will grieve me
when I awake if I have won it and then lost it; no, the
less it means to me, the less I'll mourn if I should lose it.
(*A trumpet sounds.*)

CLARIN. On a swift steed (pardon me, for I have a compulsion to exaggerate when I tell a story), on whom a map
seems drawn, since his body is the earth and fire is the
spirit in his breast; his foam is the sea, his breath the air—in
all, a confusion where chaos may be glimpsed, for in his
spirit, foam, body, and breath, he is a very monster of fire,
earth, water, and wind; on such a steed, then, dappled silvery gray, and spurred on by a rider under whom he does
not run, but flies—on such a steed there comes a graceful
woman to your presence.

SEGISMUNDO. Her light blinds me.

CLARIN. As God lives, it's Rosaura! (*He withdraws.*)

SEGISMUNDO. Heaven has restored her to me.
(*Enter* ROSAURA *in a loose jacket, wearing sword and
dagger.*)

ROSAURA. Generous Segismundo, whose heroic majesty
rises from a night of shadows into a day of deeds and dawns
like the sun which, in the arms of Aurora, returns shining
to plants and roses, over mountains and seas. Crowned with
flashing rays of light, it shines forth, bathing the hilltops
with brilliance, painting the edges of the foam. So may you,
O radiant sun of Poland, dawn on the world as on this unhappy woman, who today throws herself at your feet. Give
her your aid because she is a woman, and unfortunate: two
reasons, either of which is enough, and more than enough
to obligate a man who boasts of his chivalry. Three times
have you seen me, without knowing who I am, for each

time I was dressed in different clothing. At first you thought me a man, in that rough prison where your life made my misfortunes seem a pleasure. The second time you saw me as a woman, when your pomp and majesty were only a dream, a vision, a shadow. The third time is today, when, like a monstrosity of both the sexes, I bear the weapons of a warrior, though I wear a woman's dress. And, so that pity may the better dispose you to grant me protection, hear, I pray, the story of my tragic fortunes. In the Court of Muscovy I was born of a noble mother, who, since she was unhappy, must have been very beautiful. On her a traitor cast his eyes. I do not name him because I do not know him, and yet I know that he was valiant; my own valor tells me this. Since I am his offspring, I am sorry now not to have been born a pagan, so that I might fondly persuade myself he was a god, like one of those who in metamorphosis rained showers of gold on Danaë, or came as swan or bull to Leda or Europa.

I thought I was stretching out my tale too long, with these stories of perfidy, but now I find that I have told you all in these few words: my mother, lovelier than any woman, but unhappy as all of us, was persuaded, alas, to love more passionately than wisely. That foolish excuse, that promise of marriage, so carried her away that even today she weeps to think of it. As Aeneas when he fled Troy, so this tyrant when he fled my mother left his sword. Its blade is sheathed here, but I will bare it before this story ends. From this imperfect knot which neither ties nor binds, this marriage, or this crime, for it's all one, was I then born, so like my mother that I was a portrait of her, a true copy, not indeed of her beauty, but of her fortunes and misfortunes. Thus I need not say that as heiress of unhappiness, I have met a fate like hers. The most I can tell you about myself is that the man who robbed the spoils, the trophies of my honor . . . is Astolfo! Alas! When I name him—quite naturally, since he is my enemy—my heart fills with rage and passion. Astolfo was that ingrate, then, who forgot all our delights (since even the memory of a love that is over will fade), and came here to Poland, called from his notorious conquest, to marry Estrella, a star rising against my setting sun. Who will believe that since a star brought two lovers together, a star—Estrella—would separate them now?

I was hurt and mocked, I was crazed, grieved, and almost dead. I was indeed my ill-starred self, with all the con-

fusion of Hell enclosed within my mind. But I kept silent,
for there are pains and anxieties which the feelings express
better than the tongue, and I told my troubles wordlessly
until one day, when we were alone, my mother, Violante,
broke open the prison of my woes. Then in troops they
surged out of my breast, stumbling over one another. It
did not embarrass me to tell her, for when one knows that
the person in whom she confides her weaknesses has erred
herself, it seems that this provides a balm and ease from
pain; and thus at times a bad example has a use.

She listened sympathetically to my sorrows, and wanted
to console me with her own. How easily can a judge who
has sinned pardon sin in others! Having learned by her
own experience that neither idleness nor lapse of time
brought remedy to her lost honor, my mother decided on
another course for me. Her best advice was that I follow
him and compel him, by unrelenting effort, to repay his
debt of honor. To accomplish this more easily, it was my
fate to dress myself in man's clothing. My mother took down
an ancient sword, which I now wear. Now is the time its
blade should be unsheathed, as I promised her when,
trusting in its sign, she said to me: "Go to Poland, and arrange for this sword you are wearing to be seen in your
possession by the highest nobles. For it may be that in one
of them your fortunes may find a merciful reception, and
your woes some consolation."

I did arrive in Poland. Let us pass over, since it is not
important, and you already know, the fact that a wild
horse brought me to your cave, where you were amazed to
see me. Let us pass over, too, the fact that there Clotaldo,
passionately taking my part, begged the King for my life,
which the King granted; that when Clotaldo learned who
I was, he persuaded me to put on my own clothing and
to serve Estrella. There ingeniously I obstructed Astolfo's
love and marriage to Estrella. Nor do we need to mention
the fact that, once more confused, you saw me here again,
this time in woman's dress, and by these changes you were
quite confounded. But let us come to the fact that Clotaldo,
persuaded that it was important to him that Astolfo and
the fair Estrella marry and rule the kingdom, advised me,
against my honor, to lay aside my claim.

Therefore, since it is your turn, O valiant Segismundo,
to take vengeance today—for heaven wishes you to break
through the barriers of this rustic prison where your body

has been a wild beast to feeling, a rock to suffering—and since your sword is lifted against your father and your country, I come to help you. On me the armor of Pallas is covered with the rich robes of Diana; I wear both cloth and steel. For both of us, then, great leader, it is important to impede and destroy these planned nuptials; for me, to keep him who is my husband from marrying another; and for you, to prevent the joining of their states, with increased power and strength, from placing our victory in doubt. As a woman, I come to persuade you to give aid to my honor, and as a man I come to encourage you to recover your crown. As a woman, I come to move you to pity when I throw myself at your feet, and as a man I come to serve you with my sword and with my person. And bear in mind that if today you court me as a woman, as a man I shall kill you in honorable defense of my honor. For I must be, in this war of love, a woman to tell you my complaints, and a man to gain honor.

SEGISMUNDO (aside). If it is true, O heavens, that I'm dreaming, suspend my memory, for it is not possible for so many things to fit into one dream. Would to God that I might either escape from all these difficulties or think of none of them! Who ever saw such troublesome uncertainties? If I merely dreamed of that grandeur in which I saw myself, how can this woman now relate such apparent proof to me? Then it was true, and not a dream. And if it was true, which would be more, not less confusing, how can my life be called a dream? Then are glories so much like dreams that the true ones are taken for false, and the false for true? There is so little difference between them that it's doubtful one can know whether what one sees or tastes is false or true! Is the copy so similar to the original that there is doubt in knowing which is real? If it is thus, and the grandeur and power, pomp and majesty are to vanish among shadows, then let us take advantage of the moment allotted to us, for in that moment we enjoy only what we can snatch between dreams.

Rosaura is in my power; my heart adores her beauty. Then let us profit from this occasion; let love break the laws of chivalry and of the trust with which she prostrates herself at my feet. This is a dream; and since it is, let us dream happiness now, for sorrows will come later. But again I convince myself with my own reasoning! If this is a dream, if this is mere vanity, then who for human vanity would lose a heavenly glory? What past blessedness is not a dream? Who has had great happiness who would not say to himself, when he recalls it in memory: "Beyond a doubt, all that I saw was just a dream." Then if this will bring me disappointment, if I know that pleasure is only a splendid flame reduced to ashes by any wind that blows, let us turn to the eternal, which is ever-living fame, where happiness does not sleep nor greatness rest. Rosaura is without honor; but a prince should give honor, not take it away. As God lives, I must win back her honor, before my crown! Let us flee from this temptation, then, for it is very strong! (*to a soldier*) Sound arms! For today I must give battle before the shadows of darkness bury the day's golden light in the dark green waves.

Rosaura. My lord, why do you withdraw so? Do not my worry and my anxiety merit even a single word from you? How is it possible, Sire, for you neither to look at me nor to hear me? Won't you even turn your face toward me?

Segismundo. Rosaura, for your honor's sake, if I am to be merciful to you, I must be cruel now. My voice does not answer you, in order that my honor may. I do not speak to you, because I wish my deeds to speak to you for me. Neither do I look at your, for it's necessary, in this moment of pain, that he who must look to your honor should not look at your beauty.   (*Exit* Segismundo, *with the soldiers.*)

Rosaura. Oh heavens, what are these riddles? After so much agony, I'm still left in doubt with these ambiguous replies!

Clarin. Señora, is this a good time to see you?

Rosaura. Ah, Clarin! Where have you been?

Clarin. Locked up in a tower, checking a hand at cards to see whether or not death is going to strike me. The face card that turned up seemed to mean that my life was at stake. But I was on the point of bursting.

Rosaura. Why?

Clarin. Because I know the secret of who you are. Indeed, Clotaldo . . . But what is that noise?

(*Sound of drums.*)

Rosaura. What can it be?

Clarin. An armed squadron, coming out of the besieged palace, to oppose or conquer the forces of fierce Segismundo.

Rosaura. How cowardly I am, not to be at his side, the wonder of the world, when such cruelty hems us in with lawlessness and disorder.   (*Exit.*)

SOME VOICES. Long live our unconquerable king!

OTHER VOICES. Long live our liberty!

CLARIN. May liberty and king both have long life! And welcome too! But to me it makes no difference whose side I'm on. For today, in the midst of all this hubbub, I'll play the role of Nero, who grieved at nothing. If I must grieve about something, let it be about myself. Well hidden here, I can see all the merriment. This spot, among these rocks, is strong and secret. Here death will not find me, so—two figs for death! (*He hides; the sound of drums and arms.*)

(*Enter* BASILIO, CLOTALDO *and* ASTOLFO, *fleeing.*)

BASILIO. Is there anywhere a more unhappy king, or a father more beset?

CLOTALDO. Your conquered army runs away in full disorder.

ASTOLFO. The traitors, winning, hold the field.

BASILIO. In such battles those who win are loyal; the losers, traitors. Then let us fly, Clotaldo, from the inhuman cruelty of a tyrant son.

(*Shots are heard offstage;* CLARIN *falls wounded from his hiding-place.*)

BASILIO. Heaven help me!

ASTOLFO. Who is this unhappy bloodstained soldier, who has fallen at our feet?

CLARIN. I am an unlucky man who, in trying to keep myself away from death, found it. Fleeing from it, I met it, for there is no place secret from death. A clear argument, this, that he who runs from it most is the one who first reaches it. Turn back, therefore, into the bloody battle; for in the midst of arms and firing there is more safety than in the most hidden mountain. There is no path secure against the might of destiny and inclement Fate. And thus, although you seek to free yourself from death by fleeing, behold that you will die when it is God's will that you die. (*He falls.*)

BASILIO. "When it's God's will that you die!" How well, oh heavens, does this corpse, which speaks to us through the mouth of a wound, guide our error and our ignorance to greater knowledge! This bloody tongue teaches us that all man's diligence is useless when it opposes a higher power. So it is with me. For, intending to save my country from murders and sedition, I delivered it over to the very evils from which I tried to save it.

CLOTALDO. Sire, although fate knows all the roads, and

finds the man it seeks even among the mountain thickets, it is not a Christian judgment to say there is no refuge from its rage. For there is; and a prudent man can attain a victory over fate. If you are not already exempted from pain and misfortune, do what you can to find yourself a shelter.

ASTOLFO. Clotaldo, Sire, speaks to you as a prudent man who has reached mature age; I, as a valiant youth: in the thick undergrowth of this mountain there is a horse, a swift monster born of the wind. Flee on it, and I, meanwhile, shall guard your flight.

BASILIO. If it is God's will that I should die, or if death awaits me here, then today I wish to find him, and meet him face to face. (*Call to arms.*)

(*Enter* SEGISMUNDO, ESTRELLA, ROSAURA, SOLDIERS, ATTENDANTS.)

SOLDIER. In the tangles of this mountain, among its thick branches, the King is hiding.

SEGISMUNDO. Follow him! Let no tree remain on these heights which you have not carefully searched, trunk by trunk and branch by branch.

CLOTALDO. Flee, Sire!

BASILIO. Why?

ASTOLFO. What is your intention?

BASILIO. Withdraw, Astolfo.

CLOTALDO. What do you wish?

BASILIO. To take a remedy, Clotaldo, that I need. (*to* SEGISMUNDO) If it is me you seek, prince, here at your feet I am. (*kneeling*) Let these snowy hairs of mine be a white rug under your feet. Step on my neck and tread upon my crown. Humble my dignity and drag my reverence in the dust. Take vengeance on my honor, and use me as a slave. After all I have done to prevent this, let Fate now demand its due; let heaven fulfill its prophecy.

SEGISMUNDO. Illustrious Court of Poland, you who have witnessed so many wonders, give ear, for now your prince speaks to you. What Heaven has determined and God's finger has written on the sky's blue tablet, whose ciphers and printed figures are so many sheets of azure adorned with gilded letters, never deceives, never lies. No, he who lies and deceives is he who attempts to penetrate and unfathom these mysteries to make evil use of them. My father, here at my feet, to free himself from the rage of my nature, made of me a brute, a human beast; so that even if I, be-

cause of my inborn nobility, my honorable blood, and my
gallant nature, had been born mild and gentle, this way of
living, this kind of upbringing would have been enough to
transform me into a beast. What a strange way to keep me
from becoming one! If a man were told, "A wild animal is
going to kill you," would it be wise for him to wake that
creature from its sleep? If he were warned, "This sword
you're wearing will kill you," to pull it from its sheath and
point it at his breast would be a foolish way to evade the
doom. Or if he were told, "Great seas of water, with monu-
ments of silver foam, will be your burying place," he would
do wrong to plunge into the proud sea while it raised curled
hills of snow and angry steeps of crystal water. And as that
man who wakes from sleep the wild beast that threatens him;
or he who, fearing a sword, unsheathes it; or he who chal-
lenges the waves of a storm, so is my father. And though—
listen to me—my fierceness were a sleeping beast, my wrath
a tempered sword, my rage a calm and quiet sea, injustice
and vengeance would never ward off the fate predicted, but
rather urge it on. And thus, whoever hopes to control his
fate must do it with prudence and with moderation. Not before a harm arrives can he who foresees it save himself from
it. By humility, he may protect himself from it, but only
after it occurs; there is no way to prevent it. Let this rare
spectacle, this strange wonder, this horror, this prodigy serve
as an example. Never was there a greater one than this, that
in spite of so many efforts to prevent it, my father should
lie conquered at my feet, a king trampled on. It was a judgment of heaven; however much he sought to stop it, he
could not. And can I, younger than he in age, lesser in
courage and in wisdom, conquer it? Sire, arise. (*to the*
KING) Give me your hand. For now that heaven has made
clear to you your error in the way you opposed its decree,
humbly my neck awaits your vengeance. I yield myself at
your feet.

BASILIO. Oh son, so noble an action gives you new birth
in my heart. You are the Prince. To you belong the laurel
and the palm. You have conquered! Your deeds crown you!

ALL. Long live Segismundo!

SEGISMUNDO. Though my valor hopes to make great con-
quests, today the greatest must be a victory over myself.
Astolfo, give your hand now to Rosaura, for it is a debt of
honor, and I must retrieve it for her.

Astolfo. Although it's true I owe a debt to her, consider that she knows not who she is. It would be base and dishonorable for me to marry a woman who . . .

Clotaldo. Wait! Go no further! Rosaura is as noble as you, Astolfo, and my sword will defend her in mortal combat. She's my daughter, and that should suffice.

Astolfo. What are you saying?

Clotaldo. That I did not wish to make known her identity until I saw her nobly and honorably married. This makes too long a story, but the sum is brief: that she's my daughter.

Astolfo. Since this is so, I will fulfill my promise.

Segismundo. So that Estrella will not be left disconsolate, by losing such a valiant and glorious prince, with my own hand I shall marry her to a husband who, if he does not exceed, at least equals him in merit and in fortune. Give me your hand.

Estrella. I gain in deserving such good fortune.

Segismundo. As for Clotaldo, who loyally served my father, my arms await him with the thanks that whatever he wishes shall be given him.

Soldier. If in this way you honor one who has not served you, then how about me? I started the great uproar in the kingdom, and I freed you from the tower in which you were imprisoned. What will you give me?

Segismundo. The very same tower. And so that you will never leave it till your death, you will be kept there under guard. The treason past, the traitor is no longer needed.

Basilio. Your wisdom fills us all with wonder.

Astolfo. How changed his character!

Rosaura. How wise and prudent!

Segismundo. What makes you wonder? What surprises you, if a dream taught me this wisdom, and if I still fear I may wake up and find myself once more confined in prison? And even if this should not happen, merely to dream it is enough. For this I have come to know, that all human happiness finally ceases, like a dream.

And now I wish to profit from the time that remains to me by asking pardon for our faults; for to noble hearts, it is natural and right to grant forgiveness.

WHEN A GIRL SAYS YES

(*El sí de las niñas*)

by *Leandro Fernández de Moratín*

TRANSLATED BY

William M. Davis

⟨⟩⟨⟩

These are the assurances that parents and tutors give, and how far they should be trusted when a girl says yes.

—Act III

CHARACTERS

Don Diego	Rita
Don Carlos	Simon
Doña Irene	Calamocha
Doña Paquita	

SCENE: *A hostelry in Alcalá de Henares.*

The stage represents the common room in a hostelry, with four guest-room doors, all numbered. Large door backstage, with a staircase leading to the ground floor. Window with breast-high sill to one side. In the middle, a table, with bench, chairs, etc.

The action begins at seven o'clock at night and ends at five the next morning.

Leandro Fernández de Moratín

(1760-1828)

Moratín is most representative of the neoclassic or Frenchified trend which characterized the end of the eighteenth century and the beginning of the nineteenth. Born in Madrid, the son of the distinguished poet and playwright Nicolás Fernández de Moratín (1737-1780), Leandro was apprenticing to a goldsmith when at the age of nineteen he won, to even his father's surprise, a literary award. One of the literary and political figures of the day, Gaspar Melchor de Jovellanos (1744-1811), took him under his wing and had him sent as secretary to the Spanish embassy in Paris. Soon thereafter, as Godoy's protégé, he traveled in France, England, and Italy, finally becoming Director of the National Library in Madrid. During the French occupation of Spain Moratín sided with Joseph Bonaparte, retreating with the latter's troops in 1814. From then until his death he lived in Paris; he was buried at the Père Lachaise between his beloved Molière and La Fontaine. Moratín's psychology is magnificently reflected in Goya's portrait of him: a sly intellectual, hesitant, melancholy, opportunistic, cowardly.

His one great passion was the theater: its history, its theories, its mechanics; he translated *Hamlet* (1795) and adapted most successfully Molière's *Le médecin malgré lui* and *L'école des maris;* and, finally, wrote five plays, one of which at least, *El sí de las niñas* (*When a Girl Says Yes,* 1805), remains a landmark in the panorama of the Spanish theater. In all his plays Moratín followed faithfully the spirit of French neoclassicism: he adhered to the unities, used a small number of characters (or types), and developed a moral thesis through humorous and sparklingly natural dialogue. The action is quick and the psychological motivation is subtle and convincing. All these qualities are especially outstanding in *El sí de las niñas* wherein he highlights the struggles between the young and old generations, censuring the rancid Spanish custom of marriage through parental imposition.

BEST EDITION: F. Ruiz Morcuende (ed.), *Teatro de Moratín.* Madrid, 1924.
ABOUT: M. S. Oliver, *Los españoles en la revolución francesa.* Madrid, n.d. F. Ruiz Morcuende, *Vocabulario de las obras de Moratín.* Madrid, 1946.

ACT I

(*Enter* Don Diego *from his room.* Simon, *who is seated in a chair, gets up.*)

Don Diego. Aren't they back yet?

Simon. No, sir.

Don Diego. They're not exactly hurrying.

Simon. After all, her aunt is pretty fond of her; and she hasn't seen her since they took her to Guadalajara.

Don Diego. Not that she shouldn't see her; but a half-hour visit and a couple of tears should have put an end to it.

Simon. Then, too, you were singularly determined to stay cooped up here at the inn for two whole days. Reading's a bore, and so is sleeping, but what makes it worse is this filthy room, the rickety chairs, the cheap prints of the Prodigal Son, the noise of doorbells and cowbells, and the coarse chatter of mule drivers and peasants who won't give you a moment's peace.

Don Diego. It's better this way. Everyone knows me here—the judge, the abbot, the priest, the rector from Malaga, and plenty more besides. I don't want anyone to see me.

Simon. I can't understand why you need such seclusion. Is there more to this than your trip with Doña Irene to Guadalajara to get the girl out of the convent and drive them back to Madrid?

Don Diego. Of course. Something more than meets the eye.

Simon. I'm listening.

Don Diego. Well, you'll find out eventually, and it can't be long. Look, Simon, swear you won't tell. You're an honest man, and you've served me faithfully for years. You know, we got the girl out of the convent and we're taking her back to Madrid.

Simon. Yes, sir.

Don Diego. Well, then . . . But I repeat, swear you won't tell a soul. That's an order.

Simon. Right, sir. I've never been fond of gossip.

Don Diego. I know. That's why I can trust you. I must confess, I never really saw the girl, Doña Paquita, but since I'm friendly with her mother, I've had frequent news of her; I've read many of the letters she wrote; I've seen some from her aunt, the nun she lived with in Guadalajara; in short, I've heard just about as much about her inclinations and behavior as I could wish.

Finally, I got to see her; I've tried to observe her closely these last few days, and to tell the truth, I think they hardly praised her enough.

Simon. I know what you mean. She's very beautiful, and . . .

Don Diego. She's very beautiful, very charming, very humble . . . But above all, what candor, what innocence! Take it from me, you won't find much of *that* kind around here. And talent. Yes, *sir*, lots of talent. So, to make a long story short, I've decided that . . .

Simon. You don't have to tell me.

Don Diego. No? Why?

Simon. I can guess. And I think it's an excellent idea.

Don Diego. What did you say?

Simon. Excellent.

Don Diego. So you knew at once?

Simon. Can't you see? Well, if you want my opinion, I think it's a perfect match, just perfect!

Don Diego. That's what I say. I've given it plenty of thought, and decided it's quite proper.

Simon. It sure is.

Don Diego. But not a word to anyone till it's done.

Simon. That's very wise of you.

Don Diego. Because not everyone sees things the same way, and there'd be no lack of gossip, or talk of madness, and I . . .

Simon. Madness! Some madness! To a girl like her?

Don Diego. That's just it. She's poor, I'll admit. Because, just between you and me, good old Doña Irene was in such a hurry to spend all she had as soon as her husband died, that if it wasn't for her two blessed sisters, the nuns, and her brother-in-law, the Canon of Castrojeriz, she wouldn't have enough to put a stew on the fire. And how she puts on airs and sticks up her nose, always talking about her relatives, and saying my late husband this and my late husband that, and such a lot of rigmarole, that . . . But never mind. I'm not looking for money; I've got plenty of that. I want modesty, composure, virtue.

SIMON. That's the main thing. Besides, what would you do with all that money?

DON DIEGO. You're right. But do you know the value of a thrifty, practical woman, who can keep house, economize, and see to everything? Always wrangling with housekeepers, one worse than the next, spoiled gossips and hysterical old busybodies who are ugly as sin, besides! No, sir, I'm turning over a new leaf. I'll have a faithful, loving helpmate, and we'll live like a couple of saints. So let people talk and gossip, and . . .

SIMON. But if you're both willing, what can they say?

DON DIEGO. I'll tell you what they'll say, only . . . They'll say it's a poor match, that there's too much difference in age, that there's . . .

SIMON. Well, I don't think it's so great: seven or eight years at most.

DON DIEGO. What? Seven or eight years? When she was sixteen only a few months ago?

SIMON. What of it?

DON DIEGO. And I, though thank God I'm strong and . . . but even so, I'll never be fifty-nine again.

SIMON. Who's talking about that?

DON DIEGO. Then what are you talking about?

SIMON. I mean . . . Well, either you can't quite explain yourself, or I understood you wrong. In short, who is this dear Doñ Paquita supposed to marry?

DON DIEGO. Now you ask? Why, me, of course!

SIMON. *You?*

DON DIEGO. Yes, me.

SIMON. Well, I'll be damned.

DON DIEGO. What! What's that?

SIMON. And to think I guessed wrong.

DON DIEGO. Well, out with it. Who did you think I meant?

SIMON. Your nephew, Don Carlos. He's a talented young man with a good education, a fine soldier, and attractive in every way. I thought you'd keep such a girl for him.

DON DIEGO. Not on your life.

SIMON. All right, then.

DON DIEGO. Marry her to him, what an idea! Not on your life. Let him study his mathematics.

SIMON. He does. And teaches it, too.

DON DIEGO. Let him earn his laurels, and . . .

SIMON. Laurels! What laurels does he need when as an officer in the last war, with a handful of only the bravest men, he captured two batteries, spiked the cannons, took several prisoners, and then returned to camp, covered with blood and wounds? Well, you were quite satisfied with your nephew's laurels then, and I saw you weep for joy more than four times when the king promoted him to lieutenant colonel and awarded him the Alcantara Cross.

DON DIEGO. All right, that's true, but not to the point. She's marrying me.

SIMON. If you're really sure she loves you, if she isn't afraid of the difference in age, if she chose you of her own free will . . .

DON DIEGO. Well, why shouldn't she? What would they gain by deceiving me? You saw the nun of Guadalajara: there's a sensible woman for you. And her other aunt from Alcala—though I still haven't made her acquaintance—I'm sure she must be a woman of excellent qualities. Then again, Doña Irene must want what's best for her daughter. And they all give me every assurance I could wish for. The maid, who served her in the convent in Madrid for more than four years, praises her to the skies; but above all, she informed me that she never saw the child show the slightest inclination for any of the few men she could see in that retreat . . . Embroidery, sewing, reading pious books, going to Mass, chasing butterflies through the garden, and pouring water down ant holes—such tasks and amusements occupied all her time . . . Now, what do you say?

SIMON. Me? Nothing, sir.

DON DIEGO. And don't you think that in spite of so many assurances, I've made good use of every chance I've had to win her friendship and confidence, and to get her to speak her mind completely freely? Though there's still time . . . Except that Doña Irene is always butting in: she does all the talking . . . But she's a fine woman, very fine . . .

SIMON. Well, sir, I hope it turns out to suit you.

DON DIEGO. Yes, I hope to God it won't go badly. Though you hardly approve of the bridegroom. And what a time to commend my dear nephew! Why, do you know how mad I am at him?

SIMON. Jesus, what's he done?

DON DIEGO. He's up to his old tricks. I found out about it

only a few days ago. You remember last year when he spent two months in Madrid . . . The visit cost me a mint . . . Well, he *is* my nephew, that's for sure, but here's the story. His regiment happened to be going to Saragossa . . . And you remember how a few days after leaving Madrid, he sent word of his arrival?

SIMON. Yes, sir.

DON DIEGO. And how he still wrote me, though not on schedule, always dating his letters from Saragossa?

SIMON. Indeed he did.

DON DIEGO. Well, the rascal wasn't there.

SIMON. You don't say!

DON DIEGO. I do. On the third of July he left my house, and at the end of September he still hadn't returned to his colors . . . Don't you think that for someone going by stage, the coaching was awfully slow?

SIMON. Maybe he got sick on the road, and to save you worry . . .

DON DIEGO. Nothing of the sort. Love affairs and flirtations are driving him out of his mind! In one of those garrison towns . . . Who knows? Let him see a pair of pretty black eyes, and he's a goner. God forbid, he may fall for one of those hussies who barter their honor for marriage.

SIMON. Oh, there's nothing to fear! And if he meets up with some love-sharp, she'll need pretty good cards to pull a fast one on *him*.

DON DIEGO. It looks as if they're here . . . They are. Go get the driver and tell him to come in so we can set a time for us to leave tomorrow.

SIMON. Very well, sir.

DON DIEGO. Now remember: I don't want any of this to leak out, or . . . You follow me?

SIMON. Don't worry, I won't tell a soul.

(SIMON *goes out the door backstage.* DOÑA IRENE, DOÑA PAQUITA, *and* RITA, *all wearing mantillas and black skirts, enter the same way.* RITA *places a knotted handkerchief on the table, then takes the mantillas and starts to fold them.*)

DOÑA PAQUITA. Well, here we are.

DOÑA IRENE. Oh, what stairs!

DON DIEGO. You are most welcome, ladies.

DOÑA IRENE. And you, my dear sir, haven't you been out?

(DOÑA IRENE *and* DON DIEGO *sit down.*)

DON DIEGO. No, madam. Later on I'll go out for a little

stroll . . . I read for a while, then I tried to sleep, but in this place you can't sleep a wink.

Doña Paquita. You really can't. And what mosquitoes! A plague on them! They kept me up all night. But look, look what I've got! (*unties the handkerchief and points*) Mother-of-pearl rosaries, cypress-wood crosses, Saint Benedict's rule, a fount for holy water . . . Look how pretty! And two little hearts of talc! Lord knows what else. Oh, and a little clay bell that's been blessed for thunder . . . So many things!

Doña Irene. Trinkets the sisters gave her. They were crazy about her.

Doña Paquita. How they all love me! And poor, dear auntie, she cried so much . . . she's such a dear old thing.

Doña Irene. She was very sorry not to have made your acquaintance.

Doña Paquita. She was. She kept saying, "Why didn't the gentleman come?"

Doña Irene. The priest and the rector of the Academy for Youths took us right to the gate.

Doña Paquita. Here. (*She ties up the handkerchief again and gives it to* Rita, *who takes it along with the mantillas to* Doña Irene's *room.*) Keep it all for me there in the sewing basket. Here, take it by the corners like this. Oh, dear, the candy Saint Gertrude is broken already!

Rita. Never mind, miss, I'll eat her. (*leaves*)

Doña Paquita. Shall we go inside, mamma, or stay out here?

Doña Irene. Wait, child. Let me catch my breath.

Don Diego. It's really been hot today.

Doña Irene. And how cool they keep that locutory! It's a real Heaven. (Doña Paquita *sits down beside her mother.*)

Doña Paquita (*aside*). But, still, that fat nun called Mother Angustias—how she could sweat. Ay, how that poor woman did sweat!

Doña Irene. My sister's the one who's always been rather delicate. She suffered terribly this winter . . . But, you know, she simply couldn't do enough for her niece. And she's so thrilled with our choice.

Don Diego. I'm glad it's so agreeable to everyone you are personally obliged to.

Doña Irene. Yes, Trinidad is so thrilled, and as for Circuncisión, you've seen for yourself. It was such an effort to pry herself loose, but she realized that where Paquita's

welfare is concerned, we must put up with everything . . .
You must remember how expressive she was, and . . .

DON DIEGO. Indeed I do. If only the interested party is as
happy as those who love her . . .

DOÑA IRENE. She's an obedient child, and would never
go against her mother's wishes.

DON DIEGO. I'm sure of that, but . . .

DOÑA IRENE. She's a thoroughbred, and must think and
act accordingly.

DON DIEGO. I understand. But couldn't she, without com-
promising her honor or her breeding . . . ?

DOÑA PAQUITA. Shall I go, mamma? (*rises, and sits down
again*)

DOÑA IRENE. No, sir, she certainly could not. A well-
bred girl, the daughter of a good family, can't help behaving
on all occasions as is fitting and proper. Look at her. She's
the spit and image of her grandmother, Doña Jeronima de
Peralta, God forgive her . . . The portrait is at home . . . I'm
sure you must have seen it. And His Grace told me it was
made to be sent to his own uncle, Bishop Serapion of San
Juan Crisostomo, bishop-elect of Michoacan.

DON DIEGO. I see.

DOÑA IRENE. And the good priest died at sea, which was
a shock to the whole family . . . Even to this very day we
still mourn him; especially my cousin Don Cucufate, per-
petual alderman of Zamora. He can't hear anyone speak of
His Grace without bursting into tears.

DOÑA PAQUITA. Bless us! What pesky flies.

DOÑA IRENE. Then he died in the odor of sanctity.

DON DIEGO. Good thing he did.

DOÑA IRENE. Yes, sir. But as the family's been coming
down so much in the world, what can you expect? No money,
no property . . . Though just in case something happens, his
biography's being written. Who knows? Maybe tomorrow
it will get published with the blessings of the Church.

DON DIEGO. Of course. They print everything nowadays.

DOÑA IRENE. I'm sure the author, the nephew of my
brother-in-law, the Canon of Castrojeriz, doesn't leave writing it for a single moment. And by this time he's already
finished the ninth volume of the manuscript, covering the
first nine years of the blessed bishop's life.

DON DIEGO. You mean a volume for every year?

DOÑA IRENE. Yes, sir, that's how he planned it.

DON DIEGO. And what did the venerable man die of?

Doña Irene. Of his eighty-two years, three months, and fourteen days.

Doña Paquita. Shall I go, mamma?

Doña Irene. Yes, yes, go along now. Dear me, what a hurry you're in!

Doña Paquita. Would you like to see me curtsy as they do in France, Don Diego?

Don Diego. Yes, child, do.

Doña Paquita (*curtsying*). Like this, see?

Don Diego. Charming! Hooray for Paquita, hooray!

Doña Paquita. A curtsy for you, and a kiss for mamma! (*She kisses* Doña Irene *and goes to the latter's room.*)

Doña Irene. She's oh so cute and clever.

Don Diego. Her natural charm is captivating.

Doña Irene. What did you expect? Raised unpretentiously and far from worldly pleasures, happy to be back beside her mother, and even happier to be settled so soon, is it any wonder that whatever she says or does is a delight, and especially to one who has been so eager to favor her?

Don Diego. I only wish she would express herself freely about our projected union, and . . .

Doña Irene. She would only repeat what I've been telling you.

Don Diego. I don't doubt it. But knowing she deems me worthy of her affection, and hearing her say so with that pretty little mouth of hers, would give me untold satisfaction.

Doña Irene. Don't trouble yourself the slightest on that account. You must realize that it's not right for a girl to state frankly what she feels. It would look bad for a well-bred young lady raised in a God-fearing home to be so bold as to say to a man, "I love you."

Don Diego. Yes, if he were a man she happened to find on the street and surprised him with such a favor straight away, of course it would be very bad. But to the man she's about to marry in just a few days, she could at least say something that . . . Besides, there are certain ways of expressing oneself . . .

Doña Irene. She's franker with me. We talk about you constantly, and she shows her special love for you in everything. How sensibly she spoke last night after you retired. I would have given anything for you to have heard her.

Don Diego. What? She spoke of me?

Doña Irene. And about how much wiser it is for a child

her age to have a middle-aged husband, a mature man of experience, whose conduct . . .

DON DIEGO. Really? She said that?

DOÑA IRENE. No, but that's what I told her, and she listened to me more carefully than a woman of forty . . . I told her plenty. And she has lots of insight, though it's wrong of me to say so . . . But isn't it a shame, sir, to see the way marriages are made today? A girl of fifteen gets married off to some young puppy of eighteen, a girl of seventeen to a boy of twenty-two: she, a mere child without judgment or experience, and he, a child, too, without an ounce of common sense or knowledge of the world. Well, sir, I ask you, who would run the house? Who'd give orders to the servants? Who would teach and correct the children? Because it just so happens that such giddy children are usually plagued with babies at a moment's notice, which is a pity.

DON DIEGO. Certainly it's a shame to see children flock about many who lack the talent, experience, and virtue needed to guide their education.

DOÑA IRENE. I assure you, sir, I was less than nineteen when I married my dear departed first husband, Don Epifanio, God rest his soul. And he was a man who, present company excepted, was the most respectful, courteous gentleman who ever lived . . . And the most amusing and entertaining, too. And if you please, he was already well past fifty-six when he married me.

DON DIEGO. A good age . . . He was no youngster, but . . .

DOÑA IRENE. I was coming to that. Nor would I have been satisfied at the time with some pretty boy with red lips and brains in his stirrups. No, sir. Which is not to say he was sickly or broken in health. Nothing of the kind. He was sound as a bell, thank God, and never laid up a day in his life, except for a little touch of epilepsy now and then. But as soon as we got married, it began to attack him so often and so hard, that in seven months' time I found myself a widow and carrying a child that was born later, and died at length of the measles.

DON DIEGO. Well! So good old Don Epifanio left an heir!

DOÑA IRENE. Indeed he did. And why not?

DON DIEGO. Because there are always some who say . . . Though if one were to pay them heed . . . And was it a boy or a girl?

DOÑA IRENE. A very beautiful little boy. A dear little angel, as good as gold.

Don Diego. It must be such a comfort to have a child like that, and . . .

Doña Irene. Lord almighty, they're troublesome at times, but who cares? They're a real pleasure. They really are.

Don Diego. I should say they are.

Doña Irene. Yes, sir.

Don Diego. Of course, it would be wonderful if . . .

Doña Irene. Why shouldn't you!

Don Diego. A delight to see them laugh and play, and to hug and kiss them and deserve their innocent caresses.

Doña Irene. Darling children! I've been blessed with twenty-two in my three marriages so far, and only this girl survived; but I assure you . . .

Simon (enters through door backstage). The driver's waiting, sir.

Don Diego. Tell him I'ι̱. coming. Ah! First bring me my hat and cane. I must get a breath of air. (Simon enters Don Diego's room, takes out a hat and cane, gives them to his master.) So you think we'll leave early tomorrow.

Doña Irene. Why not? Whenever you like.

Don Diego. Around six. All right?

Doña Irene. Fine.

Don Diego. The sun will be on our backs. I'll tell him to come half an hour early.

Doña Irene. That's best. There are still so many little things to attend to.

(Don Diego leaves with Simon.)

Doña Irene. Goodness! Now that I think of it . . . Rita! They probably let him die. Rita!

Rita (with sheets and pillows in her arms). Yes, ma'am?

Doña Irene. What have you done with the thrush? Did you feed him?

Rita. Yes, ma'am. He ate like an ostrich. I put him in the hall window.

Doña Irene. Did you make the beds?

Rita. Yours is all done. I'll do the others before it gets dark, 'cause otherwise, since there's only one candle and that has no wick, I'd be lost.

Doña Irene. And my daughter—what's she up to?

Rita. She's crumbling up a biscuit for Polly's supper.

Doña Irene. How I hate to write! (gets up and goes to her room.) But I suppose I'll have to, or poor Circuncisión will be on pins and needles.

RITA. What nonsense! Not two hours, so to speak, since we left the place, and already the notes are flying. These female prudes and flatterers make me sick. (*goes into* DOÑA PAQUITA's *room*)

>(CALAMOCHA *enters through door backstage with a few valises, boots, and a whip. He puts everything on the table and then sits down.*)

CALAMOCHA. So this must be room number three. Oh, fine. We're old friends. Biggest collection of bugs this side of the Museum of Natural History. I'm scared to go in. Ow! Ow! What aches! I ache all over. Patience, Calamocha, patience . . . Thank heaven the horsies said, "We're all in." Or else I'd never see this number three—and these plagues of Pharaoh it has inside . . . Anyway, if the nags live through the night, that's nothing to sneeze at. They're ready to drop. (RITA *sings inside.* CALAMOCHA *gets up and stretches.*) Hey, listen to that! A pretty voice, too. Come on now, time for adventure. Ow! Ow-w-w! I'm falling apart.

RITA (*entering*). Better lock up, or they'll steal our clothes, and . . . (*struggling to turn the key*) They might even oil the lock.

CALAMOCHA. Want some help, sweetheart?

RITA. Thanks, dearie.

CALAMOCHA. Well, I'll be! Rita!

RITA. Calamocha!

CALAMOCHA. What a find!

RITA. And your master?

CALAMOCHA. We both just got here.

RITA. Really?

CALAMOCHA. No, I'm joking. As soon as he got Doña Paquita's letter, I don't know where he went, who he spoke to, or how he arranged it; all I know is, we left Saragossa that very night. We rode here like two streaks of lightning and arrived in Guadalajara this morning, and our first inquiries brought us the comforting news that the birds had flown. So to horse again, and more racing and sweating and cracking the whip. In short, the nags are all in and we're half dead, so we stopped here, intending to leave tomorrow. My lieutenant's gone off now to see a friend of his at the Colegio Mayor while they fix us something for supper . . . That's the story.

RITA. You mean he's here?

CALAMOCHA. And more in love than ever, jealous, ready

to kill anything and everything, and cure the hiccups of anyone who disputes his claim to his adored little Doña Paquita.

RITA. How you talk!

CALAMOCHA. Plain and simple.

RITA. I'm delighted. Now you can see it's really love.

CALAMOCHA. Love? Frenzy, you mean! Compared with him, Romeo was a laughingstock, Medoro a schemer, and Gaiferos a first-grader.

RITA. Just wait till missy finds out!

CALAMOCHA. But you haven't told me. How did you get here? Who are you with? When did you come? What . . .

RITA. Well, it's this way. Doña Paquita's mother started writing letter after letter, telling us she'd arranged for her darling to be married in Madrid to a wealthy, honest, esteemed, and respected gentleman—one, in short, as perfect as could be desired. Worried by these proposals, and heartsick over being preached at by that confounded nun, she answered that she was ready to do anything they told her . . . You simply can't imagine how much the poor girl wept, and how unhappy she was. She wouldn't eat and couldn't sleep . . . And at the same time she had to hide her feelings, so her aunt wouldn't guess the truth. So when the first shock was over, and there was time to think of ways and means, we decided the only thing to do was warn your master. We hoped that if his love was really true and genuine, he wouldn't let his poor Paquita fall into the hands of a stranger, or let so many caresses, so many tears, and so many sighs be lost forever on the walls of the convent yard.

A few days after she wrote him, up rolls the six-horse coach and the driver, Gasparet, with his blue stockings, and the mother and the groom. We pick up our clothes, close our trunks, take leave of the blessed nuns, and in two cracks o' the whip we arrive day before yesterday at Alcala. The stop-off was so Doña Paquita could visit another aunt of hers who's a nun and lives around here—one as wrinkled up and deaf as the one we left behind. She's already seen her and been kissed by all the nuns one by one. Now I think we'll be leaving early tomorrow. In case we do, we'll . . .

CALAMOCHA. Say no more . . . But . . . So the groom is at the inn?

RITA. That's his room. (*points to* DON DIEGO'S *room,* DOÑA IRENE'S, *and* DOÑA PAQUITA'S) That's the old lady's, and that's ours.

CALAMOCHA. Ours? You mean yours and mine?

RITA. Of course not! That's where Doña Paquita and I will sleep tonight, because yesterday when the three of us squeezed into the one across the hall, there was no room for us standing; we couldn't sleep a wink, or even breathe.

CALAMOCHA. All right. Goodbye. (*picks up the things he put on the table, and starts to go.*)

RITA. Where to?

CALAMOCHA. I don't know . . . But did that suitor of hers bring along a bunch of friends or relatives to parry the first thrust?

RITA. There's a servant with him.

CALAMOCHA. That's not much . . . Look, for pity's sake, tell him to make his will, 'cause he's in danger.

RITA. Will you be back soon?

CALAMOCHA. You bet. These things require speed, and though I can hardly move, my lieutenant will have to cut short the visit, come back here, take care of his treasure, arrange to bury the guy from Madrid, and . . . So this is our room, eh?

RITA. Yes. The Señorita's and mine.

CALAMOCHA. Wench!

RITA. Rascal. Goodbye.

CALAMOCHA. Goodbye, hateful! (*takes things to* DON CARLOS' *room*)

RITA. How awful! But . . . Bless us, Don Felix here! Yes, he loves her, that's quite plain . . . (CALAMOCHA *comes out of* DON CARLOS' *room and exits through the door backstage.*) Oh, no matter what people say, there are some who are very refined; and then, what can a girl do? . . . Love them— it can't be helped—just love them . . . But what will my mistress say when she sees him? She's head over heels in love. Poor little thing! Wouldn't it be a shame if . . . ? Here she comes.

(*Enter* DOÑA PAQUITA.)

DOÑA PAQUITA. Oh, Rita!

RITA. What's wrong? Have you been crying?

DOÑA PAQUITA. Well, shouldn't I? If you could see my mother . . . She insists I've got to love that man. If she only knew what you know, she wouldn't ask the impossible. But she keeps saying he's so good, and rich, and that we'd get along so well . . . She got so angry, she called me a disobedient hussy . . . Poor me! Because I won't lie and I can't pretend, they call me a hussy.

RITA. Please, Miss, you'll worry yourself sick.

DOÑA PAQUITA. Well, you should have heard her. And she says that Don Diego is complaining because I don't say anything to him. I tell him plenty, and I've really tried to act happy with him, which I certainly am not, and laugh and talk nonsense . . . And all just to please my mother, otherwise . . . But the Virgin well knows I don't feel it in my heart. (*Stage slowly darkens.*)

RITA. Now, now, there's still no reason for so much anguish. Who knows? Don't you remember the holiday we took last year at the intendant's country house?

DOÑA PAQUITA. Oh, how can I forget it? But, what were you going to say?

RITA. I was about to say that the gentleman we saw there with the green cross, so gallant and refined . . .

DOÑA PAQUITA. What hedging! Don Felix. What about him?

RITA. And who rode us into town . . .

DOÑA PAQUITA. All right. And then he came back, and I saw him, to my misfortune, many times . . . badly advised by you.

RITA. Why, Miss? Who did we shock? No one suspects anything at the convent. He never came in through the gates, and when he talked to you at night, there was such a great distance between you that you cursed it more than once. But that's not what I was getting at. What I meant to say was that a lover like that one couldn't forget his darling Paquita so quickly. Just see if all the things we read on the sly in novels can hold a candle to what we've seen in him. Remember the three claps we heard between eleven and midnight, and how he played the guitar with such delicacy and expression?

DOÑA PAQUITA. Oh, Rita, I remember it all. I'll remember it as long as I live . . . But he's away . . . and perhaps engaged in some new love affair.

RITA. I can't believe that.

DOÑA PAQUITA. Well, he's a man, and they're all . . .

RITA. What nonsense! Don't fool yourself, Miss. With men and women it's just like Anover melons. There are all kinds; the hard thing is to know how to choose them. Let whoever picks a bad one complain of his bad luck, but don't discredit the goods. Oh, I'll grant you, some men are cheats and liars, but I can't believe that of someone who's given such repeated proofs of constancy and devotion. For three months he courted you under your window and talked to you in the dark, and in all that time, you know very well that we never saw him act immodestly or utter a bold or indecent word.

Doña Paquita. It's true. That's why I loved him so much, and he'll always be in here, here. (*Points to her heart.*) What do you suppose he said when he got my letter? Oh, I can imagine what he said. Bless us! It's a shame. Poor Paquita . . . That's all. Not another word . . . Nothing more.

Rita. No, Miss, he didn't say that.

Doña Paquita. How do you know?

Rita. Never mind, I know. As soon as he read the letter he must have saddled up and come flying to comfort his sweetheart . . . But . . . (*She goes toward* Doña Irene's *room.*)

Doña Paquita. Where are you going?

Rita. I want to see if . . .

Doña Paquita. She's writing.

Rita. She'll have to stop soon. It's getting dark . . . Miss, what I told you is the God's honest truth. Don Felix is in Alcala.

Doña Paquita. What? You're joking.

Rita. There's his room. I just spoke to Calamocha.

Doña Paquita. Really?

Rita. Yes. And he came looking for you to . . .

Doña Paquita. So he loves me! Oh, Rita, aren't you glad we warned him? See what refinement! I wonder if he arrived safely. To ride so many leagues just to see me . . . because I asked him to! How can I thank him enough? Oh, I promise he won't be sorry. I'll be grateful and loving forever.

Rita. I'll go get some lights. I'll try to stay downstairs till they come. I'll see what their plans are, 'cause if they find us here, there'll be a deuce of a scene, with mother, daughter, groom, and suitor. And if we don't really watch our step, we'll end up the losers.

Doña Paquita. You're right. But he has talent and courage, and he'll be able to figure out what's best . . . How will you let me know? I want to see him as soon as he gets here.

Rita. Don't worry, I'll bring him up, and the moment you hear that little dry cough . . . Understand?

Doña Paquita. Yes, I know.

Rita. Now all you have to do is find some excuse. I'll stay

with the old lady; I'll talk to her about all her husbands and about her relatives-in-law, and about the bishop who died at sea . . . Besides, if Don Diego's around . . .

DOÑA PAQUITA. Well, go, and as soon as he gets here . . .

RITA. The very moment.

DOÑA PAQUITA. Don't forget to cough.

RITA. No fear of that.

DOÑA PAQUITA. If you only knew how happy I am!

RITA. You don't have to swear. I believe you.

DOÑA PAQUITA. You remember when he told me he could never forget me, that there were no dangers that could stop him, or hardships he wouldn't face for me?

RITA. Yes, I remember very well.

DOÑA PAQUITA. Ah, you can see he was telling the truth.

(DOÑA PAQUITA *goes to* DOÑA IRENE'S *room;* RITA *exits backstage.*)

ACT II

Stage dark.

Doña Paquita. No one here yet . . . (*goes over to the door upstage and comes back*) I can hardly wait! . . . And my mother keeps telling me I'm a silly goose, and only think of laughing and playing, and don't know what love is . . . Well, maybe I'm still not seventeen, but I know what it is to love, and the tears and worries it brings.

(*Enter* Doña Irene.)

Doña Irene. You left me here alone in the dark.

Doña Paquita. You were finishing your letter, mamma, and I didn't want to disturb you, so I came out here for a little fresh air.

Doña Irene. But what's that girl doing without a light? It takes her a year to get something done. And me, with a temper like gunpowder! (*She sits.*) God's will be done! What about Don Diego? Hasn't he come?

Doña Paquita. I don't think so.

Doña Irene. Well, child, you can depend on what I told you. And you know I hate to repeat things. That gentleman is grieved, and has every right to be.

Doña Paquita. All right, mother, I know. Stop scolding me.

Doña Irene. I'm not scolding, dear, just giving you a piece of advice. Because you don't have sense enough to realize what a blessing walked in our own front door . . . Or how many debts I have—I can't imagine what would become of your poor mother . . . Always in bed one day and up the next . . . Doctors, medicines . . . When I had to plead with that old brute Don Bruno (may God crown him with glory) for as much as twenty or thirty reals for every little packet of colocynth or asafetida pills . . . Mind you, very few girls get a chance for a marriage like yours. I haven't the least doubt we owe all this good fortune to your aunts' prayers, blessed saints that they are, and not to your merits or my efforts . . . What did you say?

261

Doña Paquita. Me? Nothing, mamma.

Doña Irene. You never say a thing. Good Lord, girl! . . . Whenever I mention *that*, you never have a thing to say.

(Rita *enters through the door backstage with candles, and places them on the table.*)

Doña Irene. There you are. I thought you'd take all night.

Rita. I'm late, ma'am, because I had to go and buy the candles. You know how the fumes from the oil-lamp always affect you . . .

Doña Irene. Of course they're very bad for me, especially on top of this headache. I had to take off the camphor plasters; they didn't do a bit of good. These capsules are better. Look, leave a candle here and take the other one to my room, and draw the curtain, so it won't be swarming with mosquitoes.

Rita. Yes, ma'am. (*takes a candle and starts to leave*)

Doña Paquita. (*aside to* Rita). Hasn't he come?

Rita. No, but he will.

Doña Irene. Listen, give that letter over there on the table to the boy downstairs, and tell him to hurry with it to the post office . . . (Rita *goes.*) And you, child, what do you want for supper? Because we'll have to retire early if we're to start out early in the morning.

Doña Paquita. But, mother, the nuns gave me a big lunch . . .

Doña Irene. Never mind. You need some soup to warm your stomach . . . (Rita *enters with a letter in her hand, and keeps starting to go and coming back, as the dialogue indicates.*) Rita, heat up the leftover stew. And make us a couple of bowls of soup. You may bring them as soon as they're ready.

Rita. Anything else?

Doña Irene. No, nothing . . . Oh! Make it very thin, with plenty of broth.

Rita. Yes, I know.

Doña Irene. Rita!

Rita (*aside*). Again! (*to* Doña Irene) What is it?

Doña Irene. Make sure that boy takes the letter at once . . . No, wait; better tell him not to bother. They're such a bunch of drunks, you can't get a single . . . Now, go get Simon and tell him I want him to do me a favor and put it in the mail, understand?

Rita. Yes, ma'am.

Doña Irene. Oh, wait a minute.

RITA (*aside*). Not again.

DOÑA IRENE. Don't be in such a hurry . . . First get the thrush and hang the cage in here, so he won't fall and get hurt . . . (RITA *goes out through the door backstage.*) What a bad night he gave me! Up the whole blessed night singing litanies and masses! I must say it was edifying, but when you're trying to get some sleep!

I wouldn't be surprised if Don Diego had an appointment that detained him. He's always so considerate and punctual! Such a good Christian! So attentive and well spoken! How fine and generous he is! It stands to reason, a person of wealth and means . . . And what a house he has! It fairly sparkles! What linens! What kitchen utensils, and what a pantry, full of everything in Creation! I don't think you've been listening to a word I said.

DOÑA PAQUITA. Yes, mother, I heard you. Only I didn't want to interrupt.

DOÑA IRENE. There you'll be like a fish in water, you'll have birds on the wing, if you want them, and everything your heart could wish for, because he loves you so much, and he's such a God-fearing gentleman . . . But, look, Paquita, this is really growing tiresome. Whenever I mention *that*, you have a habit of never answering a word . . . And that's not the only time, either!

DOÑA PAQUITA. Don't get angry, mamma.

DOÑA IRENE. Why shouldn't I? Do you think I don't have a good idea what's at the bottom of this? Can't you see I know what crazy notions they stuffed in that wild head? God forgive me!

DOÑA PAQUITA. But . . . well, what do you know?

DOÑA IRENE. You think you can fool me, eh? Oh, daughter, I've lived a long time, and I've got too much brains and backside for you to fool me.

DOÑA PAQUITA. (*aside*). I'm lost!

DOÑA IRENE. Without taking her mother into consideration . . . As if she had no right . . . I can assure you that even if it hadn't been for this occasion, I would have had to get you out of the convent anyway. Even if I had to come alone and on foot along the highway, I would have got you out of there . . . Look at how much sense the girl has! Just because she's lived a bit with nuns, she's got it in her head that she'll be a nun, too . . . A lot she knows about it, a lot she . . . People serve God in all walks of life, Paquita, but to please one's mother, to help her, to accompany her and be the comfort of her days, that is the first duty of an obedient daughter . . . You'd better learn that, if you didn't know it before.

Doña Paquita. It's true, mamma . . . But I never thought of abandoning you.

Doña Irene. Yes, as if I didn't know.

Doña Paquita. No, madam, believe me. Your Paquita will never leave her mother, or cause her trouble.

Doña Irene. Do you mean that?

Doña Paquita. Yes, madam. I can't tell a lie.

Doña Irene. Well, child, you know what I've been telling you. You can see for yourself what you'd be losing, and the grief you'd cause me if you didn't do everything right and proper . . . See that you do!

Doña Paquita. (*aside*). Woe is me!

(Don Diego *enters through door backstage and places his hat and cane on the table.*)

Doña Irene. Why so late?

Don Diego. I'd hardly turned the corner when who should I bump into but the rector from Malaga and Dr. Padilla, and they wouldn't let me go till they'd stuffed me full of chocolate and rolls. (*sits near* Doña Irene) But let's talk about you; how are you getting on?

Doña Irene. Fine, thank you.

Don Diego. And Doña Paquita?

Doña Irene. Always talking about her nuns. I've been telling her it's high time she changed her tune, and thought about pleasing her mother and obeying her.

Don Diego. Dash it! So she's still so wrapped up in . . .

Doña Irene. Is it any wonder? They're such children . . . they don't know what they love or hate . . . at such a tender age . . .

Don Diego. No, I beg to disagree. That's just the age when the passions are more energetic and decisive than at ours, when inasmuch as the mind is still weak and imperfect, the impulses of the heart are much more violent . . . (*takes* Doña Paquita *by the hand and seats her next to him*) But really, Doña Paquita, would you like to go back to the convent? The truth, now.

Doña Irene. But if she doesn't . . .

Don Diego. Wait, madam, let her answer for herself.

Doña Paquita. You know what I just told her. God forbid I should cause her any trouble.

Don Diego. But you say that so wistfully, and . . .

DOÑA IRENE. It's only natural . . . Can't you see?

DON IRENE. For God's sake, Doña Irene, keep quiet and stop telling me what's natural. It's only natural for Paquita to be scared stiff, and not to dare to say a word out of turn. But if that's the case, on my life, we'd be in a fine kettle of fish.

DOÑA PAQUITA. No, sir. What madam says, I say, too; exactly. Because whatever she tells me to do, I obey her.

DON DIEGO. *Tells* you, child? In these delicate matters, parents with a grain of sense don't *tell* you. They hint, suggest, and advise. That they do, but they never *tell* you. And who can escape the sad results of what they tell? How often do we see unhappy marriages, monstrous unions brought about only because a foolish father was bold enough to *tell* what he had no right to? How often does some unhappy woman go to an early grave in the confines of a nunnery because her mother or her uncle insisted on giving God what God did not want? No, sir, that won't do. Look, Doña Paquita, I'm not the sort of man to hide my defects. I know that neither my face nor my age are calculated to make anyone fall hopelessly in love; but neither do I think it impossible for a girl of good judgment and breeding to come to love me with that calm, constant love that so closely resembles friendship, the only kind that makes for happy marriages. To achieve this, I didn't go looking for a young lady in one of those families that lives in proper independence. (I say *proper* because I attach no blame to what does not oppose the exercise of virtue.) But who among them would not already be prejudiced in favor of some suitor more tempting than I? And in Madrid. Imagine, in a place like Madrid! Full of these ideas, I thought that perhaps I'd find in you all that I desired.

DOÑA IRENE. And can you believe for a single instant that my daughter . . .

DON DIEGO. I was about to finish, madam, so let me finish. I quite understand, dear Paquita, how much a girl so well inclined as you have probably been influenced by the pious customs you saw practiced in that innocent refuge of virtue and devotion. But if nonetheless your inflamed imagination or unforeseen circumstances have already inspired you to make some more worthy choice, I want you to know that I will never resort to violence. I am sincere: my heart and my tongue never contradict each other. And that's what I ask of you, Paquita: sincerity. The love I bear you must not make you unhappy. Your mother cannot want to do an injustice, and knows very well that no one can be made happy by force. If you do not find me to your liking, if you feel some other little care in your heart, believe me, the slightest dissimulation on your part will make us all profoundly unhappy.

Doña Irene. May I speak, sir?

Don Diego. *She's* the one who must speak, and without a prompter or interpreter.

Doña Irene. When I tell her to.

Don Diego. Well, you can tell her to right now, because it's her turn to answer. I'm supposed to marry her, not you.

Doña Irene. Well, señor Don Diego, I don't think you'll have either one of us! What do you take us for? Her godfather was right, and right plain he wrote me, too, just a few days ago, when I told him about the wedding. And though he hasn't seen her since he held her at the font, he loves her very dearly, and always asks everyone passing through Burgos de Osma how she is, and he's continually sending us keepsakes by mail.

Don Diego. Very well, madam, what did her godfather write? Or rather, what does any of *that* have to do with what we're talking about?

Doña Irene. It's got something to do, all right. And though I do say so myself, I assure you that not even a priest of Antocha could have drawn up a letter any better than the one he sent me about the child's wedding. And he's no professor or bachelor of arts, or anything like that, but just an ordinary individual, a man of cape and sword, as they say, with a wretched little job that barely keeps him alive. But he's very clever, and knows about everything, and it's a real pleasure the way he writes and talks. Nearly the whole letter was in Latin. Just imagine! And very good advice he gave me in it, too, since he must have guessed what's going on.

Don Diego. But, madam, if nothing is going on, and nothing has displeased you . . .

Doña Irene. Well, don't you think I have a right to be displeased when I hear you talk about my daughter in terms that . . . Other loves or attachments! The very idea! Why, if I thought . . . Good God, I'd beat her to death, I would. Answer him, since he wants you to speak, and me not to say a word. Tell him about the sweethearts you left in Madrid when you were twelve, and the ones you acquired in the convent under the care of your blessed aunt. Tell him so he'll calm down and . . .

Don Diego. Madam, I'm calmer than you.

Doña Irene. Answer him!

Doña Paquita. I don't know what to say. If you're going to get angry . . .

Don Diego. No, dear. Your mother's a little excited. But not angry. Of course not. Doña Irene knows how highly I regard her.

Doña Irene. Yes, sir, I know, and I'm exceedingly grateful for all the favors you've done us. For that very reason . . .

Don Diego. Please, let's not speak of gratitude. It's little enough I can do . . . I only want Doña Paquita to be happy.

Doña Irene. Of course she is! Answer him!

Doña Paquita. Yes, sir, I am.

Don Diego. And the change that has come into your life isn't causing you the least sorrow or regret?

Doña Irene. No, sir, on the contrary . . . It would be hard to imagine a wedding more to everyone's liking.

Don Diego. If that's the case, I can assure her that she'll have no reason to repent later. In our company she will be loved and adored, and I trust that by dint of favors I shall deserve her friendship and esteem.

Doña Paquita. Thank you, sir. A poor, destitute orphan like me!

Don Diego. But with such admirable qualities, that they make you worthy of even greater fortune.

Doña Irene. Come here, come on now . . . Over here, Paquita.

Doña Paquita. *Mamma!* (*She gets up, hugs her mother, and they embrace.*)

Doña Irene. See how much I love you?

Doña Paquita. Yes, madam.

Doña Irene. And how much I look out for your interests, and want only to see you settled before I die?

Doña Paquita. Oh, I know.

Doña Irene. My little baby! Will you be good?

Doña Paquita. Yes, madam.

Doña Irene. Oh, you can never know how much your mother loves you!

Doña Paquita. Well, don't I love you, too?

Don Diego. Now, now, we'd better go. (Don Diego *gets up, followed by* Doña Irene.) Or else someone will come and find the three of us bawling like three schoolchildren.

Doña Irene. Yes, you're quite right.

(Don Diego *and* Doña Irene *go to* Doña Irene's *room.* Doña Paquita *is about to follow them, but is stopped by* Rita, *who enters through the door backstage.*)

Rita. Señorita . . . Hey! Psst! Señorita!

Doña Paquita. What is it?

Rita. He's here!

Doña Paquita. What?

Rita. He just got here. I gave him a hug for you, and he's coming up the stairs.

Doña Paquita. Goodness, what will I do?

Rita. A fine question! Look, the important thing is not to waste time billing and cooing. Get down to business. And use your head. Don't forget, this is no place for long conversations. Ah, here he is.

Doña Paquita. Yes, it's he.

Rita. I'll keep an eye on those folks. Steady, Miss, be firm. (Rita *goes to* Doña Irene's *room.*)

Dona Paquita. No, no, I'll go, too. But he doesn't deserve that.

(Don Carlos *enters by the door upstage.*)

Don Carlos. Paquita, my love, I'm here! How goes it, my beauty, how goes it?

Doña Paquita. Welcome.

Don Carlos. Why so sad? Don't I deserve a smile?

Doña Paquita. Of course. But so much has been happening that I'm beside myself. You know. Yes, but if you only knew. After I wrote that letter, they came for me. Tomorrow we're going to Madrid . . . My mother is in there.

Don Carlos. In where?

Doña Paquita. There, in that room. (*points to* Doña Irene's *room*)

Don Carlos. Alone?

Doña Paquita. No, sir.

Don Carlos. I'll bet she's with the husband-to-be. (*He goes toward the door, stops, and comes back.*) So much the better . . . But isn't anyone else with her?

Doña Paquita. No one. They're alone. What are you thinking of?

Don Carlos. If I gave way to the passion which your eyes

inspire in me, I'd do something rash . . . But there's time . . . Then, too, he must be a gentleman, and it would not be right to insult him for loving a woman so worthy of being loved. I don't know your mother, or . . . Well, nothing can be done now. Your honor deserves attention first.

Doña Paquita. She's very determined for me to marry him.

Don Carlos. Don't worry about it.

Doña Paquita. She wants the wedding to take place as soon as we get to Madrid.

Don Carlos. What? No, not that.

Doña Paquita. They're both agreed, and they say . . .

Don Carlos. Well, let them talk. But there won't be any.

Doña Paquita. That's all my mother talks about. She threatens me, she scares me half to death . . . He urges me, too, and offers me so many things, he . . .

Don Carlos. And you, what hope do you give him? Did you promise to love him dearly?

Doña Paquita. Ingrate! Don't you know . . . Ingrate!

Don Carlos. Don't think I don't know, Paquita . . . I was your first love.

Doña Paquita. And my last.

Don Carlos. And I'd rather lose my life than my place in your heart. It's all mine, isn't it? (*takes her hands in his*)

Doña Paquita. Well, whose should it be?

Don Carlos. You lovely creature! What sweet hope drives me on! A single word from those lips of yours assures me . . . It gives me courage to face everything . . . Yes, I'm here. Did you call me to defend you, free you, and live up to a promise we made a thousand times a thousand times over? Well, that's just what I've come for. If you go to Madrid tomorrow, I shall go, too. Your mother shall know who I am. There I can rely on the favor of a respectable and virtuous old man who is my uncle, but whom I prefer to call father and friend. He has no relative nearer or dearer than me; he is a very rich man, and if worldly goods have an attraction for you, that circumstance might add happiness to our union.

Doña Paquita. What do I care for all the wealth in the world?

Don Carlos. I know. Ambition cannot trouble such an innocent soul.

Doña Paquita. To love and be loved . . . I can wish for nothing more, and know no greater fortune.

Don Carlos. There is none. But you must calm yourself, and trust that luck will change our present affliction into lasting happiness.

Doña Paquita. And what can I do to spare my mother from suffering? She loves me so much! I've just been telling her I would never displease her or leave her; that I'll always be good and obedient . . . And she embraced me so tenderly! She was so comforted by the few words I managed to say. I don't know; I simply don't know what way you can find out of this trouble.

Don Carlos. I'll find one. Don't you have confidence in me?

Doña Paquita. What a question! Do you think I'd be alive if that hope didn't drive me on? Alone and a stranger to everyone, what could I do? If you hadn't come, my grief would have killed me, with no one to turn to, and no one to tell the reason for it . . . But you have acted like a gentleman and a suitor; your coming gave me the greatest proof of how much you love me. (*She is touched, and bursts into tears.*)

Don Carlos. What weeping! Ah, those tears are irresistible. Yes, Paquita, I love you enough to defend you against all who, wish to oppress you. Who can oppose a favored suitor? There's nothing to fear.

Doña Paquita. Is it possible?

Don Carlos. Nothing. Love has united our souls in tender bonds, and only death can break them.

Rita (*entering*). Inside, Miss. Your mother's been asking for you. I'll fetch supper, and then everyone goes straight to bed. And you, sir gallant, you can make yourself scarce.

Don Carlos. Yes, it's best not to arouse suspicion . . . I have nothing to add.

Doña Paquita. Nor do I.

Don Carlos. Till tomorrow, then. At daybreak we'll see our happy rival.

Rita. A very worthy gentleman, very rich and very wise. With his long waistcoat, his clean stiff shirt, and his sixty years under his wig. (*goes out through door upstage*)

Doña Paquita. Until tomorrow.

Don Carlos. Goodbye, Paquita.

Doña Paquita. Go to bed, and rest.

Don Carlos. Rest, when jealous?

Doña Paquita. Jealous of whom?

DON CARLOS. Good night. Sleep well, Paquita.

DOÑA PAQUITA. Sleep, when love . . . ?

DON CARLOS. Goodbye, my darling.

DOÑA PAQUITA. Goodbye. (*enters* DOÑA IRENE'S *room*)

DON CARLOS. Take her away from me! (*pacing up and down*) No, whoever he is, he won't take her away from me. Nor will her mother be unwise enough to insist on a marriage her daughter objects to, while I . . . But sixty! Of course he must be very rich. Money! A curse on money, the root of so many evils.

CALAMOCHA. Well, sir (*enters through door upstage*), we've got half a roast kid, and . . . at least it looks like kid. And a fine watercress salad, without any wolfsbane or other strange materials, well washed, drained, and seasoned by these sinning hands, as good as you could ask for. Bread from Meco, and wine from Tercia. So if we've got to eat and drink, we might as well . . .

DON CARLOS. Let's go. And where might that be?

CALAMOCHA. Down below. I fixed up a narrow, shaky table, that looks like a blacksmith's bench.

RITA. Who wants soup? (*comes in the door upstage with several dishes, a cup, a ladle, and a napkin*)

DON CARLOS. Eat hearty.

CALAMOCHA. If there's some pretty girl who'd like roast kid for supper, let her raise her finger.

RITA. Some pretty girl's already eaten half a potful of meatballs . . . But thank you, Mister Soldier. (*goes into* DOÑA IRENE'S *room*)

CALAMOCHA. I like you so appreciative, sweetheart!

DON CARLOS. Ready?

CALAMOCHA. Ay, ay, ay! (CALAMOCHA *heads for door upstage, and returns; he and* DON CARLOS *talk quietly until* CALAMOCHA *goes over to greet* SIMON.) Hey, Pssst!

DON CARLOS. What?

CALAMOCHA. Look who's coming.

DON CARLOS. Is it Simon?

CALAMOCHA. Big as life. Who the devil . . . ?

DON CARLOS. What are we going to do?

CALAMOCHA. How should I know? Pump him, lie, and . . . Do you give me permission?

DON CARLOS. Yes, lie as much as you like. What do you suppose brings that fellow here?

(SIMON *enters by door upstage.*)

CALAMOCHA. Hey, Simon, what are you doing here?

SIMON. Hi, Calamocha! How are things?

CALAMOCHA. Just fine.

SIMON. I'm so glad to . . .

DON CARLOS. Man alive, you in Alcala! Well, what's the good news?

SIMON. Oh, that you're here, sir! By all the saints!

DON CARLOS. How's my uncle?

SIMON. Same as usual.

CALAMOCHA. Did he stay in Madrid, or . . .

SIMON. Who would have told me? What a coincidence . . . It never would have occurred to me . . . And you . . . better-looking than ever! So you're going to see your uncle, eh?

CALAMOCHA. You must have come on some errand for the old gentleman.

SIMON. What a hot trip, and how dusty the road was. Whew, whew!

CALAMOCHA. Doing some collecting, maybe, hmmm?

DON CARLOS. Could be. Since my uncle has that piece of property at Ajalvar. Is that why you're here? And what a rotten sneak that agent turned out to be! You won't find a wickeder, more rascally farmer in all the country . . . So you're just coming from Saragossa?

DON CARLOS. Well . . . You ought to know.

SIMON. Or are you on your way there?

DON CARLOS. Where?

SIMON. To Saragossa. Isn't his regiment there?

CALAMOCHA. But, man alive, if we left Madrid last summer, wouldn't we have made more than four leagues by now?

SIMON. How should I know? Some go by the post, and take more than four months to get here. It must be a very bad road.

CALAMOCHA (*aside, stepping away from* SIMON). Damn you and your road, and the wench that gave you suck!

DON CARLOS. But you still haven't told me if my uncle's in Madrid or Alcala, or why you're here, or . . .

SIMON. I'm coming to that. Yes, sir, I'll tell you . . . Well, then . . . Well, the master told me . . .

DON DIEGO (*from within*). No, never mind. There's light here. Good night, Rita. (DON CARLOS *gets flustered and moves to one side of the stage.*)

DON CARLOS. My uncle!

(DON DIEGO *enters on his way from* DOÑA IRENE'S

room to his own; he notices Don Carlos *and comes toward him.* Simon *lights his way, and puts the light back on the table.*)

Don Diego. Simon!

Simon. Here I am, sir!

Don Carlos (*aside*). All is lost!

Don Diego. Well now, who is it?

Simon. A friend of yours, sir.

Don Carlos. I'm dead!

Don Diego. What do you mean, "friend?" What? Bring that light closer.

Don Carlos. Uncle! (*makes a move to kiss the hand of* Don Diego, *who pushes him away angrily*)

Don Diego. Get out of here!

Don Carlos. Sir?

Don Diego. Get out . . . I don't know why I don't . . . What are you doing here?

Don Carlos. If you upset yourself, and . . .

Don Diego. What are you doing here?

Don Carlos. My misfortune brought me.

Don Diego. Always giving me cause for sorrow, always! But (*approaching* Don Carlos) what did you say? Is there really some misfortune? Well, what's been happening to you? Why are you here?

Calamocha. Because he's loyal to you, and loves you, and . . .

Don Diego. I didn't ask *you!* Why did you come to Saragossa without letting me know? Why are you so frightened to see me? You've done something. Yes, you've been up to some sort of mischief that will be the death of your poor uncle . . .

Don Carlos. No, sir, I'll never forget the principles of wisdom and honor with which you inspired me so often.

Don Diego. Well, why did you come? Was it a duel? Was it debts? Was it some quarrel with your superiors? Relieve me of this worry, Carlos . . . Relieve me of this anxiety, my boy.

Calamocha. Why, the whole thing is no more than . . .

Don Diego. I told you to keep quiet. Come here. (*takes* Carlos *by the hand to one side of the stage and speaks to him in a low voice*) Tell me what it was.

Don Carlos. An indiscretion, a lack of submission to you. First, coming to Madrid without asking your permission. I'm really sorry, considering how worried you were when you saw me.

DON DIEGO. And what else is there?

DON CARLOS. Nothing else, sir.

DON DIEGO. Then what was the misfortune you spoke of?

DON CARLOS. None. That of finding you in this place . . . and of having displeased you so much when I was hoping to surprise you in Madrid, stay with you for a few weeks, and return happy because I had seen you.

DON DIEGO. Isn't there more?

DON CARLOS. No, sir.

DON DIEGO. Think hard.

DON CARLOS. No, sir. Just that. Nothing more.

DON DIEGO. But you don't mean to tell me . . . Such escapades can't . . . No, sir. How can an officer be allowed to come and go when he pleases, and desert his post like that? If such examples were followed, discipline would vanish. Well, it's got to stop.

DON CARLOS. But, look, uncle, this is peacetime, and Saragossa doesn't need to be watched all the time, like some places where the garrison is never relieved. And besides, I want you to know that this journey was authorized with the full approval of my superiors; that I, too, have some regard for my good name; and that when I came, I made sure I was not needed.

DON DIEGO. An officer is always needed by his men. The King keeps him there to instruct them, protect them, and give them an example of subordination, valor, and virtue.

DON CARLOS. Very well. But I told you the reasons why . . .

DON DIEGO. Your reasons aren't worth a damn. Because he felt like seeing his uncle! What your uncle wants from you is not to see you every weekend, but to know that you're a sensible man and fulfill your obligations. That's what he wants. But (*raises his voice and paces the floor nervously*) I'll take steps to see that these pranks are not repeated. What you must do now is leave at once.

DON CARLOS. Sir, if I . . .

DON DIEGO. There's no other way. And right now. You can't sleep here.

CALAMOCHA. But the horses aren't ready to travel . . . They can't even move.

DON DIEGO. Then take these. (*to* CALAMOCHA) And take the bags to the inn outside the walls. (*to* DON CARLOS) You can't sleep here . . . Let's go. (*to* CALAMOCHA) And you, smart aleck, bestir yourself. Take everything downstairs.

Pay the bill, get out the horses, and go . . . (*to* SIMON) You help him . . . How much do you have?

SIMON. Maybe four to six *onzas*. (*takes some gold coins out of a pocket and gives them to* DON DIEGO)

DON DIEGO. Give them here. Well, what are you waiting for? (*to* CALAMOCHA) Didn't you hear me say at once? Step lively! (*to* SIMON) And you, go with him, help him, and don't leave until they're gone.

(*The two servants go into* DON CARLOS' *room.*)

DON DIEGO. Here. (*gives him the money*) This will cover the cost of the journey. You know that when I arrange matters this way, I know what I'm doing. Don't you realize it's all for your own good, and that what you did was a piece of folly? But you mustn't worry about it, or think it's a lack of affection . . . You know that I've always loved you, and that if you behave right, you will find me now as ever your staunchest friend.

DON CARLOS. I know.

DON DIEGO. All right, then, do as I tell you.

DON CARLOS. I'll do it without fail.

DON DIEGO. Go to the inn outside the walls. (*to the two servants, who carry out the bags from* DON DIEGO'S *room and exit through the door upstage*) There you can sleep while the horses eat and rest. And don't come back here or go into town for any reason. Watch your step. And at about three or four o'clock, leave the place. Remember, I'll know just when you leave. Understand?

DON CARLOS. Yes, sir.

DON DIEGO. See that you do.

DON CARLOS. Yes, sir; I'll do as you say.

DON DIEGO. Very well. Goodbye, Carlos. I forgive you for everything. Go with God. And I'll know when you get to Saragossa, too; don't think I'm unaware of what you did last time.

DON CARLOS. But what did I do?

DON DIEGO. If I tell you that I know, and I forgive you, what more do you want? There's no time to discuss that now. Go!

DON CARLOS. Stay with God. (*makes a move to go, but comes back.*)

DON DIEGO. Without kissing your uncle's hand, eh?

DON CARLOS. I didn't dare. (*kisses* DON DIEGO'S *hand*)

DON DIEGO. And give me a hug, in case we don't see each other again. (*They embrace.*)

DON CARLOS. What did you say? God forbid!

Don Diego. Who knows, my boy? Do you have some debts? Is there anything you need?

Don Carlos. No, sir, not now.

Don Diego. It's a wonder, when you always spend so freely. And count on your uncle's purse . . . Well, then, I'll write to señor Aznar and tell him to give you a hundred doubloons on my account. And be careful how you spend them. Do you gamble?

Don Carlos. No, sir. Never in my life.

Don Diego. See that you don't. So, pleasant journey. And don't get overheated: easy day stages and nothing more . . . Are you going away happy?

Don Carlos. No, sir. Because you love me so much, and overwhelm me with kindness, and I reward you ill.

Don Diego. Let's not speak of the past.

Don Carlos. Are you still mad at me?

Don Diego. No, of course not. I was very displeased, but that's all over. Don't cause me any more trouble. (*Places both hands on his nephew's shoulders.*) Conduct yourself like an officer.

Don Carlos. Have no fear of that.

Don Diego. And a gentleman.

Don Carlos. I promise.

Don Diego. Goodbye, Carlos. (*They embrace.*)

Don Carlos (*aside, as he exits rear*). I must leave her! And lose her forever!

Don Diego (*alone*). That was a bit too easy. But he'll know soon enough, when it's time. Only it isn't the same writing him as . . . After it's done, it won't matter. But always such respect for his uncle! He's as gentle as a lamb. (*He wipes away a few tears, takes a candle, and goes to his room. For a moment the stage remains empty and dark.*)

(*Doña Paquita and Rita enter from Doña Irene's room. Rita holds a light, which she places on the table.*)

Rita. It's awfully quiet around here.

Doña Paquita. They must have gone to bed. They're probably exhausted.

Rita. They sure looked it.

Doña Paquita. What a long ride!

Rita. And all for love!

Doña Paquita. You can say that again. My love . . . What wouldn't I do for him?

Rita. Just wait a while, this isn't the last miracle. When we get to Madrid, you'll see fireworks. Poor Don Diego. How disappointed he'll be! But then again, what a fine gentleman. It's certainly a pity.

Doña Paquita. There's the rub. If he were a man to be despised, my mother would never have arranged the match, nor would I have to hide my repugnance. But times have changed, Rita. Don Felix has come, and now I'm not afraid of anyone. My fate is in his hands, and I'm the happiest of women.

Rita. Oh, now that I think of it . . . She was pretty positive about it, too. Of course, with all these love affairs, my head simply . . . I'll get it! (*heads for* Doña Irene's *room*)

Doña Paquita. What?

Rita. The thrush. I forgot all about him.

Doña Paquita. Yes, get him, or he'll start praying again like last night. I put him near the window. Careful, don't wake mamma.

Rita. Listen to those hoofbeats down there . . . Until we get to our Wolf Street, number seven, second story, there's no use thinking of sleep. And this damn gate that squeaks till . . .

Doña Paquita. Here, you take the candle.

Rita. Never mind, I know where it is. (*goes to* Doña Irene's *room*)

(Simon *enters through the door upstage.*)

Doña Paquita. I thought you'd gone to bed.

Simon. The master's probably performed that necessary act by now, but I still don't know where I'm supposed to set up camp . . . Or whether I'll get much sleep, either.

Doña Paquita. Who just came?

Simon. Nobody. Some folks were here but they've already gone.

Doña Paquita. The mule drivers?

Simon. No, Miss. An officer and a servant of his. I think they were bound for Saragossa.

Doña Paquita. Who did you say?

Simon. A lieutenant colonel and his orderly.

Doña Paquita. They were here?

Simon. Yes, Miss, here in this room.

Doña Paquita. I haven't seen them.

Simon. It seems they arrived this evening and . . . Apparently they must have attended to whatever business they had . . . So they left. Good night, Miss. (*goes to* Don Diego's *room*)

Doña Paquita. Merciful heavens! What's this? Oh no, it can't be. (*sits in a chair next to the table*)

RITA (*entering*). This will be the death of me. (*takes cage and puts it on the table: opens the door of* DON CARLOS' *room, and comes back*)

DOÑA PAQUITA. Oh, it's true! Did you know . . . ?

RITA. Wait. I still can't believe my eyes. But they're gone . . . bag and baggage, clothes, and . . . But how could I be so blind? When I saw them leave myself.

DOÑA PAQUITA. You're sure?

RITA. Yes, Miss. Both of them.

DOÑA PAQUITA. But did they go outside the town?

RITA. I didn't lose sight of them till they left the Martyr's Gate. It's only a few steps from here.

DOÑA PAQUITA. And is that the road to Aragon?

RITA. It is.

DOÑA PAQUITA. Unworthy! An unworthy man!

RITA. Señorita!

DOÑA PAQUITA. How did this unhappy girl offend you?

RITA. I'm trembling all over. But . . . I can't understand it . . . Why should he make such a sudden change in plans?

DOÑA PAQUITA. Well, didn't I love him more than my life? Didn't he see me mad with love?

RITA. I don't know what to say when I consider such an infamous act.

DOÑA PAQUITA. What can you say? That he never loved me, that he's not a gentleman, that he came for this? To deceive me, to desert me this way! (*rises, and* RITA *sustains her*)

RITA. To think that he came for some other purpose doesn't seem to make sense. Jealousy . . . why should he be jealous? And even if he was, that would make him love her more . . . He's not a coward, and it can't be said he was afraid of his rival.

DOÑA PAQUITA. You'll wear yourself out in vain. Say he's false, say he's a monster of cruelty, and you've said it all.

RITA. Let's get out of here. Somebody might come, and . . .

DOÑA PAQUITA. Yes, let's go. And let's have a good cry. Look at the situation he left me in! Isn't that wicked?

RITA. Yes, Miss. Indeed it is.

DOÑA PAQUITA. How good he was at pretending. And with whom? With me! Did I deserve to be so treacherously deceived? Did my love deserve this reward? Merciful God! What is it, what have I done? (RITA *takes the candle and both go to* DOÑA PAQUITA'S *room.*)

ACT III

Stage dark. On the table, a candlestick with a dimly lit candle and the birdcage. SIMON *is asleep, sprawled out on the bench.* DON DIEGO *enters from his room putting on his robe.*

DON DIEGO. Here, at least, if I can't get to sleep, I won't melt . . . You know, if a bedroom like that would just not . . . Whew, what a snore! We'll have to sit up and watch him till dawn. It won't be long now. (SIMON *awakens, and hearing* DON DIEGO, *sits up and rises.*) What ails you? Mind you don't fall.

SIMON. What, are you here, sir?

DON DIEGO. Yes, I came out here. You can't get a wink of sleep in there.

SIMON. Well I, thank God, though the bed's pretty hard, I slept like an emperor.

DON DIEGO. Poor comparison! Say you slept like a poor man; without money, ambition, troubles, or remorse.

SIMON. As a matter of fact, you're right . . . What time do you suppose it is?

DON DIEGO. San Justo's clock rang a minute ago, and if I didn't count wrong, it struck three.

SIMON. Oh! By this time our gentlemen must be galloping down the road with sparks flying.

DON DIEGO. Yes, I'm pretty sure they're gone. He promised he would, and I trust he will.

SIMON. You should have seen how bad he felt when I left him! And how sad he was!

DON DIEGO. It couldn't be helped.

SIMON. I know.

DON DIEGO. Can you imagine a more untimely arrival?

SIMON. It's true. Without your permission, without letting you know, without there being an urgent reason . . . Well, he acted very badly. Though on the other hand, he has enough good qualities so that one could forgive him this

279

one indiscretion. I mean . . . I don't think the punishment will go any further, will it?

DON DIEGO. No, indeed! No, sir. It's one thing to make him go back . . . You can see what a position we were in . . . I'll admit that when he left, I felt a lump in my throat. (*Sound of hands clapping three times in the distance, and soon after, the strumming of a guitar.*) What's that I hear?

SIMON. I don't know. People walking down the street. Maybe farmers.

DON DIEGO. Quiet.

SIMON. Looks like we'll have some music.

DON DIEGO. Yes, if they can play.

SIMON. What unhappy lover do you suppose would be serenading at this time of night in this filthy alley? I'll bet someone has a crush on the maid at the inn—the one who looks like a monkey.

DON DIEGO. Maybe so.

SIMON. They're starting. Listen. (*A sonata is played from within.*) Well, I must say, that rogue of a barber plays very well.

DON DIEGO. No, no barber could play that, however well he shaves.

SIMON. Shall we peek out a little and see?

DON DIEGO. No, leave them alone. Poor folks! Who knows what importance they give to such music! I don't like to embarrass anybody. (DOÑA PAQUITA *and* RITA *leave their room and go to the window.* DON DIEGO *and* SIMON *retire to one side, and watch.*)

SIMON. Sir! . . . Psst! . . . Quick, stand aside.

DON DIEGO. What is it?

SIMON. They've opened the door to that bedroom. It smells of skirts, and no mistake.

DON DIEGO. It does? Let's go before they see us.

(DOÑA PAQUITA *enters with* RITA.)

RITA. Careful, Miss!

DOÑA PAQUITA. Follow the wall, right? (*Guitar playing resumes.*)

RITA. Yes, madam . . . They're playing again . . . Shhh.

DOÑA PAQUITA. Wait. Let's find out first if it's he.

RITA. Of course it is. Signals don't lie.

DOÑA PAQUITA. Shh. Yes, it's he. Goodness! (RITA *goes to the window, opens the sash, and claps three times. The music stops.*) Hurry, answer. Oh joy, my heart! It's he.

SIMON. Hear that?

Don Diego. Yes.

Simon. What do you suppose it means?

Don Diego. Quiet.

Doña Paquita (*leans out the window.* Rita *remains behind her. The dots indicate more or less lengthy pauses*). —Here I am . . . And what was I to think, seeing what you'd just done . . . What flight is this? (*turns away from the window, then looks out again*) (He. For Heaven's sake, be careful, and if you hear any noise, warn me right away . . .) Forever? Woe is me! All right, throw it . . . But I don't quite understand . . . Ay, Don Felix! I've never seen you so timid! (*A letter is thrown from inside the scenes. It falls from the window onto the stage.* Doña Paquita *starts to look for it, and not finding it, leans out again*.) No, I didn't find it; but it must be here . . . And must I wait until daybreak for you to tell me why you left me here dying? . . . Yes, I want to hear it from your own lips. Your Paquita demands it . . . And how do you think mine is? . . . There's no room in my breast for it . . . Tell me. (Simon *takes a few steps forward, stumbles on the birdcage, and lets it fall.*)

Rita. Let's get out of here, Miss . . . Quick, someone's coming.

Doña Paquita. Oh, dear . . . Guide me.

Rita. Let's go. (Rita *stumbles against* Simon. *The two girls hurry to* Doña Paquita's *room*) Alas!

Doña Paquita. I'm dead.   (*They leave.*)

Don Diego. What was that scream?

Simon. One of the lady ghosts, who bumped into me in retreat.

Don Diego. Come over to this window, and see if you can find a note on the floor . . . What a pickle!

Simon (*groping along the floor, near the window*). Can't find a thing, sir.

Don Diego. Look carefully. It must be there.

Simon. Did they throw it in from the street?

Don Diego. Yes . . . What lover is this? Only sixteen and brought up in a convent! All my illusions have vanished.

Simon. Here it is. (*finds the letter, and gives it to* Don Diego)

Don Diego. Go downstairs and light a candle . . . There must be a lantern in the stable or the kitchen . . . And come back with it at once.   (Simon *exits backstage.*)

Don Diego. And whom should I blame? (*leaning over*

the back of a chair) Is she the guilty party? Or is it her mother, her aunts, or me? On whom . . . on whom must I vent this rage, which, however much I try, I cannot repress? Nature made her so lovely in my eyes! What sweet hopes I cherished! What happiness she promised . . . What? Am I jealous? What an age to be jealous! It's a shame . . . But this anxiety I feel, this indignation, these desires for vengeance—where do they come from? What shall I call them? On the other hand, it seems that . . . (*hears noise from* DoÑA PAQUITA's *room, and hides at one end of the stage*) Yes.

RITA (*entering*). They're gone now. (*watches, listens, then leans out and looks for the letter on the floor*) That letter may be very well written, but so help me God, señor Don Felix is a great big rascal . . . Poor little darling! . . . It will just about kill her . . . Nothing, not even dogs on the street . . . I wish we'd never met him! Where is that confounded paper? We're really in hot water if it doesn't turn up . . . Wonder what it says? . . . Lies, lies, all lies.

(*Enter* DON DIEGO *with lantern.* RITA *is startled.*)

RITA. I'm lost!

DON DIEGO (*coming closer*). Rita! Is that you?

RITA. Yes, sir, because . . .

DON DIEGO. What are you looking for at this time of night?

RITA. I was looking . . . I'll tell you . . . Because we heard such an awful racket . . .

SIMON (*returning*). You did, eh?

RITA. We sure did . . . A racket and . . . and just look. (*picks up the cage, which i on the floor*) Guess it was the birdcage. Well, it *was* the cage, there's no doubt about it. Good God! I wonder if he's been killed. No, he's alive, see?

SIMON. Must have been some cat, to be sure.

RITA. Poor birdie. Look how scared he is!

SIMON. He has good reason to be . . . Don't you think, if the cat got hold of him?

RITA. He'd have gulped him down. (*Hangs the cage on a nail.*)

SIMON. Without any pepper sauce . . . feathers and all.

DON DIEGO. Bring me that light.

RITA. Oh, let it be. We'll light this one. (*lights the candle on the table*) What with all the sleep we got . . .

DON DIEGO. And Doña Paquita?

RITA. Fast asleep, sir.

SIMON. It's a wonder, with the thrush making all that racket . . .

DON DIEGO. Come on. (*Goes to his room.* SIMON *follows him, taking one of the candles.*)

DOÑA PAQUITA (*coming from her room*). Have you found that note yet?

RITA. No, Miss.

DOÑA PAQUITA. Were they both here when you went out?

RITA. I don't know. But I do know that the servant went and got a light, and all of a sudden there I was, as if by magic, between him and his master, without a chance of escape or any excuse to give them. (*Takes the light, and looks again near the window.*)

DOÑA PAQUITA. They must have been here when I spoke from the window. Is it there?

RITA. I can't find it, Miss.

DONA PAQUITA. They must have it. Don't wear yourself out. That's all I need to make my misery complete . . . Stop looking. They have it.

RITA. Here, at least . . .

DOÑA PAQUITA. It's enough to drive you crazy! (*sinks into a chair*)

RITA. And him, not explaining himself, or saying a word . . .

DOÑA PAQUITA. He was about to, when you warned me, and we had to get away . . . I can't tell you how fearful and nervous he was. He told me that the letter would explain why he had to return, and that he had written it intending to put it into the hands of a trustworthy person who would give it to me, assuming it would be impossible to see me. All excuses, Rita, trumped up by a deceitful man who made promises he never meant to keep . . . He came, found a rival, and must have said: Well, why should I bother anyone or become the defender of a woman? There are so many women! Let them marry her off . . . I have nothing to lose . . . My peace of mind is worth more than the life of that unhappy girl. Oh Lord, forgive me! Forgive me for loving him so much!

RITA. Oh, Miss! (*looking toward* DON DIEGO's *room*) They seem to be going.

DOÑA PAQUITA. Never mind, leave me.

RITA. What if Don Diego sees you this way?

DOÑA PAQUITA. If everything is lost, what's there to be afraid of? I don't have the strength to move . . . Let them come. Nothing matters any more.

(DON DIEGO *enters with* SIMON.)

SIMON. I understand perfectly; say no more.

DON DIEGO. And listen, have *El Moro* saddled first thing on your way. If they're out, come back and get the horse, and with a fast trot you can overtake them. (*sees* DOÑA PA-QUITA *and* RITA) Both of them here, eh? Hurry now, there's not a moment to lose.

SIMON. I'm flying!   (*Exits rear.*)

DON DIEGO. You're up very early, Doña Paquita.

DOÑA PAQUITA. Yes, sir.

DON DIEGO. Has Doña Irene called yet?

DOÑA PAQUITA. No, sir . . . (*to* RITA) Better go in and see if she's awake and wants to get dressed.

(RITA *goes to* DOÑA IRENE's *room.*)

DON DIEGO. Did you sleep well?

DOÑA PAQUITA. No, sir. Did you?

DON DIEGO. No, I didn't either.

DOÑA PAQUITA. It's been too hot.

DON DIEGO. Do you feel indisposed?

DOÑA PAQUITA. A little.

DON DIEGO. What's wrong? (*sits beside* DOÑA PAQUITA)

DOÑA PAQUITA. Nothing. Just a little . . . nothing . . . It's really nothing.

DON DIEGO. It must be something. You look so downcast, so tearful, and worried. What's the matter, Paquita? Don't you know I love you dearly?

DOÑA PAQUITA. Yes, sir.

DON DIEGO. Then why don't you confide in me more? Don't you know I get the greatest pleasure out of finding ways to please you?

DOÑA PAQUITA. I know.

DON DIEGO. Then why, when you know you have a friend, won't you open your heart to him?

DOÑA PAQUITA. Because that very thing compels me to be silent.

DON DIEGO. That means that perhaps I am the cause of your trouble.

DOÑA PAQUITA. No, sir, you have in no way offended me . . . It's not you I have to complain of.

DON DIEGO. Then who is it, my child? Here, now. (*comes closer*) For once at least let's speak plainly and frankly. Tell me, isn't it true that you look on this proposed marriage with something akin to repugnance? What would you wager that if you were entirely free to choose, you wouldn't marry me?

Doña Paquita. Or anyone else.

Don Diego. Is it possible that you don't know someone more lovable than me, who loves you, and requites your love as you deserve?

Doña Paquita. No, sir. No.

Don Diego. Are you very sure?

Doña Paquita. Didn't I just tell you?

Don Diego. Then am I to believe perchance that you still have such a longing for that refuge where you spent your childhood, that you would prefer the austerity of a convent to a life more . . . ?

Doña Paquita. Not at all. No, sir . . . It never entered my mind.

Don Diego. All right, I won't insist. But in all you've just told me, there's a most serious contradiction. It seems you don't feel disposed to convent life. You assure me that you have no complaint to make of me, that you are persuaded of my great esteem for you, that you have not thought of marrying anyone else, that I ought not to suspect that anyone will dispute your love with me. Then why these tears? What is the cause of that deep sadness which in so short a time has altered your appearance to such an extent that I hardly know you? Are they signs that you love only me, that you will gladly marry me in just a few days? Is this the way love and happiness announce themselves?

(*The stage lights up gradually, as if by approaching dawn.*)

Doña Paquita. And what reasons have I given you for such a lack of trust?

Don Diego. What reasons? Why, if I make light of all these considerations, if I hasten the preparations for the wedding, if your mother continues her approval, and things reach a point . . .

Doña Paquita. I'll do what my mother tells me, and marry you.

Don Diego. And afterwards, Paquita?

Doña Paquita. Afterwards . . . So long as I live, I'll be an honest woman.

Don Diego. I don't doubt that in the least. But if you look on me as the one who is to be your friend and companion till death do us part, tell me: don't those titles give me some right to expect more confidence from you? Can't I induce you to tell me the reason for your grief? Not to satisfy my idle curiosity, but' to give myself wholly to the task of consoling you, of improving your luck, of making you happy, if my efforts and zeal can accomplish so much.

DOÑA PAQUITA. Happiness for me . . . That's all over.

DON DIEGO. Why?

DOÑA PAQUITA. I'll never say why.

DON DIEGO. But, what stubborn, foolish silence! When you yourself might at least surmise that I'm not unaware of how things stand.

DOÑA PAQUITA. If you don't know, señor Don Diego, for Heaven's sake don't pretend you do; and if you really know, don't ask me.

DON DIEGO. All right. Seeing there's nothing to say: this sorrow and these tears are a joke; today we'll reach Madrid; and in a week you'll be my wife.

DOÑA PAQUITA. And please my mother.

DON DIEGO. And live unhappily ever after.

DOÑA PAQUITA. I know.

DON DIEGO. These are the fruits of education. This is what we call bringing up a girl right: teaching her to belie and hide the most innocent passions with perfidious dissimulation. They are judged honest as soon as they become expert in the art of silence and lying. We insist that temperament, age, or disposition must not affect their inclinations in the least; that their will must be bent to the caprice of those who guide them. They may do anything, except be sincere. As long as they don't say what they feel, as long as they pretend to hate what they most desire, as long as they utter, when called upon, that perjured, sacrilegious *yes,* the source of so many scandals, we call them well brought up, and praise the excellent education which inspires in them the fear, the cunning, and silence of a slave.

DOÑA PAQUITA. You're right, sir, it's true. That's what they demand of us, that's what they teach us in school. But the reason for my grief is much greater.

DON DIEGO. Whatever it is, my child, you must cheer up. If your mother saw you like this, what would she say? Listen . . . I think she must be up now.

DOÑA PAQUITA. Heaven help us!

DON DIEGO. Yes, Paquita, you must get hold of yourself.

Don't lose hope. Have faith in Providence. You know, our misfortunes are never as great as our imagination paints them. Just look how upset you are. What excitement! What tears! Now, do you give me your word that you'll be this way . . . a bit calm, and . . . all right?

Doña Paquita. And you, sir. You know my mother's temper. If you don't defend me, who shall I turn to? Who will take pity?

Don Diego. Your good friend . . . I myself . . . How could I desert you, child? In the sorry state you're in? (*takes her by the hand*)

Doña Paquita. Really?

Don Diego. You know my heart very little.

Doña Paquita. I know it well. (*Tries to kneel;* Don Diego *prevents her.*)

Don Diego. What are you doing, child?

Doña Paquita. How little I deserve such kindness. Oh, if you only knew!

Don Diego. I know you are as grateful as you can be for the love I bear you. The rest has been . . . how shall I say? A mistake of mine, and nothing more. But it was no fault of yours, and I won't let you take the blame.

Doña Paquita. Let's go. Aren't you coming?

Don Diego. Not just now, Paquita. In a little while.

Doña Paquita. Yes, but come soon. (*heads for* Doña Irene's *room, turns quickly, runs to* Don Diego *and kisses his hands, then leaves*)

Don Diego. I'll come.

Simon. They're here, sir.

Don Diego. What did you say?

Simon. When I came out the gate, I saw them in the distance, riding down the road. I started shouting and waving my handkerchief; they stopped, and as soon as I caught up with them I told the young gentleman what you told me to; he turned his horse around, and now he's down below. I told him not to come up till I said he could, in case there were people around, and that you didn't want him to be seen.

Don Diego. What did he say when you gave him the message?

Simon. Never a word . . . He was like dead. No, sir, never a word. It made me heartsick to see him like that, so . . .

Don Diego. Don't start pleading for him again.

SIMON. I, sir?

DON DIEGO. Yes, you. As if I didn't have ears. Heartsick! He's a scoundrel.

SIMON. Since I don't know what he's done . . .

DON DIEGO. He's a rascal, and he'll be the death of me yet. I've already told you, don't plead his case.

SIMON. Yes, sir. (SIMON *exits rear.* DON DIEGO *sits down, looking worried and angry.*)

DON DIEGO. Tell him to come up.

(DON CARLOS *enters.*)

DON DIEGO. Come here, young man, come here. Where have you been since we saw each other last?

DON CARLOS. At the inn outside the walls.

DON DIEGO. And you didn't stir from there all night, eh?

DON CARLOS. Forgive me, sir, I went into town and . . .

DON DIEGO. What! Sit down.

DON CARLOS. I had to speak to someone . . .

DON DIEGO. Had to?

DON CARLOS. Yes, sir. I owe him many favors, and I couldn't go back to Saragossa without seeing him first.

DON DIEGO. I see. Since you owe him so much . . . But to go and see him at three in the morning is very thoughtless . . . Why didn't you write him a note? Like this, for instance. By sending him a note like this at the opportune time, there'd be no need to keep him up all night or bother anyone. (*Hands him the note.* As soon as DON CARLOS *recognizes it, he rises as if to go.*)

DON CARLOS. Well, now that you know everything, why call me? Why not let me go my way, and we'll avoid a dispute that will make neither one of us very happy.

DON DIEGO. Your uncle would like to know what this is all about, and wants you to tell him.

DON CARLOS. Why do you want to know more?

DON DIEGO. Because I want to. That's an order. Understand?

DON CARLOS. Very well.

DON DIEGO. Sit down here. (DON CARLOS *sits down.*) Where did you meet this girl? What sort of love affair is there? What brought it about? What are your mutual obligations? Where and when did you see her?

DON CARLOS. On the way back to Saragossa last year. I was passing through Guadalajara without intending to stay; but the intendant, who put us up at his country house, insisted I spend the day there, it being his wife's birthday,

and promised that on the following day, he'd let me proceed
on my journey. Among the invited guests was Doña Paquita,
whom the lady of the house had brought out of the convent
that day to give her a bit of an airing. There was something
about her that made me restless and aroused in me a constant, irresistible longing to see her, to hear her speak, to be
at her side, to chat with her, and charm her . . . The intendant said among other things—jokingly, of course—that
I was very much in love, and suggested I call myself Don
Felix of Toledo. I went along with him, because from the
first I had conceived the idea of staying for some time in
that town, taking care to avoid your notice. I observed that
Doña Paquita treated me with particular courtesy, and when
we separated at night, I was full of vanity and hopes, seeing
she preferred me to all the many other suitors she had had
that day. As a matter of fact . . . But I shouldn't like to
offend you by referring to . . .

DON DIEGO. Go on.

DON CARLOS. I discovered she was the daughter of a poor
widow from Madrid, but came from a very good family. I
found it necessary to confide in my friend the love intrigues
that obliged me to remain in his company, and he, without approving or disapproving, found the most ingenious excuses so that none of his family would suspect my motives
for staying on. As his country house is quite close to the
city, I had no trouble coming and going at night . . . I
arranged for Doña Paquita to read a few of my letters; and
the few replies she sent me were enough to plunge me into
a passion that will make me unhappy as long as I live.

DON DIEGO. Well, well, go on.

DON CARLOS. My orderly, who, as you know, is a re-
sourceful fellow, and knows his way around, invented new
tricks ever step of the way and helped me overcome the
many obstacles we found at first . . . The signal was to
clap three times, and she would answer with three more
from a little window overlooking the convent yard. We would
converse every night until a very untimely hour, with all
the cautions and precautions you can easily imagine. To her
I was always Don Felix of Toledo, a regiment officer esteemed
by my superiors, and a man of honor. I never told her more
than that, or spoke to her of my relatives and ambitions,
or suggested that by marrying me she could hope to im-
prove her luck; it wouldn't have been proper to mention
you, or to tell her she should favor me out of interest

rather than love. Every time I saw her she was more precious, more beautiful, more worthy of being adored. For nearly three months I stayed there; but at last we had to separate and one dismal night I took leave of her, and left her prey to a mortal faint. I fled, blind with love, whence duty called. Her letters consoled me for some time in my exile, and in one she sent me only a few days ago, she told me how her mother was trying to marry her off, and that she would rather die than give her hand to anyone but me. She reminded me of my promises, and begged me to keep them. I got on my horse, raced down the road, tried to find her in Guadalajara, and then came here . . . The rest you know well enough . . . There's no need to tell you.

Don Diego. And what did you plan to do here?

Don Carlos. Comfort her, swear an eternal love to her again, stop and see you in Madrid, throw myself at your feet, tell you the whole story, and ask you not for wealth or property, protection, or . . . Not for that . . . But only for your blessing and consent to bring about a longed-for union on which she and I had founded all our happiness.

Don Diego. You know that's out of the question.

Don Carlos. Yes, sir.

Don Diego. You love her, but I love her, too. Her mother and her whole family approve of the marriage. She . . . whatever promises she may have made you . . . She herself, not half an hour ago, said she was ready to obey her mother and give me her hand, as soon as . . .

Don Carlos. But not her heart. (*Rises.*)

Don Diego. What are you saying?

Don Carlos. No, I tell you. That would be to insult her. You may celebrate the wedding when you please; she will always behave as befits her modesty and her virtue; but the first and only object of her affection was and always will be me. You may call yourself her husband, but if you catch her once or many times with her beautiful eyes flooded with tears, she will be shedding them for me . . . Never ask her why she is sad . . . I will be the reason. The sighs she tries to repress will be favors for an absent sweetheart.

Don Diego. What boldness! (*rises angrily, goes toward* Don Carlos, *who takes a few steps back*)

Don Carlos. I told you I couldn't speak without offending you. But let us put an end to this odious conversation. May you live happily ever after, and not hate me, for I never meant to displease you. The greatest proof I can give you of my obedience and respect is to leave her at once. But don't deny me the comfort of knowing you forgive me.

DON DIEGO. What, you're really going?

DON CARLOS. At once, sir. And this absence will be very long.

DON DIEGO. Why?

DON CARLOS. Because I must never see her again as long as I live. If the present rumors of an impending war are borne out, then . . .

DON DIEGO. What do you mean? (*grabs* DON CARLOS *by the arm and drags him forward*)

DON CARLOS. Nothing, except that I love war because I'm a soldier.

DON DIEGO. Carlos! How terrible! And you have the heart to tell me?

DON CARLOS. Someone's doming. (*looks restlessly toward* DOÑA IRENE's *room, breaks away from* DON DIEGO, *and starts toward the door upstage.* DON DIEGO *tries to stop him*) Maybe it's she . . . God be with you.

DON DIEGO. Where are you going? No, sir, you mustn't go.

DON CARLOS. There's no other way. I mustn't see her. A single glance of ours might plunge you into despair.

DON DIEGO. I've told you it must not be. Go in there.

DON CARLOS. But if . . .

DON DIEGO. Do what I tell you.

(DON CARLOS *goes into* DON DIEGO's *room.*)

DOÑA IRENE (*entering*). So, señor Don Diego, is it time for us to go? Good morning. (*Puts out the light on the table.*) Are you praying?

DON DIEGO (*pacing restlessly*). Yes, I'm just in the mood for praying.

DOÑA IRENE. If you like, they can put the chocolate on the fire, and tell the driver to harness up as soon as . . . But what ails you, sir? Bad news?

DON DIEGO. Yes. Never a lack of that.

DOÑA IRENE. Well, what? For Heaven's sake, speak up! Don't you know how frightened I am? Anything sudden like that gets me all upset and I . . . Since my last stillbirth, my nerves have been so delicate . . . And now it's going on nineteen years, if not twenty; but ever since, every little trifle throws me into a panic . . . And nothing I try—hot baths, snake broths, tamarind preserves—seems to do me any good, so . . .

Don Diego. Let's save stillbirths and preserves for another day . . . There's something more important to discuss. What are the girls doing?

Doña Irene. Getting their things together and packing our trunk, so everything will be ready, and there'll be no delay.

Don Diego. Very well. Sit down. And there's no need to get frightened or excited (Don Diego *and* Doña Irene *sit*.) about anything I may say. And remember, let's not lose our wits when we need them most. Your daughter is in love . . .

Doña Irene. Well, haven't I told you that a thousand times? Yes, sir, she is. And it's enough for me to tell you, so that . . .

Don Diego. That confounded habit of interrupting at every turn! Let me speak.

Doña Irene. Well, all right; speak.

Don Diego. She's in love, but she's not in love with me.

Doña Irene. What did you say?

Don Diego. What you heard. ·

Doña Irene. But who ever told you such nonsense?

Don Diego. No one. I know it, I've seen it, no one told me, and when I tell it to you, I'm quite sure it's true . . . Well, what are you crying for?

Doña Irene (*weeping*). Oh dear, oh dear!

Don Diego. Why?

Doña Irene. Because I'm a poor widow and alone and without means, it seems that everybody hates me and is plotting against me.

Don Diego. Señora Doña Irene . . .

Doña Irene. At the end of my days and my monthlies, to be treated this way, like a dishmop, like a wayside Cinderella, I must say . . . Who would have thought it of you? Heaven help us! Why, if my three dead husbands were alive . . . If my last dead husband was alive—he had a temper like a snake.

Don Diego. Look, madam, I'm losing my patience.

Doña Irene. And all you had to do was answer him back, and he'd turn into a fury straight from hell, and one Corpus Christi Day, over some trifle or other, he gave such a beating to a commissary officer that if it hadn't been for a couple of Carmelites who broke it up he would have dashed out his brains on the posts of Santa Cruz.

Don Diego. Is it possible that you haven't been paying attention to a thing I said?

DOÑA IRENE. Oh, no, sir, but I'll have you know that I'm no fool. No, sir! Now you don't want the girl, and you're looking for excuses so you can throw her over . . . Daughter of my heart and soul!

DON DIEGO. Madam, please be good enough to listen to me, and not answer back or spout nonsense, and as soon as you know what it's all about, you can weep and groan and scream and say whatever you please . . . But meanwhile, don't prolong the suffering, for the love of God!

DOÑA IRENE. Say whatever you feel like.

DON DIEGO. Just let's not start crying again and . . .

DOÑA IRENE. No, sir; I'm not crying now. (dabs her eyes with a handkerchief)

DON DIEGO. Well, for about a year now, Doña Paquita has had another suitor. They've spoken to each other often, they've written each other, they've promised each other to be loving, faithful, and constant . . . And finally, there exists in both of them a passion so tender, that obstacles and absence, far from diminishing it, have actually made it greater. This being the case . . .

DOÑA IRENE. But can't you see, sir, that this is all a piece of gossip thought up by some evil tongue who bears us no great love?

DON DIEGO. Let's get back to our subject. It's not gossip, madam. I repeat, I know whereof I speak.

DOÑA IRENE. What can you know, sir, and what shadow of truth is there in this? My dear, darling child, shut up in a convent, kept under the strictest religious principles, watched over all the time by those saintly nuns . . . A child with no idea of the world, who still isn't out of the shell, so to speak. It's pretty obvious you don't know what a temper Circuncisión has! She's just the one to gloss over the least backsliding on the part of her niece . . .

DON DIEGO. We're not speaking of backsliding, of which, as far as we know, there has been no intimation. Your daughter is above reproach, and is incapable of backsliding. What I am saying is that Mother Circuncision, and Soledad, and Candelaria, and all the other sisters, and you and I especially, have made a colossal blunder. The girl wants to marry someone else, and not me. We've come to our senses late; you relied too thoroughly on your daughter's will. Well, what's the use of wearing ourselves out? Read this note, and you'll see if I'm not right! (He hands her the note.

DOÑA IRENE *gets up excitedly without reading it and goes to the door of her room.* DON DIEGO *rises and tries in vain to calm her.*)

DOÑA IRENE. You're driving me out of my mind! Paquita! Virgin of the Quagmire! Rita! Paquita!

DON DIEGO. But what's the good of calling them?

DOÑA IRENE. Well, sir, I want her to come, and see for herself what kind of man you are.

DON DIEGO. She's upset everything . . . That's what you get when you rely on a woman's prudence.

(DOÑA PAQUITA *and* RITA *enter from their room.*)

RITA. Madam!

DOÑA PAQUITA. Were you calling me?

DOÑA IRENE. Yes, daughter, yes. Because señor Don Diego has been treating us intolerably. What love affairs have you had, child? Who did you promise to marry? What sort of plot . . . ? (*to* RITA) And you, you rascally girl . . . You must know something, too . . . I'll make you tell. Who wrote this note? Read it! (*handing the open letter to* DOÑA PAQUITA)

RITA (*aside to* DOÑA PAQUITA). His handwriting.

DOÑA PAQUITA. What wickedness! Señor Don Diego, is this how you keep your word?

DON DIEGO. God only knows, I'm not to blame . . . Come here. (*takes* DOÑA PAQUITA *by the hand and seats her beside him*) There's nothing to be afraid of . . . And you, madam, listen and be quiet, and don't make me do something foolish. Give me that letter. (*takes the note from her*) Paquita, you remember the three handclaps tonight.

DOÑA PAQUITA. I'll remember as long as I live.

DON DIEGO. Well, this is the paper they threw in the window. I told you, there's nothing to be afraid of. (*He reads.*) "My darling: If I can't get to speak with you, I'll do my best to see that this letter reaches your hands. Almost as soon as I left you I met the man I called my enemy at the inn. When I saw him I was struck dumb with sorrow and amazement. He ordered me to leave the city at once, and I had to obey him. My name is Don Carlos. Don Diego is my uncle. I hope you will be happy, and forget forever your unhappy suitor, Carlos de Urbina."

DOÑA IRENE. So that's how it is!

DOÑA PAQUITA. Woe is me!

DOÑA IRENE. So it's true what the gentleman said, you conniving hussy! I'll give you something to remember, all right. (*She goes to* DOÑA PAQUITA *in a rage, as if to strike her.* RITA *and* DON DIEGO *prevent her.*)

DOÑA PAQUITA. Mother, forgive me!

DOÑA IRENE. No, girl. I'll kill you!

DON DIEGO. What madness is this?

DOÑA IRENE. I'll kill her!

(DON CARLOS *dashes in from* DON DIEGO'S *room, grabs* DOÑA PAQUITA *by the arm, runs with her backstage, and stands in front of her to defend her.* DOÑA IRENE *gets scared and draws back.*)

DON CARLOS. None of that. Before me, no one shall offend her.

DOÑA PAQUITA. Carlos!

DON CARLOS (*to* DON DIEGO). Pardon my boldness . . . I saw she was being insulted, and I couldn't contain myself.

DOÑA IRENE. What's going on? Good God, who are you? What sort of behavior . . . ? What a scandal!

DON DIEGO. There are no scandals here. This is the man your daughter is in love with. To separate them and to kill them amounts to the same thing. Carlos . . . Never mind . . . Embrace your wife.

(CARLOS *goes over to* PAQUITA, *they embrace, and kneel before* DON DIEGO.)

DOÑA IRENE. What? Your nephew?

DON DIEGO. Yes, madam. My nephew, who with his hand claps, his music, and his letter gave me the most terrible night of my life . . . What is this, children, what is it?

DOÑA PAQUITA. So you'll forgive us and make us happy?

DON DIEGO. Yes, my darlings. Yes. (*bids them rise, with tender expression*)

DOÑA IRENE. Is it possible that you've decided to make a sacrifice?

DON DIEGO. I could separate them forever and claim this lovable child for myself, but my conscience won't let me. Carlos! Paquita! How my heart aches for the effort I just made . . . Because, after all, I am a weak and wretched man.

DON CARLOS (*kissing his hands*). If our love and gratitude can suffice to console you for such a loss . . .

DOÑA IRENE. So it's good old Don Carlos! Now if only . . .

DON DIEGO. He and your daughter were madly in love, while you and the aunts built castles in the air and filled my head with illusions that have vanished like a dream. This is the result of the abuse of authority, and the oppression our young people suffer. These are the assurances that parents and tutors give, and how far they should be trusted when a girl says yes . . . By accident I discovered my mistake in time. Woe to those who discover it too late!

DOÑA IRENE. Well, God bless them and grant them a long and happy life. Come here, sir. Come on now, I want to hug you. (*Embraces* DON CARLOS. DOÑA PAQUITA *kneels and kisses her mother's hand.*) Paquita, darling. Well! You made a good choice. You can see he's very gallant. A little swarthy, but what flashing eyes!

RITA. Yes, tell her that. She may not have noticed. Señorita, a million kisses! (DOÑA PAQUITA *and* RITA *kiss.*)

DOÑA PAQUITA. Did you ever see such happiness? And you, you love me so much! You'll always, always be my friend.

DON DIEGO. Lovely Paquita (*kisses* DOÑA PAQUITA), receive the first embraces of your new father. I no longer fear the terrible loneliness that threatened my old age . . . You two (*taking* DOÑA PAQUITA *and* DON CARLOS *by the hand*) will be the delight of my heart, and the first fruit of your love, yes, children, that one—without fail—that one's for me. And when I hold him in my arms, I can say: this innocent child owes his life to me; if his parents live and are happy, it's because of me.

DON CARLOS. Blessings on so much goodness!

DON DIEGO. Blessings and thanks to God!

THE GREAT GALEOTO
(*El gran galeoto*)

by José Echegaray

TRANSLATED BY
Hannah Lynch

ᏬᏇᏬ

CHARACTERS

TEODORO, *wife of*
DON JULIAN
DOÑA MERCEDES, *wife of*
DON SEVERO

PEPITO, *their son*
ERNEST
A WITNESS
TWO SERVANTS

SCENE: *Madrid during the 1880's*

José Echegaray
(1832-1916)

By the time Echegaray produced his first play, *El libro talonario* (1874)—on a challenge, to prove to his brother, a noted playwright, how easy it was to write a play—he was known as a brilliant mathematician and economist, and he had occupied important positions in the government, including that of Minister of Finance.

After completing his studies at the School of Engineering, where he had been considered a prodigy and mathematical wizard, he became professor of mathematics there, but soon drifted into economics and politics and was instrumental in organizing the Bank of Spain. Encouraged by the reception accorded *El libro talonario,* however, he gave up most of his political activities and devoted himself to the writing of plays, sixty-eight of them, mostly spectacular successes. At first Echegaray followed the Romantic path. Such plays as *La esposa del vengador* (1874), *O locura o santidad* (1877), and *En el seno de la muerte* (1879) were frankly melodramatic, verbose, hypertense; but when in the '80's Ibsen, Strindberg, Hauptmann, Sudermann, the so-called "realists" and "naturalists," took over the European stage, Echegaray followed suit. And yet the melodramatic and Romantic quality of his first period persisted. *El hijo de Don Juan* (1892) is an embarrassing mixture of the Romantic school and the Ibsen of *Ghosts;* all he did was to tag on a "thesis," thus giving the semblance of a problem-play to a basically Romantic melodrama.

As a good mathematician, Echegaray treated a play as a game of chess, a series of generally exciting moves. Somehow the human potentialities of the characters failed to come through—they were moved about like chess pieces or cardboard puppets. To compensate for this lack of human warmth, Echegaray let loose a barrage of words.

Most attractive to contemporary taste is *El gran galeoto* (*The Great Galeoto,* 1881), a success in many European capitals, which facilitated his entrance into the Royal Spanish Academy and to half a Nobel Prize (1905)—the other half going to the Provençal poet Frederic Mistral.

BEST EDITION: *Obras.* Madrid, Sociedad de Autores Españoles.
ABOUT: H. Courson, *Le Théâtre de J. Echegaray.* Paris, 1913. I. Goldberg, *Don José Echegaray: A Study in Modern Spanish Drama* (dissertation, Harvard University). H. Merimée, "José Echegaray et son œuvre dramatique," *Bulletin Hispanique,* XVIII (1916). G. B. Shaw, *Dramatic Opinions and Essays.* London, 1916, I, 81-89; II, 186-194.

PROLOGUE

SCENE: *A study; to the left a balcony, on the right a door; in the middle a table strewn with papers and books, and a lighted lamp upon it. Toward the right a sofa. Night.*

ERNEST (*seated at table and preparing to write*). Nothing —impossible! It is striving with the impossible. The idea is there; my head is fevered with it; I feel it. At moments an inward light illuminates it, and I see it. I see it in its floating form, vaguely outlined, and suddenly a secret voice seems to animate it, and I hear sounds of sorrow, sonorous sighs, shouts of sardonic laughter . . . a whole world of passions alive and struggling . . . They burst forth from me, extend around me, and the air is full of them. Then, then I say to myself: 'Now is the moment.' I take up my pen, stare into space, listen attentively, restraining my very heart-beats, and bend over the paper . . . Ah, the irony of impotency! The outlines become blurred, the vision fades, the cries and sighs faint away . . . and nothingness, nothingness encircles me . . . The monotony of empty space, of inert thought, of dreamy lassitude! and more than all the monotony of an idle pen and lifeless paper that lacks the life of thought! Ah! How varied are the shapes of nothingness, and how, in its dark and silent way, it mocks creatures of my stamp! So many, many forms! Canvas without color, bits of marble without shape, confused noise of chaotic vibrations. But nothing more irritating, more insolent, meaner than this insolent pen of mine (*throws it away*), nothing worse than this white sheet of paper. Oh, if I cannot fill it, at least I may destroy it—vile accomplice of my ambition and my eternal humiliation. Thus, thus . . . smaller and still smaller. (*tears up paper. Pauses*) And then! How lucky that nobody saw me! For in truth such fury is absurd and unjust. No, I will not yield. I will think and think, until either I have conquered or am crushed. No, I will not give up. Let me see, let me see . . . if in that way——

DON JULIAN (*at the door, without entering.*) Ernest!

299

ERNEST. Don Julian!

DON JULIAN. Still working? Do I disturb you?

ERNEST (*rising*). Disturb me! What a question, Don Julian! Come in, come in. And Teodora?

(DON JULIAN *enters.*)

DON JULIAN. We have just come from the Opera. She has gone upstairs with my brother, to see something or other that Mercedes has bought, and I was on my way to my room when I saw your light, so I stopped to say good night.

ERNEST. Was there a good house?

DON JULIAN. As usual. All our friends inquired after you. They wondered you were not there too.

ERNEST. That was kind of them.

DON JULIAN. Not more than you deserve. And how have you improved the shining hours of solitude and inspiration!

ERNEST. Solitude, yes; inspiration, no. It shuns me though I call on it never so humbly and fondly.

DON JULIAN. It has failed at the rendezvous?

ERNEST. And not for the first time, either. But if I have done nothing else, at least I have made a happy discovery.

DON JULIAN. What?

ERNEST. That I am a poor devil.

DON JULIAN. Nonsense! That's a famous discovery.

ERNEST. Nothing less.

DON JULIAN. But why are you so out of sorts with yourself? Is the play you talked of the other day not going smoothly?

ERNEST. How can it? The only *going* is me going out of my wits.

DON JULIAN. How's that? Both the drama and inspiration are faithless to my poor friend.

ERNEST. That's how I stand. When I first conceived the idea, I imagined it full of promise, but when I attempt to give it form, and put it in an appropriate stage garb, the result shows something extraordinary, difficult, undramatic, and impossible.

DON JULIAN. How it is impossible? Come, tell me. You've excited my curiosity. (*Sits down on the sofa.*)

ERNEST. Imagine the principal character, one who creates the drama and develops it, who gives it life and provokes the catastrophe, who, broadly, fills and possesses it, and yet who cannot make his way to the stage.

DON JULIAN. Is he so ugly, then? So repugnant or bad?

ERNEST. Not so. Bad as you or I may be—not worse. Neither good nor bad, and truly not repugnant. I am not such a cynic—neither a misanthrope, nor one so out of love with life as to fall into such unfairness.

DON JULIAN. Then what's the reason?

ERNEST. The reason, Don Julian, is that there is no material room in the scenario for this personage.

DON JULIAN. Holy Virgin! What do you mean? Is it a mythological drama with Titans in it?

ERNEST. Titans, yes, but in the modern sense of the word.

DON JULIAN. That is to say——?

ERNEST. That is to say, this person is . . . *everybody*.

DON JULIAN. *Everybody!* You are right. There is no room for everybody on the stage. It is an incontrovertible truth that has been demonstrated more than once.

ERNEST. Then you agree with me?

DON JULIAN. Not entirely. Everybody may be condensed in a few types and characters. This is matter beyond my depth, but I have always understood that the masters have more than once accomplished it.

ERNEST. Yes, but in my case it is to condemn me not to write my drama.

DON JULIAN. Why?

ERNEST. For many reasons it would be difficult to explain —above all, at this late hour.

DON JULIAN. Never mind. Give me a few.

ERNEST. Look! Each individual of this entire mass, each head of this monster of a thousand heads, of this Titan of the century, whom I call *everybody*, takes part in my play for a flying moment, utters but one word, flings a single glance. Perhaps his action consists of a smile. He appears but to vanish. Listless and absent-minded, he acts without passion, without anger, without guile, often for mere distraction's sake.

DON JULIAN. What then?

ERNEST. These light words, these fugitive glances, these indifferent smiles, all these evanescent sounds and this trivial evil, which may be called the insignificant rays of the dramatic light, condensed to one focus, to one group, result in conflagration or explosion, in strife and in victims. If I represent the whole by a few types or symbolical personages, I bestow upon each one that which is really dispersed among many, and such a result distorts my idea. I must bring types on the stage whose guile repels and is the less natural because evil in them has no object. This exposes me to a worse consequence, to the accusation of meaning to paint a cruel, corrupted, and debased society, when my sole intention is to prove that not even the most insignificant actions are in themselves insignificant or lost for good or evil. For, concentrated by the mysterious influences of modern life, they may reach to immense effects.

DON JULIAN. Say no more, my friend. All this is metaphysics. A glimmer of light, perhaps, but through an infinitude of cloud. However, you understand these things better than I do. Letters of exchange, shares, stock, and discount, now —that's another matter.

ERNEST. No, no; you've common sense, and that's the chief thing.

DON JULIAN. You flatter me, Ernest.

ERNEST. But you follow me?

DON JULIAN. Not in the least. There ought to be a way out of the difficulty.

ERNEST. If that were all!

DON JULIAN. What! More?

ERNEST. Tell me what is the great dramatic spring?

DON JULIAN. My dear fellow, I don't exactly know what you mean by a dramatic spring. All I can tell you is that I have not the slightest interest in plays where love does not preponderate—above all unfortunate love, for I have enough of happy love at home.

ERNEST. Good, very good! Then in my play there can be little or no love.

DON JULIAN. So much the worse. Though I know nothing of your play, I suspect it will interest nobody.

ERNEST. So I have been telling you. Nevertheless, it is possible to put in a little love—and jealousy too.

DON JULIAN. Ah, then, with an interesting intrigue skilfully developed, and some effective situations——

ERNEST. No, nothing of the sort. It will be all simple, ordinary, almost vulgar . . . so that the drama will not have any external action. The drama evolves within the characters: it advances slowly: today takes hold of a thought, tomorrow of a heart-beat, little by little, undermines the will.

DON JULIAN. But who understands all this? How are these interior ravages manifested? Who recounts them to the audience? In what way are they evident? Must we spend a whole evening hunting for a glance, a sigh, a gesture, a single word? My dear boy, this is not amusement. To cast us into such depths is to hurl us upon philosophy.

ERNEST. You but echo my own thought.

DON JULIAN. I have no wish to discourage you. You best know what you are about—there. Though the play seems rather colorless, heavy, uninteresting, perhaps if the dénoûment is sensational—and the explosion—eh?

ERNEST. Sensation! Explosion! Hardly, and that only just upon the fall of the curtain.

DON JULIAN. Which means that the play begins when the curtain falls?

ERNEST. I am inclined to admit it. But I will endeavor to give it a little warmth.

DON JULIAN. My dear lad, what you have to do is to write the second play, the one that begins where the first ends. For the other, according to your description, would be difficult to write, and is not worth the trouble.

ERNEST. That's the conclusion I have come to myself.

DON JULIAN. Then we agree, thanks to your skill and logic. And what is the name?

ERNEST. That's another difficulty. I can find none.

DON JULIAN. What do you say? No name either?

ERNEST. No, unless, as Don Hermogenes * says, we could put it into Greek for greater clarity.

DON JULIAN. Surely, Ernest, you were dozing when I came in. You have been dreaming nonsense.

ERNEST. Dreaming! yes. Nonsense! perhaps. I talk both dreams and nonsense. But you are sensible and always right.

DON JULIAN. In this case it does not require much penetration. A drama in which the chief personage cannot appear; in which there is hardly any love; in which nothing happens but what happens every day; that begins with the fall of the curtain upon the last act, and which has no name. I don't know how it is to be written, still less how it is to be acted, how it is to find an audience, nor how it can be called a drama.

ERNEST. Nevertheless, it is a drama, if I could only give it proper form, and that I can't do.

DON JULIAN. Do you wish to follow my advice?

ERNEST. Can you doubt it? You, my friend, my benefactor, my second father! Don Julian!

DON JULIAN. Come, come, Ernest, don't let us drop into a sentimental drama on our own account instead of yours,

---

* A pedant in Moratin's Comedia Nueva, who quotes Greek incessantly to make himself better understood.

which we have declared impossible. I asked you if you would take my advice.

ERNEST. And I said yes.

DON JULIAN. Then leave aside your plays. Go to bed, rest yourself, and come out shooting with me tomorrow. Kill a few partridges, and that will be an excuse for your not killing one or two characters, and not exposing yourself to the same fate at the hands of the public. After all, you may thank me for it.

ERNEST. I'll do no such thing. I mean to write that play.

DON JULIAN. But, my poor fellow, you've conceived it in mortal sin.

ERNEST. I don't know, but it is conceived. I feel it stir in my brain. It clamors for life, and I must give it to the world.

DON JULIAN. Can't you find another plot?

ERNEST. But this idea?

DON JULIAN. Send it to the devil.

ERNEST. Ah, Don Julian, you believe that an idea which has gripped the mind can be effaced and destroyed at our pleasure. I wanted to think out another play, but this accursed idea won't give it room, until it itself has seen the light.

DON JULIAN. God grant you a happy delivery.

ERNEST. That's the question, as Hamlet says.

DON JULIAN (*conspiratorially*). Couldn't you cast it into the literary foundling hospital of anonymity?

ERNEST. Don Julian, I am a man of conscience. Good or bad, my children are legitimate. They bear my name.

DON JULIAN (*preparing to go*). I have nothing more to say. What must be done will be done.

ERNEST. I wish it were so. Unfortunately, it is not done. But no matter; if I don't do it, somebody else will.

DON JULIAN. Then to work, and good luck, and may nobody rob you of your laurels.

TEODORA (*outside*). Julian, Julian!

DON JULIAN. It's Teodora.

TEODORA. Are you there, Julian?

DON JULIAN (*going to the door*). Yes, I'm here. Come in.

TEODORA (*entering*). Good evening, Ernest.

ERNEST. Good evening, Teodora. Was the singing good?

TEODORA. As usual; and have you been working much?

ERNEST. As usual; nothing.

TEODORA. Then you'd have done better to come with us. They all asked after you.

ERNEST. It seems that everybody is interested in me.

DON JULIAN. I should think so, since *everybody* is to be the principal personage of your play. You may imagine if they are anxious to be on good terms with you.

TEODORA. A play?

DON JULIAN. Hush! It's a mystery. Ask no questions. Neither title, nor characters, nor action, nor catastrophe—the sublime! Good night, Ernest. Come, Teodora.

ERNEST. Adieu, Don Julian.

TEODORA. Till tomorrow.

ERNEST. Good night.

TEODORA (*to* DON JULIAN). How preoccupied Mercedes was!

DON JULIAN. And Severo was in a rage.

TEODORA. Why, I wonder.

DON JULIAN. How do I know? On the other hand, Pepito chattered enough for both.

TEODORA. He always does, and nobody escapes his tongue.

DON JULIAN. He's a character for Ernest's play.

(*Exit* TEODORA, *and* DON JULIAN *by right.*)

ERNEST. Let Don Julian say what he will, I won't abandon the undertaking. That would be signal cowardice. Never retreat—always forward. (*rises and begins to walk about in an agitated way. Then approaches the balcony*) Protect me, night. In thy blackness, rather than in the azure clearness of day, are outlined the luminous shapes of inspiration. Lift your roofs, you thousand houses of this great town, as well for a poet in dire necessity as for the devil on two sticks who so wantonly exposed you. Let me see the men and women enter your drawing-rooms and boudoirs in search of the night's rest after fevered pleasures abroad. Let my acute hearing catch the stray words of all those who inquired for me of Don Julian and Teodora. As the scattered rays of light, when gathered to a focus by diaphanous crystal, strike flame, and darkness is forged by the crossed bars of shadow; as mountains are made from grains of earth, and seas from drops of water: so will I use your wasted words, your vague smiles, your eager glances, and build my play of all those thousand trivialities dispersed in cafés, at reunions, theaters, and spectacles, and that float now in the air. Let the modest crystal of my intelligence be the lens which will concentrate light and shadow, from which will spring the dramatic conflagration and the tragic explosion of the catastrophe. Already my play takes shape. It has even a title now, for there, under the lamp-shade, I see the immortal work of the immortal Florentine. It offers me in Italian what in good Spanish it would be risky and futile audacity either to write on paper or pronounce on the stage. Francesca and Paolo, assist me with the story of your loves! (*sits down and prepares to write*) The play . . . the play begins . . . First page—there, it's no longer white. It has a name. (*writing*) *The Great Galeoto.* (*Writes feverishly.*)

ACT I

SCENE: *A drawing-room in* DON JULIAN'S *house. At the back of stage a large door, and beyond a passage separating it from the dining-room door, which remains closed throughout the act. On the left a balcony, and beyond it a door. On the right two doors. On the stage a table, and a handsome, luxurious armchair. Hour: toward sunset.*

(TEODORA *and* DON JULIAN. TEODORA *near the balcony;* DON JULIAN *seated on the sofa, lost in thought.*)

TEODORA. What a lovely sunset! what clouds and light, and what a sky! Suppose it were true, as the poets say, and our fathers believed, that our fate is stamped upon the azure heaven! Were the mysterious secret of human destiny traced by the stars upon the sapphire sphere, and this splendid evening should hold the cipher of ours, what happiness it must disclose! What a smiling future! What a life in our life, and what radiance in our heaven! Is it not so, Julian? (*She approaches* DON JULIAN.) Ah, plunged in thought, I see! Come and look out. What, no word for me?

DON JULIAN (*absently*). What is it?

TEODORA (*coming near*). You have not been listening to me!

DON JULIAN. You have my heart ever—who are its magnet and its center. But my mind is apt to be besieged by preoccupations, cares, business——

TEODORA. They are the plague of my life, since they rob me, if not of my husband's affections, at least of some of his attention. But what is the matter, Julian? (*affectionately*) Something worries you. Is it serious, that you are so solemn and so silent? If it should be trouble, Julian, remember that

307

I have a right to share it. My joys are yours, and your sorrows are no less mine.

DON JULIAN. Sorrows! Troubles! Are you not happy? Do I not possess in you the living embodiment of joy? With those cheeks so ruddy in the glow of health, and those dear eyes, clear like your soul and resplendent as the sky, and I the owner of all you, could pain, or shadow, or grief teach me I am other than the happiest man alive?

TEODORA. It is a business annoyance, perhaps?

DON JULIAN. Money never yet forced sleep or appetite to forsake me. I have never felt aversion, much less contempt for it, so it follows that the article has flowed easily into my coffers. I was rich, I am rich; and until Don Julian of Garagarga dies of old age, please God and his own good fortune, he will remain, if not the wealthiest, certainly the surest, banker of Madrid, Cadiz, and Oporto.

TEODORA. Then what is your preoccupation?

DON JULIAN. I was thinking—it's a good thought, too.

TEODORA. Naturally, since it's yours.

DON JULIAN. Flatterer! you would spoil me.

TEODORA. But I am still unenlightened.

DON JULIAN. There is an important matter I want to achieve.

TEODORA. Connected with the new works?

DON JULIAN. No; it has nothing to do with stone or iron.

TEODORA. What, then?

DON JULIAN. It is a question of kindness—a sacred debt of old date.

TEODORA (*gleefully*). Oh, I can guess now.

DON JULIAN. So!

TEODORA. You mean Ernest.

DON JULIAN. You are right.

TEODORA. Yes, yes, you must. Poor lad! he's so good and noble and generous.

DON JULIAN. Quite his father's son—the model of a loyal hidalgo.

TEODORA. And then so clever! Only twenty-six, and a prodigy! What doesn't he know?

DON JULIAN. Know! I should think he *did* know. That's nothing—rather, that's the worst of it. While he is wandering in the sphere of sublime thought, I fear he's not likely to learn much of a world so deceptive and prosaic as ours, which takes no interest in the subtleties of the mind until three centuries after genius has been buried.

TEODORA. But with you for a guide, Julian—you don't intend to abandon him yet a while, surely?

DON JULIAN. God forbid. I should be black-hearted indeed if I would so readily forget all I owe his father. Don Juan of Acedo risked name and wealth—for my family, yes, almost his life. Should this lad need mine, he might ask it, and welcome. It would be but just payment of the debt my name represents.

TEODORA. Well said, Julian. It is like you.

DON JULIAN. You remember, about a year ago, I heard my good friend was dead, and his son was left badly off. I lost no time, caught the train to Gerona, nearly used force, and carried the boy back here. When he stood in the middle of this room I said to him: "You are master here; you may command me and mine. Since I owe your father everything, you must regard me in the light of his representative. If I fall short, my desire is to come as near as possible to him. As for the amount of affection I have to dispose of—we'll see if I don't outrace him there."

TEODORA. I remember it well. The soft-hearted fellow burst out crying, and clung to you like a child.

DON JULIAN. He's but a child, as you say. That's why we must think and plan for him. And it was of that I was so seriously thinking a moment ago. I was meditating a half-formed project, while you, dear, wanted me to contemplate a panorama of radiant cloud and scarlet sun that cannot compare with the sun that shines in my own heaven.

TEODORA. I cannot divine your idea. What is it you project doing for Ernest?

DON JULIAN. Those are my words.

TEODORA. But is there something yet undone that you expect to discover? He has lived with us for the past year like one of ourselves. Were he your son, or a brother of mine, could you show him more tenderness, I more affection?

DON JULIAN. It is much, but not enough.

TEODORA. Not enough! I fancy——

DON JULIAN. You are thinking of the present, and I of the future.

TEODORA. Oh! the future! That is easily settled. See, he lives here with us as long as he likes, for years. It is his home. Then when the just and natural law prompts him to fall in love and desire another, we will marry him. You will nobly share your wealth with him, and we will lead them

from the altar to their own house—*he* and *she*! The proverb,
you know, says wisely, "For each wedded pair a house."
He will live just a little away from us, but that will be
no reason for our forgetting him, or loving him less. I see
it all distinctly. They are happy, and we even happier. They
have children, of course, and we perhaps more—well, at
least, one little girl, who will fall in love with Ernest's son,
and to whom we will marry her by and by.

(*Spoken playfully, with volubility, grace, blushes, and
lively gesture, according to the actress's talents.*)

Don Julian. But where in heaven's name are you going
to stop? (*Laughing.*)

Teodora. You spoke of his future, Julian, and I've
sketched it. If not this one, I will neither approve nor accept it.

Don Julian. How like you, Teodora! but——

Teodora. Ah, there is a but already.

Don Julian. Listen, Teodora. It is but a debt we owe to
look after the poor fellow as if he were a relative, and obligation runs with the exactions of our affection. So much for
himself, so much for his father's son. But every human action
is complex, has two points of view, and every medal has its
reverse. Which means, Teodora, that you must understand
it is a very different matter to give and receive favors; and
that in the end Ernest might feel my protection a humiliation. He's a high-spirited, fine lad, a trifle haughty perhaps,
and it is imperative there should be an end to his present
position. We may, if we can, do more for him, but we must
seem to do less.

Teodora. How so?

Don Julian. We'll see—but here he comes—— (*Looks
down the stage.*)

Teodora. Hush!

(Ernest *enters.*)

Don Julian. Welcome!

Ernest. Don Julian!—and Teodora! (*Salutes absently. Sits
down near the table in pensive silence.*)

Don Julian (*approaching him*). What's the matter?

Ernest. Nothing.

Don Julian. You look as if something ailed you—your
preoccupation reveals it. No trouble, I hope?

Ernest. Nonsense.

Don Julian. Nor disappointment?

Ernest. None whatever.

DON JULIAN. I don't annoy you?

ERNEST. You! good heavens! (*rises and comes toward him effusively*) You speak out of the right of friendship and affection, and you read me through and through. Yes, sir; there is indeed something the matter. I will tell you, if you, and you also, Teodora, out of your pity, will hold me excused. I am an ungrateful fool, a mere boy, in truth, deserving neither of your kindness nor of your affection. Possessing such a father and such a sister, I ought to be happy, with no care for the morrow. But it is not so. I blush to explain it —can't you understand?—Yes, yes, you must see how false my position is. I live here on alms. (*with energy*)

TEODORA. Such a word—

ERNEST. Teodora!

TEODORA. —affronts us.

ERNEST. I expressed myself ill—but it is so.

DON JULIAN. I say it is not so. If anyone in this house lives upon alms, and those no slight ones, it is I and not you.

ERNEST. I am acquainted, sir, with the story of two loyal friends, and of some money matters long forgotten. It does honor to my father and to his hidalgic race. But I am shamed in profiting by it. I am young, Don Julian, and although I may not be worth much, there ought still to be some way for me to earn my bread. It may be pride or folly, I cannot say. But I remember what my father used to say: "What you can do yourself, never ask another to do. What you can earn, never owe to anyone else."

DON JULIAN. So that my services humiliate and degrade you. You count your friends importunate creditors.

TEODORA. Reason may be on your side, Ernest, and in knowledge you are not deficient, but, believe me, in this case the heart alone speaks with wisdom.

DON JULIAN. Your father did not find me so ungenerous or so proud.

TEODORA. Ah, friendship was then a very different thing.

ERNEST. Teodora!

TEODORA (*to* DON JULIAN). What a noble anxiety he displays!

ERNEST. I know I seem ungrateful—I feel it—and an idiot to boot. Forgive me, Don Julian.

DON JULIAN. His head is a forge.

TEODORA (*also apart to* DON JULIAN). He doesn't live in this world.

Don Julian. Just so. He's full of depth and learning, and lets himself be drowned in a pool of water.

Ernest (*meditatively*). True, I know little of life, and am not well fitted to make my way through it. But I divine it, and shudder, I know not why. Shall I founder on the world's pool as upon the high sea? I may not deny that it terrifies me far more than the deep ocean. The sea only reaches the limit set by the loose sand: over all space travel the emanations of the pool. A strong man's arms can struggle with the waves of the sea, but no one can struggle against subtle miasma. But if I fall, I must not feel the humiliation of defeat. I wish and pray that at the last moment I may see the approach of the sea that will bear me away at its will; see the sword that is to pierce me, the rock against which I am to be crushed. I must measure my adversary's strength, and despise it falling, despise it dying, instead of tamely breathing the venom scattered through the ambient air.

Don Julian (*to* Teodora). Didn't I tell you he was going out of his mind?

Teodora. But, Ernest, where are you wandering?

Don Julian. Yes. What has all this to do with the matter?

Ernest. Sir, I have come to the conclusion that others, seeing me housed and fed here, are saying of me what I long have thought. They see me constantly driving out with you, in the morning walking with Teodora or Mercedes, in your opera-box, hunting on your lands, and daily occupying the same place at your table. Though you would like to think otherwise, in one way or another the gossip runs: Who is he? Is he a relation? Not so. The secretary? Still less. A partner? If a partner, it may be accepted he brings little or nothing to the general fund. So they chatter.

Don Julian. By no means. You are raving.

Ernest. I beg to contradict you.

Don Julian. Then give me a name.

Ernest. Sir——

Don Julian. One will do.

Ernest. There is one at hand—upstairs.

Don Julian. Name him.

Ernest. Don Severo.

Don Julian. My brother?

Ernest. Exactly, your brother! Will that suffice? or shall we add his respected wife, Doña Mercedes? and Pepito, their son? What have you to say then?

Don Julian. That Severo is a fool, Mercedes an idle chatterer, and the lad a puppy.

Ernest. They only repeat what they hear.

Don Julian. It is not true. This is false reasoning. Between gentlemen, when the intention is honorable, what can the opinion of the world really matter? The meaner it is, the loftier our disdain of it.

Ernest. That is nobly said, and is what all well-bred men feel. But I have been taught that gossip, whether inspired by malice or not, which is according to each one's natural tendency, begins in a lie and generally ends in truth. Does gossip, as it grows, disclose the hidden sin? Is it a reflex of the past, or does it invent evil and give it existence? Does it set its accursed seal upon an existent fault, or merely breed that which was yet not, and furnish the occasion for wrong? Should we call the slanderer infamous or severe? the accomplice or the divulger? the public avenger or the tempter? Does he arrest or precipitate our fall? wound through taste or duty? And when he condemns, is it from justice or from spite? Perhaps both, Don Julian. Who can say? though time, occasion, and facts may show.

Don Julian. See here, Ernest, I don't understand an iota of all this philosophizing. I presume it is on such nonsense you waste your intelligence. But I don't want you to be vexed or worried. It's true—you really wish for austere independence, to stand alone at a post of honor?

Ernest. Don Julian!

Don Julian. Answer me.

Ernest (*joyously*). Yes.

Don Julian. Then count it gained. At this very moment I have no secretary. I am expecting one from London. But nobody would suit me better than a certain young fool, who is enamoured of poverty. (*speaks in pleasant reproach*) His work and salary will, of course, be settled as anyone else's, though he be a son to one who cherishes him as such.

Ernest. Don Julian!

Don Julian (*affecting comical severity*). Remember, I am an exacting businessman, and I have not the habit of giving my money away for nothing. I intend to get as much as possible out of you, and work you hard. In my house the bread of just labor alone is consumed. By the clock, ten hours, starting at daybreak, and when I choose to be severe, you will see that Severo himself is no match for me. So, before the world you pose as the victim of my selfishness . . . but in private, dear boy, ever the same, the center of my dearest affections. (*Unable to maintain former tone*, Don Julian *breaks off, and holds his hand out to* Ernest.)

Ernest (*deeply moved*). Don Julian!

Don Julian. You accept, then?

Ernest. I am yours to command.

Teodora (*to* Don Julian). At last you have tamed the savage.

Ernest (*to* Don Julian). Anything for your sake.

Don Julian. So would I have you always, Ernest. And now I have to write to my London correspondent, and thank him, and while recognizing the extraordinary merit of his Englishman, whom he extols to the skies, regret that I have already engaged a young man. (*walks toward the first door on the right hand*) This is how we stand for the present; but in the future—it will be as partners. (*Returns with an air of mystery.*)

Teodora. Stop, Julian, I beg of you. Can't you see that he will take alarm? (Don Julian *goes out on the right, and laughs to himself, looking back at* Ernest.)

(*Twilight has fallen, so that at this moment the room is in deep shadow.*)

Ernest. I am dazed by so much kindness. How can I ever repay it? (*He sits down on the sofa, displaying great emotion.* Teodora *walks over and stands beside him.*)

Teodora. By ejecting the spirit of pride and distrust; by being sensible and believing that we truly love you, that we will never change; and by putting full faith in all Julian's promises. His word is sacred, Ernest, and in him you will always have a father, in me a sister.

(*Enter* Doña Mercedes *and* Don Severo. *They remain behind. The room is quite dark, save for a glimmer of light shed from the balcony, toward which* Ernest *and* Teodora *have moved.*

Ernest. How good you are!

Teodora. And you, what a boy! After today I hope you have done with sadness—eh?

Ernest. Quite.

Mercedes (*outside, speaking low*). How dark it is!

Severo (*in same tone*). Come away, Mercedes.

Mercedes (*crossing the threshold*). There is nobody here.

Severo (*detaining her*). Yes, there is. (*Both stand a while peering.*)

ERNEST. Teodora, my whole life, a thousand lives would still not be enough to offer you in return for your kindness. Don't judge me by my morose temper. I cannot lend a showy front to my affections, but, believe me, I do know how to love—and hate as well. My heart can beat to bursting under the lash of either sentiment.

MERCEDES (*to* SEVERO). What are they saying?

SEVERO. Something odd, but I hear imperfectly. (TEODORA *and* ERNEST *go out on the balcony, speaking low.*)

MERCEDES. It's Ernest.

SEVERO. And she—I suppose—is—

MERCEDES. Teodora.

SEVERO. Their eternal tricks—always together. I can stand no more of this. And their words? I musn't put it off any longer—

MERCEDES. True, Severo. Come away. It is certainly your duty, since everybody is talking.

SEVERO. Yes, I must open Julian's eyes—today, at once.

MERCEDES. The fellow has impudence enough, and to spare.

SEVERO. By all that's holy—so has she.

MERCEDES. Poor girl! She's but a child. Leave her to me.

TEODORA. Another house? Surely no. You wouldn't leave us? What an idea! Julian would never consent.

SEVERO (*to* DOÑA MERCEDES). I should think not indeed, neither would I. (*aloud*) Ah, Teodora, you didn't see me? This is how you receive your guests.

TEODORA (*coming from the balcony*). Don Severo! I am delighted.

MERCEDES. Is there no dinner this evening? It's near the hour.

TEODORA. Mercedes too!

MERCEDES. Yes, Teodora.

SEVERO (*aside*). She is a capital actress. What a creature!

TEODORA. I must ring for lights. (*Touches the bell on the table.*)

SEVERO. Quite so. Everyone likes plenty of light.

SERVANT. Madam?

TEODORA. Bring the lamps, Genaro. (*Exit* SERVANT.)

SEVERO. He who follows the narrow path of loyalty and duty, and is always that which he appears to be, need never fear the light, nor blush in its glare.

(*The* SERVANT *enters with lamps, the stage is brilliantly illuminated. After a pause.*)

TEODORA (*laughing naturally*). So I should think, and such, I imagine, is the general opinion. (*Looks at* MERCEDES.)

MERCEDES. I suppose so.

SEVERO. Hello, Don Ernest! what were you doing out there? Were you with Teodora when we came in! (*Speaks with marked intention.*)

ERNEST (*coldly*). I was here as you see.

SEVERO. The deuce you were! It is rather dark to see. (*approaches him with outstretched hand, looking fixedly at him.* TEODORA *and* MERCEDES *converse apart. Aside*) His face is flushed, and he appears to have been crying. In this world only children and lovers weep. (*aloud*) And Julian?

TEODORA. He went away to write a letter.

ERNEST (*aside*). Though I have patience to spare, this man tries me hard.

SEVERO (*to* TEODORA). I am going to see him. There is still time before dinner?

TEODORA. Plenty.

SEVERO. Good. (*aside, rubbing his hands, and looking back at* ERNEST *and* TEODORA) Then to work. (*aloud*) Goodbye.

TEODORA. Goodbye.

SEVERO (*rancorously, from the door*). My faith!

MERCEDES (*to* ERNEST). We did not see you today.

ERNEST. No, madam.

MERCEDES. Nor Pepito?

ERNEST. No.

MERCEDES. He is upstairs alone.

ERNEST (*aside*). Let him stop there.

MERCEDES (*gravely and mysteriously to* TEODORA). I wish he would go. I want to speak to you.

TEODORA. Indeed?

MERCEDES (*in same tone*). Yes, it is something very serious.

TEODORA. Well, begin!

MERCEDES. Why doesn't he go?

TEODORA (*in a low voice*). I don't understand you.

MERCEDES. Courage! (*takes her hand and clasps it affectionately.* TEODORA *looks at her in somber question*) Send him about his business.

TEODORA. If you insist. Ernest, will you do me a favor?

ERNEST. Gladly—with a thousand wills.

MERCEDES (*aside*). One were still too many.

TEODORA. Then go upstairs—to Pepito— But it might bore you to carry a message.

ERNEST. By no means.

MERCEDES (*aside*). In what a sweet, soft voice he speaks to her!

TEODORA. Tell him—ask him if he has renewed our subscription at the Opera as I told him. He knows about it.

ERNEST. With pleasure—this very moment.

TEODORA. Thanks, Ernest, I am sorry——

ERNEST. Nonsense. (*Exit.*)

TEODORA. Adieu! (*to* MERCEDES) Something serious? You alarm me, Mercedes. Such mystery! What can it mean?

MERCEDES. It is indeed very serious.

TEODORA. Concerning whom?

MERCEDES. All of you.

TEODORA. All of us?

MERCEDES. Julian, Ernest, and you.

TEODORA. All three?

MERCEDES. Yes, all three. (*Short pause. Both women stare at each other.*)

TEODORA. Then make haste.

MERCEDES (*aside*). I should like to—but, no; I must go gently in this unsavory affair. (*aloud*) Listen, Teodora. My husband is, after all, your husband's brother, and in life and death our fortunes are one. So that we owe one another in all things protection, help, and advice—is it not so? Today it may be I who offer assistance, and tomorrow, should I need it, I unblushingly claim it of you.

TEODORA. You may count upon it, Mercedes. But come to the end of the matter now.

MERCEDES. Up to today, Teodora, I shrank from this step, but Severo urges me. "It can't go on," he insists. "My brother's honor and my own self-esteem forbid me to witness that which fills me with shame and sorrow. On all sides am I assailed with innuendoes, with the smiles, the covert glances and the reproaches of my friends. There must be an end to this low gossip about us."

TEODORA. Continue, pray.

MERCEDES. Then heed me. (*They exchange a prolonged gaze.*)

TEODORA. Tell me, what is the gossip?

MERCEDES. The murmuring of the river tells us that its waters are swollen.

TEODORA. I understand nothing of your river and its swollen waters, but do not drive me wild.

MERCEDES (*aside*). Poor child! My heart grieves for her. *aloud*) So you do not understand me?

TEODORA. I? not in the least.

MERCEDES (*aside*). How stupid she is! (*aloud, energetically*) You make a laughing-stock of him.

TEODORA. Of whom?

MERCEDES. Why, of your husband, of course.

TEODORA (*impetuously, rising*). Julian! what a falsehood! What wretch could say so? Julian would strike him!

MERCEDES (*endeavoring to soothe her and make her sit down*). He would need a good many hands, then; for, if report speak truly, he would have to strike the entire town.

TEODORA. But what does it all mean? What is the mystery, and what is this talk of the town?

MERCEDES. So you're sorry?

TEODORA. I am sorry. But what is it?

MERCEDES. You see, Teodora, you are quite a child. At your age one is so often thoughtless and light, and then such bitter tears are afterwards shed. You still don't understand me?

TEODORA. No, what has such a case to do with me?

MERCEDES. It is the story of a scoundrel and the story of a lady——

TEODORA (*eagerly*). Whose name——?

MERCEDES. Her name——

TEODORA. Oh, what does it matter?

(TEODORA *moves away from* MERCEDES, *who shifts her seat on the sofa to follow her. The double movement of repugnance and aloofness on* TEODORA's *part, and of insistence and protection on* MERCEDES' *is very marked.*)

MERCEDES. The man is a shabby-hearted betrayer, who, for one hour of pleasure, would thrust upon the woman a life of sorrow: the husband's dishonor, the ruin of a family, and she left shamed and condemned to social penitence in the world's disdain, and to keener punishment still at the whip of her own conscience.

(*Here* TEODORA, *avoiding* MERCEDES, *reaches the edge of the sofa, bows her head and covers her face with both hands. At last she understands.*)

MERCEDES (*aside*). Poor little thing! She touches me. (*aloud*) This man is not worthy of you, Teodora.

TEODORA. But, madam, what is the drift of all this blind

emotion? Do not imagine that my eyes are dimmed with fear or horror or tears. They burn with the flame of anger. To whom can such words be addressed? What man do you mean? Is it, perchance——?

MERCEDES. Ernest.

TEODORA. Ah! (*pause*) And the woman I? Not so? (MERCEDES *nods and* TEODORA *rises again.*) Then listen to me, though I may offend you. I know not who is the viler, the inventor of this tale or you who repeat it. Shame upon the meanness that formed the idea, and shame upon the villainy that spreads it! It is so abominable, so fatal, that I almost feel myself criminal because I cannot instantly reject the thought and forget it. Heavens! Could I suppose or credit such baseness? Because of his misfortunes I loved him. He was like a brother to me, and Julian was his providence. And he so noble and thorough a gentleman! (*stands staring at* MERCEDES, *then turns away her face. Aside*) How she inspects me! I scarcely like to say a good word for him to her. My God! I am compelled already to act a part.

MERCEDES. Be calm, child.

TEODORA (*raising her voice*). Oh, what anguish! I feel cold and inconsolable. Stained in this way by public opinion! Oh, my dearest mother, and you, Julian, my heart's beloved. (*She falls sobbing into a chair on the left, and* MERCEDES *strives to console her.*)

MERCEDES. I did not imagine—forgive me—don't cry. There, I didn't really believe it was serious. I knew your past exonerated you. But as the case stands, you must admit that out of every hundred a hundred would accuse you and Julian of excessive rashness, or say you had led the world to conclude the worst. You a girl of twenty, Julian a man of forty, and Ernest between you, with his head full of romantic thoughts. On the one hand, a husband given up to business, on the other a youth to dreams, every day bringing its opportunity, and you there, unoccupied, in the flush of romance. It was wrong for people to conclude the worst because they saw you walking with him, and saw him so often at the theater with you. But, Teodora, in reason and justice I think that, if the world was bent on seeing evil, you furnished the occasion. Permit me to point out to you that the fault which society most fiercely chastizes, pursues most relentlessly and cruelly, and in every varied imaginable way, both in man and woman is—don't frown so, Teodora—is *temerity*.

TEODORA (*turning to* MERCEDES *without having heard her*). And you say that Julian——

MERCEDES. Is the laughing-stock of the town, and you——

TEODORA. Oh, I! That's no matter. But Julian!—Oh, oh, so good, so chivalrous! If he only knew——

MERCEDES. He will know, for at this very moment Severo is telling him.

TEODORA. What!

JULIAN (*inside*). That will do.

TEODORA. Oh, goodness!

JULIAN. Let me alone.

TEODORA. Come away, quickly.

MERCEDES (*rushing with* TEODORA *toward first door on the right*). Yes, yes, quickly. What folly! (TEODORA *and* MERCEDES *go to the right.*)

TEODORA (*stopping suddenly*). But why, since I am not guilty? Not only does miserable calumny stain us, but it degrades us. It is so steeped in evil, that, against all evidence, its very breath takes the bloom off our consciences. Why should an idle terror cast its mean influence over me? (*At this moment* DON JULIAN *appears on the threshold of the first door on the right hand side, and behind him stands* DON SEVERO.)

TEODORA. Julian!

DON JULIAN. Teodora! (*She runs over to him, and he folds her in a passionate embrace.*) Here in my arms, dearest. It is the home of your honor. (*to* DON SEVERO) Let it pass for this once, but, please God! there's an end of it. Whoever in future shall stain this face with tears (*pointing to* TEODORA), I swear, and mean it, will never again cross the threshold of my house—though he should be my own brother. (*Pause.* DON JULIAN *soothes and comforts* TEODORA.)

DON SEVERO. I only mentioned common report.

DON JULIAN. Infamous!

DON SEVERO. It may be so.

DON JULIAN. It is.

DON SEVERO. Well, let me tell you what everyone says.

DON JULIAN. Filth! abominable lies.

DON SEVERO. Then repeating them—

DON JULIAN. —is not the way to put an end to them. (*Pause.*)

DON SEVERO. You are wrong.

DON JULIAN. Right—more than right. A fine thing it would be if you carry the mire of the street into my drawing-room!

DON SEVERO. But I will do so.

DON JULIAN. You shall not.

DON SEVERO. You bear my name.

DON JULIAN. Enough.

DON SEVERO. And your honor——

DON JULIAN. Remember that you are in my wife's presence. (*Pause.*)

DON SEVERO (*in a low voice to* DON JULIAN). If our father saw you——

DON JULIAN. What do you mean, Severo?

MERCEDES. Hush! Here is Ernest.

TEODORA (*aside*). How dreadful! If he should know—— (TEODORA *turns away her face, and holds her head bent.* DON JULIAN *looks at her questioningly.* ERNEST *enters and walks over to* TEODORA.)

ERNEST (*looking at* DON JULIAN *and* TEODORA. *Aside*). He and she! It is no illusion. Can it be what I feared? what that fool told me. (*referring to* PEPITO, *who at that moment enters behind*) It was not his invention.

PEPITO (*staring strangely about*). My salutations to all, and good appetite—as it is dinner-time. Here are the tickets, Teodora. Don Julian——

TEODORA. Thanks, Pepito. (*Accepts them mechanically.*)

ERNEST (*to* DON JULIAN *in a low voice*). What's the matter with Teodora?

DON JULIAN. Nothing.

ERNEST (*in same tone*). She is pale, and has been crying.

DON JULIAN (*angrily*). Don't busy yourself about my wife. (*Pause.* DON JULIAN *and* ERNEST *exchange glances.*)

ERNEST (*aside*). The wretches! They've completed their work.

PEPITO (*in a low voice to his mother, pointing to* ERNEST). He ought to have a straitjacket. I quizzed him about Teodora. Poof! Upon my word, I thought he'd kill me.

ERNEST (*aloud, with resolution and sadness*). Don Julian, I have thought over your generous offer, and much as I've already abused your kindness, it goes sorely against me to refuse it now. But, sir, I feel that I ought to reject this post you offer me.

DON JULIAN. Why?

ERNEST. Because I am so fashioned—a poet and a dreamer. My father, sir, trained me for no career. I want to travel; I am restless and liable to revolt. I am not capable of settling down like another. Like a new Columbus, I am bitten by the spirit of adventure. But we will appeal to Don Severo. He will decide if I am right.

DON SEVERO. You speak like the book of wisdom and like a man of sense. I have been thinking as you do for a long while.

DON JULIAN. Since when have you felt this itch for new worlds and travel? When did you make up your mind to leave us? And the means?—where are they?

DON SEVERO. He wants to go away—to some place more to his taste than here. To be just, Julian, the rest is your affair. Give him as much as he wants, too, for this is no time for economy.

ERNEST (*to* DON SEVERO). I don't traffic with dishonor, nor receive alms. (*pause*) Well, it must be so; and as our parting would be a sad one—for in this life, who knows? I may never come back, and may not see them again—it is better that we should shake hands now, here, Don Julian, and have it over. Thus we snap the tie, and you forgive my selfishness. (*Deeply moved.*)

DON SEVERO (*aside*). How they stare at one another!

TEODORA (*aside*). What a noble fellow!

ERNEST (*to* DON JULIAN). Why do you withhold your hand? It is our last adieu, Don Julian. (*Goes toward him with outstretched hands.* DON JULIAN *embraces him.*)

DON JULIAN. No, lad. The question well considered, this is neither the first nor the last. It is the cordial embrace of two honorable men. You must not mention your mad project again.

DON SEVERO. Then he is not going away?

DON JULIAN. Never. I have not the habit of changing my mind or the plans I have matured because of a boy's caprice or a madman's folly. And I have still less intention of weakly subjecting my actions to the town's idle gossip.

DON SEVERO. Julian!

DON JULIAN. Enough. Dinner is served.

ERNEST. Father, I cannot——

DON JULIAN. But what if I believe you can? Or does my authority begin to bore you?

ERNEST. I beg you——

DON JULIAN. Come, dinner is ready. Give your arm to Teodora, and take her in.

ERNEST (*looking at her, but holding back*). To Teodora!

TEODORA (*with a similar emotion*). Ernest!

DON JULIAN. Yes, as usual.

(*There is a movement of uncertainty on both sides;
finally* ERNEST *approaches and* TEODORA *takes his arm,
but neither dares to look at the other, and both are
abrupt and violently agitated.*)

DON JULIAN (*to* PEPITO). And you! The deuce, why don't
you offer your arm to your mother? My good brother Severo
will take mine. So, quite a family party, and now let pleasure
flow with the wine in our glasses. So there are gossips about?
Well, let them chatter and scream. A farthing for all they can
say. I shouldn't object to a glass house, that they might
have the pleasure of staring in at Teodora and Ernest together, and learn how little I care for their spite and their
calumnies. Each man to his fancy.

(*Enter* SERVANT *in black suit and white tie.*)

SERVANT. Dinner is served.

(*The dining-room door opens and displays a well-ap-
pointed table.*)

DON JULIAN. Let us look after our life, since it will be the
affair of others to look after our death. Come. (*Invites the
others to pass.*)

TEODORA. Mercedes.

MERCEDES. Teodora.

TEODORA. I pray you, Mercedes.

(DOÑA MERCEDES *passes in with* PEPITO *and takes her
place at the table.* ERNEST *and* TEODORA *stand plunged
in thought,* ERNEST *looking anxiously at her.*)

DON JULIAN (*aside*). He is looking at her, and there are
tears in her eyes. (TEODORA, *walking unsteadily and struggling with emotion, slowly follows the others inside.*)

DON JULIAN (*to* SEVERO). Are they talking together?

DON SEVERO. I don't know, but I think it very probable.

DON JULIAN. Why are they looking back at us? Both! Did
you notice? I wonder why.

DON SEVERO. You see, you are growing reasonable at
last!

DON JULIAN. No, I've caught your madness. Ah, how sure
a thing is calumny! It pierces straight to the heart.

ACT II

SCENE: *A small room almost poorly furnished. Door at the end, on the right another door, and on the left a balcony. A bookcase, a table, an armchair. On the table* DON JULIAN's *portrait in a frame, beside it an empty frame; both small and alike. On the table an unlighted lamp,* The Divine Comedy, *open at the Francesca episode, and close to it a morsel of burnt paper. Papers scattered about, and the manuscript of a play. A few chairs. Time: Day.*

(*Enter* DON JULIAN. DON SEVERO *and* SERVANT *below.*)

DON SEVERO. Don Ernest is out?

SERVANT. Yes, sir. He went out early.

DON SEVERO. No matter. We'll wait. I suppose he will be in sooner or later.

SERVANT. I should think so. Nobody could be more punctual than he.

DON SEVERO. That will do.

SERVANT. Certainly, sir. If you want anything, you'll find me downstairs. (*Exit* SERVANT.)

DON SEVERO (*looking round*). How modest!

DON JULIAN. Poor is a better word.

DON SEVERO. What a lodging! (*opens the door and peeps in*) An alcove, this study, and an outer room—and that's all.

DON JULIAN. And thereby hangs the devil's own tale of human ingratitude, of bastard sentiment, of miserable passions, and of blackguard calumny. And whether you tell it quickly or at length, there's never an end to it.

DON SEVERO. It is the work of chance.

DON JULIAN. Not so, my dear fellow. It was the work of—well, I know whom.

DON SEVERO. Meaning me?

DON JULIAN. Yes, you as well. And before you the empty-

324

pated idlers whom it behoved to busy themselves shame-
lessly about my honor and my wife's. And I, coward, mean,
and jealous, I let the poor fellow go, despite my evidence of
his upright nature. I responded to his nobler conduct by black
ingratitude. Yes, ingratitude. You see my ostentatious wealth,
the luxury of my surroundings and equipages, and the credit
of my firm. Well, do you know where all that comes from?

DON SEVERO. I have quite forgotten.

DON JULIAN. Justly said—forgotten! Such is the natural
reward of every generous action, of every unusual impulse
that prompts one man to help another quietly, without a
flourish of trumpet or self-advertisement—just for friendship's
or for honesty's sake.

DON SEVERO. You are unjust to yourself. To such an
excess have you pushed gratitude, that you have almost sac-
rificed honor and fortune to it. What more could be expected
—even of a saint? There's a limit to all things, good and evil.
He is proud and obstinate, and, however much you may oppose him, it is none the less a fact that he's his own master.
If he chooses to leave your palace in a fit of despair, for
this shanty—it's his right. I admit, my dear boy, that it's very
sad—but then, who could have prevented it?

DON JULIAN. The world in general, if it would mind its
own business instead of tearing and rending reputations by
the movement of its tongue and the sign of its hand. What
did it matter to the public if we, fulfilling a sacred duty,
treated Ernest, I as a son, and Teodora as a brother? Is it
reason enough to assume the worst, and trumpet scandal because a fine lad sits at my table, walks out with my wife, and
has his seat in my opera-box? Is by chance impure love
the sole supreme bond between man and woman in this
world of clay? Is there no friendship, gratitude, sympathy, esteem, that youth and beauty should only meet in the mire?
And even supposing that the conclusion of the fools was
the right one, is it their business to avenge me? I have my
own eyes to look after my own affairs, and to avenge my
wrongs have I not courage, steel, and my own right hand?

DON SEVERO. Well, accepting that outsiders were wrong
to talk, did you expect me, who am of your blood and bear
your name, to hold my tongue?

DON JULIAN. By heavens, no! But you should have been
more careful. You might have told me alone of this sorry
business, and not have set flame to a conflagration under my
very roof.

DON SEVERO. I erred through excess of affection, I admit. But while I confess that the world and I have done the mischief—it by inventing the situation, and I by weakly crediting, and by giving voice to the shabby innuendoes—you, Julian (*approaches him and speaks with tender interest*), have nothing to reproach yourself with. You have the consolation of having acted throughout as a gentleman.

DON JULIAN. I cannot so easily console myself, while my heart gives shelter to that same story which my lips and my intelligence reject. I indignantly turn away from the world's calumny, and to myself I say: "What if it should be no lie: if perchance the world should be right?" So I stand in strife between two impulses, sometimes judge, sometimes accomplice. This inward battle wears me out, Severo. Doubt increases and expands, and my heart groans, while before my bloodshot vision stretches a reddened field.

DON SEVERO. Delirium!

DON JULIAN. No, it's not raving. You see, I bare myself to you as a brother. Do you think Ernest would have left my house if I had firmly stood in his way and opposed his crossing the threshold? If so, why does a traitorous voice keep muttering in my disturbed consciousness: "It was wise to leave the door open to his exit, and lock it well afterward, for the confiding man is but a poor guardian of honor's fortress." In my heart I wish what my lips deny. "Come back, Ernest," aloud, and to myself, "Do not come back," and while I show him a frank front, I am a hypocrite and a coward, watchful and worn with mistrust. No, Severo, this is not to act like an honest man. (*He drops into the armchair beside the table in deep dejection.*)

DON SEVERO. It is how any husband would act who had a beautiful young wife to look after, especially one with a romantic temperament.

DON JULIAN. Don't speak so of Teodora. She is a mirror that our breath tarnishes by any imprudent effort to bring it to our level. It gave back the sun's pure light before the million vipers of the earth gathered to stare at it. Today they crawl within the glass in its divine frame, but they are insubstantial shadows. My hand can wave them away, and once more you will see the clear blue of heaven.

DON SEVERO. All the better.

DON JULIAN. No, not so.

DON SEVERO. Then what the deuce do you want?

DON JULIAN. Oh, so much. I told you that this inward struggle of which I spoke is changing me to another man. Now my wife finds me always sad, always distant. I am not the man I was, and no effort will ever make me so again. Seeing me so changed, she must ask, "Where is Julian? this is not my dear husband; what have I done to forfeit his confidence, and what shabby feeling causes this aloofness?" A shadow lies between us, ever deepening, and slowly, step by step, we move more apart. None of the old dear confidence, none of the old delightful talks; smiles frozen, tones embittered, in me through unjust resentment, in her through tearful grief—I wounded in my love, and she, by my hand, wounded in her woman's dignity. There's how we stand.

DON SEVERO. Then you stand upon the verge of perdition. If you see your position so plainly, why don't you remedy it?

DON JULIAN. It's of no use. I know I am unjust to doubt her. No, it's worse still. I don't doubt her now. But who will say that, I losing little by little, and he gaining as steadily, the lie of today will not tomorrow be truth? (*He seizes* DON SEVERO *by the arm, and speaks with voluble earnestness and increasing bitterness.*) I, jealous, somber, unjust, and hard, he noble and generous, resigned and inalterably sweet-natured, with that halo of martyrdom which, in the eyes of women, sits so becomingly on the brow of a brave and handsome youth. Is it not clear that his is the better part, and that my loss is his gain? While I can do nothing to alter the injustice of it. You see it, too? And if the ignoble talk of the town should compel those two to treason, though they may now truthfully assert: "We are not lovers," the force of repetition of the word may eventually drive them to the fact.

DON SEVERO. If that's how you feel about it, Julian, I think the safest thing would be to let Ernest carry out his project.

DON JULIAN. That I've come to prevent.

DON SEVERO. Then you are insane. He purposes to go to Buenos Aires. Nothing could be better. Let him go—in a sailing vessel, fresh wind to his sail, and good speed.

DON JULIAN. Do you wish me to show myself so miserably ungrateful and jealous before Teodora? Don't you know, Severo, that a woman may despise a lover and love him still, but not so a husband? Contempt is his dishonor. You would not have my wife follow the unhappy exile across the ocean with sad regrets? And I, should I see the trace of a tear upon her cheek, the mere thought that it might be for Ernest would drive me to strangle her in my arms. (*Speaks with rancor and rage.*)

DON SEVERO. What is it then you do want?

DON JULIAN. I must suffer. The care of unraveling the knot belongs to the world that conceived the drama solely by looking at us—so fertile is its glance for good and ill.

DON SEVERO (*moving back*). I think somebody is coming.

SERVANT (*from without, not seen on the stage*). Don Ernest cannot be much later.

(*Enter* PEPITO.)

DON SEVERO. You here?

PEPITO (*aside*). By Jove, I see they know all about it. (*aloud*) We are all here. How do you do, uncle? How do, father? (*aside*) Easy. They know what's in the wind. (*aloud*) What brings you?—but I suppose you are looking for Ernest.

DON SEVERO. What else could bring us here?

DON JULIAN. I daresay you know what this madman is up to?

PEPITO. What he's up to! Well, yes—rather. I know as much as another.

DON SEVERO. And it's tomorrow?

PEPITO. No, tomorrow he is going away, so it must be today.

DON JULIAN (*surprised*). What do you say?

PEPITO. That's what Pepe Uceda told me last night at the club. He is Nebreda's second, so he ought to know. But why do you stare so oddly? Didn't you know——

DON JULIAN (*hastily covering his brother's movement*). Everything.

DON SEVERO. We——

DON JULIAN (*aside*). Hold your tongue, Severo. —He starts tomorrow, and today he stakes his life—and we are here, of course, to prevent both, the duel and the departure. (DON JULIAN *makes it evident that he is only sounding* PEPITO's *knowledge of facts, and that he is only aware of the pending departure.*)

DON SEVERO. What duel?

DON JULIAN (*aside to* SEVERO). I know nothing about it, but I shall presently.

PEPITO (*aside*). Come, I haven't been such a duffer after all.

DON JULIAN (*speaking with an air of certainty*). We know there is a viscount—

PEPITO. Yes.

DON JULIAN. With whom Ernest proposes to fight—a certain trustworthy person has informed us, who was at once appraised of it. They say it's a serious matter (PEPITO *nods.*), a disgraceful quarrel in the presence of several witnesses (PEPITO *nods again.*)—the lie direct, and a deluge of bad language—

PEPITO (*interrupts excitedly, glad of his more accurate information*). Language indeed!—a blow bigger than a monument.

DON SEVERO. On which side?

PEPITO. Ernest struck the viscount.

DON JULIAN. Of course Ernest struck the viscount. I thought you knew that, Severo. The viscount insulted him. Patience is not the lad's strong point—hence the blow.

PEPITO. Exactly.

DON JULIAN (*confidently*). I told you we knew the whole story. (*then anxiously*) The affair is serious?

PEPITO. Most serious. I don't like discussing it, but since you know so much, there is no need for further mystery.

DON JULIAN. None whatever. (*He approaches* PEPITO *eagerly.*)

PEPITO (*after a pause, adopts an ominous air to announce bad news.*) It is a matter of life and death. (*looks round triumphantly.* DON JULIAN *and* DON SEVERO *start.*) The viscount is neither a chicken nor a skulk. He can handle a sword.

DON JULIAN. And the quarrel? What was it? Nebreda is supposed to be—

PEPITO. It was hardly a quarrel. I'll tell you the facts. (*Both men draw near eagerly.*) Ernest, you know, means to leave Madrid tomorrow, and take passage in the *Cid* lying in Cadiz. Luiz Alcaraz had promised him a letter of introduction, and the poor fellow went off to meet him at the café and get it, with the best of intentions. Luiz wasn't there, so he waited. Some of the frequenters of Alcaraz's table, who did not know him, were in the full swing of glorious slander, and did not notice his clenched teeth. A name mentioned meant a reputation blasted. Broad-handed, ready-tongued, every living soul passed in their review. In this asylum of charity, in the midst of more smoke than an express train emits, between lifted glass and dropped cigarette ashes, with here and there a lump of sugar, the marble was converted for the moment into a dissecting-table: each woman dishonored, another glass of the old tap: a shout of laughter for each tippler's cut. In four clippings these lads left reputations ragged and the ladies rent to tatters. Yet what did it all come to? They but echoed society at a café-table. I don't say all this for myself, nor think it, but it was how Ernest spoke when he recounted the quarrel to me.

Don Julian. Well, make an end of it.

Pepito. The end of it is, that between name and name, there was mention of one that Ernest could not endure. "Who dares to ridicule an honorable man?" he shouts. Somebody retorts: "A lady," and names a woman. His head was instantly on fire, and he flings himself upon Nebreda. The poor viscount fell like a ninepin, and there you have an Agramante's camp. The day's business is now a duel—in a room somewhere—I don't know where.

Don Julian (seizing his arms). The man was I!

Pepito. Sir?

Don Julian. And Teodora the woman! How have we fallen —she, myself, our love? (Sits down and covers his face with both hands.)

Severo. What have you done, you blockhead!

Pepito. Didn't he say he knew all about it? and I naturally believed him.

Don Julian. Dishonored, dishonored!

Severo (approaching him). Julian, my dear fellow.

Don Julian. It is true. I ought to be calm, I know. But what heart can I have when faith is gone? (seizes his brother's hand) Just Heaven! Why are we so disgraced? What reason have they to turn and throw mud at us? No matter. I know my duty as a gentleman. I can count on you, Severo?

Severo. On me? Till death, Julian. (They shake hands cordially.)

Julian (to Pepito). The duel?

Pepito. For three o'clock.

Julian (aside). I'll kill him—yes, kill him. (to Severo) Come.

Severo. Whither?

Don Julian. To look for this viscount.

Severo. Do you mean——?

Don Julian. I mean to do what I ought and can to avenge

myself and save Don Juan of Acedo's son. (*to* PEPITO) Who
are the seconds?

PEPITO. Alcaraz and Rueda.

DON JULIAN. I know them both. Let him stay here (*pointing to* PEPITO) so that in the event of Ernest's return——

SEVERO. Of course.

DON JULIAN (*to* PEPITO). Without arousing his suspicion,
find out where the duel takes place.

SEVERO. You hear.

DON JULIAN (*to his brother*). Come.

SEVERO. What's the matter with you, Julian?

DON JULIAN. It's a long while since I've felt so overjoyed.
(*Catches* SEVERO's *arm feverishly.*)

SEVERO. The deuce! overjoyed! You're beside yourself.

DON JULIAN. I shall meet that fellow.

SEVERO. Nebreda?

DON JULIAN. Yes. Observe, until today calumny was impalpable. There was no seizing its shape. I have now discovered it, and it has taken a human form. There it is at hand, in
the person of a viscount. Swallowing blood and gall for the
past three months—the devil!—and now—fancy, face to face
—he and I!   (*Exeunt* DON JULIAN *and* DON SEVERO.)

PEPITO. Well, here we are in a nice fix, and all for nothing! However, in spite of my uncle's belief, it was little short
of madness to leave a resplendent creature under the same
roof and in continual contact with a handsome fellow like
Ernest, with a soul on fire, or given to romanticism. He swears
there's nothing in it, and that his feeling for her is pure affection, that he loves her like a sister, and that my uncle
is a father to him. But I am a sly fox, and, young as I am,
I know a thing or two of this world. I've no faith in this sort
of relations, when the brother is young and the sister is beautiful, and brotherhood between them a fiction. But suppose it
were as he says, all square. What do outsiders know about
that? Nobody is under any obligation to think the best of
his fellows. The pair are seen everywhere together, and, seeing them, haven't their neighbors a right to talk? No, swears
Ernest. *We hardly ever went out alone.* Once, perhaps?
That's enough. If a hundred persons saw them on that occasion, it is quite the same as if they had been seen in public
a hundred times. Good Lord! How are you going to confront all the witnesses to prove whether it was once or often
they chose to give an airing to this pure sympathy and brotherly love? It's absurd—neither just nor reasonable. What we

see we may mention—it's no lie to say it. "I saw them once," says one, "And I," another. One and one make two. "And I also"—that makes three. And then a fourth, and a fifth, and so, summing which, you soon enough reach infinity. We see because we look, and our senses are there to help us to pass the time, without any thought of our neighbor. He must look out for himself, and remember that, if he shuns the occasion, calumny and peril will shun him. (*pause*) And take notice that I admit the purity of the affection, and this makes it so serious a matter. Now, in my opinion, the man who could be near Teodora, and not fall in love with her, must be a stone. He may be learned and philosophical, and know physics and mathematics, but he has a body like another, and she's there with a divine one, and, body of Bacchus! that's sufficient to found an accusation on. Ah! If these walls could speak. If Ernest's private thoughts, scattered here, could take tangible form! By Jove! What's this? An empty frame, and beside it Don Julian's likeness in its fellow. Teodora was there, the pendant of my respected uncle. Why has she disappeared? To avoid temptation? (*sits down at the table*) If that's the reason—it's bad. And still worse if the portrait has left its frame for a more honorable place near his heart. Come forth, suspected imps that float about, and weave invisible meshes. Ruthlessly denounce this mystic philosopher. (*looks about the table and sees the open Dante*) Here's another. I never come here but I find this divine book open on Ernest's table. *The Divine Comedy!* His favorite poem, and I note that he seems never to get beyond the Francesca page. I conceive two explanations of the fact. Either the fellow never reads it, or he never reads any other. But there's a stain, like a tear-drop. My faith! what mysteries and abysses! And what a difficult thing it is to be married and live tranquilly. A paper half burnt—(*picks it up*)— there's still a morsel left. (*Goes over to the balcony trying to read it. At this moment* ERNEST *enters, and stands watching him.*)

ERNEST. What are you looking at?

PEPITO. Hello! Ernest. Only a paper I caught on the wing. The wind blew it away.

ERNEST (*takes it and returns it after a short inspection*). I don't remember what it is.

PEPITO. Verses. You may remember (*reads with difficulty*) "The flame that consumes me." (*aside*) *Devora* rhymes with *Teodora.*

ERNEST. It is nothing important.

PEPITO. No, nothing. (*Throws away the paper.*)

ERNEST. That worthless bit of paper is a symbol of our life—a few sobs of sorrow, and a little flake of ashes.

PEPITO. Then they were verses?

ERNEST. Yes. When I've nothing better to do, sometimes —my pen runs away with me—I write them at night.

PEPITO. And to prick enthusiasm, and get into harness, you seek inspiration in the master's book.

ERNEST. It would seem——

PEPITO. Say no more. It's truly a gigantic work. The episode of Francesca. (*Pointing to the page.*)

ERNEST (*ironically and impatiently*). You can't guess wrong today.

PEPITO. Not entirely, by Jove. Here, where the book is open, I find something I can't guess, and you must explain it to me. Reading a love tale together to pass the time, we are told that Francesca and Paolo reached that part where the gallant author, proving himself no amateur in the business, sings the loves of Launcelot and Queen Guinevere. The match fell pat. The kiss in the book was repeated by the passionate youth on the girl's mouth. And at this point of the story, with rare skill and sublime truth, the Florentine poet tells us what happens. (*points to the line*) But this is what I do not understand. *Galeoto was the book they were reading, and they read no more.* They stopped reading? That's easy enough to understand. But this Galeoto, tell me where he comes in, and who was he? You ought to know, since he has given his name to the play that is to make you famous. Let me see. (*Takes up the manuscript and examines it.*)

ERNEST. Galeoto was the go-between for the Queen and Launcelot and in all loves the *third* may be truthfully nicknamed Galeoto, above all when we wish to suggest an ugly word without shocking an audience.

PEPITO. I see, but have we no Spanish word to express it?

ERNEST. We have one, quite suitable and expressive enough. It's an office that converts desires into ducats, overcomes scruples, and is fed upon the affections. It has a name, but to use it would be putting a fetter upon myself, forcing myself to express what, after all, I would leave unsaid. (*takes the manuscript from* PEPITO *and flings it upon the table*) Each case, I have remarked, has its own special go-between. Sometimes it is the entire social mass that is Galeoto. It then unconsciously exercises the office under the influence of a vice of quite another aspect, but so dexterously does it work against honor and modesty that no greater Galeoto can ever be found. Let a man and woman live happily, in tranquil and earnest fulfilment of their separate duties. Nobody minds them, and they float along at ease. But God be praised, this is a state of things that does not last long in Madrid. One morning somebody takes the trouble to notice them, and from that moment, behold society engaged in the business, without aim or object, on the hunt for hidden frailty and impurity. Then it pronounces and judges, and there is no logic that can convince it, nor living man who can hope to persuade it, and the most honest has not a rag of honor left. And the terrible thing is, that while it begins in error it generally ends in truth. The atmosphere is so dense, misery so envelops the pair, such is the press and torrent of slander, that they unconsciously seek one another, unite lovelessly, drift toward their fall, and adore each other until death. The world was the stumbling-stone of virtue, and made clear the way for shame—was Galeoto and—(*aside*) stay! what mad thought inflames me!

PEPITO (*aside*). If that's the way he discourses to Teodora, heaven help poor Don Julian. (*aloud*) I suppose last night's verses dealt with the subject.

ERNEST. Yes, they did.

PEPITO. How can you waste your time so coolly, and sit there so calm, doing nothing, when in another hour you will be measuring swords with Nebreda, who, for all his dandy's cane, is a man when put upon his mettle? Wouldn't it be saner and wiser to practise fencing instead of expounding questions of verse and rhyme? You look so mighty cool that I almost doubt if you regard your meeting with the viscount as serious.

ERNEST. No—for a good reason. If I kill him, the world gains; if he kills me, I gain.

PEPITO. Well, that's good.

ERNEST. Don't say any more about it.

PEPITO (*aside*). Now I must warily find out. (*approaches him and speaks in a low voice*) Is it for today?

ERNEST. Yes, today.

PEPITO. Outside the town?

ERNEST. No, there's no time for that. Besides, we wish to keep it quiet.

PEPITO. In a house, then?

ERNEST. So I proposed.

PEPITO. Where?

ERNEST. Upstairs. (*speaks with cold indifference*) There's an empty room upstairs, with a side window, through which nobody can look. Under the circumstances it's better than a field, and will be had for a handful of silver.

PEPITO. And now all you need——

ERNEST. The swords!

PEPITO. I hear voices outside. Somebody is coming—the seconds?

ERNEST. Maybe.

PEPITO. It sounds like a woman's voice. (*Approaches the door.*)

ERNEST (*approaching also*). But who's keeping them?
(SERVANT *enters.*)

SERVANT (*mysteriously*). Somebody wants to see you, sir.

ERNEST. Who?

SERVANT. A lady.

ERNEST. How extraordinary!

PEPITO (*aside to servant*). What does she want?

SERVANT (*to* PEPITO). She is crying.

PEPITO (*aloud*). Is she young?

SERVANT. Really, sir, I can't say. It's very dark outside, and the lady's face is so thickly veiled that the devil himself couldn't tell what she's like, and she speaks so low you can't even hear her.

ERNEST. Who can she be?

PEPITO. Who could want to see you?

ERNEST. I cannot think.

PEPITO (*aside*). This is startling. (*takes up his hat and holds out his hand*) Well, I'll leave you in peace. Goodbye and good luck. (*to the servant*) What are you waiting for, you fool?

SERVANT. For orders to show the lady in.

PEPITO. In such a case it's your business to anticipate them. And afterward, until the veiled one has departed, you mustn't let anyone in unless the sky were falling.

SERVANT. Then I am to show her in?

ERNEST. Yes. (*to* PEPITO *at the door*) Goodbye.

PEPITO. Goodbye, Ernest.   (*Exit* SERVANT *and* PEPITO.)

ERNEST. A lady? On what pretext? What does this mean? (*Enter* TEODORA, *thickly veiled; she stands without approaching.*) Ah, there she is! . . . You desire to speak to me, madam? Kindly be seated. (*Offers her a chair.*)

TEODORA (*unveiling*). Forgive me, Ernest.

ERNEST. Teodora!

TEODORA. I am wrong to come—am I not?

ERNEST (*abruptly and stammering*). I can't say—since I don't know to what I owe this honor. But what am I saying? Alas! (*with devotion*) Here, in my rooms, madam, reverence attends you, than which you cannot find a greater. But what wrong can you possibly fear here, lady?

TEODORA. None—and there was a time—but that *once* is forever past. No thought of doubt or fear was then. I might have crossed any room on your arm without blush or fluttering pulse. But now! They tell me that you are starting for America tomorrow—and I—yes—like those who go away—perhaps not to return—it is so sad to lose a friend!—before Julian—before the whole world—thinking only of our affection —I myself, Ernest, would have held out my arms to you—in farewell.

ERNEST (*starts and quickly restrains himself*). Oh, Teodora!

TEODORA. But now I suppose it is not the same thing. There is a gulf between us.

ERNEST. You are right, madam. We may no longer care for one another, be no longer brother and sister. The mutual touch of palm would leave our hands unclean. It's all forever past. What we have now to learn is to hate one another.

TEODORA (*in naïve consternation*). Hate! surely not!

ERNEST. Have I used that word—and to you! Poor child!

TEODORA. Yes.

ERNEST. Don't heed me. If you needed my life, and the occasion offered itself, claim it, Teodora, for, to give my life for you would be— (*with passion*) it would be my duty. (*with a sudden change of voice. Pause*) Hate! if my lips pronounced the word, I was thinking of the misery—I was thinking of the injury I have unwittingly brought one to whom I owe so much. Yes, you, Teodora, must hate me—but I—ah, no!

TEODORA (*sadly*). They have made me shed tears enough; yes, you are right in that, Ernest (*with tenderness*) but you I do not accuse. Who could condemn or blame you for all this talk? You have nothing to do with the venomous solicitude with which evil minds honor us, nor with poor Julian's clouded temper. It is sorrow that makes him restive, and his suffering wounds me, for I know that it springs from doubt of my devotion.

ERNEST. That is what I cannot understand (*angrily*) and in him less than in another. It is what drives me wild: by the living God, I protest it is not worthy of pity, and there is no excuse for it. That the man should exist who could doubt a woman like you!

TEODORA. Poor fellow, he pays a heavy price for his savage distrust.

ERNEST (*horrified to find he has been blaming* DON JULIAN *to* TEODORA). What have I said? I don't accuse him—no—I meant——(*He hastens to exculpate* DON JULIAN *and modify his former words.*) Anybody might feel the same, that is, if he were very much in love. In our earthly egoism, don't we doubt the very God in heaven? And the owner of a treasure jealously watches it as gold, and cannot but fear for it. I, too, in his place, would be full of doubt—yes—even of my own brother. (*Speaks with increasing fervor, and again restrains himself, perceiving that he is on the brink of a peril he would avoid.* TEODORA *hears voices outside and rushes to the door.*)

ERNEST. Where are you leading me, rebel heart? What depth have I stirred? I accuse the world of calumny, and would now prove it right.

TEODORA. Do you hear? Somebody is coming.

ERNEST (*following her*). It is hardly two o'clock. Can it be——?

TEODORA (*with terror*). It is Julian's voice. —He is coming in!

ERNEST. No, they have prevented him.

TEODORA (*turns to* ERNEST, *still frightened*). If it were Julian? (*Moves towards the bedroom door.* ERNEST *detains her respectfully.*)

ERNEST. Should it be he, stay here. Loyalty is our shield. Were it one of those who distrust us—then there, Teodora. (*points to the door*) Ah, nobody. (*Listening.*)

TEODORA. How my heart throbs!

ERNEST. You need not be afraid. The person who wanted to come in has gone away—or it was an illusion. For God's sake, Teodora——! (*Advances up the stage.*)

TEODORA. I had so much to say to you, Ernest, and the time has passed so quickly.

ERNEST. The time has flown.

TEODORA. I wanted——

ERNEST. Teodora, pray forgive me—but is it prudent? If any one came in—and, indeed, I fear someone will.

TEODORA. That is why I came—to prevent it.

ERNEST. So that——?

TEODORA. I know everything, and I am stricken with horror at the thought that blood should be shed on my account. My head is on fire, my heart is bursting. (*Strikes her breast.*)

ERNEST. It is the affront that burns and shames you until my hand has struck at Nebreda's life. He wanted mud! Well, let him have it stained with blood.

TEODORA. You would kill him?

ERNEST. Certainly. (*represses* TEODORA's *movement of supplication*) You can dispose of me in all else but in this one thing. Do not ask me to feel compassion for a man whose insult I remember.

TEODORA (*prayerfully, with a sob*). For my sake!

ERNEST. For your sake?

TEODORA. It would be such a horrible scandal.

ERNEST. That is possible.

TEODORA. You can say it so coolly, and not endeavor to avoid it, not even when it is I who implore you!

ERNEST. I cannot avoid it, but I can chastize it: so I think and say, and this is my business. Others will look for the insult, I for the punishment.

TEODORA (*coming nearer and speaking softly, as if afraid of her own voice*). And Julian?

ERNEST. Well?

TEODORA. If he were to know about it?

ERNEST. He will know about it.

TEODORA. What will he say?

ERNEST. What?

TEODORA. That only my husband, the man who loves me, has a right to defend me.

ERNEST. Every honorable man has the right to defend a lady. He may not even know her, be neither a friend, nor a relative, nor a lover. It is enough for him to hear a woman insulted. Why do I fight this duel? Why do I defend her? Because I heard the calumny. Because I am myself. Who is so base as to give his protection by scale and measure? Was I not there? Then whoever it was—I or another—who was first on the scene——

TEODORA (*listens eagerly, dominated by him, and holds out her hand to him*). This is noble and honorable, and worthy of you, Ernest. (*then restrains herself and moves backward*) But it leaves Julian humiliated. (*With conviction.*)

ERNEST. He? Humiliated!

TEODORA. Most surely.

ERNEST. Why?

TEODORA. For no reason whatever.

ERNEST. Who will say so?

TEODORA. Everybody.

ERNEST. But wherefore?

TEODORA. When the world hears of the affront, and learns that it was not my husband who avenged me, and above all (*drops her eyes ashamed*) that it was you who took his place —have we not then a new scandal topping the old?

ERNEST (*convinced but protests*). If one had always to think of what people will say, by Heaven there would be no manner or means of living then!

TEODORA. It is so, nevertheless.

ERNEST. Just so. It's horrible.

TEODORA. Then yield.

ERNEST. Impossible.

TEODORA. I beseech you.

ERNEST. No. Looking into the matter, as nobody can know what will happen, it is better that I should face Nebreda. For, after all, if the fellow lacks a sense of honor, he can use a sword.

TEODORA (*wounded and humiliated in the protection* ERNEST *seems to offer* DON JULIAN). My husband is not lacking in courage.

ERNEST. Fatality again! Either I have expressed myself ill, or you do not understand me. I know his worth. But when a desperate injury lies between men of courage, who knows what may happen? which of them may fall, and which may kill? And if this man's sword must strike Don Julian or Ernest, can you doubt which it ought to be? (*Questions her with sad sincerity.*)

TEODORA (*in anguish*). You!—oh, no—not that either.

ERNEST. Why? If it is my fate? Nobody loses by my death, and I lose still less.

TEODORA. For Heaven's sake, do not say that. (*Barely able to repress her sobs.*)

ERNEST. What do I leave behind me? Neither friendship nor strong love. What woman is there to follow my corpse shedding a lover's tears?

TEODORA (*vehemently*). Last night I prayed for you— and you say that nobody— I could not bear you to die.

ERNEST (*with passion*). Ah, we pray for anyone; we only weep for one.

TEODORA (*startled*). Ernest!

ERNEST (*terrified by his own words*). What!

TEODORA (*moving further away*). Nothing.

ERNEST (*also moving away and looking nervously down*). I told you a little while ago I was half mad. Do not heed me. (*Pause. Both remain silent and pensive, at some distance, not looking at each other.*)

TEODORA (*starting and glancing anxiously down the stage*). Again!

ERNEST (*following her movement*). Somebody has come.

TEODORA. They are trying to get in.

ERNEST (*listening*). There can be no doubt of it. There, Teodora. (*Points to the bedroom door.*)

TEODORA. My honor is my shield.

ERNEST. But it is not your husband.

TEODORA. Not Julian?

ERNEST (*leading her to the door*). No.

TEODORA. I hoped—(*detains him with an air of supplication*) Will you give up this duel?

ERNEST. Give it up? When I've struck him!

TEODORA. I didn't know that. (*despairingly, but understands that nothing can be done*) Then fly.

ERNEST. I fly!

TEODORA. For my sake, for his sake—for God's sake!

ERNEST (*despairingly*). You must loathe me to propose such a thing to me. Never!

TEODORA. One word only. Are they coming for you now?

ERNEST. It is not yet time.

TEODORA. Swear it to me.

ERNEST. Yes, Teodora. And you—say you don't hate me.

TEODORA. Never.

PEPITO (*outside*). Nothing. I must see him.

ERNEST. Quickly.

TEODORA. Yes. (*Hides in the bedroom.*)

PEPITO (*outside*). Why do you keep me out?

ERNEST. Ah, calumny is working to make the lie truth.
(*Enter* PEPITO, *without his hat, exhibiting strong excitement.*)

PEPITO. Go to the devil—I will go in—Ernest.

ERNEST. What has happened?

PEPITO. I hardly know how to tell you—yet I must——

ERNEST. Speak.

PEPITO. My head is in a whirl. Christ above, who would think——

ERNEST. Quickly. A clear account of what has happened.

PEPITO. What has happened? A great misfortune. Don Julian heard of the duel. He came here to look for you, and you were out. He went away to find the seconds, and marched them off to Nebreda's house.

ERNEST. Nebreda's! How?

PEPITO. The Lord send you sense. Don Julian's way, of course, who makes short work of convention and the will of others.

ERNEST. Go on——

PEPITO (*going to the door*). They're coming, I believe.

ERNEST. Who?

PEPITO. They—they're carrying Don Julian.

ERNEST. You terrify me. Explain at once. (*Catches his arm violently, and drags him forward.*)

PEPITO. He compelled him to fight. There was no way out of it. The viscount cried: "Very well, between us two." It was settled it should take place here. Don Julian came upstairs. Your servant sent him away, protesting you were engaged with a lady, and swearing nobody could enter.

ERNEST. And then?

PEPITO. Don Julian went downstairs muttering "Better so. I have the day's work for myself." And he, my father, Nebreda, and the seconds came back together, and went upstairs.

ERNEST. They fought?

PEPITO. Furiously, as men fight when their intent is deadly, and their enemy's heart is within reach of the sword's point.

ERNEST. And Don Julian! No—it must be a lie.

PEPITO. Here they are.

ERNEST. Silence. Tell me who it is, but speak softly.

PEPITO. There.

(*Enter* DON JULIAN, DON SEVERO, *and* RUEDA. *The two men support* DON JULIAN, *who is badly wounded.*)

ERNEST. Heaven preserve us! . . . Don Julian! my friend, my father, my benefactor! (*hurries excitedly toward him, and speaks brokenly*)

DON JULIAN (*weakly*). Ernest!

ERNEST. Oh, wretched I!

SEVERO. Quick, come away.

ERNEST. Father!

SEVERO. He is fainting with pain.

ERNEST. For my sake!

DON JULIAN. It is not so.

ERNEST. Through me—pardon! (*takes* DON JULIAN's *hand and bends on one knee before him*)

DON JULIAN. No need to ask it, lad. You did your duty, and I did mine.

SEVERO. A couch. (*loosens his hold of* DON JULIAN, *and* PEPITO *takes his place*)

PEPITO (*pointing to the bedroom*). Let us carry him in there.

ERNEST (*shouting terribly*). Nebreda!

SEVERO. Let there be an end to folly. Is it your intention to kill him outright?

ERNEST (*with frenzy*). Folly, oh, we'll see. I have two to avenge now. It is my right. (*rushes down the stage*)

SEVERO (*moving to the right*). We'll take him into your room and lay him on the bed. (ERNEST *wheels round in terror.*)

ERNEST. Where?

SEVERO. In here.

PEPITO. Yes.

ERNEST. No. (*strides back, and stands before the door. The group are on the point of lifting* DON JULIAN, *desist, and stare at* ERNEST *in indignant surprise.*)

SEVERO. You forbid it?

PEPITO. Are you mad?

SEVERO. Back: can't you see he is dying?

DON JULIAN. What is it? He doesn't wish it? (*raises himself and looks at* ERNEST *in distrust and fear*)

RUEDA. I don't understand it.

PEPITO. Nor I.

ERNEST. He is dying—and implores me—and doubts me—father!

SEVERO. Come, we must. (*pushes open the door above* ERNEST's *shoulder.* TEODORA *is discovered.*)

ERNEST. My God!

SEVERO *and* PEPITO. She!

RUEDA. A woman!

TEODORA (*coming forward to her husband and embracing him*). Julian!

DON JULIAN. Who is it? (*pushes her away to stare at her, drags himself to his feet with a violent effort, and shakes himself free of all aid*) Teodora! (*falls unconscious to the ground*)

ACT III

SCENE: *The same decoration as first act: an armchair instead of a sofa. It is night; a lighted lamp stands on the table.*

(PEPITO *listens at the door on the right, then comes back into the middle of the stage.*)

PEPITO. The crisis is past at last. I hear nothing. Poor Don Julian! He's in a sad way. His life hangs in the balance: on one side death awaits him, and on the other another death, that of the soul, of honor—either abyss deeper than hopeless love. The devil! All this tragedy is making me more sentimental than that fellow with his plays and verses. The tune of disaster, scandal, death, treason, and disgrace hums in my brain. By Jove, what a day, and what a night! And the worst is yet to come. Well, it certainly was madness to move him in his condition; but when once my uncle gets an idea into his head, there's no reasoning with him. And, after all, he was right. No honorable man, in his place, could have stayed, and he is a man of spirit. Who is coming? My mother, I believe—yes.

(*Enter* DOÑA MERCEDES.)

MERCEDES. Where's Severo?

PEPITO. He has not left my uncle for a moment. I had no idea he was so attached to him. If what I fear should happen——

MERCEDES. How is your uncle?

PEPITO. He suffers greatly, but says nothing. Sometimes he calls out "Teodora" in a low harsh voice, and sometimes "Ernest"; and then he tugs violently at the sheets, and lies quiet again as a statue, staring vacantly into space. Now his brow is bathed in the cold sweat of death, and then fever seizes him. He sits up in bed, listens attentively, and shouts that *he* and *she* are waiting for him. He tries to jump out

343

of bed to rush at them, and all my father's entreaties and commands barely suffice to restrain him or soothe him. There's no quieting him. Anger races hot through his veins, and thought is a flame. It is shocking, mother, to see the bitter way his lips contract, and how his fingers close in a vise, with head all wild, and pupils dilated as though they drank in with yearning and despair every shadow that floats around the chamber.

MERCEDES. How does your father bear it?

PEPITO. He groans and breathes of vengeance. He, too, mutters the names of Teodora and Ernest. I hope to God he will not meet either, for if he should, small chance there is of restraining his fury.

MERCEDES. Your father is a good man.

PEPITO. Yes, but with a temper——

MERCEDES. It is not easily aroused, however. But when he has cause——

PEPITO. With all due respect, he's then a very tiger.

MERCEDES. Only when provoked.

PEPITO. I don't know about other occasions, but this time he certainly has provocation enough. And Teodora?

MERCEDES. She is upstairs. She wanted to come down—and cried—like a Magdalen.

PEPITO. Already! Repentant or erring?

MERCEDES. Don't speak so. Unhappy girl, she is but a child.

PEPITO. Who, innocent and candid, sweet and pure and meek, kills Don Julian. So that, if I am to accept your word, and regard her as a child, and such is her work on the edge of infancy, we may pray God in his mercy to guard us from her when she shall have put on years.

MERCEDES. She is hardly to be blamed. The infamy lies with your fine friend—he of the dramas, the poet and dreamer. He it is who is the culprit.

PEPITO. I don't deny it.

MERCEDES. Where is he?

PEPITO. Where is he? At this moment racing about the streets and public places, flying from his conscience, and unable to get away from it.

MERCEDES. He has a conscience?

PEPITO. So it would seem.

MERCEDES. Oh, what a tragedy!

PEPITO. A misfortune!

MERCEDES. Such a deception!

PEPITO. A cruel one.

MERCEDES. What shocking treason!

PEPITO. Unparalleled.

MERCEDES. Poor Julian!

PEPITO. Melancholy fate!

(*Enter* SERVANT.)

SERVANT. Don Ernest.

MERCEDES. He dares——

PEPITO. This is too much.

SERVANT. I thought——

PEPITO. You had no business to think anything.

SERVANT. He is only passing. There is a cab waiting, so——

PEPITO. What are we to do?

MERCEDES. Let him come in.   (*Exit* SERVANT.)

PEPITO. I'll give him his dismissal.

MERCEDES. Do it cleverly.

(ERNEST *enters.* DOÑA MERCEDES *is seated in the armchair,* PEPITO *standing, and* ERNEST *remains behind; neither salute nor look at him.*)

ERNEST (*aside*). Hostile silence, anger, and contempt. Through no fault of my own, I now appear to them a prodigy of evil and insolence, and they all despise me.

PEPITO. Listen to me, Ernest. (*Turns round to him and speaks in a hard voice.*)

ERNEST. Well.

PEPITO. I have to tell you——

ERNEST. To go away, perhaps.

PEPITO (*changing his tone*). Good heavens! What a notion! I only—wanted to ask you—if it is true (*hunts for something to say*) that you afterward—the viscount, you know?

ERNEST (*gloomily looking away*). Yes.

PEPITO. How did it happen?

ERNEST. I ran downstairs—half mad—I found them—we went upstairs again—locked the door. Two men—two witnesses—two swords—and afterwards—I hardly know what happened. Swords clashed—there was a cry—a thrust—blood spouted—an assassin stood—and a man lay stretched on the ground.

PEPITO. The devil! Sharp work. Did you hear, mother?

MERCEDES. More blood shed.

PEPITO. Nebreda deserved it.

ERNEST (*approaching her*). Mercedes, for pity's sake—

one word—Don Julian? How is he? If you could know what
my anguish is—my sorrow—what do they say?

MERCEDES. That the wound, since his removal, is mortal,
and it would be worse for him if you went near the bed of
suffering and death. Leave this house.

ERNEST. I must see him.

MERCEDES. Go, instantly.

ERNEST. I will not.

PEPITO. What insolence!

ERNEST. It is befitting. (*to* PEPITO) Pardon me, madam
(*turning respectfully to* MERCEDES); you see I am achieving
the general opinion of me.

MERCEDES. For pity's sake, Ernest——

ERNEST. Listen, Mercedes. When a man such as I am is
abused, and for no reason on earth treated as a blackguard,
and finds himself snared, with crime thrust upon him, it is
indeed a perilous case—for others rather than for himself.
I, in this fierce struggle with miserable fate, have lost honor,
friendship, and love, and have now nothing more to lose
but the shabby shreds of an insipid and dreary existence. I
have come here solely to know if there is any hope—only
for that—and then—but you cannot deny me so slight a consolation? (*pleading*) One word!

MERCEDES. Very well. They say—that he is better.

ERNEST. True? You are not deceiving me? You are sure—
quite sure? Oh! you are merciful, you are kind. It is true,
quite true! May God spare him! Not his death. Let him live
and be happy once more; let him forgive me and embrace
me once again! Only let me see him. (*Falls into the armchair beside the table sobbing, and covers his face with his
hands. Pause.*)

MERCEDES. If your father should hear—if he should come
out. Courage, Ernest, be sensible. (DOÑA MERCEDES *and*
PEPITO *endeavor to screen* ERNEST.)

PEPITO. These nervous creatures are terrible. They sob
and kill in the same breath.

ERNEST. If you see me crying, while sobs shake my throat
in an hysterical convulsion, and I seem as weak as a child,
or a woman, believe me, it is not for myself, but for him—
for her—for their lost happiness, for this indelible blot upon
their name—for the affront I am the cause of, in return for all
their love and kindness. It is not my fault, but my utter
misfortune. That is why I weep. My God, if I could wipe out

this wretched past with tears, I would gladly weep away my blood to the last drop.

MERCEDES. Silence, I implore you!

PEPITO. There, we will discuss tears and sorrows another time.

ERNEST. If everybody else is discussing them today, why should we too not speak of them? The whole town is astir and on tiptoe with excitement. It has swallowed up, devoured and blighted three reputations, three names, three persons, and floated them on the froth of laughter and a wave of degrading chatter down the straits of human misery, into the social abysm of shame, where forever lie engulfed the conscience, and fame, and future of the unfortunates.

MERCEDES. Not so loud, Ernest.

ERNEST. Why? since the others are not murmurs, but voices, that thunder through the air? The tragic event is known all over the town, and each one has his own way of telling it. Wonderful! everything is known except the truth. It's fatality. (DOÑA MERCEDES *and* PEPITO *exhibit keen interest in hearing the reports.*) Some say that Don Julian discovered Teodora in my rooms, and that I attacked him in blind fury and killed him on the spot. Others—and these would seem to be my friends, since they raise me from the rank of vulgar assassin to the noble level of duelist—aver that we fought loyally like gentlemen. And there are others, again, who have the tale more accurately, and recount how Don Julian took my place in the arranged meeting with Nebreda—that I arrived late on the scene—either from design or fear, or because I was in the arms—but, no; it would burn my lips to give this version—the thought of it sets my brain on fire. Seek the basest, the vilest, that which most blackens—the filth of the mind, the mire of the soul, the dross of degraded consciences; cast it to the wind as it whistles along the streets upon bespattering tongues, and you will have the tale, and may see what reputation remains for an innocent woman and two honest men when the town takes to jabbering about them.

MERCEDES. It is sad, I admit; but perhaps public opinion is not altogether to blame.

PEPITO. Teodora did go to your rooms—she was there——

ERNEST. To prevent the duel with Nebreda.

PEPITO. Then why did she hide herself?

ERNEST. Because we feared her presence would be misconstrued.

PEPITO. The explanation is easy and simple. The difficult thing, Ernest, is to get us to believe it, for there is another still more easy and simple.

ERNEST. Which dishonors more, and that's the beauty of it.

PEPITO. Well, at least, admit that Teodora was giddy, if not really culpable.

ERNEST. Guilt is prudent and cautious. On the other hand, how imprudent is innocence!

PEPITO. Look here, if your rule holds good for everybody, the worst of us is an angel or a saint.

ERNEST. You are right. What does it matter? What is the weight or value of such calumny? The worst of it is that thought is degraded by mean contact with a mean idea. From force of dwelling upon a crime, the conscience becomes familiar with it. It shows itself terrible and repellent—*but it shows itself*—at night, in dark solitude! Yes—(*aside*) but what! why are they listening to me so strangely, almost in suspense? (*aloud*) I am myself; my name is an honorable one. If I killed Nebreda solely because of a lie, what would I not do to myself if guilt threatened to give the truth to calumny?

PEPITO (*aside to* MERCEDES). He denied it! Why, it is as clear as daylight.

MERCEDES (*aside to* PEPITO). He's wandering.

PEPITO. It's only his confession he's making.

MERCEDES (*aloud*). That will do, Ernest. Go, now.

ERNEST. Impossible, madam. I should go mad if I had to spend tonight away from this sickroom—out of my mind.

MERCEDES. But if Severo came and found you?

ERNEST. What do I care? He is a loyal gentleman. Better still, let him come. We fly from fear, and only the guilty are afraid. Nothing will make me run away, or acknowledge fear.

PEPITO (*listening*). Somebody is coming.

MERCEDES. Is it he?

PEPITO (*going down the stage*). No, it's Teodora.

ERNEST. Teodora! Teodora! I want to see her.

MERCEDES (*sternly*). Ernest!

ERNEST. Yes, I must ask her to forgive me.

MERCEDES. You don't remember——

ERNEST. I remember everything and understand. We two together! Ah, no. Enough. You need not fear. For her would I shed my blood, lay down my life, sacrifice my future, honor—all! But see her? Never. It's no longer possible. The mist of blood has risen between us. (*Goes out on the left.*)

MERCEDES. Leave me alone with her. Go inside to your father. I want to see into her heart, and shall be able to probe its depths with my tongue.

PEPITO. Then I will leave you together.

MERCEDES. Goodbye.

PEPITO. Goodbye. (*Goes out on the right.*)

MERCEDES. Now to put my plan to work.

(TEODORA *enters timidly, and stands near* DON JU-LIAN's *door on the right, listening anxiously, and muffling her sobs with her handkerchief.*)

MERCEDES. Teodora.

TEODORA. It is you. (*Advances to her.*)

MERCEDES. Courage! what good does crying do?

TEODORA. How is he? How is he? The truth!

MERCEDES. Much better.

TEODORA. Will he recover?

MERCEDES. I think so.

TEODORA. My God! My life for his.

MERCEDES (*draws her affectionately forward*). And then —I have faith in your good sense. I can measure your remorse by your tears and anxiety.

TEODORA. Yes (DOÑA MERCEDES *sits down with a satisfied air.*), I did wrong, I know, in going to see him (DOÑA MERCEDES *looks disappointed the confession is no worse.*), but last night you told me about the outrage and the duel. I was grateful to you for doing so, although I did not then suspect the harm you did me, nor could I now explain it to you. Oh, what a night! (*crosses her hands and glances upward*) I have cried and raved, thinking of Julian's plight, of the scandal, of the violent quarrel and the bloodshed. Everything passed before my eyes—and then—poor Ernest dying, perhaps for my sake! But why do you look at me so strangely? There can be no harm in it, surely! Or are you unconvinced, and do you think as the rest do?

MERCEDES (*drily*). I think your fear for that fellow's life altogether superfluous.

TEODORA. Why? with so skilled an antagonist! You have seen it—Julian——

MERCEDES. Julian has been avenged. The man who killed him no longer lives, so that you have been wasting your fears and your tears. (*With deliberate hardness.*)

TEODORA (*eagerly*). It was Ernest——

MERCEDES. Yes, Ernest.

TEODORA. He met the viscount?

MERCEDES. Face to face.

TEODORA (*unable to restrain herself*). How noble and brave!

MERCEDES. Teodora!

TEODORA. What do you mean? Tell me.

MERCEDES (*sternly*). I can read your thought.

TEODORA. My thought!

MERCEDES. Yes.

TEODORA. Which?

MERCEDES. You know very well.

TEODORA. Have I no right to be glad because Julian is avenged? Is that an impulse I could be expected to repress?

MERCEDES. That was not your feeling.

TEODORA. You know so much more about it than I do!

MERCEDES (*pointedly*). Believe me, admiration is not far from love.

TEODORA. What do I admire?

MERCEDES. This youth's courage.

TEODORA. His nobility.

MERCEDES. Quite so, but that's the beginning.

TEODORA. What folly!

MERCEDES. It *is* folly—but on your side.

TEODORA. You persist! Ever this accursed idea!—while it is with immense, with infinite pity that I am filled.

MERCEDES. For whom?

TEODORA. For whom else but Julian?

MERCEDES. Have you never learnt, Teodora, that in a woman's heart pity and forgetfulness may mean one and the same thing?

TEODORA. I beseech you—Mercedes—silence!

MERCEDES. I wish to let light in upon the state of your mind—to turn upon it the lamp of truth, lit by my experience.

TEODORA. I hear you, but while I listen, it seems no longer a sister, a friend, a mother that speaks to me, so hateful are your words. Your lips seem to speak at inspiration of the devil's prompting. Why should you strive to convince me that little by little I am ceasing to love my husband, and that more and more I am imbued with an impure tenderness, with a feeling that burns and stains? I who love Julian as dearly as ever, who would give the last drop of blood in my body for a single breath of life for him—for him, from whom I am now separated (*points to his room*) —why, I should like to go in there this moment, if your husband did not bar my way, and press Julian once more in my arms. I would so inundate him with my tears, and so close him round with the passion of my love, that its warmth would melt his doubts, and his soul would respond to the fervor of mine. But it is not because I adore my husband that I am bound to abhor the faithful and generous friend who so nobly risked his life for me. And if I don't hate him, is that a reason to conclude that I love him? The world can think such things. I hear such strange stories, and such sad events have happened, and calumny has so embittered me, that I find myself wondering if public opinion can be true—in doubt of myself. Can it be that I really am the victim of a hideous passion, unconsciously influenced by it? and in some sad and weak moment shall I yield to the senses, and be subjugated by this tyrannous fire?

MERCEDES. You are speaking the truth?

TEODORA. Can you doubt it?

MERCEDES. You really do not love him?

TEODORA. Mercedes, what words have I that will convince you? At another time, such a question would drive the blood of anger to my brow, and today, you see, I am discussing with you whether I am honest or not. Yes, am I really so? To the depth of the soul? No, for endurance of this humiliation proves me worthy of it. (*Hides her face in her hands and flings herself down in the armchair.*)

MERCEDES. Do not cry so, Teodora. I believe in you. Enough. No more tears. Let me but add one more word, and there's an end to the matter. Ernest is not what you believe him to be. He is not worthy of your trust.

TEODORA. He is good, Mercedes.

MERCEDES. No.

TEODORA. He is fond of Julian.

MERCEDES. He would betray him.

TEODORA. Again! My God!

MERCEDES. I no longer accuse you of responding to his passion, but I only assert—I would warn you that *he loves you*.

TEODORA (*rising in anger*). Loves me!

MERCEDES. It is known to everybody. In this very room, a moment ago, before Pepito and me—you understand?

TEODORA. No, explain at once—what?

MERCEDES. He openly confessed it. He made a violent declaration, swore that he was ready to sacrifice life, honor, soul, and conscience for you. And when you came, he wanted to see you. He only yielded to the force of my entreaties and went away. I tremble lest he should meet Severo and their encounter lead to an explosion. And you—what have you to say now?

TEODORA (*who has listened to* MERCEDES *intently, held in an indefinable gloomy terror*). Heavens above! Can it be true? and I who felt—who professed so sincere an affection for him!

MERCEDES. There, you are on the point of crying again.

TEODORA. The heart has no tears for the manifold deceptions of this miserable life. A lad so pure and finely natured —and to see him now so debased and spotted! And you say that he actually uttered those words here—he!—Ernest. Oh, oh, Mercedes! send him away from this house.

MERCEDES. Ah, that is what I wanted. Your energy consoles me. (*With evidence of honest satisfaction.*) Pardon me—now I fully believe you. (*Embraces her.*)

TEODORA. And before? No? (*The actress must strongly accentuate this line.*)

MERCEDES. Hush! He is coming back.

TEODORA (*impetutously*). I will not see him. Tell him so. Julian expects me. (*Goes to the right.*)

MERCEDES (*detaining her*). Impossible! You must know it. He will not heed my orders, and now that I understand so fully how you feel for him, I should be glad to have him suffer at your hands the contempt he has already endured at mine.

TEODORA. Then leave me.

(*Enter* ERNEST.)

ERNEST. Teodora!

MERCEDES (*aside to* TEODORA). It is late, do your duty quickly. (*aloud to* ERNEST) The command you heard a little while ago from me, you will receive again from Teodora's lips, and she is the mistress of this house.

TEODORA (*in a low voice to* MERCEDES). Don't go away.

MERCEDES (*to* TEODORA). Are you afraid?

TEODORA. I afraid! I am afraid of nothing. (*Makes a sign for her to go. Exit* DOÑA MERCEDES *on the right.*)

ERNEST. The command was—that I should go away. (*Pause. Both remain silent without looking at each other.*) And you? Are you going to repeat it? (TEODORA *nods, but still does not look at him*) Have no fear, Teodora. I will respect and obey your order. (*submissively*) The others could not get me to obey them, little as they may like to hear it (*harshly*), but nothing you could say, even though you wound me— From you I will endure anything! (*Sadly.*)

TEODORA. I wound you! No, Ernest, you cannot believe that—— (*Still does not look at him, is half vexed and afraid.*)

ERNEST. I do not believe it. (*Pause.*)

TEODORA. Adieu. I wish you all happiness.

ERNEST. Adieu, Teodora. (*remains waiting for a moment to see if she will turn and offer him her hand. Then walks down the stage, turns back again, and approaches her.* TEODORA *shows that she feels his movement, and is distressed, but continues to keep her face averted.*) If with my death at this very instant I could blot out all the misery that lies to my account, not through any fault of mine, but through an implacable fate, I should not now be standing here alive. You may believe it on the word of an honorable man. No shadow of the past would remain—neither sighs nor pain to remember, nor that sorrowful pallor of your face (TEODORA *starts and glances at him in terror.*), nor the grieved fear of those eyes, nor sobs that tear the throat, nor tears that line the cheek. (TEODORA *sobs.*)

TEODORA (*aside, moving further away*). Mercedes was right, and I, blind and thoughtless that I was——

ERNEST. Bid me goodbye—once—for kindness' sake.

TEODORA. Goodbye! Yes; and I forgive you all the injury you have done us.

ERNEST. I, Teodora!

TEODORA. Yes, you.

ERNEST. What a look! What a tone!

TEODORA. No more, Ernest, I beseech you.

ERNEST. What have I done to deserve——?

TEODORA. It is all over between us. Regard me as one who no longer exists for you.

ERNEST. Is this contempt?

TEODORA. Go.

ERNEST. Go? In this way?

TEODORA. My husband is dying in there—and here I feel as if I too were dying. (*Staggers back and clutches the armchair to keep from falling.*)

ERNEST. Teodora. (*Rushes forward to support her.*)

TEODORA (*angrily drawing herself away*). Don't touch me. (*pause*) Ah, I breathe again more freely. (*Tries to walk, staggers again weakly, and a second time* ERNEST *offers to assist her. She repulses him.*)

ERNEST. Why not, Teodora?

TEODORA. Your touch would soil me.

ERNEST. I soil you!

TEODORA. Exactly.

ERNEST. I! (*pause*) What does she mean, Almighty God! She also! Oh, it is not possible! Oh, death is preferable to this—it cannot be true—I am raving—say it is not true, Teodora—only one word—for justice—one word of pardon, of pity, of consolation, madam. I am resigned to go away, never to see you again, although it were to break, and mutilate, and destroy my life. But it will, at least, be bearable if I may carry into solitude your forgiveness, your affection, your esteem—only your pity, then. So that I still may think you believe me loyal and upright—that I could not, that I have not degraded you, much less be capable of insulting you. I care nothing about the world, and despise its affronts. Its passions inspire me with the profoundest disdain. Whether its mood be harsh or cruel, however it may talk of me and of what has happened, it will never think so ill of me as I do of it. But you, the purest dream of man's imagining—you for whom I would gladly give—not only my life, but my right to heaven, yes, a thousand times—eagerly, joyously—you, to suspect me of treason, of hypocrisy! Oh, this, Teodora—I cannot bear! (*Deeply moved, speaks despairingly.*)

TEODORA (*with increasing nervousness*). You have not understood me, Ernest. We must part.

ERNEST. But not like this!

TEODORA. Quickly, for mercy's sake. Julian suffers. (*Points to the sickroom.*)

ERNEST. I know it.

TEODORA. Then we should not forget it.

ERNEST. No; but I also suffer.

TEODORA. You, Ernest! why?

ERNEST. Through your contempt.

TEODORA. I feel none.

ERNEST. You have expressed it.

TEODORA. It was a lie.

ERNEST. No; not entirely. So that our sufferings are not equal. In this implacable strife *he* suffers as those on earth suffer, *I* as those in hell.

TEODORA. Spare me, Ernest—my head is on fire.

ERNEST. And my heart aches.

TEODORA. That will do, Ernest. I entreat you to pity me.

ERNEST. That was all I asked of you.

TEODORA. Mercy.

ERNEST. Yes, mercy. But why should you claim it? What is it you fear? of what are you thinking? (*Approaches her.*)

TEODORA. Forgive me if I have offended you.

ERNEST. Offended me, no! The truth, that is what I crave —and I implore it on my knees. See, Teodora, my eyes are wet. (*Bends his knee before her and takes her hand.* DON JULIAN's *door opens, and* DON SEVERO *stands staring at them.*)

DON SEVERO (*aside*). Miserable pair!

TEODORA. Don Severo!

(ERNEST *stands apart on the right.* DON SEVERO *places himself between him and* TEODORA.)

DON SEVERO (*in a low voice of concentrated anger, so that* DON JULIAN *may not hear*). I can find no word or epithet adequate to the passion of contempt I would express, so I must be content to call you a blackguard. Leave this house at once.

ERNEST (*also in a low voice*). My respect for Teodora, for this house, and for the sick man lying in yonder room, sir, compels me to put my retort—in silence.

DON SEVERO (*ironically, under the impression that* ERNEST *is going*). It's the best thing you can do—obey and hold your tongue.

ERNEST. You have not understood me. I do not intend to obey.

SEVERO. You remain?

ERNEST. Until Teodora commands me to go. I was on the point of going away for ever a moment ago, but the Almighty or the devil deterred me. Now you come and order me out, and as if your insult were an infernal message, it roots my heels to the floor in revolt.

SEVERO. We'll see that. There are servants to kick you out, and sticks if necessary.

ERNEST. Try it. (*Approaches* DON SEVERO *with a threatening air.* TEODORA *rushes between them.*)

TEODORA. Ernest! (*turns commandingly to* DON SEVERO) You seem to forget that this is my house as long as my husband lives and is its owner. Only one of us two has the right to command here. (*softens to* ERNEST) Not for him— but for my sake, because I am unhappy——

ERNEST (*unable to contain his joy at hearing himself defended by* TEODORA). You wish it, Teodora?

TEODORA. I beg it. (ERNEST *bows and turns away.*)

SEVERO. Your audacity confounds and shocks me as much
—no, far more, than his. (*strides menacingly toward her.*
ERNEST *turns swiftly round, then makes a strong effort to
control himself and moves away again*) You dare to raise
your head, wretched woman, and before me too! Shame on
you! (ERNEST *repeats previous movements and gestures, but
this time more accentuated.*) You, so fearful and cowardly,
where have you found courage to display this energy in
his defence? How eloquent is passion! (ERNEST *stands, looking back.*) But you forget that, before pitching him out, I
had the authority to forbid the door of this house to you,
who have stained its threshold with Julian's blood. Why have
you returned? (*Seizes her brutally and drags her roughly
toward himself.*)

ERNEST. No. I can't stand this—I cannot! (*He thrusts himself between* SEVERO *and* TEODORA.) Off, you scoundrel.

SEVERO. Again!

ERNEST. Again.

SEVERO. You have dared to return?

ERNEST. You insolently affront Teodora. I still live. What
do you expect me to do, if not return and chastise you, and
brand you as a coward?

SEVERO. Me?

ERNEST. Precisely.

TEODORA. No!

ERNEST. He has brought it on himself. I have seen him
lift his hand in anger to you—you, you! So now—— (*Seizes*
DON SEVERO *violently.*)

SEVERO. You impudent puppy!

ERNEST. True, but I'll not release you. You loved and respected your mother, I presume. For that reason you must
respect Teodora, and humbly bow before a sorrow so immense
as hers. This woman, sir, is purer, more honest than the
mother of such a man as you.

SEVERO. This to me?

ERNEST. Yes, and I have not yet done.

SEVERO. Your life——

ERNEST. Oh, my life, as much as you like—but afterward.
(TEODORA *endeavors to part them, but he pushes her gently
away, without releasing* DON SEVERO.) You believe in a God
—in a Maker—in hope. Well, then, as you bend your knee
before the altar of that God above, so will I compel you to
kneel to Teodora—and that instantly, sir. Down—in the dust.

TEODORA. For mercy's sake——

ERNEST. To the ground! (*Forces* DON SEVERO *to kneel.*)

TEODORA. Enough, Ernest.

SEVERO. A thousand thunders.

ERNEST. At her feet!

SEVERO. You!

ERNEST. Yes, I.

SEVERO. For her?

ERNEST. For her.

TEODORA. That will do. Hush! (*She points in terror to* DON JULIAN'S *door.* ERNEST *releases* DON SEVERO, *who rises and moves backward.* TEODORA *retreats and forms with* ERNEST *a group in the background.*)

DON JULIAN (*inside*). Let me go.

MERCEDES (*inside*). No. You must not.

DON JULIAN. It is they. Don't you hear them?

TEODORA (*to* ERNEST). Go.

SEVERO (*to* ERNEST). Avenged!

ERNEST. I don't deny it.

(*Enter* DON JULIAN, *pale and dying, leaning on* DOÑA MERCEDES' *arm.* DON SEVERO *stations himself on the right*, ERNEST *and* TEODORA *remain in the background.*)

DON JULIAN. Together! Where are they going? Who detains them here? Away with you, traitors. (*Wants to rush at them, but strength fails him, and he staggers back.*)

SEVERO (*hurrying to his assistance*). No, no.

DON JULIAN. Severo, they deceived me—they lied to me —the miserable pair! (*While he speaks* DON SEVERO *and* DOÑA MERCEDES *lead him to the armchair.*) There, look at them—both—she and Ernest! Why are they together?

TEODORA AND ERNEST (*separating*). No.

DON JULIAN. Why don't they come to me? Teodora!

TEODORA (*stretches out her arms but does not advance.*) Julian!

DON JULIAN. Here in my arms. (TEODORA *runs forward and flings herself into* DON JULIAN'S *arms, who clasps her feverishly. Pause*) You see—you see—(*to* DON SEVERO) I know well enough they are deceiving me. I hold her thus in my arms. I crush and subdue her—I might kill her—so! and it's only what she deserves. But I look at her—*I look at her*— and then I cannot!

TEODORA. Julian——

DON JULIAN (*pointing to* ERNEST). And that fellow?

ERNEST. Sir!

DON JULIAN. I loved him! Silence, and come hither. (ER-

NEST *approaches.*) You see, I am still her owner. (*He holds* TEODORA *more tightly clasped.*)

TEODORA. Yes—I am yours.

DON JULIAN. Drop pretense. Don't lie.

MERCEDES (*striving to soothe him*). For pity's sake——

DON SEVERO. Julian!

DON JULIAN (*to both*). Peace. (*to* TEODORA) I see through you. I know well that you love him. (TEODORA *and* ERNEST *try to protest, but he will not let them.*) All Madrid knows it too—all Madrid.

ERNEST. No, father.

TEODORA. No.

DON JULIAN. They deny it—they deny it! Why, it is as clear as noonday. Why, I feel it in every fiber—by the beat of fevered pulse, by the consuming flame of inward illumination!

ERNEST. It is the fever of your blood and the delirium of bodily weakness that feed the delusion. Listen to me, sir——

DON JULIAN. To hear how well you can lie?

ERNEST (*pointing to* TEODORA). She is innocent.

DON JULIAN. But I do not believe you.

ERNEST. Sir, by my father's memory——

DON JULIAN. Don't insult his name and memory.

ERNEST. By my mother's last kiss——

DON JULIAN. That kiss has long since been wiped from your brow.

ERNEST. What then do you want, father? I will swear by anything you wish. Oh, my father!

DON JULIAN. No oaths, or protests, or deceitful words.

ERNEST. Then what? Only tell me.

TEODORA. Yes, what, Julian?

DON JULIAN. Deeds.

ERNEST. What does he wish, Teodora? What does he ask of us?

TEODORA. I don't know. Oh, what are we to do, Ernest?

DON JULIAN (*watching them in feverish distrust*). Ah, you would even deceive me to my face! You are plotting together, wretched traitors! I see it.

ERNEST. It is fever that misleads you—not the testimony of your eyes.

DON JULIAN. Fever, yes. And since fever is fire, it has burnt away the bandage with which before you two had blinded me, and at last I see you for what you are. And now!—but why these glances at one another? Why, traitors? Why do your eyes gleam so? Tell me, Ernest. There are no tears in them to make them shine. Come nearer—nearer to me. (*draws* ERNEST *to him, bends his head, and then succeeds in thrusting him upon his knees. Thus* TEODORA *is on one side of* DON JULIAN *and* ERNEST *at his feet.* DON JULIAN *passes his hand across the young man's eyes.*) You see—no tears—they are quite dry.

ERNEST. Forgive me, forgive me!

DON JULIAN. You ask my forgiveness? Then you acknowledge your sin?

ERNEST. No.

DON JULIAN. Yes.

ERNEST. I say it is not so.

DON JULIAN. Then here before me, look at her.

DON SEVERO. Julian!

MERCEDES. Sir!

DON JULIAN (*to* TEODORA *and* ERNEST). Perhaps you are afraid? So it is not like a brother that you cherish her? If so, prove it. Let me see what sort of light shines in your eyes as they meet—whether, to my close inspection, the rays dart passion's flame, or mild affection. Come here, Teodora. Both—so—still nearer. (*Drags* TEODORA *until she stumbles, so that both faces are compelled toward each other.*)

TEODORA (*frees herself with a violent effort*). Oh, no.

ERNEST (*also strives to free himself, but is held in* DON JULIAN's *grasp*). I cannot.

DON JULIAN. You love one another—you can't deny it, for I've seen it. (*to* ERNEST) Your life!

ERNEST. Yes.

DON JULIAN. Your blood!

ERNEST. All.

DON JULIAN (*forcing him to his knees*). Stay still.

TEODORA. Julian!

DON JULIAN. Ah, you defend him, you defend him.

TEODORA. Not for his sake.

DON SEVERO. In God's name——

DON JULIAN (*to* SEVERO). Silence. (*still holds* ERNEST *down*) Bad friend, bad son!

ERNEST. My father.

DON JULIAN. Disloyal! Traitor!

ERNEST. No, father.

DON JULIAN. Here is my shameful seal upon your cheek —Today with my hand—soon with steel—so! (*With a supreme effort strikes* ERNEST. ERNEST *jumps up with a terrible cry, and turns away, covering his face.*)

ERNEST. Oh!

DON SEVERO (*stretches out his hand to* ERNEST). Justice.

TEODORA. My God! (*Hides her face in both hands, and drops on a chair.*)

MERCEDES (*turning to* ERNEST *to exculpate* DON JULIAN). It was only delirium.

(*These four exclamations very hurried. A moment of stupor.* DON JULIAN *stands still staring at* ERNEST, *and* DOÑA MERCEDES *and* DON SEVERO *endeavor to calm him.*)

DON JULIAN. It was not delirium, it was chastisement, Heaven be praised. What did you think, ungrateful boy?

MERCEDES. That will do.

DON SEVERO. Come, Julian.

DON JULIAN. Yes, I am going. (*Is led away with difficulty between* DON SEVERO *and* DONA MERCEDES, *and stops to look back at* TEODORA *and* ERNEST.)

MERCEDES. Quickly, Severo.

DON JULIAN. Look at them, the traitors! It was only justice—was it not? Say so—at least I believe it.

DON SEVERO. For God's sake, Julian—well, at any rate, for *mine*—

DON JULIAN. Yes, for yours, Severo, only for yours. You alone have loved me truly. (*Embraces him.*)

DON SEVERO. Yes, yes, it is so.

DON JULIAN (*stops at the door and looks back again*). She is crying for him—and does not follow me. Not even a look. She does not see that I am dying—yes, dying.

DON SEVERO. Julian, Julian!

DON JULIAN (*on the threshold*). Wait, wait. Dishonor for dishonor. Goodbye, Ernest.

(*Exit* DON JULIAN, DON SEVERO, *and* MERCEDES. ERNEST *drops into a chair near the table.* TEODORA *remains standing on the right. Pause.*)

ERNEST (*aside*). What is the use of loyalty?

TEODORA. And what is the use of innocence?

ERNEST. Conscience grows dark.

TEODORA. Pity, my God! Pity!

ERNEST. Pitiless destiny.

TEODORA. Oh, most miserable fate!

ERNEST. Poor child!

TEODORA. Poor Ernest! (*Both remain apart until now.*)

DON SEVERO (*in anguish from within*). My brother.

MERCEDES. Help!

PEPITO. Quickly. (ERNEST *and* TEODORA *move together.*)

TEODORA. They are crying.

ERNEST. He is dying.

TEODORA. Come at once.

ERNEST. Where?

TEODORA. To him.

ERNEST. We cannot. (*Detains her.*)

TEODORA. Why not? I want him to live.

ERNEST. And I!—but I cannot. (*Points to* DON JULIAN's *room.*)

TEODORA. Then I will. (*Rushes to the door of* DON JULIAN's *room.* PEPITO *and, behind him,* DON SEVERO, *bar the way.*)

PEPITO. Where are you going?

TEODORA (*in desperation*). I must see him.

PEPITO. It is impossible.

DON SEVERO. She cannot pass. This woman must not remain in my house—turn her out at once. (*to* PEPITO) No compassion—this very moment.

ERNEST. What!

TEODORA. My mind is wandering.

DON SEVERO. Though your mother should stand in front of that woman, Pepito, you have my orders. Obey them. Never mind her prayers or supplications. If she should cry—then let her cry. (*with concentrated fury*) Away with her, away—else I might kill her.

TEODORA. Julian orders——

DON SEVERO. Yes, Julian.

ERNEST. Her husband! It cannot be.

TEODORA. I must see him.

DON SEVERO. Very well. Look at him, once more—and then—depart.

PEPITO (*interfering*). Father——

DON SEVERO (*pushing him away*). Stop, sir.

TEODORA. It can't be true.

PEPITO. This is too horrible.

TEODORA. It is a lie.

DON SEVERO. Come, Teodora—come and see. (*Seizes her arm and leads her to the door.*)

TEODORA. Oh! My husband! Julian—dead. (*Staggers shudderingly back, and falls half senseless.*)

ERNEST (*covering his face*). My father! (*Pause.* DON SEVERO *watches them rancorously.*)

DON SEVERO (*to his son*). Turn her out.

ERNEST (*placing himself before* TEODORA). What cruelty!

PEPITO (*doubting*). Sir——

SEVERO (*to* PEPITO). Such are my orders. Do you doubt my word?

ERNEST. Pity.

DON SEVERO (*pointing to the death-chamber*). Yes, such pity as she showed him.

ERNEST. Fire races through my veins. I will leave Spain, sir.

DON SEVERO. It makes no difference.

ERNEST. She will die.

DON SEVERO. Life is short.

ERNEST. For the last time——

DON SEVERO. No more. (*to his son*) Ring.

ERNEST. But I tell you she is innocent. I swear it.

PEPITO (*interceding*). Father——

DON SEVERO (*with a contemptuous gesture*). That fellow lies.

ERNEST. You impel me with the current. Then I will not struggle against it. I go with it. I cannot yet know what may be her opinion (*pointing to* TEODORA) of others, and of yout outrages. Her lips are silent, mute her thoughts. But what I think of it all—yes, I will tell you.

DON SEVERO. It is useless. It won't prevent me from—— (*Approaches* TEODORA.)

PEPITO (*restraining him*). Father——

ERNEST. Stay. (*pause*) Let nobody touch this woman. She is mine. The world has so desired it, and its decision I accept. It has driven her to my arms. Come, Teodora. (*He raises her, and sustains her.*) You cast her forth from here. We obey you.

DON SEVERO. At last, you blackguard!

ERNEST. Yes; now you are right. I will confess now. Do you want passion? Then passion and delirium. Do you want love? Then love—boundless love. Do you want more? Then more and more. Nothing daunts me. Yours the invention, I give it shelter. So you may tell the tale. It echoes through all this heroic town. But should any one ask you who was the infamous intermediary in this infamy, you will reply, "Ourselves, without being aware of it, and with us the stupid chatter of busybodies." Come, Teodora; my mother's spirit kisses your pure brow. Adieu, all. She belongs to me, and let heaven choose its day to judge between you and me. (*Gathers* TEODORA *into his embrace, with a glance of defiance around.*)

Jacinto Benavente

(1866-1954)

El nido ajeno (1894), Benavente's first play, was something like a lethal blow to Echegaray's theater. This newcomer, the son of a noted Madrid pediatrician, left law school to travel through Europe and write mordant newspaper sketches satirizing the aristocracy and upper middle class. The stage attracted him like a magnet and the unexpected happened: his début became a hit. Tired of Echegaray's tirades, the public wanted amusing plays, witty, sparkling, sophisticated, and here was Benavente to become the untiring purveyor of these. He had nothing positive to say, no message, but he enjoyed, and the public with him, gamboling about wickedly, shooting firecrackers, pulling people's legs. Until his death at the age of eighty-eight, he was at it continuously. He attained world recognition, and then ironically enough, the iconoclast was elected in 1913 to the Spanish Royal Academy; and in 1922 he was awarded the Nobel Prize. Among his 150 plays the most memorable were *Señora ama* (1908) and *La malquerida* (1913), tragedies of rural life; *El príncipe que todo lo aprendió de los libros* (1919), a lovely children's play; and many social satires, such as *Gente conocida* (1896), *La ciudad alegre y confiada* (1916), and the allegorical *Los intereses creados* (*Bonds of Interest*, 1907), undoubtedly his finest achievement, in which, using a *commedia dell'arte* technique, he claimed the necessity of evil in human relationships.

BEST EDITION: *Obras completas.* Madrid, Aguilar, 1942-1946, 8 vols.

ABOUT: John Dos Passos, *Rocinante to the Road Again.* New York, 1922, pp. 182-195. I. S. Estevan, *Jacinto Benavente y su teatro.* Barcelona, 1954. A. Lázaro, *Jacinto Benavente: de su vida y de su obra.* Madrid, 1925. F. de Onís, *Jacinto Benavente.* New York, 1923. W. Starkie, *Jacinto Benavente.* Oxford, 1924.

THE BONDS OF INTEREST
(*Los intereses creados*)

by Jacinto Benavente

TRANSLATED BY
John Garrett Underhill

 ⌒~⚭~⌒

CHARACTERS

Doña Sirene
Silvia
The Wife of Polichinelle
Columbine
Laura
Risela
Leander
Crispin
The Doctor

Polichinelle
Harlequin
The Captain
Pantaloon
The Innkeeper
The Secretary
1st and 2d Servants at the Inn
1st and 2d Constables

The action takes place in an imaginary country at the beginning of the seventeenth century.

PROLOGUE

A conventional drop at the front, having a door in the middle, curtained.

CRISPIN. Here you have the mummer of the antique farce who enlivened in the country inns the hard-earned leisure of the carter, who made the simple rustics gape with wonder in the square of every rural town and village, who in the populous cities drew about him great bewildering assemblages, as in Paris where Tabarin set up his scaffold on the *Pont-Neuf* and challenged the attention of the passers-by, from the learned doctor pausing a moment on his solemn errand to smooth out the wrinkles on his brow at some merry quip of old-time farce, to the light-hearted cutpurse who there whiled away his hours of ease as he cheated his hunger with a smile, to prelate and noble dame and great grandee in stately carriages, soldier and merchant and student and maid. Men of every rank and condition shared in the rejoicing —men who were never brought together in any other way— the grave laughing to see the laughter of the gay rather than at the wit of the farce, the wise with the foolish, the poor with the rich, so staid and formal in their ordinary aspect, and the rich to see the poor laugh, their consciences a little easier at the thought: "Even the poor can smile." For nothing is so contagious as the sympathy of a smile.

Sometimes our humble farce mounted up to Princes' Palaces on the whims of the mighty and the great; yet there its rogueries were not less free. It was the common heritage of great and small. Its rude jests, its sharp and biting sentences it took from the people, from that lowly wisdom of the poor which knows how to suffer and bear all, and which was softened in those days by resignation in men who did not expect too much of the world and so were able to laugh at the world without bitterness and without hate.

From its humble origins Lope de Rueda and Shakespeare

and Molière lifted it up, bestowing upon it high patents of nobility, and like enamored princes of the fairy-tales, elevated poor Cinderella to the topmost thrones of Poetry and of Art. But our farce tonight cannot claim such distinguished lineage, contrived for your amusement by the inquiring spirit of a restless poet of today.

This is a little play of puppets, impossible in theme, without any reality at all. You will soon see how everything happens in it that could never happen, how its personages are not real men and women, nor the shadows of them, but dolls or marionettes of paste and cardboard, moving upon wires which are visible even in a little light and to the dimmest eye. They are the grotesque masks of the Italian *Commedia dell'Arte*, not as boisterous as they once were, because they have aged with the years and have been able to think much in so long a time. The author is aware that so primitive a spectacle is unworthy of the culture of these days; he throws himself upon your courtesy and upon your goodness of heart. He only asks that you should make yourselves as young as possible. The world has grown old, but art never can reconcile itself to growing old, and so, to seem young again, it descends to these fripperies. And that is the reason that these outworn puppets have presumed to come to amuse you tonight with their child's play.

ACT I

A plaza in a city. The façade of an Inn is at the right, having a practicable door, with a knocker upon it. Above the door is a sign which reads INN.

(LEANDER *and* CRISPIN *enter from the left.*)

LEANDER. This must be a very great city, Crispin. Its riches and its power appear in everything.

CRISPIN. Yes, there are two cities. Pray God that we have chanced upon the better one!

LEANDER. Two cities do you say, Crispin? Ah! Now I understand—an old city and a new city, one on either side of the river.

CRISPIN. What has the river to do with it, or newness or age? I say two cities just as there are in every city in the world; one for people who arrive with money and the other for persons who arrive like us.

LEANDER. We are lucky to have arrived at all without falling into the hands of Justice. I should be heartily glad to stop here awhile and rest myself, for I am tired of this running about the world so continually.

CRISPIN. Not I! No, it is the natural condition of the free-born subjects of the Kingdom of Roguery, of whom am I, not to remain seated long in any one place, unless it be through compulsion, as to say in the galleys, where, believe me, they are very hard seats. But now since we have happened upon this city, and to all appearances it is a well fortified and provisioned one, let us like prudent captains map out our plan of battle beforehand, if we are to conquer it with any advantage to ourselves.

LEANDER. A pretty army we shall make to besiege it.

CRISPIN. We are men and we have to do with men.

LEANDER. All our wealth is on our backs. You were not

willing to take off these clothes and sell them, when by doing so we could easily have obtained money.

CRISPIN. I would sooner take off my skin than my good clothes. As the world goes nothing is so important as appearances, and the clothes, as you must admit, are the first things to appear.

LEANDER. What are we going to do, Crispin? Hunger and fatigue have been too much for me. I am overcome; I cannot talk.

CRISPIN. There is nothing for us to do but to take advantage of our talents and our effrontery, for without effrontery talents are of no use. The best thing, as it seems to me, will be for you to talk as little as possible, but be very impressive when you do, and put on the airs of a gentleman of quality. From time to time then I will permit you to strike me across the back. When anybody asks you a question, reply mysteriously and if you open your mouth upon your own account, be sure that it is with dignity, as if you were pronouncing sentence. You are young; you have a fine presence. Until now you have known only how to dissipate your resources; this is the time for you to begin to profit by them. Put yourself in my hands. There is nothing so useful to a man as to have some one always at his heels to point out his merits, for modesty in one's self is imbecility, while self-praise is madness, and so between the two we come into disfavor with the world. Men are like merchandise; they are worth more or less according to the skill of the salesman who markets them. I tell you, though you were but muddy glass, I will so contrive that in my hands you shall pass for pure diamond. And now let us knock at the door of this inn, for surely it is the proper thing to have lodgings on the main square.

LEANDER. You say at this inn? But how are we going to pay?

CRISPIN. If we are to be stopped by a little thing like that then we had better search out an asylum or an almshouse or else beg on the streets, if so be that you incline to virtue. Or if to force, then back to the highway and cut the throat of the first passer-by. If we are to live upon our means, strictly speaking, we have no other means to live.

LEANDER. I have letters of introduction to persons of importance in this city, who will be able to lend us aid.

CRISPIN. Then tear those letters up; never think of such baseness again! Introduce yourself to no man when you are in need. Those would be pretty letters of credit indeed! Today you will be received with the greatest courtesy; they will tell you that their houses and their persons are to be considered as yours. The next time you call, the servant will tell you that his master is not at home. No, he is not expected soon . . . and at the next visit nobody will trouble so much as to open the door. This is a world of giving and taking, a shop, a mart, a place of exchange, and before you ask you have to offer.

LEANDER. But what can I offer when I have nothing?

CRISPIN. How low an opinion you must have of yourself! Is a man in himself, then, worth nothing? A man may be a soldier, and by his valor win great victories. He may be a husband or a lover, and with love's sweet, oblivious medicine, restore some noble dame to health, or some damsel of high degree, who has been pining away through melancholy. He may be the servant of some mighty and powerful lord, who becomes attached to him and raises him up through his favor, and he may be so many other things besides that I have not the breath even to begin to run them over. When one wants to climb, why any stair will do.

LEANDER. But if I have not even that stair?

CRISPIN. Then accept my shoulders, and I will lift you up. I offer you the top.

LEANDER. And if we both fall down upon the ground?

CRISPIN. God grant that it may be soft! (*knocking at the inn-door*) Hello! Ho, within there! Hello, I say, in the inn! Devil of an innkeeper! Does no one answer? What sort of a tavern is this?

LEANDER. Why are you making all this noise when as yet you have scarcely begun to call?

CRISPIN. Because it is monstrous that they should make us wait like this! (*calling again more loudly*) Hello within! Who's there, I say? Hello in the house! Hello, you thousand devils!

INNKEEPER (*within*). Who's there? What knocking and what shouting at my door! Is this the way to stand and wait? Out, I say!

CRISPIN. It is too much! And now he will tell us that this dilapidated old tavern is a fit lodging for a gentleman.

(*The* INNKEEPER *and* TWO SERVANTS *come out of the Inn.*)

INNKEEPER. Softly, sirs, softly; for this is not a tavern but an inn, and great gentlemen have been lodged in this house.

CRISPIN. I would like to have seen those same great gentlemen—gentle, a little more or less. What? It is easy enough to see by these rascals that they are not accustomed to waiting on persons of quality. They stand there like blockheads without running to do our service.

INNKEEPER. My life! But you are impertinent!

LEANDER. My servant is a little forward, perhaps. You will find him somewhat hasty in his temper. However, your inn will be good enough for the brief time that we shall be able to remain in it. Prepare an apartment for me and another for my servant, and let us spare these idle words.

INNKEEPER. I beg your pardon, sir. If you had only spoken before . . . I don't know how it is, but somehow gentlemen are always so much more polite than their servants.

CRISPIN. The fact is my master is so good-natured that he will put up with anything. But I know what is proper for his service, and I have no mind to wink at villainy. Lead us to our apartments.

INNKEEPER. But where is your luggage?

CRISPIN. Do you suppose that we are carrying our luggage with us on our backs, like a soldier's knapsack, or trundling it like students' bundles in our hands? Know that my master has eight carts coming after him, which will arrive if he stays here long enough, and at that he will only remain for the time which is absolutely necessary to conclude the secret mission with which he has been intrusted in this city.

LEANDER. Will you be silent and hold your tongue? What secret is it possible to keep with you? If I am discovered through your impudence, through your misguided talk . . . (*He threatens and strikes* CRISPIN *with his sword.*)

CRISPIN. Help! He is killing me! (*Running.*)

INNKEEPER (*interposing between* LEANDER *and* CRISPIN). Hold, sir!

LEANDER. Let me chastise him! The most intolerable of vices is this desire to talk.

INNKEEPER. Do not beat him, sir!

LEANDER. Let me at him! Let me at him! Will the slave never learn?

(*As he is about to strike* CRISPIN, CRISPIN *runs and hides himself behind the* INNKEEPER, *who receives all the blows.*)

CRISPIN (*crying out*). Ay! Ay! Ay!

INNKEEPER. Ay, say I! For I got all the blows!

LEANDER (*to* CRISPIN). Now you see what you have done.

This poor man has received all the blows. Down! Down! Beg his pardon!

INNKEEPER. It will not be necessary, sir. I pardon him willingly. (*to the servants*) What are you doing standing there? Prepare the rooms in which the Emperor of Mantua is accustomed to reside when he is stopping in this house, and let dinner be made ready for these gentlemen.

CRISPIN. Perhaps it would be as well if I saw to that myself, otherwise they may delay and spoil everything, and commit a thousand blunders for which I shall be held responsible, for my master, as you see, is not a man to submit to insult. I am with you, sirrahs—and remember who it is you serve, for the greatest good fortune or the direst calamity in the world enters at this moment behind you through these doors.

(*The* SERVANTS, *followed by* CRISPIN, *re-enter the Inn.*)

INNKEEPER (*to* LEANDER). Will you be good enough to let me have your name, where you come from, and the business which brings you to this city?

LEANDER (*seeing* CRISPIN *re-enter from the Inn*). My servant will let you have them. Learn not to bother me with foolish questions. (*He goes into the Inn.*)

CRISPIN. What have you done now? You have not dared to question my master? If you want to keep him so much as another hour in your house, never speak to him again. No! Not one word!

INNKEEPER. But the laws are very strict. It is absolutely necessary that the questions should be answered. The law in this city——

CRISPIN. Never mention the law to my master! Silence! Silence! And for shame! You do not know whom you have in your house; no, and if you did, you would not be wasting your time on these impertinences.

INNKEEPER. But am I not to be told at least——

CRISPIN. Bolt of Heaven! Silence! Or I will call my master, and he will tell you whatever he sees fit—and then you will not understand. Take care! Look to it that he wants for nothing! Wait on him with every one of your five senses, or you will have good reason to regret it! Have you no knowledge of men? Can't you read character? Don't you see who my master is? What? How is that? What do you say? No reply? . . . Come! Come! . . . In! . . .

(*He goes into the Inn, pushing the* INNKEEPER *before*

him. The CAPTAIN *and* HARLEQUIN *enter from the left.*)

HARLEQUIN. As we return from the fields which surround this fair city—and beyond a doubt they are the best part of it—it seems that without intending it we have happened upon this Inn. What a creature of habit is man! And surely it is a vile habit, this being obliged to eat every day.

CAPTAIN. The sweet music of your verses had quite deprived me of all thought. Delightful privilege of the poet!

HARLEQUIN. Which does not prevent him from being equally lacking upon his own part. The poet wants everything. I approach this Inn with fear. Will they consent to trust us today? If not, we must rely upon your sword.

CAPTAIN. My sword? The soldier's sword, like the poet's lyre, is little valued in this city of merchants and traders. We have fallen upon evil days.

HARLEQUIN. We have. Sublime poesy, which sings of great and glorious exploits, is no more. It is equally profitless to offer your genius to the great to praise or to lampoon them. Flattery and satire are both alike to them. They neither thank you for the one nor fear the other, nor do they read them. Aretino himself would have starved to death in these days.

CAPTAIN. But tell me, how is it with us? What is the position of the soldier? Because we were defeated in the late wars—more through these base traffickers who govern us and send us to defend their interests without enthusiasm and without arms, than through any power of the enemy, as if a man could fight with his whole heart for what he did not love—defeated by these traffickers who did not contribute so much as a single soldier to our ranks or lend one single penny to the cause but upon good interest and yet better security; who, as soon as they scented danger and saw their pockets in jeopardy, threatened to make common cause with the enemy—now they blame us, they abuse us and despise us, and seek to economize out of our martial misery, which is the little pay that they give us, and would dismiss us if they dared, if they were not afraid that some day all those whom they have oppressed by their tyranny and their greed would rise up and turn against them. And woe to them when they do, if we remember that day on which side lie duty and justice!

HARLEQUIN. When that day comes you will find us at your side.

CAPTAIN. Poets cannot be depended upon for anything.

Your spirits are like the opal, which looks different in every light. You are in an écstasy today over what is about to be born, and tomorrow over what is in the last stages of dissolution. You have a special weakness for falling in love with ruins, which to my mind is a melancholy thing. And since as a rule you sit up all night, you more often see the sun set than the day break; you know more about going down than you do of rising.

HARLEQUIN. That cannot truthfully be said of me. I have often seen the sun rise when I had no place to lay my head. Besides, how can you expect a man to hail the day as blithely as the lark when it always breaks so unfortunately for him— What say you? Shall we try our fate?

CAPTAIN. It cannot be avoided. Be seated, and let us await what our good host has in store.

HARLEQUIN (*calling into the Inn*). Hello, there! Ho! Who serves today?

(*The* INNKEEPER *enters.*)

INNKEEPER. Ah, gentlemen! Is it you? I am sorry, but there is no entertainment at the Inn today.

CAPTAIN. And for what reason, if it is proper to ask the question?

INNKEEPER. A proper question for you to ask. Do you suppose that I trust nobody for what is consumed in this house?

CAPTAIN. Ah! Is that the reason? And are we not persons of credit, who are to be trusted?

INNKEEPER. No; not by me. And as I never expect to collect anything, you have had all that courtesy requires out of me already. This being the case, you will be so kind as to remove yourselves from my door.

HARLEQUIN. Do you imply that there is nothing to be counted between us but money? Are all the praises that we have lavished upon your house in all parts of the country to go for nothing? I have even composed a sonnet in your honor, in which I celebrate the virtues of your stewed partridges and hare pie! And as for my friend, the Captain, you may rest assured that he alone would uphold the reputation of your hostelry against an army. Is that a feat which is worth nothing? Is there nothing but clinking of coins in your ears?

INNKEEPER. I am not in a jesting mood; it does not suit my humor. I want none of your sonnets, nor the Captain's sword either, which might better be employed in other business.

CAPTAIN. Name of Mars! You are right. Better employed upon an impudent rascal's back, flaying off his hide! (*Threatening him and striking him with his sword.*)

INNKEEPER (*crying out*). What? How is this? You strike me? Help! Justice!

HARLEQUIN (*restraining the* CAPTAIN). Don't run your head into a noose on account of such a worthless scamp.

CAPTAIN. I shall kill him. (*Striking him.*)

INNKEEPER. Help! Justice!

(*The* TWO SERVANTS *enter, running, from the Inn.*)

SERVANTS. They are killing our master!

INNKEEPER. Save me!

CAPTAIN. Not one of them shall remain alive!

INNKEEPER. Will no one come?

(CRISPIN *and* LEANDER *enter.*)

LEANDER. What is this brawl?

CRISPIN. In the presence of my master? Before the house where he resides? Is there no rest possible, nor quiet? Hold! Or I shall summon Justice. Order! Quiet!

INNKEEPER. This will be the ruin of me! With such a dignitary stopping in my house!——

HARLEQUIN. Who is he?

INNKEEPER. Never dare to ask me his name!

CAPTAIN. Your pardon, sir, if we have disturbed your rest, but this rascally villain——

INNKEEPER. It wasn't my fault, my lord. These unblushing scoundrels——

CAPTAIN. What? I? Unblushing—I? I can bear no more!

CRISPIN. Hold, sir Captain, for one is here who is able to redress your wrongs, if so be you have had them of this man.

INNKEEPER. Consider, sir, that for more than a month these fellows have eaten at my expense without the payment of one penny—without so much as the thought of payment; and now because I refuse to serve them today, they turn upon me.

HARLEQUIN. I do not turn because I am accustomed to face that which is unpleasant.

CAPTAIN. Is it reasonable that a soldier should not be given credit?

HARLEQUIN. Is it reasonable that a sonnet should be allowed to pass for nothing, although it is written with the best of flourishes in praise of his stewed partridges and hare pies? And all this upon credit on my part, for I have never tasted one of them, but only his eternal mutton and potatoes.

CRISPIN. These two noble gentlemen are right. It is infamous that a poet and a soldier should be denied in this manner.

HARLEQUIN. Ah, sir! You have a great soul!

CRISPIN. No, I have not—but my master, who is here present. Being a grand gentleman, there is nothing which appeals to him so much in the world as a poet or a soldier.

LEANDER. To be sure. I agree with you.

CRISPIN. You need have no doubt but that while he remains in this city you will be treated with the consideration you deserve. You shall want for nothing. Whatever expense you may be at in this Inn, is to be placed upon his account.

LEANDER. To be sure. I agree with you.

CRISPIN. And let the landlord look to it that you get your deserts!

INNKEEPER. Sir! . . .

CRISPIN. And don't be so stingy with those partridges and hairy pies. It is not proper that a poet like Signor Harlequin should be obliged to draw upon his imagination in his descriptions of such material things.

HARLEQUIN. What? Do you know my name?

CRISPIN. No, I do not; but my master, being such a great gentleman, knows all the poets who exist or who ever did exist in the world, provided always that they were worthy of the name.

LEANDER. To be sure. I agree with you.

CRISPIN. And none of them is more famous than you, Signor Harlequin. Whenever I consider that you have not been treated here with the respect which is your due——

INNKEEPER. Your pardon, sir. They shall be made welcome, as you desire. It is sufficient that you should be their security.

CAPTAIN. Sir, if I can be of service to you in any way . . .

CRISPIN. What? Is it a small service to be permitted to know you? O glorious Captain, worthy only to be sung by this immortal poet!

HARLEQUIN. Sir!

CAPTAIN. Sir!

HARLEQUIN. So my verses are known to you?

CRISPIN. How? Known? And if known would it ever be possible to forget them? Is not that wonderful sonnet yours, which begins:

"The soft hand which caresses and which slays" . . .

HARLEQUIN. What?
CRISPIN. What?

"The soft hand which caresses and which slays" . . .

It does not say what.
HARLEQUIN. Nonsense! No, that is not my sonnet.
CRISPIN. Then it is worthy of being yours. And you, Captain! Who is not familiar with your marvelous exploits? Was it not you who, alone, with twenty men, assaulted the Castle of the Red Rock in the famous battle of the Black Field?
CAPTAIN. You know, then?
CRISPIN. How? . . . Do I know? Oh! Many a time, transported, I have listened to my master recount the story of your prowess! Twenty men, twenty, and you in front of them, and in front of you the castle. Boom! Boom! Boom! from the castle, shots and bombards, darts and flaming squibs and boiling oil! And the twenty men all standing there like one man, and you in front of them! And from above: Boom! Boom! Boom! And the roll of the drums: Rum-a-tum-tum! And the blare of the trumpets: Tara! Tara-ra! And you all the while there alone with your sword: Swish! Swish! Swish! A blow here, a blow there. Or without your sword . . . Above, below . . . A head, an arm . . .
(*He begins to rain blows about him right and left, and to kick, using his fists, his feet, and the flat side of his sword indifferently.*)
SERVANTS. Ay! Ay! Oh! Oh!
INNKEEPER. Hold! Hold! Restrain yourself! You don't know what you are doing. You are all excited . . . It is as if the battle were really taking place . . .
CRISPIN. How? I am excited? Know that I always feel in my breast the *animus belli,* the thirst for war!
CAPTAIN. It seems almost as if you must have been there.
CRISPIN. To hear my master describe it is the same as being there. No, it is preferable to it. And is such a soldier, the hero of the Red Rocks in the Black Fields, to be insulted thus? Ah! How fortunate it is that my master was present, and that important business had brought him to this city, for he will see to it that you are accorded the consideration you deserve. So sublime a poet, so great a captain! . . .

(*to the* SERVANTS) Quick! What are you doing there? Bring the best food that you have in the house and set it before these gentlemen. And first of all get a bottle of good wine; it will be a rare pleasure to my master to drink with them. He will esteem himself indeed fortunate. Don't stand there and stare! Quick! Bestir yourselves!

INNKEEPER. Run, run! I go . . . We are getting something out of this after all.

(*The* INNKEEPER *and the* TWO SERVANTS *run into the Inn.*)

HARLEQUIN. Ah, sir! How can we ever repay you?

CAPTAIN. How? We certainly never shall . . .

CRISPIN. Let nobody speak of payment before my master. The very thought gives offense. Be seated, be seated. My master, who has wined and dined so many princes, so many noblemen at his table, will deem this an even greater pleasure.

LEANDER. To be sure. I agree with you.

CRISPIN. My master is not a man of many words; but, as you see, the few that he does speak, are, as it were, fraught with wisdom.

HARLEQUIN. His grandeur appears in everything.

CAPTAIN. You have no idea what a comfort it is to our drooping spirits to find a noble gentleman like you who condescends to treat us with consideration.

CRISPIN. Why, this is nothing to what he will condescend to do! I know that my master will never rest satisfied to stop at such a trifle. He will elevate you to his own level, and then hold you up beside him on the same exalted plane. He is just that kind of a man.

LEANDER (*to* CRISPIN). Don't let your tongue run away with you, Crispin.

CRISPIN. My master is averse to foolish talk; but you will soon know him by his deeds.

(*The* INNKEEPER *and the* SERVANTS *re-enter, bringing wine and provisions which they place upon the table.*)

INNKEEPER. Here is the wine—and the dinner.

CRISPIN. Drink, drink and eat! See that they want for nothing; my master is agreeable. He will be responsible. His responsibility is fortunately not in question. If you would like anything you don't see, don't hesitate to ask for it. My master will order it. And let the landlord look to it that it is brought promptly, for verily at this business, he is the sorriest kind of a knave.

INNKEEPER. To be sure . . . I don't agree with you.

CRISPIN. Not another word! You insult my master.

CAPTAIN. Your very good health!

LEANDER. Your good healths, gentlemen! To the health of the greatest poet and the best soldier in the world!

HARLEQUIN. To the health of the noblest gentleman!

CAPTAIN. The most liberal and the most generous!

CRISPIN. In the world! Excuse me, but I must drink too, though it may seem presumptuous. But on a day like this, this day of days, which has brought together the sublimest poet, the bravest captain, the noblest gentleman, and the most faithful servant in the universe . . . (*They drink.*) Now you will permit my master to retire. The important business which brings him to the city admits of no further delay.

LEANDER. To be sure.

CRISPIN. You will not fail to return every day and present your respects to him?

HARLEQUIN. Every hour! And I am going to bring with me all the poets and all the musicians of my acquaintance, to serenade him with music and songs.

CAPTAIN. I shall bring my whole company with me with torches and banners.

LEANDER. You will offend my modesty.

CRISPIN. And now eat, drink! Mind you, sirrahs! About it! Quick! Serve these gentlemen. (*to the* CAPTAIN) A word in your ear. Are you out of money?

CAPTAIN. What shall I say?

CRISPIN. Say no more. (*to the* INNKEEPER) Eh! This way! Let these gentlemen have forty or fifty crowns on my master's account, as a present from him. Omit nothing! See that they are satisfied.

INNKEEPER. Don't worry, sir. Forty or fifty, did you say?

CRISPIN. While you are about it, better make it sixty. Your health, gentlemen!

CAPTAIN. Long life to the noblest gentleman in the world!

HARLEQUIN. Long life!

CRISPIN. Shout long life, too, you uncivil people.

INNKEEPER AND SERVANTS. Long life! Long life!

CRISPIN. Long life to the sublimest poet and the best soldier in the world!

ALL. Long life!

LEANDER (*to* CRISPIN). Are you mad, Crispin? What are you doing? How are we ever going to get out of this?

CRISPIN. The same way that we got in. You see now poesy

and arms are ours. On! We shall achieve the conquest of the world!

(*All exchange bows and salutations, after which* LEANDER *and* CRISPIN *go out upon the left, as they came in. The* CAPTAIN *and* HARLEQUIN *attack the dinner which is set before them by the* INNKEEPER *and the* SERVANTS, *who wait upon them assiduously with anticipation of their every want.*)

ACT II

A garden with the façade of a pavilion opening upon it.

(Doña Sirena *and* Columbine *enter from the pavilion.*)

Sirena. Is it not enough to deprive a woman of her five senses, Columbine? Can it be possible that a lady should see herself placed in so embarrassing a position and by low, unfeeling people? How did you ever dare to show yourself in my presence with such a tale?

Columbine. But sooner or later wouldn't you have had to know it?

Sirena. I had rather have died first. But did they all say the same?

Columbine. All, one after the other, exactly as I have told it to you. The tailor absolutely refuses to send you the gown until you have paid him everything that you owe.

Sirena. Impudent rascal! Everything that I owe *him.* The barefaced highwayman! And does he not stand indebted for his reputation and his very credit in this city to me? Until I employed him in the decoration of my person he did not know, so to speak, what it was to dress a lady.

Columbine. All the cooks and musicians and servants say the same. They refuse to play tonight or to appear at the fête unless they are all paid beforehand.

Sirena. The rogues! The brood of vipers! Whence does such insolence spring? Were these people not born to serve? Are they to be paid nowadays in nothing but money? Is money the only thing which has value in the world? Woe unto her who is left without a husband to look after her, as I am, without male relatives, alas, without any masculine connection! A woman by herself is worth nothing in the world, be she never so noble or virtuous. O day foretold of the Apocalypse! Surely Antichrist has come!

Columbine. I never saw you so put out before. I hardly

know you. You have always been able to rise above these calamities.

SIRENA. Those were other days, Columbine. Then I had my youth to count on, and my beauty, as powerful allies. Princes and great grandees cast themselves at my feet.

COLUMBINE. But on the other hand you did not have the experience and knowledge of the world which you have now. And as far as beauty is concerned, surely you never shone with such refulgence as today—that is, if you will listen to me.

SIRENA. Don't attempt to flatter me. Do you suppose that I should ever have got myself into such a fix if I had been the Doña Sirena of my twenties?

COLUMBINE. Your twenty suitors?

SIRENA. What do you think? I had no end of suitors. And you who have not yet begun upon twenty, you have not the sense to perceive what that means and to profit by it. I would never have believed it possible. Otherwise should I have adopted you for my niece if I had, though I saw myself abandoned by every man in the world and reduced to live alone with a maidservant? If instead of wasting your youth on this impecunious Harlequin, this poet who can bring you nothing but ballads and verses, you had had the sense to make a proper use of your time, we should not be languishing now in this humiliating dilemma.

COLUMBINE. What do you expect? I am too young to resign myself to being loved without loving. If I am ever to become skillful in making others suffer for love of me, surely I must learn first what it is one suffers when one loves. And when I do, I am positive I shall be able to profit by it. I have not yet turned twenty, but you must not think because of that I have so little sense as to marry Harlequin.

SIRENA. I would not trust you. You are capricious, flighty, and allow yourself to be run away with by your imagination. But first let us consider what is to be done. How are we to extricate ourselves from this horrible dilemma? In a short time the guests will arrive—all persons of quality and importance, and among them Signor Polichinelle and his wife and daughter, who, for various reasons, are of more account to me than the rest. You know my house has been frequented of late by several noble gentlemen, somewhat frayed in their nobility, it is true, as I am, through want of means. For any one of them, the daughter of Signor Polichinelle,

with her rich dowry and the priceless sum which she will inherit upon her father's death, would be an untold treasure.
She has many suitors, but I interpose my influence with
Signor Polichinelle and with his wife in favor of them all.
Whichever one should be fortunate I know that he will requite my good offices with his bounty, because I have made
them all sign an agreement which assures me of it. I have
no other means than this to repair my state. If now some
rich merchant or some trader by some lucky chance should
fall in love with you . . . Ah, who can say? This house might
become again what it was in other days. But if the insolence
of these people breaks out tonight, if I cannot give the fête
. . . No! I cannot think of it! It would be the death of me!

COLUMBINE. Do not trouble yourself, Doña Sirena. We
have enough in the house to provide the entertainment. As
for the music and the servants, Signor Harlequin will be
able to supply them—he is not a poet and in love with me
for nothing. Many singers and choice spirits of his acquaintance will willingly lend themselves to any adventure. You
will see that nothing will be lacking, and your guests will all
say that they have never been present at so marvelous a
fête in their lives.

SIRENA. Ah, Columbine! If that could only be, how greatly
you would rise in my estimation! Run, run and seek out
your poet . . . There is no time to lose.

COLUMBINE. My poet? Surely he is walking up and down
now on the other side of the garden, waiting for a sign.

SIRENA. I fear it would not be proper for me to be present
at your interview. I ought not to demean myself by solicit-
ing his favors. I leave all that to you. Let nothing be want-
ing at the fête and you shall be well repaid, for these terrible straits through which we are passing tonight cannot
continue forever—or else I am not Doña Sirena!

COLUMBINE. All will be well. Have no fear.

(DOÑA SIRENA *goes out through the pavilion.*)

COLUMBINE (*stepping toward the right and calling*). Harlequin! Harlequin! (CRISPIN *enters.*) It isn't he!

CRISPIN. Be not afraid, beautiful Columbine, mistress of
the mightiest poet, who yet has not been able to heighten
in his verses the splendors of your charm. If the picture must
always be different from reality, the advantage in this case
is all on the side of reality. You can imagine, no doubt, what
the picture must have been.

COLUMBINE. Are you a poet, too, or only a courtier and a flatterer?

CRISPIN. I am the best friend of your lover Harlequin, although I only met him today; but he has had ample proof of my friendship in this brief time. My greatest desire has been to salute you, and Signor Harlequin would not have been the poet that I take him for, had he not trusted to my friendship implicitly. But for his confidence I should have been in danger of falling in love with you simply upon the opportunity which he has afforded me of seeing you.

COLUMBINE. Signor Harlequin trusted as much in my love as he did to your friendship. Don't take so much credit to yourself. It is as foolish to trust a man while he lives as a woman while she loves.

CRISPEN. Now I see that you are not so fatal to the sight as to the ear.

COLUMBINE. Pardon me. Before the fête tonight I must speak with Signor Harlequin, and . . .

CRISPIN. It will not be necessary. That is why I have come, a poor ambassador from him and from my master, who stoops to kiss your hand.

COLUMBINE. Who is your master, if I may ask that question?

CRISPIN. The noblest and most powerful gentleman in the world. Permit me for the present not to mention his name. Soon it will be known. My master desires to salute Doña Sirena and to be present at her fête tonight.

COLUMBINE. At her fête? Don't you know . . .

CRISPIN. I know everything. That is my business—to investigate. I know that there were certain inconveniences which threatened to becloud it; but there will be none. Everything is provided for.

COLUMBINE. What! Then you do know?

CRISPIN. I assure you everything is provided for—a sumptuous reception, lights and fireworks, musicians and sweet song. It will be the most brilliant fête which ever was in the world.

COLUMBINE. Ah, then you are an enchanter?

CRISPIN. Now you begin to know me. But I shall only tell you that I do not bring good fortune with me for nothing. The people of this city are so intelligent that I am sure they will be incapable of frowning upon it and discouraging it with foolish scruples when they see it arrive. My master

knows that Signor Polichinelle and his only daughter, the
beautiful Silvia, the richest heiress in the city, are to be present at the fête tonight. My master has to fall in love with
her, my master has to marry her; and my master will know
how to requite in fitting fashion the good offices of Doña
Sirena and of yourself in the matter, if so be that you do him
the honor to assist in his suit.

COLUMBINE. Your speech is impertinent. Such boldness
gives offense.

CRISPIN. Time presses and I have no leisure to pay compliments.

COLUMBINE. If the master is to be judged by the man . . .

CRISPIN. Reassure yourself. You will find my master the
most courteous, the most affable gentleman in the world.
My effrontery permits him to be modest. The hard neces-
sities of life sometimes compel the noblest cavalier to descend to the devices of the ruffian, just as sometimes they
oblige the noblest ladies, in order to maintain their state, to
stoop to menial tricks, and this mixture of ruin and nobility
in one person is out of harmony with nature. It is better to
divide among two persons that which is usually found confused clumsily and joined in one. My master and myself, as
being one person, are each a part of the other. Would it
could be always so! We have all within ourselves a great
and splendid gentleman of lofty hopes and towering ideals,
capable of everything that is noble and everything that is
good—and by his side, a humble servant born to forlorn
hopes and miserable and hidden things, who employs himself in the base actions to which we are enforced by life.
The art of living is so to separate the two that when we
fall into any ignominy we can say: "It was not my fault; it
was not I. It was my servant." In the greatest misery to
which we sink there is always something in us which rises
superior to ourselves. We should despise ourselves too much
if we did not believe that we were better than our lives. Of
course you know who my master is: he is the one of the
towering thoughts, of the lofty, beautiful ideals. Of course
you know who I am: I am the one of the forlorn and hidden
things, the one who grovels and toils on the ground, delving
among falsehood and humiliation and lies. Only there is
something in me which redeems me and elevates me in my
own eyes. It is the loyalty of my service, this loyalty which
humiliates and abases itself that another may fly, that he

may always be the lord of the towering thoughts, of the lofty, beautiful ideals.

(*Music is heard in the distance.*)

COLUMBINE. What is this music?

CRISPIN. The music which my master is bringing with him to the fête with all his pages and all the attendants of his train, accompanied by a great court of poets and singers presided over by Signor Harlequin, and an entire legion of soldiers with the Captain at their head, illuminating his coming with torches, with rockets and red fire.

COLUMBINE. Who is your master, that he is able to do so much? I run to tell my lady . . .

CRISPIN. It will not be necessary. She is here.

(DOÑA SIRENA *enters from the pavilion.*)

SIRENA. What is this? Who has prepared this music? What troop of people is arriving at my door?

COLUMBINE. Ask no questions. Know that today a great gentleman has arrived in this city, and it is he who offers you this fête tonight. His servant will tell you everything. I hardly know myself whether I have been talking to a great rogue or a great madman. Whichever it is, I assure you that he is a most extraordinary man.

SIRENA. Then it is not Harlequin?

COLUMBINE. Ask no questions. It is all a work of magic!

CRISPEN. Doña Sirena, my master begs permission to kiss your hand. So great a lady and so noble a gentleman ought not, when they meet, to descend to indignities inappropriate to their state. That is why, before he arrives, I have come to tell you everything. I am acquainted with a thousand notable exploits of your history, which should I but refer to them, would be sufficient to assure me attention. But it might seem impertinence to mention them. (*handing her a paper*) My master acknowledges in this paper over his signature the great sum which he will be in your debt should you be able to fulfil upon your part that which he has here the honor to propose.

SIRENA. What paper and what debt is this? (*reading the paper to herself*) How? A hundred thousand crowns at once and an equal quantity upon the death of Signor Polichinelle, if your master succeeds in marrying his daughter? What insolence and what infamy have we here? And to a lady! Do you know to whom you are speaking? Do you know what house this is?

CRISPIN. Doña Sirena! Forego your wrath. There is nobody present to warrant such concern. Put that paper away with the others, and let us not refer to the matter again. My master proposes nothing which is improper to you, nor would you consent that he should do so. Whatever may happen hereafter will be the work of chance and of love. I, the servant, was the one who set this unworthy snare. You are ever the noble dame, my master the virtuous cavalier, and as you meet in this festival tonight, you will talk of a thousand gallant and priceless things, as your guests stroll by and whisper enviously in praise of the ladies' beauty and the exquisite artfulness of their dress, the splendor and magnificence of the entertainment, the sweetness of the music, the nimble grace of the dancers' feet. And who is to say that this is not the whole story? Is not life just this—a fête in which the music serves to cover up the words, the words to cover up the thoughts? Then let the music sound, let conversation flash and sparkle with its smiles, let the supper be well served—this is all that concerns the guests. See, here is my master, who comes to salute you in all courtesy.

(LEANDER, HARLEQUIN, *and the* CAPTAIN *enter from the right.*)

LEANDER. Doña Sirena, I kiss your hand.

SIRENA. Sir . . .

LEANDER. My servant has already told you in my name much more than I myself could say.

CRISPIN. Being a gentleman of discretion, my master is a man of few words. His admiration is mute.

HARLEQUIN. He wisely knows how to admire.

CAPTAIN. True merit.

HARLEQUIN. True valor.

CAPTAIN. The divine art of poesy.

HARLEQUIN. The incomparable science of war.

CAPTAIN. His greatness appears in everything!

HARLEQUIN. He is the noblest gentleman in the world.

CAPTAIN. My sword shall always be at his service.

HARLEQUIN. I shall dedicate my greatest poem to his glory.

CRISPIN. Enough! Enough! You will offend his native modesty. See how he tries to hide himself and slip away. He is a violet.

SIRENA. Surely he has no need to speak for himself who can make others talk like this in his praise.

(*After bows and salutations the men all withdraw upon the right,* DOÑA SIRENA *and* COLUMBINE *remaining alone.*)

SIRENA. What do you think of this, Columbine?

COLUMBINE. I think that the master is most attractive in his figure and the servant most captivating in his impertinence.

SIRENA. We shall take advantage of them both. For either I know nothing of the world or about men, or else fortune this day has set her foot within my doors.

COLUMBINE. Surely then it must be fortune, for you do know something of the world, and about men—what don't you know!

SIRENA. Here are Risela and Laura, the first to arrive.

COLUMBINE. When were they the last at anything? I leave them to you; I must not lose sight of our cavalier.

(*She goes out to the right.* LAURA *and* RISELA *enter.*)

SIRENA. My dears! Do you know, I was beginning to worry already for fear that you would not come?

LAURA. What? Is it really so late?

SIRENA. Naturally it is late before I worry about you.

RISELA. We were obliged to disappoint at two other fêtes so as not to miss yours.

LAURA. Though we understood that you might not be able to give it tonight. We heard that you were indisposed.

SIRENA. If only to rebuke gossipers I should have given it though I had died.

RISELA. And we should have been present at it even though we had died.

LAURA. But of course you have not heard the news?

RISELA. Nobody is talking of anything else.

LAURA. A mysterious personage has arrived in the city. Some say that he is a secret ambassador from Venice or from France.

RISELA. Others say that he has come to seek a wife for the Grand Turk.

LAURA. They say he is beautiful as an Adonis.

RISELA. If we could only manage to meet him! —What a pity! You ought to have invited him to your fête.

SIRENA. It was not necessary, my dears. He himself sent an ambassador begging permission to come. He is now in my house, and I have not the slightest doubt but that you will be talking to him soon.

LAURA. What is that? I told you that we made no mistake when we came. Something was sure to happen.

RISELA. How we shall be envied tonight!

LAURA. Everybody is mad to know him.

SIRENA. It was no effort for me. It was sufficient for him to hear that I was receiving in my house.

RISELA. Of course—the old story. No person of importance ever arrives in the city, but it seems he runs at once and pays his attentions to you.

LAURA. I am impatient to see him. Lead us to him, on your life!

RISELA. Yes! Take us where he is.

SIRENA. I beg your pardons—Signor Polichinelle arriving with his family. But, my dears, you will not wait. You need no introductions.

RISELA. Certainly not! Come, Laura.

LAURA. Come, Risela, before the crowd grows too great and it is impossible to get near.

(LAURA and RISELA *go out to the right.* POLICHINELLE, *the* WIFE OF POLICHINELLE, *and* SILVIA *enter.*)

SIRENA. O, Signor Polichinelle! I was afraid you were not coming. Until now I really did not know whether or not I was to have a fête!

POLICHINELLE. It was not my fault; it was my wife's. With forty gowns to select from, she can never make up her mind which to put on.

WIFE OF POLICHINELLE. Yes, if I were to please him I should make an exhibition of myself. Any suggestion will do. As it is, you see that I have really not had time to put on anything.

SIRENA. But you never were more beautiful!

POLICHINELLE. Well, she is not displaying one-half of her jewels. If she were, she could not support the weight of the treasure.

SIRENA. Who has a better right to be proud than you have, Signor Polichinelle? What your wife displays are the riches which you have acquired by your labor.

WIFE OF POLICHINELLE. I tell him this is the time to enjoy them. He ought to be ambitious and seek to rise in the world. Instead, all he thinks about is how he can marry his daughter to some trader.

SIRENA. O, Signor Polichinelle! Your daughter deserves a great deal better than a trader. Surely you hold your daughter far too high for trade. Such a thing is not to be thought of for one moment. You have no right to sacrifice her heart to a bargain. What do you say, Silvia?

POLICHINELLE. She would prefer some waxed-up dandy. Instead of listening to my advice, she reads novels and poetry. It disgusts me.

SILVIA. I always do as my father says, unless it is displeasing to my mother or distasteful to me.

SIRENA. You speak very sensibly.

WIFE OF POLICHINELLE. Her father has an idea that there is nothing but money to be had in the world.

POLICHINELLE. I have an idea that without money there is nothing to be had out of the world. Money is the one thing which counts. It buys everything.

SIRENA. Oh, I cannot hear you talk like that! What of virtue, what of intelligence, what of noble blood?

POLICHINELLE. They all have their price. You know it. And nobody knows it better than I do, for I have bought heavily in those lines, and found them reasonable.

SIRENA. O, Signor Polichinelle! You are in a playful humor this evening. You know very well that money will not buy everything, and if your daughter should fall in love with some noble gentleman, you would not dream of attempting to oppose her. I can see that you have a father's heart.

POLICHINELLE. I have. I would do anything for my daughter.

SIRENA. Even ruin yourself?

POLICHINELLE. That would not be anything for my daughter. Why, I would steal first, rob, murder—anything . . .

SIRENA. I felt sure that you must know some way to recoup yourself. But the fête is crowded already! Come with me, Silvia. I have picked out a handsome gentleman to dance with you. You will make a striking couple—ideal!

(*All go out upon the right except* SIGNOR POLICHINELLE, *who is detained as he is about to do so by* CRISPIN, *who enters and accosts him.*)

CRISPIN. Signor Polichinelle! With your permission . . . A word with you . . .

POLICHINELLE. Who calls me? What do you want?

CRISPIN. You don't remember me? It is not surprising. Time blots out everything, and when what has been blotted out was unpleasant, after a while we do not remember even the blot, but hurry and paint over it with bright colors, like these with which you now hide your capers from the world. Why, when I knew you, Signor Polichinelle, you had hard work to cover your nakedness with a couple of muddy rags!

POLICHINELLE. Who are you and where did you know me?

CRISPIN. I was a mere boy then; you were a grown man. But you cannot have forgotten so soon all those glorious exploits on the high seas, all those victories gained over the Turks, to which we contributed not a little with our heroic strength, both pulling chained at the same noble oar in the same victorious galley?

POLICHINELLE. Impudent scoundrel! Silence, or——

CRISPIN. Or you will do with me as you did with your first master in Naples, or with your first wife in Bologna, or with that usurious Jew in Venice?

POLICHINELLE. Silence! Who are you who know so much and talk so freely?

CRISPIN. I am—what you were. One who will come to be what you are—as you have done. Not with the same violence as you, for these are other days and only madmen commit murder now, and lovers, and poor ignorant wretches who fall armed upon the wayfarer in dark alleys or along the solitary highway. Despicable gallows-birds! Negligible!

POLICHINELLE. What do you want of me? Money, is it not? Well, we can meet again; this is not the place . . .

CRISPIN. Do not trouble yourself about your money. I only want to be your friend, your ally, as in those days.

POLICHINELLE. What can I do for you?

CRISPIN. Nothing; for today I am the one who is going to do for you, and oblige you with a warning. (*directing him to look off upon the right*) Do you see your daughter there— how she is dancing with that young gentleman? How coyly she blushes at his gallant compliments! Well, that gentleman is my master.

POLICHINELLE. Your master? Then he must be an adventurer, a rogue, a blackguard, like . . .

CRISPIN. Like us, you were going to say? No, he is more dangerous than we, because, as you see, he has a fine figure, and there is a mystery and an enchantment in his glance and a sweetness in his voice which go straight to the heart, and which stir it as at the recital of some sad tale. Is not this enough to make any woman fall in love? Never say that I did not warn you. Run and separate your daughter from this man and never permit her to dance with him again, no, nor to speak to him, so long as she shall live.

POLICHINELLE. Do you mean to say that he is your master and is this the way you serve him?

CRISPIN. Are you surprised? Have you forgotten already how it was when you were a servant? And I have not planned to assassinate him yet.

POLICHINELLE. You are right. A master is always despicable. But what interest have you in serving me?

CRISPIN. To come safe into some good port, as we often did when we rowed together at the oar. Then sometimes you used to say to me: "You are stronger than I, row for me." In this galley in which we are today, you are stronger than I. Row for me, for your faithful friend of other days, for life is a horrible vile galley and I have rowed so long.

(*He goes out by the way he came in.* DOÑA SIRENA, *the* WIFE OF POLICHINELLE, RISELA, *and* LAURA *re-enter.*)

LAURA. Only Doña Sirena could have given such a fête!

RISELA. Tonight she has outstripped all the others.

SIRENA. The presence of so distinguished a gentleman was an added attraction.

POLICHINELLE. But Silvia? Where is Silvia? What have you done with my daughter?

SIRENA. Do not disturb yourself, Signor Polichinelle. Your daughter is in excellent hands, and you may rest assured that she will remain in them as long as she is in my house.

RISELA. There were no attentions for any one but her.

LAURA. All the smiles were for her.

RISELA. And all the sighs!

POLICHINELLE. Whose? This mysterious gentleman's? I do not like it. This must stop——

SIRENA. But Signor Polichinelle!

POLICHINELLE. Away! Let me be! I know what I am doing. (*He rushes out.*)

SIRENA. What is the matter? What infatuation is this?

WIFE OF POLICHINELLE. Now you see what sort of man he is. He is going to commit an outrage on that gentleman. He wants to marry his daughter to a trader, does he—a clinker of worthless coin? He wants to make her unhappy for the rest of her life.

SIRENA. No, anything rather than that! Remember—you are her mother and this is the time for you to interpose your authority.

WIFE OF POLICHINELLE. Look! He has spoken to him and

the cavalier drops Silvia's hand and retires, hanging his head.

LAURA. And now Signor Polichinelle is attacking your daughter!

SIRENA. Come! Come! Such conduct cannot be tolerated in my house.

RISELA. Signora Polichinelle, in spite of your riches you are an unfortunate woman.

WIFE OF POLICHINELLE. Would you believe it, he even forgets himself sofar sometimes as to turn upon me?

LAURA. Is it possible? And are you a woman to submit to that?

WIFE OF POLICHINELLE. He makes it up afterward by giving me a handsome present.

SIRENA. Well, there are husbands of my acquaintance who never even think of making up . . .

(*They all go out.* LEANDER *and* CRISPIN *enter.*)

CRISPIN. What is this sadness, this dejection? I expected to find you in better spirits.

LEANDER. I was never unfortunate till now; at least it never mattered to me whether or not I was unfortunate. Let us fly, Crispin, let us fly from this city before anyone can discover us and find out who we are.

CRISPIN. If we fly it will be after everyone has discovered us and they are running after us to detain us and bring us back in spite of ourselves. It would be most discourteous to depart with such scant ceremony without bidding our attentive friends goodbye.

LEANDER. Do not jest, Crispin; I am in despair.

CRISPIN. So you are. And just when our hopes are under fullest sail.

LEANDER. What could you expect? You wanted me to pretend to be in love, but I have not been able to pretend it.

CRISPIN. Why not?

LEANDER. Because I love—I love in spirit and in truth!

CRISPIN. Silvia? Is that what you are complaining about?

LEANDER. I never believed it possible a man could love like this. I never believed that I could ever love. Through all my wandering life along the dusty roads, I was not only the one who passed, I was the one who fled, the enemy of the harvest and the field, the enemy of man, enemy of sunshine and the day. Sometimes the fruit of the wayside tree, stolen, not given, left some savor of joy on my parched lips, and sometimes, after many a bitter day, resting at night beneath the stars, the calm repose of heaven would invite and soothe me to a dream of something that might be in my life like that calm night sky, brooding infinite over my soul —serene! And so tonight, in the enchantment of this fête, it seemed to me as if there had come a calm, a peace into my life—and I was dreaming! Ah! How I did dream! But tomorrow it will be again the bitter flight with justice at our heels, and I cannot bear that they should take me here where she is, and where she may ever have cause to be ashamed at having known me.

CRISPIN. Why, I thought that you had been received with favor! And I was not the only one who noticed it. Doña Sirena and our good friends, the Captain and the poet, have been most eloquent in your praises. To that rare excellent mother, the wife of Polichinelle, who thinks of nothing but how she can relate herself by marriage to some nobleman, you have seemed the son-in-law of her dreams. As for Signor Polichinelle . . .

LEANDER. He knows . . . he suspects . . .

CRISPIN. Naturally. It is not so easy to deceive Signor Polichinelle as it is an ordinary man. An old fox like him has to be cheated truthfully. I decided that the best thing for us to do was to tell him everything.

LEANDER. How so?

CRISPIN. Obviously. He knows me of old. When I told him that you were my master, he rightly supposed that the master must be worthy of the man. And upon my part, in appreciation of his confidence, I warned him not to permit you under any circumstances to come near to or speak with his daughter.

LEANDER. You did? Then what have I to hope?

CRISPIN. You are a fool! Why, that Signor Polichinelle will exert all his authority to prevent you from meeting her.

LEANDER. I do not understand.

CRISPIN. In that way he will become our most powerful ally, for if he opposes it, that will be enough to make his wife take the opposite side, and the daughter will fall in love with you madly. You have no idea what a young and beautiful daughter of a rich father, who has been brought up to the gratification of her every whim, can do when she finds out for the first time in her life that somebody is opposing her wishes. I am certain that this very night, before the fête is over, she will find some way of eluding the vigilance of her father at whatever cost, and return to speak with you.

LEANDER. But can't you see that Signor Polichinelle is nothing to me, no, nor the wide world either? It is she, only she! It is to her that I am unwilling to appear unworthy or mean, it is to her—to her that I cannot lie.

CRISPIN. Bah! Enough of this nonsense! Don't tell me that. It is too late to draw back. Think what will happen if we vacillate now and hesitate in going on. You say that you have fallen in love? Well, this real love will serve us better than if it were put on. Otherwise you would have wanted to get through with it too quickly. If insolence and effrontery are the only qualities which are of use elsewhere, in love a faint suggestion of timidity is of advantage to a man. Timidity in a man always makes the woman bolder. If you don't believe it, here is the innocent Silvia now, skulking in the shadows and only waiting for a chance to come near until I retire or am concealed.

LEANDER. Silvia, do you say?

CRISPIN. Hush! You may frighten her. When she is with you, remember, discretion—only a few words, very few. Adore her, admire her, contemplate her, and let the enchantment of this night of pallid blue speak for you, propitious as it is to love, and whisper to her in the music whose soft notes die away amid the foliage and fall upon our ears like sad overtones of this festival of joy.

LEANDER. Do not trifle, Crispin! Do not trifle with my love! It will be my death.

CRISPIN. Why should I trifle with it? I know, too, it is not always well to grovel on the ground. Sometimes we must soar and mount up into the sky better to dominate the earth. Mount now and soar—and I will grovel still. The world lies in our hands!

(*He goes out to the right.* SILVIA *enters.*)

LEANDER. Silvia!

SILVIA. Is it you? You must pardon me. I did not expect to find you here.

LEANDER. I fly from the festival. I am saddened by this joy.

SILVIA. What? You, too?

LEANDER. Too, do you say? Does joy sadden you, too?

SILVIA. My father is angry with me. He never spoke to you forgive him?

me like this before. And he was discourteous to you. Will

LEANDER. Yes. I forgive him everything. But you must not make him angry upon my account. Return to the company. They will be looking for you. If they find you here with me . . .

SILVIA. You are right. But you must come, too. Why should you be so sad?

LEANDER. No, I must slip away without anybody seeing me, without their knowing I am gone. I must go far away.

SILVIA. What? But you have important business in the city. I know you have . . . You will have to stay a long, long time.

LEANDER. No, no! Not another day, not another hour!

SILVIA. But then . . . You have not lied to me?

LEANDER. Lied? No! Don't say that I have lied! No; this is the one truth of my whole life—this dream from which there should be no awakening!

(*The music of a song is heard in the distance, continuing until the curtain falls.*)

SILVIA. It is Harlequin, singing . . . What is the matter? You are crying. Is it the music which makes you cry? Why will you not tell me what it is that makes you cry?

LEANDER. What makes me cry? The song will tell you. Listen to the song!

SILVIA. We can hear only the music; the words are lost, it is so far away. But don't you know it? It is a song to the silence of the night. It is called the "Kingdom of the Soul." You must know it.

LEANDER. Say it over to me.

SILVIA.

The amorous night above the silent lover
Across the blue heaven spreads a nuptial veil.
The night has strewn its diamonds on the cover
Of a moonlit sky in drowsy August pale.
The garden in the shade now knows no color,
Deep in the shadow of its obscurity
Lightly the leaflets flutter, sweetly smells the flower,
And love broods there in silent sympathy.

You voices which sigh, you voices which sing,
You voices which whisper sweet phrases of love,
Intruders you are and a blasphemous thing,
Like an oath at night-tide in a prayer sped above.

Great Spirit of Silence, whom I adore,
There is in your silence the ineffable voice
Of those who have died loving in silence of yore,
Of those who were silent and died of their love;
Of those in their lives whose great love was such
They were unable to tell it, their love was so much!
Yours are the voices which nightly I hear,
Whispers of love and eternity near.

    Mother of my soul, the light of this star,
      Is it not the light of your eyes,
    Which, like a drop of God's blood,
      Trembles in the night
      And fades at sunrise?
    Tell him whom I love, I never shall love
      More than him on the earth,
    And when he fades away, light of my eyes,
      I shall kiss at sunrise
      But the light of thy star!
LEANDER.
    Mother of my soul, I never have loved
      More than you on the earth.
    And when you fade away, light of my eyes,
      I shall kiss at sunrise
      The light of thy star.
(*They remain in silence, embracing and gazing into
each other's eyes.*)
CRISPIN (*who appears at the right—to himself*).
    Poesy and night and madness of the lover . . .
      All has to serve us that to our net shall come.
    The victory is sure! Courage, charge and over!
    Who shall overcome us when love beats the drum?
(SILVIA *and* LEANDER *move slowly off to the right,
locked in each other's arms.* CRISPIN *follows them in silence, without being seen. Slowly the Curtain descends.*)

ACT III

A room in LEANDER's *house.*

(CRISPIN, *the* CAPTAIN, *and* HARLEQUIN *enter from the right.*)

CRISPIN. Enter, gentlemen, and be seated. Will you take something? Let me give orders to have it brought. Hello there! Ho!

CAPTAIN. No! By no means! We can accept nothing.

HARLEQUIN. We came merely to offer our services to your master after what we have just heard.

CRISPIN. Incredible treachery, which, believe me, shall not be suffered to remain unpunished! I promise you if Signor Polichinelle ever puts himself within the reach of my hands——

HARLEQUIN. Ah! Now you see what an advantage is possessed by us poets! I have him always within the reach of my verses. Oh! What a terrible satire I am thinking of writing against him! The cutthroat! Old reprobate!

CAPTAIN. But you say your master was not so much as even wounded?

CRISPIN. It might have killed him just the same. Imagine! Set upon by a dozen ruffians absolutely without warning . . . Thanks, though, to his bravery, to his skill, to my cries . . .

HARLEQUIN. Do you say that it happened at night as your master was talking to Silvia over the wall of her garden?

CRISPIN. Naturally, my master had already been advised of what might happen. But you know what sort of man he is. He is not a person to be deterred by anything.

CAPTAIN. He ought to have notified us, however.

HARLEQUIN. He ought, certainly, to have notified the Captain. He would have been delighted to have lent his aid.

CRISPIN. You know what my master is. He is a host in himself.

CAPTAIN. But you say that he caught one of the ruffians by the nape of the neck, and the rascal confessed that it had all been planned and arranged by Signor Polichinelle beforehand so as to rid himself of your master?

CRISPIN. Who else could have had any interest in it? His daughter is in love with my master; her father wants to marry her to suit himself. My master is opposing his plans, and Signor Polichinelle has known all his life how to get rid of disturbances. Didn't he become a widower twice in a very short time? Hasn't he inherited all that his relatives had, irrespective of age, whether they were older or younger than he? Everybody knows it; nobody will say that I do him injustice. Ah! the riches of Signor Polichinelle are an affront to our intelligence, a discouragement to honest labor. A man like Signor Polichinelle could remain rich only among a base and degenerate people.

HARLEQUIN. I agree with you. I intend to say all this in my satire—of course, without mentioning names. Poetry does not admit of such license.

CRISPIN. Much good, then, your satire will do!

CAPTAIN. Leave him to me! Leave him to me! I promise you if he once puts himself within the reach of my sword— ah! But I am confident that he never will.

CRISPIN. My master would never consent to have an insult offered to Signor Polichinelle. After all, he is Silvia's father. The point is to let people in the city understand that an attempt has been made to assassinate my master. Is that old fox to be allowed to stifle the honest affection, the generous passion of his daughter? It is impossible.

HARLEQUIN. It is impossible. Love will find a way.

CRISPIN. If my master had been some impecunious beggar . . . Tell me, isn't Signor Polichinelle the one who ought to be congratulated that my master has condescended to fall in love with his daughter, and is willing to accept him for his father-in-law?—my master, who has rejected the advances of so many damsels of high degree; my master, for whom over four princesses have committed I know not how many absurdities! But who is here? (*looking toward the right*) Ah, Columbine! Come in, my beautiful Columbine! Do not be afraid. (COLUMBINE *enters from the right.*) We are all your friends, and our mutual friendship will protect you from our mutual admiration.

COLUMBINE. Doña Sirena has sent me for news of your master. It was scarcely day when Silvia came to our house and confided everything that had happened to my mistress. She says that she will never return to her father, nor leave

my mistress, unless it is to become the bride of Signor
Leander.

CRISPIN. Does she say that? O noble girl! O constant, true-
hearted lover!

HARLEQUIN. What an epithalamium I shall write for their
wedding!

COLUMBINE. Silvia is positive that Leander is wounded.
She heard the clash of swords beneath the balcony, your
cries for help; then she fell senseless and they found her in
a swoon at daybreak. Tell me how Signor Leander is, for she
is beside herself with anxiety to hear, and my lady also
is much distressed.

CRISPIN. Tell her that my master escaped with his life
only through the unutterable power of love. Tell her that
he is dying now only from the incurable wounds of love.
Tell her that to the last . . . (*seeing* LEANDER *approach*) Ah,
but here he is himself, and he will be able to give you
later news than I.

(LEANDER *enters.*)

CAPTAIN (*embracing him*). My dear, good friend!

HARLEQUIN (*embracing him*). My friend and master!

COLUMBINE. Ah, Signor Leander, what happiness! You
are safe!

LEANDER. What? How did you know?

CRISPIN. Nothing else is talked about in the city. People
gather in groups in the squares murmuring vengeance and
venting imprecations upon Signor Polichinelle.

LEANDER. What is this?

CAPTAIN. He had better not dare to attempt your life a
second time.

HARLEQUIN. He had better not dare to attempt to arrest
the true course of your love.

COLUMBINE. It would be useless. Silvia is in my mistress's
house and she swears that she will leave it only to become
your bride.

LEANDER. Silvia in your house? But her father . . .

COLUMBINE. Signor Polichinelle has all he can do to look
after himself.

CAPTAIN. What? I knew that man would be up to something. Oh, of what base uses money is capable!

HARLEQUIN. It is capable of everything but love; of that
it is incapable.

COLUMBINE. He tried to have you assassinated dishonor-
ably in the dark.

CRISPIN. By twelve cutthroats. Twelve! I counted them.

LEANDER. I made out only three or four.

CRISPIN. My master will end by telling you that there was no danger so as not to receive credit for his coolness and his bravery—but I saw it. There were twelve; twelve armed to the teeth, prepared to do murder. It seemed impossible that he could escape with his life.

COLUMBINE. I must run and calm Silvia and my mistress.

CRISPIN. Listen, Columbine. As to Silvia—wouldn't it be as well, perhaps, not to calm her?

COLUMBINE. Leave that to my mistress. Silvia is convinced that your master is dead, and although Doña Sirena is making the most unheard-of efforts to console her, it will not be long before she is here in spite of the consequences.

CRISPIN. I ought to have known of what your mistress was capable.

CAPTAIN. We must be going, too; there is nothing here that we can do. The point is to arouse the indignation of the people against Signor Polichinelle.

HARLEQUIN. We shall stone his house; we shall raise the whole city. Until today not a single man has dared to lift his hand against him; today we will all dare to do it together. There is an uplift, a moral earnestness in a crowd.

COLUMBINE. He will come creeping on his knees and beg you to accept his daughter as your wife.

CRISPIN. Yes, yes, he will indeed! Run, friends, run! The life of my master is not secure. A man who has once made up his mind to assassinate him is not likely to be turned aside for a trifle.

CAPTAIN. Have no fear, my good friend.

HARLEQUIN. My friend and master!

COLUMBINE. Signor Leander!

LEANDER. Thanks to you all, my friends. My loyal friends!
(*All go out but* LEANDER *and* CRISPIN.)

LEANDER. What is this, Crispin? What are you trying to do? Where do you expect to come out with all your lies? Do you know what I believe? You paid those fellows yourself; it was your idea. I should have got off badly enough among so many if they had been in earnest.

CRISPIN. Have you the temerity to reproach me when I precipitate the fulfilment of your desires so skillfully?

LEANDER. No, Crispin, no. You know you do not. I love Silvia. I am resolved: I shall never win her love through deception, come what may.

CRISPIN. You know very well, then, what will come. Do you call it love to sit down and resign yourself to losing what you love for the sake of these quibbles of conscience? Silvia herself would not thank you for it.

LEANDER. What do you mean? If she once learns who I am . . .

CRISPIN. By the time she finds out you will no longer be the one that you are. You will be her husband then, her beloved husband, who is everything that is noble and faithful and true, and whatever else you like besides, or that her heart desires. Once you are master of her heart—and her fortune—will you not be a complete and perfect gentleman? You will not be like Signor Polichinelle, who, with all his wealth which permits him so many luxuries, has not yet been able to permit himself the luxury of being honest. Deceit is natural to him, but with you it was only necessity. If you had not had me at your side you would have starved to death before this out of pure conscientiousness. Ah! do you suppose that if I had thought for one moment that you were a man of another sort, I would have been satisfied to devote your abilities to love? No, I would have put you into politics, and not merely the fortune of Signor Polichinelle would have been ours, but a chastened and admiring world. But you are not ambitious. You will be satisfied to be happy.

LEANDER. But can't you see that no good, no happiness, can come out of this? If I could lie so as to make her love me and in that way become rich, then it could only be because I did not love. And if I did not love, then how could I be happy? And if I love, how can I lie?

CRISPIN. Don't lie, then. Love, love passionately, entirely, with your whole heart and soul. Put your love before everything else upon earth. Guard and protect it. A lover does not lie when he keeps to himself what he thinks might prejudice the blind affection of his mistress.

LEANDER. These are subtleties, Crispin.

CRISPIN. Which you would have known all about before if you had really been in love. Love is all subtleties and the greatest subtlety of them all is not that lovers deceive others —it is that they can so easily deceive themselves.

LEANDER. I do not deceive myself, Crispin. I am not one of those men who, when they have sold their conscience, think that they have also been able to dispose of their intelligence as well.

CRISPIN. That is the reason I said you would never make

a good politician. You are right. For the intelligence is the conscience of truth, and the man who parts with that among the lies of this life is as one who has lost himself. He is without compass or sail. He will never be able to find himself again, nor know himself, but become in all his being just one more living lie.

LEANDER. Where did you learn all these things, Crispin?

CRISPIN. I meditated a little while in the galleys, where this conscience of my intelligence accused me of having been more of a fool than a knave. If I had had more knavery and less stupidity, instead of rowing I might have commanded the ship. So I swore never again to return to the oar. You can see now what I am willing to do for your sake since I am on the point of breaking my oath.

LEANDER. In what way?

CRISPIN. Our situation has become desperate. We have exhausted our credit, and our dupes begin to demand something more substantial than talk: the innkeeper who entertained us so long with such munificence, expecting that you would receive your remittances; Signor Pantaloon, who, hearing of the credit extended by the innkeeper, advanced us whatever was necessary to install us sumptuously in this house; tradesmen of every description, who did not hesitate to provide us with every luxury, dazzled by such display; Doña Sirena herself, who has lent us her invaluable good offices in your love affair—they have all only asked what was reasonable; it would be unjust to expect more of them or to complain of such delightful people. The name of this fair city shall ever be engraven upon my heart in letters of gold. From this hour I claim it as my adopted mother! But more than this, have you forgotten that they have been searching for us in other parts and following on our heels? Can it be that all those glorious exploits of Mantua and Florence have been forgotten? Don't you recall that famous lawsuit in Bologna? Three thousand two hundred pages of testimony already admitted against us before we withdrew in alarm at the sight of such prodigious expansive ability! Do you imagine that it has not continued to grow under the pen of that learned doctor and jurist, who has taken it under his wing? How many whereases and therefores must there now be therefore, whereas they are all there for no good? Do you still doubt? Do you still hesitate and reprove me because I give the battle today which is to decide our fate forever at a single blow?

LEANDER. Let us fly!

CRISPIN. No! Let the despairing fly! This day decides. We challenge fortune. I have given you love; give me life!

LEANDER. But how can we save ourselves? What can I do? Tell me.

CRISPIN. Nothing yet. It will be enough to accept what others offer. We have intertwined ourselves with the interests of many, and the bonds of interest will prove our salvation.

(DOÑA SIRENA *enters.*)

SIRENA. Have I your permission, Signor Leander?

LEANDER. Doña Sirena! What? You in my house?

SIRENA. I am conscious of the risk I am running—the gossip of evil tongues. What? Doña Sirena in the house of a young and gallant gentleman?

CRISPIN. My master will know how to avoid all cause of scandal, if any indeed could attach to your name.

SIRENA. Your master? I would not trust him. Men are so boastful! But it is idle to anticipate. What, sir, is this talk about an attempt to kill you last night? I have not heard another thing since I got up in the morning. And Silvia! The poor child! How she loves you! I would give a great deal to know what it was that you did to make her fall in love with you like that.

CRISPIN. My master feels that it was what you did. He owes it all to you.

SIRENA. I should be the last one to deny that he owes me anything. I have always tried to speak well of him—a thing I had no right to do, not knowing him sufficiently. I have gone to great lengths in his service. Now if you are false to your promise . . .

CRISPIN. You do not doubt my master? Have you not the papers signed in his own hand?

SIRENA. The hand is a good one and so is the name. I don't bother about them. I know what it is to trust, and I know that Signor Leander will pay me what he owes. But today has been a bitter day for me, and if you could let me have today one-half of what you have promised, I would willingly forego the other half.

CRISPIN. Today, do you say?

SIRENA. A day of tribulation! And what makes it worse, it is twenty years ago today that my second husband died, who was my first—yes, my only love.

CRISPIN. May he rest in peace with all the honors óf the first!

SIRENA. The first was forced upon me by my father. I never loved him, but in spite of it he insisted upon being faithful to me.

CRISPIN. What knowledge you have of men, Doña Sirena!

SIRENA. But let us leave these recollections, which are depressing, and turn to hope. Would you believe it? Silvia insisted upon coming with me.

LEANDER. Here? To this house?

SIRENA. Where do you suppose it was that she insisted upon coming? What do you say to that? What would Signor Polichinelle say? With all the city roused against him, there would be nothing for him to do but to have you marry.

LEANDER. No, no! Don't let her come . . .

CRISPIN. Hush! You know my master has a way of not saying what he means.

SIRENA. I know. What would he give to see Silvia at his side, never to be separated from him more?

CRISPIN. What would he give? You don't know what he would give!

SIRENA. That is the reason I ask.

CRISPIN. Ah, Doña Sirena! If my master becomes the husband of Silvia today, today he will pay you everything that he has promised you.

SIRENA. And if he does not?

CRISPIN. Then you lose everything. Suit yourself.

LEANDER. Silence, Crispin, silence! Enough! I cannot submit to have my love treated as a bargain. Go, Doña Sirena! Say to Silvia that she must return to her father's house, that under no circumstances is she ever to enter mine; that she must forget me forever. I shall fly and hide myself in the desert places of the earth, where no man shall see me, no, nor so much as know my name. My name? I wonder—have I a name?

CRISPIN. Will you be silent?

SIRENA. What is the matter with him? What paroxysm is this? Return to your senses! Come to your proper mind! How? Renounce so glorious an enterprise for nothing? You are not the only person who is to be considered. Remember that there are others who have put their confidence in you. A lady of quality who has exposed herself for your sake is not to be betrayed with impunity. You will do no such thing. You will not be so foolish. You will marry Silvia or there will be one who will find a way to bring you to a reckoning for all your impostures. I am not so defenseless in the world as you may think, Signor Leander.

CRISPIN. Doña Sirena is right. But believe me, this fit of my master's—he is offended by your reproaches, your want of confidence.

SIRENA. I don't want confidence in your master. And I might as well say it—I don't want confidence in Signor Polichinelle. He is not a man to be trifled with, either. After the outcry which you raised against him by your stratagem of last night——

CRISPIN. Stratagem, did you say?

SIRENA. Bah! Everybody knows it. One of the rascals was a relative of mine, and among the others I had connections. Very well, sirs, very well! Signor Polichinelle has not been asleep. It is said in the city that he has given information as to who you are to Justice, and on what grounds you may be apprehended. It is said that a process has arrived today from Bologna——

CRISPIN. And a devil of a doctor with it? Three thousand nine hundred folios . . .

SIRENA. So it is said and on good authority. You see that there is no time to lose.

CRISPIN. Who is losing and who is wasting time but you? Return, return at once to your house! Say to Silvia——

SIRENA. Silvia? Silvia is here. She came along with me and Columbine as one of the attendants in my train. She is waiting in the antechamber. I told her that you were wounded horribly.

LEANDER. Oh, my Silvia!

SIRENA. She has reconciled herself to your death. She hopes for nothing else. She expects nothing else. She thinks nothing of what she risks in coming here to see you. Well? Are we friends?

CRISPIN. You are adorable! (to LEANDER) Quick! Lie down here. Stretch yourself out in this chair. Seem sick, suffer, faint—be downhearted. And remember, if I am not satisfied with the appearance, I will substitute the reality! (Threatens him and forces him into a chair.)

LEANDER. Yes, I am in your power! I see it, I know it! But Silvia shall never be! Yes, let me see her. Tell her to come in. I shall save her in spite of you, in spite of everything, in spite even of herself!

CRISPIN. You know my master has a way of not meaning what he says.

SIRENA. I never thought him such a fool. Come with me.
(*She goes out with* CRISPIN. SILVIA *enters.*)

LEANDER. Silvia! My Silvia!

SILVIA. But aren't you wounded?

LEANDER. No, don't you see? It was a lie, another lie to
bring you here. But don't be afraid. Your father will come
soon; soon you will leave this house with him without having any cause to reproach me . . . Ah! None but that I
have disturbed the serenity of your soul with an illusion of
love which will be to you in the future no more than the
remembrance of a dark and evil dream!

SILVIA. But Leander? Then your love was not real?

LEANDER. My love was, yes. That is why I could not deceive you. Leave this place at once—before any but those
who brought you here discover that you came.

SILVIA. What are you afraid of? Am I not safe in your
house? I was not afraid to come. What harm can happen
to me at your side?

LEANDER. You are right. None! My love will protect you
even from your innocence.

SILVIA. I can never go back to my father's house—not after
the horrible thing which he did last night.

LEANDER. No, Silvia, do not blame your father. It was not
his fault; it was another deception, another lie. Fly from
me; forget this miserable adventurer, this nameless outcast,
a fugitive from justice . . .

SILVIA. No, it isn't true. No! It is the conduct of my father which makes me unworthy of your love. That is what
it is. I see it all now. I understand. Ay, for me!

LEANDER. Silvia! My Silvia! How cruel your sweet words
are! How cruel this noble confidence of your heart, so innocent of evil and of life!

(CRISPIN *enters, running.*)

CRISPIN. Master! Master! Signor Polichinelle is coming!

SILVIA. My father!

LEANDER. It doesn't matter. I shall lead you to him with
my own hand.

CRISPIN. But he is not coming alone. There is a great
crowd with him; the officers of justice . . .

LEANDER. What? Ah! If they should find you here? In my
house! (*to* CRISPIN) I see it all now. You have told them.
But you shall not succeed in your design!

CRISPIN. I? No. Certainly not! For this time this is in earnest and nothing can save us now.

LEANDER. No, not us. Nor shall I try. But her . . . Yes! Hide her, conceal her! We must secrete her here.

SILVIA. But you?

LEANDER. Have no fear. Quick! They are on the stair. (*He hides* SILVIS *in a room at the rear, meanwhile saying to* CRISPIN) See what these fellows want. On your life let no man set his foot within this room after I am gone! . . . The game is up! It is the end for me. (*He runs to the window.*)

CRISPIN (*holding him back*). Master! Master! Hold! Control yourself. Come to your senses. Don't throw your life away!

LEANDER. I am not throwing my life away . . . There is no escape . . . I am saving her . . .

(*He climbs through the window and rapidly up outside and disappears.*)

CRISPIN. Master! Master! H'm! Not so bad after all. I thought he was going to dash himself to pieces on the ground. Instead he has climbed higher . . . There is hope yet—he may yet learn to fly. It is his region, the clouds . . . Now I to mine, the firm ground. And more need than ever that I should make certain that it is solid beneath my feet. (*He seats himself complacently in an armchair.*)

POLICHINELLE (*without, to those who are with him*). Guard the doors! Let no man escape! No, nor woman either . . . Nor dog nor cat!

INNKEEPER. Where are they? Where are these bandits? These assassins?

PANTALOON. Justice! Justice! My money! My money!

(SIGNOR POLICHINELLE, *the* INNKEEPER, SIGNOR PANTALOON, *the* CAPTAIN, HARLEQUIN, *the* DOCTOR, *the* SECRETARY, *and two* CONSTABLES *enter, bearing in their arms enormous scrolls and protocols, or papers of the suit. All enter from the right in the order named. The* DOCTOR *and the* SECRETARY *pass at once to the table and prepare to take testimony. Such rolls and papers as cannot be accommodated upon the table the two* CONSTABLES *retain in their hands, remaining standing for that purpose at the rear.*)

CAPTAIN. But can this be possible, Crispin?

HARLEQUIN. Is it possible that such a thing can be?

PANTALOON. Justice! Justice! My money! My money!

INNKEEPER. Seize them! Put them in irons!

PANTALOON. Don't let them escape! Don't let them escape!

CRISPIN. What? How is this? Who dares to desecrate with impious clamor the house of a gentleman and a cavalier? Oh, you may congratulate yourselves that my master is not at home!

PANTALOON. Silence! Silence! For you are his accomplice and you will be held to answer to the same reckoning as he.

INNKEEPER. Accomplice, did you say? As guilty as his pretended master!—for he was the one who deceived me.

CAPTAIN. What is the meaning of this, Crispin?

HARLEQUIN. Is there any truth in what these people say?

POLICHINELLE. What have you to say for yourself now, Crispin? You thought you were a clever rogue to cut up your capers with me. I tried to murder your master, did I? I am an old miser who is battening on his daughter's heart? All the city is stirred up against me, is it, heaping me with insults? Well, we shall see.

PANTALOON. Leave him to us, Signor Polichinelle, for this is our affair. After all, you have lost nothing. But I—all my wealth which I lent him without security. I am ruined for the rest of my life. What will become of me?

INNKEEPER. What will become of me, tell me that, when I spent what I never had and even ran into debt so that he might be served—as I thought—in a manner befitting his station? It was my destruction, my ruin.

CAPTAIN. We too were horribly deceived. What will be said of me when it is known that I have put my sword at the disposition of an adventurer?

HARLEQUIN. And of me, when I have dedicated sonnet after sonnet to his praise, just as if he had been any ordinary gentleman?

POLICHINELLE. Ha! Ha! Ha!

PANTALOON. Yes, laugh, laugh, that is right. You have lost nothing.

INNKEEPER. Nobody robbed you.

PANTALOON. To work! To work! Where is the other villain?

INNKEEPER. Better see what there is in the house first.

CRISPIN. Slowly, slowly, gentlemen. If you advance one other step—— (*Threatens them with his sword.*)

PANTALOON. What? You threaten us? Again? Is such a thing to be endured? Justice! Justice!

INNKEEPER. Yes, justice!

DOCTOR. Gentlemen, unless you listen to me we shall get nowhere. No man may take justice into his own hands, inasmuch as justice is not haste nor oppression nor vengeance nor act of malice. *Summum jus, summum injuria;* the more wrong, the more justice. Justice is all wisdom, and wisdom is all order, and order is all reason, and reason is all procedure, and procedure is all logic. Barbara, Celarent, Darii, Ferio, Baralipton, deposit all your wrongs and all your disputations with me, for if they are to be of any validity they must all form a part of this process which I have brought in these protocols with me.

CRISPIN. The devil you say! Hasn't it grown enough already?

DOCTOR. Herein are set down and inscribed divers other offenses of these defendants, whereunto must be added and conjoined each and every one of those of which you may accuse them now. And I must be the advocate in all of them, for that is the only way in which it will be possible for you to obtain satisfaction and justice. Write, Signor Secretary, and let the said complainants depose.

PANTALOON. It might be better to settle our differences among ourselves. You know what justice is.

INNKEEPER. Write nothing. It will only be making the white black, and in the end we shall be left without our money and these rogues without punishment.

PANTALOON. Exactly. My money! My money! And justice afterward.

DOCTOR. You unlearned, you uncivil, you ignorant generation! What do you know of justice? It is not enough for you to say that you have suffered a wrong, unless there be plainly apparent therein an intention to make you suffer that wrong; that is to say, fraud or deceit, which are not the same, although they are confounded in the popular acceptation. But I say unto you that only in the single case——

PANTALOON. Enough! Enough! You will end by telling us that we are the guilty ones.

DOCTOR. What else am I to think when you persist in denying such a plain and obvious fact?

INNKEEPER. I like that. Good! We were robbed. Do you want any plainer or more obvious fact?

DOCTOR. Know, then, that robbery is not the same as theft, much less is it the same as fraud or deceit, which again are not the same as aforesaid. From the laws of the Twelve Tables down to Justinian, to Tribonian, to Emilian, to Triberian . . .

PANTALOON. We shall be cheated out of our money. There is no one who can reason me out of that.

POLICHINELLE. The Signor Doctor is right. We can safely leave the matter to him and everything will be attended to in the process.

DOCTOR. Then write, Signor Secretary, write.

CRISPIN. Will any one listen to me?

PANTALOON. No one, no one. Let that rascal be quiet! Silence for that villain!

INNKEEPER. You will have a chance to talk soon enough when you don't want to.

DOCTOR. He will speak at the proper moment, for justice requires that everybody should be afforded an opportunity to talk. Write, write: In the city of . . . in the matter of . . . But it would certainly not be amiss if we proceeded first to an inventory of whatever there is in the house.

CRISPIN (*before the door*). It certainly would be a miss . . .

DOCTOR. Thence to progress to the deposit of security on the part of the complainants, so that there may be no question as to their good faith when they assert that they have suffered a loss. Two thousand crowns will be sufficient from each of you, to be secured by guarantees upon all your goods and chattels.

PANTALOON. What is that? Two thousand crowns from us?

DOCTOR. I ought to make it eight; however, as you are persons of responsibility, I take that fact into account. I allow nothing to escape me.

INNKEEPER. Hold! And write no more! We cannot submit to this.

DOCTOR. What? Do you threaten justice? Open a separate process for battery and the hand of violence raised against an officer of the law in full performance of his duties.

PANTALOON. This man will be the ruin of us.

INNKEEPER. He is mad.

DOCTOR. What? Do you call me a man and mad? Speak with more respect. Write! Write! Open two more counts. There was also an assault by word of mouth . . .

CRISPIN. Now see what you have done through not listening to me.

PANTALOON. Talk, talk, for heaven's sake! Talk! Anything would be better than what is happening to us now.

CRISPIN. Then shut off this fellow, for the love of mercy! He is raising up a mountain with his protocols.

PANTALOON. Stop! Stop, I say!

INNKEEPER. Put down that pen!

DOCTOR. Let no man dare to raise his hand.

CRISPIN. Signor Captain, then lend us your sword. It also is the instrument of justice.

CAPTAIN (*going up to the table and delivering a tremendous blow with his sword upon the papers on which the* DOCTOR *is engaged*). Have the kindness to desist.

DOCTOR. You see how ready I am to comply with a reasonable request. Suspend the actions. (*They stop writing.*) There is a previous question to be adjudged. The parties dispute among themselves. Nevertheless it will be proper to proceed with the inventory . . .

PANTALOON. No! No!

DOCTOR. It is a formality which cannot be waived.

CRISPIN. I don't think it would be proper. When the proper time comes you can write as much as you like. But let me have permission first to speak for a moment with these honorable gentlemen.

DOCTOR. If you wish to have what you are about to say recorded as testimony . . .

CRISPIN. No! By no means. Not a single word, or I shall not open my mouth.

CAPTAIN. Better let the fellow talk.

CRISPIN. What shall I say? What are you complaining about? That you have lost your money? What do you want? To get it back?

PANTALOON Exactly! Exactly! My money!

INNKEEPER. Our money!

CRISPIN. Then listen to me. Where do you suppose that it is coming from when you insist upon destroying the credit of my master in this fashion, and so make his marriage with the daughter of Signor Polichinelle impossible? Name of Mars! I had rather deal with a thousand knaves than one fool. See what you have done now and how you will be obliged to compound with justice for a half share of what we owe you—I say *owe* you. How will you be any better off if you succeed in sending us to the galleys or to some worse place? Will it put money in your pockets to collect the welts on our skins? Will you be richer or nobler or more powerful because we are ruined? On the other hand, if you had not interrupted us at such an inopportune moment, to-day, this very day, you would have received your money with interest, which God knows is enough to send you all to hang on the gallows to remain suspended forever, if justice were not in these hands—and these pens. Now do as you see fit; I have told you what you ought to do.

DOCTOR. They will remain suspended until further notice.

CAPTAIN. I would never have believed it possible that their crimes could have been so great.

POLICHINELLE. That Crispin . . . He will be capable of convincing them.

PANTALOON (*to the* INNKEEPER). What do you think of this? Looking at it calmly . . .

INNKEEPER. What do you think?

PANTALOON. You say that your master was to have married the daughter of Signor Polichinelle today? But suppose he refuses to give his consent?

CRISPIN. What good would that do him? His daughter has run away with my master. All the world will soon know it. It is more important to him than it is to anyone else not to have it known that his daughter has thrown herself away upon a rapscallion, a man without character, a fugitive from justice.

PANTALOON. Suppose this should turn out to be true? What do you think?

INNKEEPER. Better not weaken. The rogue breathes deceit. He is a master.

PANTALOON. You are right. No one can tell how far to believe him. Justice! Justice!

CRISPIN. I warn you—you lose everything!

PANTALOON. Wait! . . . just a moment. We will see. A word with you, Signor Polichinelle.

POLICHINELLE. What do you want with me?

PANTALOON. Suppose that we had made a mistake in this complaint. Suppose that Signor Leander should turn out to be, after all, a noble, virtuous gentleman, incapable of the slightest dishonest thought . . .

POLICHINELLE. What is that? Say that again.

PANTALOON. Suppose that your daughter was in love with

him madly, passionately, even to the point where she had run away with him from your house?

POLICHINELLE. My daughter run away from my house with that man? Who says so? Show me the villain! Where is he?

PANTALOON. Don't get excited. It is only in supposition.

POLICHINELLE. Well, sir, I shall not tolerate it even in supposition.

PANTALOON. Try to listen more calmly. Suppose all this

should have happened. Wouldn't the best thing for you to do be to let them marry?

POLICHINELLE. Marry? I would see them dead first. But it is useless to consider it. I see what you want. You are scheming to recoup yourselves at my expense, you are such rogues yourselves. But it shall not be! It shall not be!

PANTALOON. Take care! We had better not talk about rogues while you are present.

INNKEEPER. Hear! Hear!

POLICHINELLE. Rogues, rogues!—conspiring to impoverish me. But it shall not be! It shall not be!

DOCTOR. Have no fear, Signor Polichinelle. Even though they should be dissuaded and abandon their design, do you suppose that this process will amount to nothing? Do you imagine that one line of what is written in it can ever be blotted out, though two and fifty crimes be alleged therein and proved against them, besides as many more which require no proof?

PANTALOON. What do you say now, Crispin?

CRISPIN. That though all those crimes were proved three times and those that require no proof yet three times more than the others, you would still be losing your money and wasting your time, for we cannot pay what we do not have.

DOCTOR. Not at all. That is not good law. For I have to be paid, whatever happens.

CRISPIN. Then the complainants will have to pay you. We shall have more than we can do to pay our offenses with our backs.

DOCTOR. The rights of justice are inviolable, and the first of them is to attach in its interest whatever there is in this house.

PANTALOON. But what good will that do us? How shall we get anything?

INNKEEPER. Of course not! Don't you see?

DOCTOR. Write, write, for if we were to talk forever we should never arrive at a conclusion which would be more satisfactory.

PANTALOON *and* INNKEEPER. No! No! Not a word! Not a word!

CRISPIN. Hear me, first, Signor Doctor! In your ear . . . Suppose you were to be paid at once, on the spot and without the trouble of all this writing, your . . . what is it that you call them?—crumbs of justice?

DOCTOR. Perquisites of the law.

CRISPIN. Have it your own way. What would you say to that?

DOCTOR. Why, in that case . . .

CRISPIN. Listen: my master will be rich today, influential, if Signor Polichinelle consents to his marrying his daughter. Remember that the young lady is the only child of Signor Polichinelle; remember that my master will be master indeed not only of her . . . Remember . . .

DOCTOR. H'm! It certainly does deserve to be remembered.

PANTALOON (to CRISPIN). What does he say?

INNKEEPER. What are you going to do?

DOCTOR. Let me consider. That fellow clearly is not thick-witted. It is easy to see that he is acquainted with legal precedent. For if we remember that the wrong which has been done was purely a pecuniary one, and that every wrong which can be redressed in kind suffers in the reparation the most fitting punishment; if we reflect that in the barbaric and primitive law of vengeance it was written: an eye for an eye and a tooth for a tooth, but not a tooth for an eye nor an eye for a tooth, so in the present instance it might be argued a crown for a crown and money for money. He has not taken your lives. Why not? The fact is evidence that he did not wish you to take his in return. He has not insulted your persons, impugned your honor, your reputations. Why not? Plainly because he was not willing to submit to a like indignity from you. Equity is the supremest justice. *Equitas justiciam magna est.* And from the Pandects to Tribonian, including Emilianus Tribonianus . . .

PANTALOON. Include him. So long as we get our money . . .

INNKEEPER. So long as he pays us . . .

POLICHINELLE. What is this nonsense? How can he pay? What is the use of all this talk?

CRISPIN. A great deal of use. As I was saying, you are all deeply interested in saving my master, in saving both of us, for your own advantage, for the common good of all. You, so as not to lose your money; the Signor Doctor so as not to see all this vast store of doctrine go for nothing, which he is heaping up in these sarcophagi of learning; the Signor Captain because everybody knows that he was the friend of my master, and it would not be creditable to his valor to have it said that he had been the dupe of an adventurer; you, Signor Harlequin, because your poetic dithyrambs would lose all their merit as soon as it became known with what little sense you composed them; you, Signor Polichinelle, my dear old friend, because your daughter is now, in the sight of God and before man, Signor Leander's wife.

POLICHINELLE. You lie! You lie! Impudent rascal! Cutthroat!

CRISPIN. I think then that we had better proceed with the inventory of what there is in the house. Write, write, and let all these gentlemen be our witnesses. We can begin with this apartment.

(*He throws back the tapestry from the door at the rear, and* SILVIA, LEANDER, DOÑA SIRENA, COLUMBINE, *and the* WIFE OF POLICHINELLE *appear, forming a group.*)

PANTALOON *and the* INNKEEPER. Silvia!

CAPTAIN *and* HARLEQUIN. Together! Both of them!

POLICHINELLE. Is it possible? What? Are they all against me? My wife and daughter, too? All, all, for my ruin? Seize that man, these women, this impostor, or I with my own hand . . .

PANTALOON. Signor Polichinelle, are you out of your head?

LEANDER (*advancing toward the proscenium, accompanied by the others*). Your daughter came to my house under the protection of Doña Sirena, believing that I was wounded; and I ran immediately in search of your wife, so that she too might be present with her and protect her. Silvia knows who I am, she knows the whole story of my life of misery and wandering, of cheats and deceptions and lies—how it has been utterly vile; and I am sure that no vestige of our dream of love any longer remains in her heart. Take her away from this place, take her away! That is my only request before I deliver myself up into the hands of justice.

POLICHINELLE. The punishment of my daughter shall be my affair, but as for this villain . . . Seize him, I say!

SILVIA. Father! If you do not save him it will be my death. I love him, I shall love him always; I love him now more than I ever did, because his heart is noble. He has been cruelly unfortunate; and he might have made me his by a lie—but he would not lie.

POLICHINELLE. Silence! Silence, foolish, unhappy girl! This is the result of the bringing up of your mother, of her vanity, her hallucinations, of all your romantic reading, your music to the light of the moon.

WIFE OF POLICHINELLE. Anything would be preferable to having my daughter marry a man like you, to be unhappy afterward all the rest of her life, like her mother. Of what use are my riches to me?

SIRENA. You are right, Signora Polichinelle. Of what use are riches without love?

COLUMBINE. The same use as love without riches.

DOCTOR. Signor Polichinelle, under the circumstances, the only thing for you to do is to let them marry.

PANTALOON. Or there will be a scandal in the city.

INNKEEPER. And everybody will be on his side.

CAPTAIN. And we can never consent to have you use force against your daughter.

DOCTOR. It will have to stand in the process that they were surprised here together.

CRISPIN. And after all, the only trouble with my master was that he had no money; no one could outdo him in nobility of character; your grandchildren will be gentlemen— even if that quality does not extend up to the grandfather.

ALL. Let them marry! Let them marry!

PANTALOON. Or we will all turn upon you.

INNKEEPER. And your history will be brought to light— the secret story of your life . . .

HARLEQUIN. And you will gain nothing by that.

SIRENA. A lady begs it of you on her knees, moved to tears by the spectacle of a love so unusual in these days.

COLUMBINE. Which seems more like love in a story.

ALL. Let them marry! Let them marry!

POLICHINELLE. Yes! let them marry in an evil hour. My daughter shall be cut off without dowry and without inheritance. I will ruin my estate rather than that this reprobate . . .

DOCTOR. You certainly will not do anything of the kind, Signor Polichinelle.

PANTALOON. Who ever heard of such nonsense?

INNKEEPER. I shouldn't think of it for a moment.

HARLEQUIN. What would people say?

CAPTAIN. We could never consent to it.

SILVIA. No, my dear father, I am the one who cannot accept anything. I am the one who must share the poverty of his fate. I love him so.

LEANDER. That is the only condition upon which I can accept your love.

(*All run toward* SILVIA *and* LEANDER.)

DOCTOR. What do you say? Are you crazy?

PANTALOON. Preposterous! Absurd!

INNKEEPER. You are going to accept everything.

HARLEQUIN. You will be happy and you will be rich.

WIFE OF POLICHINELLE. What? My daughter in poverty? Is this wretch the hangman?

SIRENA. Remember that love is a delicate babe and able to endure but few privations.

DOCTOR. It is clearly illegal. Signor Polichinelle, you will sign a munificent donation immediately as befits a person of your dignity and importance, who is a kind and loving father. Write, write, Signor Secretary, for this is something to which nobody will object.

ALL (*except* POLICHINELLE). Write! Write!

DOCTOR. And you, my dear, my innocent young lovers, resign yourselves to riches. You have no right to carry your prejudices to an extreme at which they become offensive to others.

PANTALOON (*to* CRISPIN). Now will you pay us?

CRISPIN. Do you doubt it? But you will have to swear first that Signor Leander never owed you anything. See how he is sacrificing himself upon your account, accepting this money which is repugnant to him.

PANTALOON. We always knew that he was a perfect gentleman.

INNKEEPER. Always.

HARLEQUIN. We all believed it.

CAPTAIN. And we shall continue to maintain our belief.

CRISPIN. Now, Doctor, this process . . . Do you suppose there is waste space enough anywhere in the world for it to be thrown away upon?

DOCTOR. My foresight has provided for everything. All that will be necessary is to change the punctuation. For example, here where it says: "Whereas I depose and declare, not without due sanction of law" . . . take out the comma and it reads: "Whereas I depose and declare not without due sanction of law." And here: "Wherefore he is not without due judgment condemned" . . . put in a comma and it reads: "Wherefore he is not, without due judgment condemned" . . .

CRISPIN. O excellent comma! O wonderful, O marvelous comma! Stupendous Genius and Miracle of Justice! Oracle of the Law! Thou Monster of Jurisprudence!

DOCTOR. Now I can rely upon the generosity of your master.

CRISPIN. You can. Nobody knows better than you do how money will change a man.

SECRETARY. I was the one who put in and took out the commas.

CRISPIN. While you are waiting for something better, pray accept this chain. It is of gold.

SECRETARY. H'm! How many carats fine?

CRISPIN. You ought to know. You understand commas and carats.

POLICHINELLE. I impose only one condition: that this rogue leave your service forever.

CRISPIN. That will not be necessary, Signor Polichinelle. Do you suppose that I am so poor in ambition as my master?

LEANDER. What? You are not going to leave me, Crispin? It will not be without sorrow on my part.

CRISPIN. It will not last long. I can be of no further use to you. With me you will be able to lay aside your lion's skin and your old man's wisdom. What did I tell you, sir? Between them all we were sure to be saved. And believe me now, when you are getting on in the world, the ties of love are as nothing to the bonds of interest.

LEANDER. You are wrong. For without the love of Silvia I should never have been saved.

CRISPIN. And is love a slight interest? I have always given due credit to the ideal and I count upon it always. With this the farce ends.

SILVIA (*to the audience*). You have seen in it how these puppets have been moved by plain and obvious strings, like men and women in the farces of our lives—strings which were their interests, their passions, and all the illusions and petty miseries of their state. Some are pulled by the feet to lives of restless and weary wandering; some by the hands, to toil with pain, to struggle with bitterness, to strike with cunning, to slay with violence and rage. But into the hearts of all there descends sometimes from heaven an invisible thread, as if it were woven out of the sunlight and the moon-beams, the invisible thread of love, which makes these men and women, as it does these puppets which seem like men, almost divine, and brings to our foreheads the smile and splendors of the dawn, lends wings to our drooping spirits, and whispers to us still that this farce is not all a farce, that there is something noble, something divine in our lives which is true and which is true and which is eternal, and which shall not close when the farce of life shall close.

BLOOD WEDDING
(*Bodas de sangre*)

by Federico García Lorca

TRANSLATED BY
James Graham Lujan and Richard L. O'Connell

❧

CHARACTERS

THE MOTHER

THE BRIDE

THE MOTHER-IN-LAW

LEONARDO'S WIFE

THE SERVANT WOMAN

THE NEIGHBOR WOMAN

YOUNG GIRLS

LEONARDO

THE BRIDEGROOM

THE BRIDE'S FATHER

THE MOON

DEATH (*as a Beggar Woman*)

WOODCUTTERS

YOUNG MEN

Federico García Lorca
(1898-1936)

The Spanish theater of the 1930's underwent a neo-romantic revival when a young poet single-handedly brought forth new myths, new techniques, and a new language, evocative, symbolic, highly poetical and often surrealistic. His name, García Lorca, was so well known that many critics included him among Spain's three greatest poets: he had published *Libro de poemas* (1921), *Canciones* (1927), *Romancero gitano* (1928), and *Poemas del canto jondo* (1931). Born in Fuentevaqueros (Granada), he studied the arts and law in Granada and Madrid; but he was more interested in his journeys across Spain studying the folk arts and collecting, by ear, the folk music of the various areas. He was deeply interested in all popular arts and was extremely gifted in music and drawing. He was especially stimulated by an old friend of his family, Manuel de Falla; and his mother, an accomplished pianist, helped him too. The young Lorca, who had begun inventing and producing his own plays at home when he was attending elementary school, was given his finest opportunity when in 1931 the republican government sponsored his traveling company, La Barraca, which went in trucks from town to town presenting classical and modern plays. The great experiment not only canalized all his energies toward the theater but also stimulated his creative genius: *Bodas de sangre* (*Blood Wedding*, 1933), *Yerma* (1934), *La casa de Bernarda Alba* (*ca.* 1934), and a dozen other dynamic plays. But, alas, this greatest promise of the Spanish drama was murdered during the chaos of the Civil War.

Bodas de sangre is Lorca's masterpiece and in it he conjugated the disparate elements of his arts, imparting a strange, cosmic force into his folk-intrigue, all of which will remind the English reader of the plays of W. B. Yeats.

BEST EDITION: *Obras completas*. Buenos Aires, 1942, 8 vols.
ABOUT: A Barea, *Lorca*. New York, 1959. G. Díaz-Plaja, *Federico García Lorca*. Buenos Aires, 1948. El Honig, *Lorca*. New York, 1939.

ACT I

SCENE 1: *A room painted yellow.*

BRIDEGROOM (*entering*). Mother.
MOTHER. What?
BRIDEGROOM. I'm going.
MOTHER. Where?
BRIDEGROOM. To the vineyard. (*He starts to go.*)
MOTHER. Wait.
BRIDEGROOM. You want something?
MOTHER. Your breakfast, son.
BRIDEGROOM. Forget it. I'll eat grapes. Give me the knife.
MOTHER. What for?
BRIDEGROOM (*laughing*). To cut the grapes with.
MOTHER (*muttering as she looks for the knife*). Knives, knives. Cursed be all knives, and the scoundrel who invented them.
BRIDEGROOM. Let's talk about something else.
MOTHER. And guns and pistols and the smallest little knife —and even hoes and pitchforks.
BRIDEGROOM. All right.
MOTHER. Everything that can slice a man's body. A handsome man, full of young life, who goes out to the vineyards or to his own olive groves—his own because he's inherited them . . .
BRIDEGROOM (*lowering his head*). Be quiet.
MOTHER. . . . and then that man doesn't come back. Or if he does come back it's only for someone to cover him over with a palm leaf or a plate of rock salt so he won't bloat. I don't know how you dare carry a knife on your body—or how I let this serpent (*She takes a knife from a kitchen chest.*) stay in the chest.
BRIDEGROOM. Have you had your say?
MOTHER. If I lived to be a hundred I'd talk of nothing else. First your father; to me he smelled like a carnation

and I had him for barely three years. Then your brother. Oh, is it right—how can it be—that a small thing like a knife or a pistol can finish off a man—a bull of a man? No, I'll never be quiet. The months pass and the hopelessness of it stings in my eyes and even to the roots of my hair.

BRIDEGROOM (*forcefully*). Let's quit this talk!

MOTHER. No. No. Let's not quit this talk. Can anyone bring me your father back? Or your brother? Then there's the jail. What do they mean, jail? They eat there, smoke there, play music there! My dead men choking with weeds, silent, turning to dust. Two men like two beautiful flowers. The killers in jail, carefree, looking at the mountains.

BRIDEGROOM. Do you want me to go kill them?

MOTHER. No . . . If I talk about it it's because . . . Oh, how can I help talking about it, seeing you go out that door? It's . . . I don't like you to carry a knife. It's just that . . . that I wish you wouldn't go out to the fields.

BRIDEGROOM (*laughing*). Oh, come now!

MOTHER. I'd like it if you were a woman. Then you wouldn't be going out to the arroyo now and we'd both of us embroider flounces and little woolly dogs.

BRIDEGROOM (*puts his arm around his mother and laughs*). Mother, what if I should take you with me to the vineyards?

MOTHER. What would an old lady do in the vineyards? Were you going to put me down under the young vines?

BRIDEGROOM (*lifting her in his arms*). Old lady, old lady —you little old, little old lady!

MOTHER. Your father, he used to take me. That's the way with men of good stock; good blood. Your grandfather left a son on every corner. That's what I like. Men, men; wheat, wheat.

BRIDEGROOM. And I, Mother?

MOTHER. You, what?

BRIDEGROOM. Do I need to tell you again?

MOTHER (*seriously*). Oh!

BRIDEGROOM. Do you think it's bad?

MOTHER. No.

BRIDEGROOM. Well, then?

MOTHER. I don't really know. Like this, suddenly, it always surprises me. I know the girl is good. Isn't she? Well behaved. Hard working. Kneads her bread, sews her skirts, but even so when I say her name I feel as though someone had hit me on the forehead with a rock.

BRIDEGROOM. Foolishness.

MOTHER. More than foolishness. I'll be left alone. Now only you are left me—I hate to see you go.

BRIDEGROOM. But you'll come with us.

MOTHER. No. I can't leave your father and brother here alone. I have to go to them every morning and if I go away it's possible one of the Felix family, one of the killers, might die—and they'd bury him next to ours. And that'll never happen! Oh, no! That'll never happen! Because I'd dig them out with my nails and, all by myself, crush them against the wall.

BRIDEGROOM (*sternly*). There you go again.

MOTHER. Forgive me. (*pause*) How long have you known her?

BRIDEGROOM. Three years. I've been able to buy the vineyard.

MOTHER. Three years. She used to have another sweetheart, didn't she?

BRIDEGROOM. I don't know. I don't think so. Girls have to look at what they'll marry.

MOTHER. Yes. I looked at nobody. I looked at your father, and when they killed him I looked at the wall in front of me. One woman with one man, and that's all.

BRIDEGROOM. You know my girl's good.

MOTHER. I don't doubt it. All the same, I'm sorry not to have known what her mother was like.

BRIDEGROOM. What difference does it make now?

MOTHER (*looking at him*). Son.

BRIDEGROOM. What is it?

MOTHER. That's true! You're right! When do you want me to ask for her?

BRIDEGROOM (*happily*). Does Sunday seem all right to you?

MOTHER (*seriously*). I'll take her the bronze earrings, they're very old—and you buy her . . .

BRIDEGROOM. You know more about that . . .

MOTHER. . . . you buy her some open-work stockings—and for you, two suits—three! I have no one but you now!

BRIDEGROOM. I'm going. Tomorrow I'll go see her.

MOTHER. Yes, yes—and see if you can make me happy with six grandchildren—or as many as you want, since your father didn't live to give them to me.

BRIDEGROOM. The first-born for you!

MOTHER. Yes, but have some girls. I want to embroider and make lace, and be at peace.

BRIDEGROOM. I'm sure you'll love my wife.

MOTHER. I'll love her. (*She starts to kiss him but changes her mind.*) Go on. You're too big now for kisses. Give them to your wife. (*pause. To herself*) When she is your wife.

BRIDEGROOM. I'm going.

MOTHER. And that land around the little mill—work it over. You've not taken good care of it.

BRIDEGROOM. You're right. I will.

MOTHER. God keep you. (THE SON *goes out.* THE MOTHER *remains seated—her back to the door. A* NEIGHBOR WOMAN *with a kerchief on her head appears in the door.*) Come in.

NEIGHBOR. How are you?

MOTHER. Just as you see me.

NEIGHBOR. I came down to the store and stopped in to see you. We live so far away!

MOTHER. It's twenty years since I've been up to the top of the street.

NEIGHBOR. You're looking well.

MOTHER. You think so?

NEIGHBOR. Things happen. Two days ago they brought in my neighbor's son with both arms sliced off by the machine. (*She sits down.*)

MOTHER. Rafael?

NEIGHBOR. Yes. And there you have him. Many times I've thought your son and mine are better off where they are—sleeping, resting—not running the risk of being left helpless.

MOTHER. Hush. That's all just something thought up—but no consolation.

NEIGHBOR (*sighing*). Ay!

MOTHER (*sighing*). Ay!

(*Pause.*)

NEIGHBOR (*sadly*). Where's your son?

MOTHER. He went out.

NEIGHBOR. He finally bought the vineyard!

MOTHER. He was lucky.

NEIGHBOR. Now he'll get married.

MOTHER (*as though reminded of something, draws her chair near* THE NEIGHBOR). Listen.

NEIGHBOR (*in a confidential manner*). Yes. What is it?

MOTHER. You know my son's sweetheart?

NEIGHBOR. A good girl!

MOTHER. Yes, but . . .

NEIGHBOR. But who knows her really well? There's nobody. She lives out there alone with her father—so far away —fifteen miles from the nearest house. But she's a good girl. Used to being alone.

MOTHER. And her mother?

NEIGHBOR. Her mother I *did* know. Beautiful. Her face glowed like a saint's—but *I* never liked her. She didn't love her husband.

MOTHER (*sternly*). Well, what a lot of things certain people know!

NEIGHBOR. I'm sorry. I didn't mean to offend—but it's true. Now, whether she was decent or not nobody said. That wasn't discussed. She was haughty.

MOTHER. There you go again!

NEIGHBOR. You asked me.

MOTHER. I wish no one knew anything about them—either the live one or the dead one—that they were like two thistles no one even names but cuts off at the right moment.

NEIGHBOR. You're right. Your son is worth a lot.

MOTHER. Yes—a lot. That's why I look after him. They told me the girl had a sweetheart some time ago.

NEIGHBOR. She was about fifteen. He's been married two years now—to a cousin of hers, as a matter of fact. But nobody remembers about their engagement.

MOTHER. How do you remember it?

NEIGHBOR. Oh, what questions you ask!

MOTHER. We like to know all about the things that hurt us. Who was the boy?

NEIGHBOR. Leonardo.

MOTHER. What Leonardo?

NEIGHBOR. Leonardo Felix.

MOTHER. Felix!

NEIGHBOR. Yes, but—how is Leonardo to blame for anything? He was eight years old when those things happened.

MOTHER. That's true. But I hear that name—Felix—and it's all the same. (*muttering*) Felix, a slimy mouthful. (*She spits.*) It makes me spit—spit so I won't kill!

NEIGHBOR. Control yourself. What good will it do?

MOTHER. No good. But you see how it is.

NEIGHBOR. Don't get in the way of your son's happiness. Don't say anything to him. You're old. So am I. It's time for you and me to keep quiet.

MOTHER. I'll say nothing to him.

NEIGHBOR (*kissing her*). Nothing.

MOTHER (*calmly*). Such things . . . !

NEIGHBOR. I'm going. My men will soon be coming in from the fields.

MOTHER. Have you ever known such a hot sun?

NEIGHBOR. The children carrying water out to the reapers are black with it. Goodbye, woman.

MOTHER. Goodbye.

(THE MOTHER *starts toward the door at the left. Halfway there she stops and slowly crosses herself.*)

(*Curtain.*)

SCENE 2: *A room painted rose with copperware and wreaths of common flowers. In the center of the room is a table with a tablecloth. It is morning.*

(LEONARDO'S MOTHER-IN-LAW *sits in one corner holding a child in her arms and rocking it. His* WIFE *is in the other corner mending stockings.*)

MOTHER-IN-LAW.
Lullaby, my baby
once there was a big horse
who didn't like water.
The water was black there
under the branches.
When it reached the bridge
it stopped and it sang.
Who can say, my baby,
what the stream holds
with its long tail
in its green parlor?

WIFE (*softly*).
Carnation, sleep and dream,
the horse won't drink from the stream.

MOTHER-IN-LAW.
My rose, asleep now lie,
the horse is starting to cry.
His poor hooves were bleeding,
his long mane was frozen,
and deep in his eyes

stuck a silvery dagger.
Down he went to the river,
Oh, down he went down!
And his blood was running,
Oh, more than the water.

WIFE.

Carnation, sleep and dream,
the horse won't drink from the stream.

MOTHER-IN-LAW.

My rose, asleep now lie,
the horse is starting to cry.

WIFE.

He never did touch
the dank river shore
though his muzzle was warm
and with silvery flies.
So, to the hard mountains
he could only whinny
just when the dead stream
covered his throat.
Ay-y-y, for the big horse
who didn't like water!
Ay-y-y, for the snow-wound
big horse of the dawn!

MOTHER-IN-LAW.

Don't come in! Stop him
and close up the window
with branches of dreams
and a dream of branches.

WIFE.

My baby is sleeping.

MOTHER-IN-LAW.

My baby is quiet.

WIFE.

Look, horse, my baby
has him a pillow.

MOTHER-IN-LAW.

His cradle is metal.

WIFE.

His quilt a fine fabric.

MOTHER-IN-LAW.

Lullaby, my baby.

WIFE.

Ay-y-y, for the big horse

who didn't like water!

MOTHER-IN-LAW.

> Don't come near, don't come in!
> Go away to the mountains
> and through the grey valleys,
> that's where your mare is.

WIFE (*looking at the baby*).

> My baby is sleeping.

MOTHER-IN-LAW.

> My baby is resting.

WIFE (*softly*).

> Carnation, sleep and dream,
> the horse won't drink from the stream.

MOTHER-IN-LAW (*getting up, very softly*).

> My rose, asleep now lie
> for the horse is starting to cry.

(*She carries the child out.* LEONARDO *enters.*)

LEONARDO. Where's the baby?

WIFE. He's sleeping.

LEONARDO. Yesterday he wasn't well. He cried during the night.

WIFE. Today he's like a dahlia. And you? Were you at the blacksmith's?

LEONARDO. I've just come from there. Would you believe it? For more than two months he's been putting new shoes on the horse and they're always coming off. As far as I can see he pulls them off on the stones.

WIFE. Couldn't it just be that you use him so much?

LEONARDO. No. I almost never use him.

WIFE. Yesterday the neighbors told me they'd seen you on the far side of the plains.

LEONARDO. Who said that?

WIFE. The women who gather capers. It certainly surprised me. Was it you?

LEONARDO. No. What would I be doing there, in that wasteland?

WIFE. That's what I said. But the horse was streaming sweat.

LEONARDO. Did you see him?

WIFE. No. Mother did.

LEONARDO. Is she with the baby?

WIFE. Yes. Do you want some lemonade?

LEONARDO. With good cold water.

WIFE. And then you didn't come to eat!

LEONARDO. I was with the wheat weighers. They always hold me up.

WIFE (*very tenderly, while she makes the lemonade*). Did they pay you a good price?

LEONARDO. Fair.

WIFE. I need a new dress and the baby a bonnet with ribbons.

LEONARDO (*getting up*). I'm going to take a look at him.

WIFE. Be careful. He's asleep.

MOTHER-IN-LAW (*coming in*). Well! Who's been racing the horse that way? He's down there, worn out, his eyes popping from their sockets as though he'd come from the ends of the earth.

LEONARDO (*acidly*). I have.

MOTHER-IN-LAW. Oh, excuse me! He's your horse.

WIFE (*timidly*). He was at the wheat buyers.

MOTHER-IN-LAW. He can burst for all of me! (*She sits down. Pause.*)

WIFE. Your drink. It is cold?

LEONARDO. Yes.

WIFE. Did you hear they're going to ask for my cousin?

LEONARDO. When?

WIFE. Tomorrow. The wedding will be within a month. I hope they're going to invite us.

LEONARDO (*gravely*). I don't know.

MOTHER-IN-LAW. His mother, I think, wasn't very happy about the match.

LEONARDO. Well, she may be right. She's a girl to be careful with.

WIFE. I don't like to have you thinking bad things about a good girl.

MOTHER-IN-LAW (*meaningfully*). If he does, it's because he knows her. Didn't you know he courted her for three years?

LEONARDO. But I left her. (*to his* WIFE) Are you going to cry now? Quit that! (*He brusquely pulls her hands away from her face.*) Let's go see the baby.

(*They go in with their arms around each other. A* GIRL *appears. She is happy. She enters running.*)

GIRL. Señora.

MOTHER-IN-LAW. What is it?

GIRL. The groom came to the store and he's bought the best of everything they had.

MOTHER-IN-LAW. Was he alone?

GIRL. No. With his mother. Stern, tall. (*She imitates her.*) And such extravagance!

MOTHER-IN-LAW. They have money.

GIRL. And they bought some open-work stockings! Oh, such stockings! A woman's dream of stockings! Look: a swallow here (*points to her ankle*), a ship here (*points to her calf*), and here (*points to her thigh*) a rose!

MOTHER-IN-LAW. Child!

GIRL. A rose with the seeds and the stem! Oh! All in silk.

MOTHER-IN-LAW. Two rich families are being brought together.

(LEONARDO *and his* WIFE *appear.*)

GIRL. I came to tell you what they're buying.

LEONARDO (*loudly*). We don't care.

WIFE. Leave her alone.

MOTHER-IN-LAW. Leonardo, it's not that important.

GIRL. Please excuse me.   (*She leaves, weeping.*)

MOTHER-IN-LAW. Why do you always have to make trouble with people?

LEONARDO. I didn't ask for your opinion. (*He sits down.*)

MOTHER-IN-LAW. Very well.

(*Pause.*)

WIFE (*to* LEONARDO). What's the matter with you? What idea've you got boiling there inside your head? Don't leave me like this, not knowing anything.

LEONARDO. Stop that.

WIFE. No. I want you to look at me and tell me.

LEONARDO. Let me alone. (*He rises.*)

WIFE. Where are you going, love?

LEONARDO (*sharply*). Can't you shut up?

MOTHER-IN-LAW (*energetically to her daughter*). Be quiet! (LEONARDO *goes out*) The baby!

(*She goes into the bedroom and comes out again with the baby in her arms. THE WIFE has remained standing, unmoving.*)

MOTHER-IN-LAW.

> His poor hooves were bleeding,
> his long mane was frozen,
> and deep in his eyes
> stuck a silvery dagger.
> Down he went to the river,
> Oh, down he went down!
> And his blood was running,
> Oh, more than the water.

WIFE (*turning slowly, as though dreaming*).
>Carnation, sleep and dream,
>the horse is drinking from the stream.

MOTHER-IN-LAW.
>My rose, asleep now lie
>the horse is starting to cry.

WIFE.
>Lullaby, my baby.

MOTHER-IN-LAW.
>Ay-y-y, for the big horse
>who didn't like water!

WIFE (*dramatically*).
>Don't come near, don't come in!
>Go away to the mountains!
>Ay-y-y, for the snow-wound,
>big horse of the dawn!

MOTHER-IN-LAW (*weeping*).
>My baby is sleeping . . .

WIFE (*weeping, as she slowly moves closer*).
>My baby is resting . . .

MOTHER-IN-LAW.
>Carnation, sleep and dream,
>the horse won't drink from the stream.

WIFE (*weeping, and leaning on the table*).
>My rose, asleep now lie,
>the horse is starting to cry.

(*Curtain.*)

SCENE 3: *Interior of the cave where* THE BRIDE *lives. At the back is a cross of large rose-colored flowers. The round doors have lace curtains with rose-colored ties. Around the walls, which are of a white and hard material, are round fans, blue jars, and little mirrors.*

SERVANT. Come right in . . . (*She is very affable, full of humble hypocrisy.* THE BRIDEGROOM *and* HIS MOTHER *enter.* THE MOTHER *is dressed in black satin and wears a lace mantilla;* THE BRIDEGROOM *in black corduroy with a great golden chain.*) Won't you sit down? They'll be right here. (*She leaves.* THE MOTHER *and* SON *are left sitting motionless as statues. Long pause.*)

MOTHER. Did you wear the watch?

BRIDEGROOM. Yes. (*He takes it out and looks at it.*)

MOTHER. We have to be back on time. How far away these people live!

BRIDEGROOM. But this is good land.

MOTHER. Good; but much too lonesome. A four-hour trip and not one house, not one tree.

BRIDEGROOM. This is the wasteland.

MOTHER. Your father would have covered it with trees.

BRIDEGROOM. Without water?

MOTHER. He would have found some. In the three years we were married he planted ten cherry trees (*remembering*), those three walnut trees by the mill, a whole vineyard and a plant called Jupiter which had scarlet flowers—but it dried up.

(*Pause.*)

BRIDEGROOM (*referring to* THE BRIDE). She must be dressing.

(THE BRIDE'S FATHER *enters. He is very old, with shining white hair. His head is bowed.* THE MOTHER *and* THE BRIDEGROOM *rise. They shake hands in silence.*)

FATHER. Was it a long trip?

MOTHER. Four hours.

(*They sit down.*)

FATHER. You must have come the longest way.

MOTHER. I'm too old to come along the cliffs by the river.

BRIDEGROOM. She gets dizzy.

(*Pause.*)

FATHER. A good hemp harvest.

BRIDEGROOM. A really good one.

FATHER. When I was young this land didn't even grow hemp. We've had to punish it, even weep over it, to make it give us anything useful.

MOTHER. But now it does. Don't complain. I'm not here to ask you for anything.

FATHER (*smiling*). You're richer than I. Your vineyards are worth a fortune. Each young vine a silver coin. But—do you know?—what bothers me is that our lands are separated. I like to have everything together. One thorn I have in my heart, and that's the little orchard there, stuck in between my fields—and they won't sell it to me for all the gold in the world.

BRIDEGROOM. That's the way it always is.

FATHER. If we could just take twenty teams of oxen and move your vineyards over here, and put them down on that hillside, how happy I'd be!

MOTHER. But why?

FATHER. What's mine is hers and what's yours is his. That's why. Just to see it all together. How beautiful it is to bring things together!

BRIDEGROOM. And it would be less work.

MOTHER. When I die, you could sell ours and buy here, right alongside.

FATHER. Sell, sell? Bah! Buy, my friend, buy everything. If I had had sons I would have bought all this mountainside right up to the part with the stream. It's not good land, but strong arms can make it good, and since no people pass by, they don't steal your fruit and you can sleep in peace.

(*Pause.*)

MOTHER. You know what I'm here for.

FATHER. Yes.

MOTHER. And?

FATHER. It seems all right to me. They have talked it over.

MOTHER. My son has money and knows how to manage it.

FATHER. My daughter too.

MOTHER. My son is handsome. He's never known a woman. His good name cleaner than a sheet spread out in the sun.

FATHER. No need to tell you about my daughter. At three, when the morning star shines, she prepares the bread. She never talks: soft as wool, she embroiders all kinds of fancy work and she can cut a strong cord with her teeth.

MOTHER. God bless her house.

FATHER. May God bless it.

(THE SERVANT *appears with two trays. One with drinks and the other with sweets.*)

MOTHER (*to* THE SON). When would you like the wedding?

BRIDEGROOM. Next Thursday.

FATHER. The day on which she'll be exactly twenty-two years old.

MOTHER. Twenty-two! My oldest son would be that age if he were alive. Warm and manly as he was, he'd be living now if men hadn't invented knives.

FATHER. One mustn't think about that.

MOTHER. Every minute. Always a hand on your breast.

FATHER. Thursday, then? Is that right?

BRIDEGROOM. That's right.

FATHER. You and I and the bridal couple will go in a carriage to the church which is very far from here; the wedding party on the carts and horses they'll bring with them.

MOTHER. Agreed.

(THE SERVANT *passes through.*)

FATHER. Tell her she may come in now. (*to* THE MOTHER) I shall be much pleased if you like her.

(THE BRIDE *appears. Her hands fall in a modest pose and her head is bowed.*)

MOTHER. Come here. Are you happy?

BRIDE. Yes, señora.

FATHER. You shouldn't be so solemn. After all, she's going to be your mother.

BRIDE. I'm happy. I've said "yes" because I wanted to.

MOTHER. Naturally. (*She takes her by the chin.*) Look at me.

FATHER. She resembles my wife in every way.

MOTHER. Yes? What a beautiful glance! Do you know what it is to be married, child?

BRIDE (*seriously*). I do.

MOTHER. A man, some children, and a wall two yards thick for everything else.

BRIDEGROOM. Is anything else needed?

MOTHER. No. Just that you all live—that's it! Live long!

BRIDE. I'll know how to keep my word.

MOTHER. Here are some gifts for you.

BRIDE. Thank you.

FATHER. Shall we have something?

MOTHER. Nothing for me. (*to* THE SON) But you?

BRIDEGROOM. Yes, thank you. (*He takes one sweet,* THE BRIDE *another.*)

FATHER (*to* THE BRIDEGROOM). Wine?

MOTHER. He doesn't touch it.

FATHER. All the better.

(*Pause. All are standing.*)

BRIDEGROOM (*to* THE BRIDE). I'll come tomorrow.

BRIDE. What time?

BRIDEGROOM. Five.

BRIDE. I'll be waiting for you.

BRIDEGROOM. When I leave your side I feel a great emptiness, and something like a knot in my throat.

BRIDE. When you are my husband you won't have it any more.

BRIDEGROOM. That's what I tell myself.

MOTHER. Come. The sun doesn't wait. (*to* THE FATHER) Are we agreed on everything?

FATHER. Agreed.

MOTHER (*to* THE SERVANT). Goodbye, woman.

SERVANT. God go with you!

(THE MOTHER *kisses* THE BRIDE *and they begin to leave in silence.*)

MOTHER (*at the door*). Goodbye, daughter.

(THE BRIDE *answers with her hand.*)

FATHER. I'll go with you.

(*They leave.*)

SERVANT. I'm bursting to see the presents.

BRIDE (*sharply*). Stop that!

SERVANT. Oh, child, show them to me.

BRIDE. I don't want to.

SERVANT. At least the stockings. They say they're all open work. Please!

BRIDE. I said no.

SERVANT. Well, my Lord. All right then. It looks as if you didn't want to get married.

BRIDE (*biting her hand in anger*). Ay-y-y!

SERVANT. Child, child! What's the matter with you? Are you sorry to give up your queen's life? Don't think of bitter things. Have you any reason to? None. Let's look at the presents. (*She takes the box.*)

BRIDE (*holding her by the wrists*). Let go.

SERVANT. Ay-y-y, girl!

BRIDE. Let go, I said.

SERVANT. You're stronger than a man.

BRIDE. Haven't I done a man's work? I wish I were.

SERVANT. Don't talk like that.

BRIDE. Quiet, I said. Let's talk about something else.

(*The light is fading from the stage. Long pause.*)

SERVANT. Did you hear a horse last night?

BRIDE. What time?

SERVANT. Three.

BRIDE. It might have been a stray horse—from the herd.

SERVANT. No. It carried a rider.

BRIDE. How do you know?

SERVANT. Because I saw him. He was standing by your window. It shocked me greatly.

BRIDE. Maybe it was my fiancé. Sometimes he comes by at that time.

SERVANT. No.

BRIDE. You saw him?

SERVANT. Yes.

BRIDE. Who was it?

SERVANT. It was Leonardo.

BRIDE (*strongly*). Liar! You liar! Why should he come here?

SERVANT. He came.

BRIDE. Shut up! Shut your cursed mouth.

(*The sound of a horse is heard.*)

SERVANT (*at the window*). Look. Lean out. Was it Leonardo?

BRIDE. It was!

(*Quick Curtain.*)

ACT II

SCENE 1: *The entrance hall of* The Bride's *house. A large door in the back. It is night.* The Bride *enters wearing ruffled white petticoats full of laces and embroidered bands, and a sleeveless white bodice.* The Servant *is dressed the same way.*

Servant. I'll finish combing your hair out here.

Bride. It's too warm to stay in there.

Servant. In this country it doesn't even cool off at dawn. (The Bride *sits on a low chair and looks into a little hand mirror.* The Servant *combs her hair.*)

Bride. My mother came from a place with lots of trees— from a fertile country.

Servant. And she was so happy!

Bride. But she wasted away here.

Servant. Fate.

Bride. As we're all wasting away here. The very walls give off heat. Ay-y-y! Don't pull so hard.

Servant. I'm only trying to fix this wave better. I want it to fall over your forehead. (The Bride *looks at herself in the mirror.*) How beautiful you are! Ay-y-y! (*She kisses her passionately.*)

Bride (*seriously*). Keep right on combing.

Servant (*combing*). Oh, lucky you—going to put your arms around a man; and kiss him; and feel his weight.

Bride. Hush.

Servant. And the best part will be when you'll wake up and you'll feel him at your side and when he caresses your shoulders with his breath, like a little nightingale's feather.

Bride (*sternly*). Will you be quiet.

Servant. But, child! What *is* a wedding? A wedding is just that and nothing more. Is it the sweets—or the bouquets of

437

flowers? No. It's a shining bed and a man and a woman.

BRIDE. But you shouldn't talk about it.

SERVANT. Oh, *that's* something else again. But fun enough too.

BRIDE. Or bitter enough.

SERVANT. I'm going to put the orange blossoms on from here to here, so the wreath will shine out on top of your hair.

(*She tries on the sprigs of orange blossom.*)

BRIDE (*looking at herself in the mirror*). Give it to me. (*She takes the wreath, looks at it and lets her head fall in discouragement.*)

SERVANT. Now what's the matter?

BRIDE. Leave me alone.

SERVANT. This is no time for you to start feeling sad. (*encouragingly*) Give me the wreath. (THE BRIDE *takes the wreath and hurls it away.*) Child! You're just asking God to punish you, throwing the wreath on the floor like that. Raise your head! Don't you want to get married? Say it. You can still withdraw. (THE BRIDE *rises.*)

BRIDE. Storm clouds. A chill wind that cuts through my heart. Who hasn't felt it?

SERVANT. You love your sweetheart, don't you?

BRIDE. I love him.

SERVANT. Yes, yes. I'm sure you do.

BRIDE. But this is a very serious step.

SERVANT. You've got to take it.

BRIDE. I've already given my word.

SERVANT. I'll put on the wreath.

BRIDE (*sits down*). Hurry. They should be arriving by now.

SERVANT. They've already been at least two hours on the way.

BRIDE. How far is it from here to the church?

SERVANT. Five leagues by the stream, but twice that by the road.

(THE BRIDE *rises and* THE SERVANT *grows excited as she looks at her.*)

SERVANT.

> Awake, O Bride, awaken,
> On your wedding morning waken!
> The world's rivers may all
> Bear along your bridal Crown!

BRIDE (*smiling*). Come now.

SERVANT (*enthusiastically kissing her and dancing around her*).

> Awake,
> with the fresh bouquet
> of flowering laurel.
> Awake,
> by the trunk and branch
> of the laurels!

(*The banging of the front-door latch is heard.*)

BRIDE. Open the door! That must be the first guests. (*She leaves. THE SERVANT opens the door.*)

SERVANT (*in astonishment*). You!

LEONARDO. Yes, me. Good morning.

SERVANT. The first one!

LEONARDO. Wasn't I invited?

SERVANT. Yes.

LEONARDO. That's why I'm here.

SERVANT. Where's your wife?

LEONARDO. I came on my horse. She's coming by the road.

SERVANT. Didn't you meet anyone?

LEONARDO. I *passed* them on my horse.

SERVANT. You're going to kill that horse with so much racing.

LEONARDO. When he dies, he's dead!

(*Pause.*)

SERVANT. Sit down. Nobody's up yet.

LEONARDO. Where's the bride?

SERVANT. I'm just on my way to dress her.

LEONARDO. The bride! She ought to be happy!

SERVANT (*changing the subject*). How's the baby?

LEONARDO. What baby?

SERVANT. Your son.

LEONARDO (*remembering, as though in a dream*). Ah!

SERVANT. Are they bringing him?

LEONARDO. No.

(*Pause. Voices sing distantly.*)

VOICES.

> Awake, O Bride, awaken,
> On your wedding morning waken!

LEONARDO.

> Awake, O Bride, awaken,
> On your wedding morning waken!

SERVANT. It's the guests. They're still quite a way off.

LEONARDO. The bride's going to wear a big wreath, isn't she? But it ought not to be so large. One a little smaller would look better on her. Has the groom already brought her the orange blossom that must be worn on the breast?

BRIDE (*appearing, still in petticoats and wearing the wreath*). He brought it.

SERVANT (*sternly*). Don't come out like that.

BRIDE. What does it matter? (*seriously*) Why do you ask if they brought the orange blossom? Do you have something in mind?

LEONARDO. Nothing. What would I have in mind? (*drawing near her*) You, you know me; you know I don't. Tell me so. What have I ever meant to you? Open your memory, refresh it. But two oxen and an ugly little hut are almost nothing. That's the thorn.

BRIDE. What have you come here to do?

LEONARDO. To see your wedding.

BRIDE. Just as I saw yours!

LEONARDO. Tied up by you, done with your two hands. Oh, they can kill me but they can't spit on me. But even money, which shines so much, spits sometimes.

BRIDE. Liar!

LEONARDO. I don't want to talk. I'm hot-blooded and I don't want to shout so all these hills will hear me.

BRIDE. My shouts would be louder.

SERVANT. You'll have to stop talking like this. (*to* THE BRIDE) You don't have to talk about what's past. (*Looks around uneasily at the doors.*)

BRIDE. She's right. I shouldn't even talk to you. But it offends me to the soul that you come here to watch me, and spy on my wedding, and ask about the orange blossom with something on your mind. Go and wait for your wife at the door.

LEONARDO. But, can't you and I even talk?

SERVANT (*with rage*). No! No, you can't talk.

LEONARDO. Ever since I got married I've been thinking night and day about whose fault it was, and every time I think about it, out comes a new fault to eat up the old one; but always there's a fault left!

BRIDE. A man with a horse knows a lot of things and can do a lot to ride roughshod over a girl stuck out in the desert. But I have my pride. And that's why I'm getting married. I'll lock myself in with my husband and then I'll have to love him above everyone else.

LEONARDO. Pride won't help you a bit. (*He draws near to her.*)

BRIDE. Don't come near me!

LEONARDO. To burn with desire and keep quiet about it is the greatest punishment we can bring on ourselves. What good was pride to me—and not seeing you, and letting you lie awake night after night? No good! It only served to bring the fire down on me! You think that time heals and walls hide things, but it isn't true, it isn't true! When things get that deep inside you there isn't anybody can change them.

BRIDE (*trembling*). I can't listen to you. I can't listen to your voice. It's as though I'd drunk a bottle of anise and fallen asleep wrapped in a quilt of roses. It pulls me along, and I know I'm drowning—but I go on down.

SERVANT (*seizing* LEONARDO *by the lapels.*) You've got to go right now!

LEONARDO. This is the last time I'll ever talk to her. Don't you be afraid of anything.

BRIDE. And I know I'm crazy and I know my breast rots with longing; but here I am—calmed by hearing him, by just seeing him move his arms.

LEONARDO. I'd never be at peace if I didn't tell you these things. I got married. Now you get married.

SERVANT. But she *is* getting married!

(*Voices are heard singing, nearer.*)

VOICES.

> Awake, O Bride, awaken,
> On your wedding morning waken!

BRIDE.

> Awake, O Bride, awaken,

(*She goes out, running toward her room.*)

SERVANT. The people are here now. (*to* LEONARDO) Don't you come near her again.

LEONARDO. Don't worry. (*He goes out to the left. Day begins to break.*)

FIRST GIRL (*entering*).

> Awake, O Bride, awaken,
> the morning you're to marry;
> sing round and dance round;
> balconies a wreath must carry.

VOICES.

> Bride, awaken!

SERVANT (*creating enthusiasm*).

> Awake,
> with the green bouquet
> of love in flower.
> Awake,
> by the trunk and the branch
> of the laurels!

SECOND GIRL (*entering*).

> Awake,
> with her long hair,
> snowy sleeping gown,
> patent leather boots with silver—
> her forehead jasmines crown.

SERVANT.

> Oh, shepherdess,
> the moon begins to shine!

FIRST GIRL.

> Oh, gallant,
> leave your hat beneath the vine!

FIRST YOUNG MAN (*entering, holding his hat on high*).

> Bride, awaken,
> for over the fields
> the wedding draws nigh
> with trays heaped with dahlias
> and cakes piled high.

VOICES.

> Bride, awaken!

SECOND GIRL.

> The bride
> has set her white wreath in place
> and the groom
> ties it on with a golden lace.

SERVANT.

> By the orange tree,
> sleepless the bride will be.

THIRD GIRL (*entering*).

> By the citron vine,
> gifts from the groom will shine.

(*Three* GUESTS *come in.*)

FIRST YOUTH.

> Dove, awaken!
> in the dawn
> shadowy bells are shaken.

GUEST.

> The bride, the white bride
> today a maiden,
> tomorrow a wife.

FIRST GIRL.

> Dark one, come down
> trailing the train of your silken gown.

GUEST.

> Little dark one, come down,
> cold morning wears a dewy crown.

FIRST GUEST.

> Awaken, wife, awake,
> orange blossoms the breezes shake.

SERVANT.

> A tree I would embroider her
> with garnet sashes wound,
> And on each sash a cupid,
> with "Long Live" all around.

VOICES.

> Bride, awaken.

FIRST YOUTH.

> The morning you're to marry!

GUEST.

> The morning you're to marry
> how elegant you'll seem;
> worthy, mountain flower,
> of a captain's dream.

FATHER (*entering*).

> A captain's wife
> the groom will marry.
> He comes with his oxen the treasure to carry!

THIRD GIRL.

> The groom
> is like a flower of gold.
> When he walks,
> blossoms at his feet unfold.

SERVANT.

> Oh, my lucky girl!

SECOND YOUTH.

> Bride, awaken.

SERVANT.

> Oh, my elegant girl!

FIRST GIRL.

> Through the windows

hear the wedding shout.

SECOND GIRL.

Let the bride come out.

FIRST GIRL.

Come out, come out!

SERVANT.

Let the bells
ring and ring out clear!

FIRST YOUTH.

For here she comes!
For now she's near!

SERVANT.

Like a bull, the wedding
is arising here!

(THE BRIDE *appears. She wears a black dress in the style of 1900, with a bustle and large train covered with pleated gauzes and heavy laces. Upon her hair, brushed in a wave over her forehead, she wears an orange blossom wreath. Guitars sound.* THE GIRLS *kiss* THE BRIDE.)

THIRD GIRL. What scent did you put on your hair?

BRIDE (*laughing*). None at all.

SECOND GIRL (*looking at her dress*). This cloth is what you can't get.

FIRST YOUTH. Here's the groom!

BRIDEGROOM. *Salud!*

FIRST GIRL (*putting a flower behind his ear*).

The groom
is like a flower of gold.

SECOND GIRL.

Quiet breezes
from his eyes unfold.

(THE GROOM *goes to* THE BRIDE.)

BRIDE. Why did you put on those shoes?

BRIDEGROOM. They're gayer than the black ones.

LEONARDO'S WIFE (*entering and kissing* THE BRIDE). *Salud!* (*They all speak excitedly.*)

LEONARDO (*entering as one who performs a duty*).

The morning you're to marry
We give you a wreath to wear.

LEONARDO'S WIFE.

So the fields may be made happy
with the dew dropped from your hair!

MOTHER (*to* THE FATHER). Are those people here, too?

FATHER. They're part of the family. Today is a day of forgiveness!

MOTHER. I'll put up with it, but I don't forgive.

BRIDEGROOM. With your wreath, it's a joy to look at you!

BRIDE. Let's go to the church quickly.

BRIDEGROOM. Are you in a hurry?

BRIDE. Yes. I want to be your wife right now so that I can be with you alone, not hearing any voice but yours.

BRIDEGROOM. That's what I want!

BRIDE. And not seeing any eyes but yours. And for you to hug me so hard, that even though my dead mother should call me, I wouldn't be able to draw away from you.

BRIDEGROOM. My arms are strong. I'll hug you for forty years without stopping.

BRIDE (*taking his arm, dramatically*). Forever!

FATHER. Quick now! Round up the teams and carts! The sun's already out.

MOTHER. And go along carefully! Let's hope nothing goes wrong.

(*The great door in the background opens.*)

SERVANT (*weeping*).

> As you set out from your house,
> oh, maiden white,
> remember you leave shining
> with a star's light.

FIRST GIRL.

> Clean of body, clean of clothes
> from her home to church she goes.

(*They start leaving.*)

SECOND GIRL.

> Now you leave your home
> for the church!

SERVANT.

> The wind sets flowers
> on the sands.

THIRD GIRL.

> Ah, the white maid!

SERVANT.

> Dark winds are the lace
> of her mantilla.

(*They leave. Guitars, castanets, and tambourines
are heard.* LEONARDO *and his* WIFE *are left alone.*)

WIFE. Let's go.

LEONARDO. Where?

WIFE. To the church. But not on your horse. You're
coming with me.

LEONARDO. In the cart?

WIFE. Is there anything else?

LEONARDO. I'm not the kind of man to ride in a cart.

WIFE. Nor I the wife to go to a wedding without her
husband. I can't stand any more of this!

LEONARDO. Neither can I!

WIFE. And why do you look at me that way? With a thorn
in each eye.

LEONARDO. Let's go!

WIFE. I don't know what's happening. But I think,
and I don't want to think. One thing I do know. I'm already cast off by you. But I have a son. And another
coming. And so it goes. My mother's fate was the same.
Well, I'm not moving from here.

(*Voices outside.*)

VOICES.

> As you set out from your home
> and to the church go
> remember you leave shining
> with a star's glow.

WIFE (*weeping*).

> Remember you leave shining
> with a star's glow!

I left my house like that too. They could have stuffed the
whole countryside in my mouth. I was that trusting.

LEONARDO (*rising*). Let's go!

WIFE. But you with me!

LEONARDO. Yes. (*pause*) Start moving! (*They leave.*)

VOICES.

> As you set out from your home
> and to the church go,
> remember you leave shining
> with a star's glow.

(*Slow Curtain*)

SCENE 2: *The exterior of* THE BRIDE's *Cave Home, in white gray and cold blue tones. Large cactus trees. Shadowy and silver tones. Panoramas of light tan tablelands, everything hard like a landscape in popular ceramics.*

SERVANT (*arranging glasses and trays on a table*).
      A-turning,
      the wheel was a-turning
      and the water was flowing,
      for the wedding night comes.
      May the branches part
      and the moon be arrayed
      at her white balcony rail.
(*in a loud voice*) Set out the tablecloths! (*in a pathetic voice*)
      A-singing,
      bride and groom were singing
      and the water was flowing
      for their wedding night comes.
      Oh, rime-frost, flash!—
      and almonds bitter
      fill with honey!
(*in a loud voice*) Get the wine ready! (*in a poetic tone*)
      Elegant girl,
      most elegant in the world,
      see the way the water is flowing,
      for your wedding night comes.
      Hold your skirts close in
      under the bridegroom's wing
      and never leave your house,
      for the Bridgeroom is a dove
      with his breast a firebrand
      and the fields wait for the whisper
      of spurting blood.
      A-turning
      the wheel was a-turning
      and the water was flowing
      and your wedding night comes.
      Oh, water, sparkle!
MOTHER (*entering*). At last!

FATHER. Are we the first ones?

SERVANT. No. Leonardo and his wife arrived a while ago. They drove like demons. His wife got here dead with fright. They made the trip as though they'd come on horseback.

FATHER. That one's looking for trouble. He's not of good blood.

MOTHER. What blood would you expect him to have? His whole family's blood. It comes down from his great-grandfather, who started in killing, and it goes on down through the whole evil breed of knife-wielding and false-smiling men.

FATHER. Let's leave it at that!

SERVANT. But how can she leave it at that?

MOTHER. It hurts me to the tips of my veins. On the forehead of all of them I see only the hand with which they killed what was mine. Can you really see me? Don't I seem mad to you? Well, it's the madness of not having shrieked out all my breast needs to. Always in my breast there's a shriek standing tiptoe that I have to beat down and hold in under my shawls. But the dead are carried off and one has to keep still. And then, people find fault. (*She removes her shawl.*)

FATHER. Today's not the day for you to be remembering these things.

MOTHER. When the talk turns on it, I have to speak. And more so today. Because today I'm left alone in my house.

FATHER. But with the expectation of having some-one with you.

MOTHER. That's my hope: grandchildren.

(*They sit down.*)

FATHER. I want them to have a lot of them. This land needs hands that aren't hired. There's a battle to be waged against weeds, the thistles, the big rocks that come from one doesn't know where. And those hands have to be the owner's, who chastises and dominates, who makes the seeds grow. Lots of sons are needed.

MOTHER. And some daughters! Men are like the wind! They're forced to handle weapons. Girls never go out into the street.

FATHER (*happily*). I think they'll have both.

MOTHER. My son will cover her well. He's of good seed. His father could have had many sons with me.

FATHER. What I'd like is to have all this happen in a day. So that right away they'd have two or three boys.

MOTHER. But it's not like that. It takes a long time. That's why it's so terrible to see one's own blood spilled out on the ground. A fountain that spurts for a minute, but costs us years. When I got to my son, he lay fallen in the middle of the street. I wet my hands with his blood and licked them with my tongue—because it was my blood. You don't know what that's like. In a glass and topaz shrine I'd put the earth moistened by his blood.

FATHER. Now you must hope. My daughter is wide-hipped and your son is strong.

MOTHER. That's why I'm hoping.

(*They rise.*)

FATHER. Get the wheat trays ready!

SERVANT. They're all ready.

LEONARDO'S WIFE (*entering*). May it be for the best!

MOTHER. Thank you.

LEONARDO. Is there going to be a celebration?

FATHER. A small one. People can't stay long.

SERVANT. Here they are!

(*Guests begin entering in gay groups.* THE BRIDE *and* GROOM *come in arm-in-arm.* LEONARDO *leaves.*)

BRIDEGROOM. There's never been a wedding with so many people!

BRIDE (*sullen*). Never.

FATHER. It was brilliant.

MOTHER. Whole branches of families came.

BRIDEGROOM. People who never went out of the house.

MOTHER. Your father sowed well, and now you're reaping it.

BRIDEGROOM. There were cousins of mine whom I no longer knew.

MOTHER. All the people from the seacoast.

BRIDEGROOM (*happily*). They were frightened of the horses.

(*They talk.*)

MOTHER (to THE BRIDE). What are you thinking about?

BRIDE. I'm not thinking about anything.

MOTHER. Your blessings weigh heavily.

(*Guitars are heard.*)

BRIDE. Like lead.

MOTHER (*stern*). But they shouldn't weigh so. Happy as a dove you ought to be.

BRIDE. Are you staying here tonight?

MOTHER. No. My house is empty.

BRIDE. You ought to stay!

FATHER (*to* THE MOTHER). Look at the dance they're forming. Dances of the faraway seashore.

(LEONARDO *enters and sits down.* HIS WIFE *stands rigidly behind him.*)

MOTHER. They're my husband's cousins. Stiff as stones at dancing.

FATHER. It makes me happy to watch them. What a change for this house!

(*He leaves.*)

BRIDEGROOM (*to* THE BRIDE). Did you like the orange blossom?

BRIDE (*looking at him fixedly*). Yes.

BRIDEGROOM. It's all of wax. It will last forever. I'd like you to have had them all over your dress.

BRIDE. No need of that.

(LEONARDO *goes off to the right.*)

FIRST GIRL. Let's go and take out your pins.

BRIDE (*to* THE GROOM). I'll be right back.

LEONARDO'S WIFE. I hope you'll be happy with my cousin!

BRIDEGROOM. I'm sure I will.

LEONARDO'S WIFE. The two of you here; never going out; building a home. I wish I could live far away like this, too!

BRIDEGROOM. Why don't you buy land? The mountainside is cheap and children grow up better.

LEONARDO'S WIFE. We don't have any money. And at the rate we're going . . . !

BRIDEGROOM. Your husband is a good worker.

LEONARDO'S WIFE. Yes, but he likes to fly around too much; from one thing to another. He's not a patient man.

SERVANT. Aren't you having anything? I'm going to wrap up some wine cakes for your mother. She likes them so much.

BRIDEGROOM. Put up three dozen for her.

LEONARDO'S WIFE. No, no. A half-dozen's enough for her!

BRIDEGROOM. But today's a day!

LEONARDO's WIFE (*to* THE SERVANT). Where's Leonardo?

BRIDEGROOM. He must be with the guests.

LEONARDO's WIFE. I'm going to go see. (*She leaves.*)

SERVANT (*looking off at the dance*). That's beautiful there.

BRIDEGROOM. Aren't you dancing?

SERVANT. No one will ask me.

(Two GIRLS *pass across the back of the stage; during this whole scene the background should be an animated crossing of figures.*)

BRIDEGROOM (*happily*). They just don't know anything. Lively old girls like you dance better than the young ones.

SERVANT. Well! Are you tossing me a compliment, boy? What a family yours is! Men among men! As a little girl I saw your grandfather's wedding. What a figure! It seemed as if a mountain were getting married.

BRIDEGROOM. I'm not as tall.

SERVANT. But there's the same twinkle in your eye. Where's the girl?

BRIDEGROOM. Taking off her wreath.

SERVANT. Ah! Look. For midnight, since you won't be sleeping, I have prepared ham for you, and some large glasses of old wine. On the lower shelf of the cupboard. In case you need it.

BRIDEGROOM (*smiling*). I won't be eating at midnight.

SERVANT (*slyly*). If not you, maybe the bride. (*She leaves.*)

FIRST YOUTH (*entering*). You've got to come have a drink with us!

BRIDEGROOM. I'm waiting for the bride.

SECOND YOUTH. You'll have her at dawn!

FIRST YOUTH. That's when it's best!

SECOND YOUTH. Just for a minute.

BRIDEGROOM. Let's go.

(*They leave. Great excitement is heard.* THE BRIDE *enters. From the opposite side* TWO GIRLS *come running to meet her.*)

FIRST GIRL. To whom did you give the first pin; me or this one?

BRIDE. I don't remember.

FIRST GIRL. To me, you gave it to me here.

SECOND GIRL. To me, in front of the altar.

BRIDE (*uneasily, with a great inner struggle*). I don't know anything about it.

FIRST GIRL. It's just that I wish you'd . . .

BRIDE (*interrupting*). Nor do I care. I have a lot to think about.

SECOND GIRL. Your pardon.

(LEONARDO *crosses at the rear of the stage.*)

BRIDE (*sees* LEONARDO). And this is an upsetting time.

FIRST GIRL. We wouldn't know anything about that!

BRIDE. You'll know about it when your time comes. This step is a very hard one to take.

FIRST GIRL. Has she offended you?

BRIDE. No. You must pardon me.

SECOND GIRL. What for? But *both* the pins are good for getting married, aren't they?

BRIDE. Both of them.

FIRST GIRL. Maybe now one will get married before the other.

BRIDE. Are you so eager?

SECOND GIRL (*shyly*). Yes.

BRIDE. Why?

FIRST GIRL. Well . . .

(*She embraces* THE SECOND GIRL. *Both go running off.* THE GROOM *comes in very slowly and embraces* THE BRIDE *from behind.*)

BRIDE (*in sudden fright*). Let go of me!

BRIDEGROOM. Are you frightened of me?

BRIDE. Ay-y-y! It's you?

BRIDEGROOM. Who else would it be? (*pause*) Your father or me.

BRIDE. That's true!

BRIDEGROOM. Of course, your father would have hugged you more gently.

BRIDE (*darkly*). Of course!

BRIDEGROOM (*embracing her strongly and a little bit brusquely.*) Because he's old.

BRIDE (*curtly*). Let me go!

BRIDEGROOM. Why? (*He lets her go.*)

BRIDE. Well . . . the people. They can see us.

(THE SERVANT *crosses at the back of the stage again without looking at* THE BRIDE *and* BRIDEGROOM.)

BRIDEGROOM. What of it? It's consecrated now.

BRIDE. Yes, but let me be . . . Later.

BRIDEGROOM. What's the matter with you? You look frightened!

BRIDE. I'm all right. Don't go.

(LEONARDO's WIFE *enters.*)

LEONARDO's WIFE. I don't mean to intrude . . .

BRIDEGROOM. What is it?

LEONARDO's WIFE. Did my husband come through here?

BRIDEGROOM. No.

LEONARDO's WIFE. Because I can't find him, and his horse isn't in the stable either.

BRIDEGROOM (*happily*). He must be out racing it.

(THE WIFE *leaves, troubled.* THE SERVANT *enters.*)

SERVANT. Aren't you two proud and happy with so many good wishes?

BRIDEGROOM. I wish it were over with. The bride is a little tired.

SERVANT. That's no way to act, child.

BRIDE. It's as though I'd been struck on the head.

SERVANT. A bride from these mountains must be strong. (*to* THE GROOM) You're the only one who can cure her, because she's yours. (*She goes running off.*)

BRIDEGROOM (*embracing* THE BRIDE). Let's go dance a little. (*He kisses her.*)

BRIDE (*worried*). No. I'd like to stretch out on my bed a little.

BRIDEGROOM. I'll keep you company.

BRIDE. Never! With all these people here? What would they say? Let me be quiet for a moment.

BRIDEGROOM. Whatever you say! But don't be like that tonight!

BRIDE (*at the door*). I'll be better tonight.

BRIDEGROOM. That's what I want.

(THE MOTHER *appears.*)

MOTHER. Son.

BRIDEGROOM. Where've you been?

MOTHER. Out there—in all that noise. Are you happy?

BRIDEGROOM. Yes.

MOTHER. Where's your wife?

BRIDEGROOM. Resting a little. It's a bad day for brides!

MOTHER. A bad day? The only good one. To me it was like coming into my own. (THE SERVANT *enters and goes toward* THE BRIDE's *room.*) Like the breaking of new ground; the planting of new trees.

BRIDEGROOM. Are you going to leave?

MOTHER. Yes. I ought to be at home.

BRIDEGROOM. Alone.

MOTHER. Not alone. For my head is full of things: of men, and fights.

BRIDEGROOM. But now the fights are no longer fights. (THE SERVANT *enters quickly; she disappears at the rear of the stage, running.*)

MOTHER. While you live, you have to fight.

BRIDEGROOM. I'll always obey you!

MOTHER. Try to be loving with your wife, and if you see she's acting foolish or touchy, caress her in a way that will hurt her a little: a strong hug, a bite, and then a soft kiss. Not so she'll be angry, but just so she'll feel you're the man, the boss, the one who gives orders. I learned that from your father. And since you don't have him, I have to be the one to tell you about these strong defenses.

BRIDEGROOM. I'll always do as you say.

FATHER (*entering*). Where's my daughter?

BRIDEGROOM. She's inside.

(THE FATHER *goes to look for her.*)

FIRST GIRL. Get the bride and groom! We're going to dance a round!

FIRST YOUTH (*to* THE BRIDEGROOM). You're going to lead it.

FATHER (*entering*). She's not there.

BRIDEGROOM. No?

FATHER. She must have gone up to the railing.

BRIDEGROOM. I'll go see!

(*He leaves. A hubbub of excitement and guitars is heard.*)

FIRST GIRL. They've started it already! (*She leaves.*)

BRIDEGROOM (*entering*). She isn't there.

MOTHER (*uneasily*). Isn't she?

FATHER. But where could she have gone?

SERVANT (*entering*). But where's the girl, where is she?

MOTHER (*seriously*). That we don't know.

(THE BRIDEGROOM *leaves. Three* GUESTS *enter.*)

FATHER (*dramatically*). But, isn't she in the dance?

SERVANT. She's not in the dance.

FATHER (*with a start*). There are a lot of people. Go look!

SERVANT. I've already looked.

FATHER (*tragically*). Then where is she?

BRIDEGROOM (*entering*). Nowhere. Not anywhere.

MOTHER (*to* THE FATHER). What does this mean? Where is your daughter?

(LEONARDO'S WIFE *enters*.)

LEONARDO'S WIFE. They've run away! They've run away! She and Leonardo. On the horse. With their arms around each other, they rode off like a shooting star!

FATHER. That's not true! Not my daughter!

MOTHER. Yes, your daughter! Spawn of a wicked mother, and he, he too. But now she's my son's wife!

BRIDEGROOM (*entering*). Let's go after them! Who has a horse?

MOTHER. Who has a horse? Right away! Who has a horse? I'll give him all I have—my eyes, my tongue even . . .

VOICE. Here's one.

MOTHER (*to* THE SON). Go! After them! (*He leaves with two young men.*) No. Don't go. Those people kill quickly and well . . . but yes, run, and I'll follow!

FATHER. It couldn't be my daughter. Perhaps she's thrown herself in the well.

MOTHER. Decent women throw themselves in water; not that one! But now she's my son's wife. Two groups. There are two groups here. (*They all enter.*) My family and yours. Everyone set out from here. Shake the dust from your heels! We'll go help my son. (*The people separate into two groups.*) For he has his family: his cousins from the sea, and all who came from inland. Out of here! On all roads. The hour of blood has come again. Two groups! You with yours and I with mine. After them! After them!

(*Curtain.*)

ACT III

SCENE 1: *A forest. It is nighttime. Great moist tree trunks. A dark atmosphere. Two violins are heard. Three* WOODCUTTERS *enter.*

FIRST WOODCUTTER. And have they found them?

SECOND WOODCUTTER. No. But they're looking for them everywhere.

THIRD WOODCUTTER. They'll find them.

SECOND WOODCUTTER. Sh-h-h!

THIRD WOODCUTTER. What?

SECOND WOODCUTTER. They seem to be coming closer on all the roads at once.

FIRST WOODCUTTER. When the moon comes out they'll see them.

SECOND WOODCUTTER. They ought to let them go.

FIRST WOODCUTTER. The world is wide. Everybody can live in it.

THIRD WOODCUTTER. But they'll kill them.

SECOND WOODCUTTER. You have to follow your passion. They did right to run away.

FIRST WOODCUTTER. They were deceiving themselves but at the last blood was stronger.

THIRD WOODCUTTER. Blood!

FIRST WOODCUTTER. You have to follow the path of your blood.

SECOND WOODCUTTER. But blood that sees the light of day is drunk up by the earth.

FIRST WOODCUTTER. What of it? Better dead with the blood drained away than alive with it rotting.

THIRD WOODCUTTER. Hush!

FIRST WOODCUTTER. What? Do you hear something?

THIRD WOODCUTTER. I hear the crickets, the frogs, the night's ambush.

FIRST WOODCUTTER. But not the horse.

THIRD WOODCUTTER. No.

FIRST WOODCUTTER. By now he must be loving her.

SECOND WOODCUTTER. Her body for him; his body for her.

THIRD WOODCUTTER. They'll find them and they'll kill them.

FIRST WOODCUTTER. But by then they'll have mingled their bloods. They'll be like two empty jars, like two dry arroyos.

SECOND WOODCUTTER. There are many clouds and it would be easy for the moon not to come out.

THIRD WOODCUTTER. The bridegroom will find them with or without the moon. I saw him set out. Like a raging star. His face the color of ashes. He looked the fate of all his clan.

FIRST WOODCUTTER. His clan of dead men lying in the middle of the street.

SECOND WOODCUTTER. There you have it!

THIRD WOODCUTTER. You think they'll be able to break through the circle?

SECOND WOODCUTTER. It's hard to. There are knives and guns for ten leagues 'round.

THIRD WOODCUTTER. He's riding a good horse.

SECOND WOODCUTTER. But he's carrying a woman.

FIRST WOODCUTTER. We're close by now.

SECOND WOODCUTTER. A tree with forty branches. We'll soon cut it down.

THIRD WOODCUTTER. The moon's coming out now. Let's hurry.

(*From the left shines a brightness.*)

FIRST WOODCUTTER.

O rising moon!
Moon among the great leaves.

SECOND WOODCUTTER.

Cover the blood with jasmines!

FIRST WOODCUTTER.

O lonely moon!
Moon among the great leaves.

SECOND WOODCUTTER.

Silver on the bride's face.

THIRD WOODCUTTER.

O evil moon!
Leave for their love a branch in shadow.

FIRST WOODCUTTER.

O sorrowing moon!

Leave for their love a branch in shadow.
(*They go out. The* MOON *appears through the shining
brightness at the left. The* MOON *is a young woodcutter
with a white face. The stage takes on an intense blue
radiance.*)

MOON.

 Round swan in the river
and a cathedral's eye,
false dawn on the leaves,
they'll not escape; these things am I!
Who is hiding? And who sobs
in the thornbrakes of the valley?
The moon sets a knife
abandoned in the air
which being a leaden threat
yearns to be blood's pain.
Let me in! I come freezing
down to walls and windows!
Open roofs, open breasts
where I may warm myself!
I'm cold! My ashes
of somnolent metals
seek the fire's crest
on mountains and streets.
But the snow carries me
upon its mottled back
and pools soak me
in their water, hard and cold.
But this night there will be
red blood for my cheeks,
and for the reeds that cluster
at the wide feet of the wind.
Let there be neither shadow nor bower,
and then they can't get away!
O let me enter a breast
where I may get warm!
A heart for me!
Warm! That will spurt
over the mountains of my chest;
let me come in, oh let me!
(*to the branches*)
I want no shadows. My rays
must get in everywhere,
even among the dark trunks I want

the whisper of gleaming lights,
so that this night there will be
sweet blood for my cheeks,
and for the reeds that cluster
at the wide feet of the wind.
Who is hiding? Out, I say!
No! They will not get away!
I will light up the horse
with a fever bright as diamonds.

(*He disappears among the trunks, and the stage goes back to its dark lighting. An* OLD WOMAN *comes out completely covered by thin green cloth. She is barefooted. Her face can barely be seen among the folds. This character does not appear in the cast.*)

BEGGAR WOMAN.

That moon's going away, just when they's near.
They won't get past here. The river's whisper
and the whispering tree trunks will muffle
the torn flight of their shrieks.
It has to be here, and soon. I'm worn out.
The coffins are ready, and white sheets
wait on the floor of the bedroom
for heavy bodies with torn throats.
Let not one bird awake, let the breeze,
gathering their moans in her skirt,
fly with them over black tree tops
or bury them in soft mud.

(*impatiently*)

Oh, that moon! That moon!

(*The* MOON *appears. The intense blue light returns.*)

MOON. They're coming. One band through the ravine and the other along the river. I'm going to light up the boulders. What do you need?

BEGGAR WOMAN. Nothing.

MOON. The wind blows hard now, with a double edge.

BEGGAR WOMAN. Light up the waistcoat and open the buttons; the knives will know the path after that.

MOON.

But let them be a long time a-dying. So the blood
will slide its delicate hissing between my fingers.
Look how my ashen valleys already are waking
in longing for this fountain of shuddering gushes!

BEGGAR WOMAN. Let's not let them get past the arroyo. Silence!

MOON. There they come!

(*He goes. The stage is left dark.*)

BEGGAR WOMAN. Quick! Lots of light! Do you hear me? They can't get away!

(THE BRIDEGROOM *and* THE FIRST YOUTH *enter.* THE BEGGAR WOMAN *sits down and covers herself with her cloak.*)

BRIDEGROOM. This way.

FIRST YOUTH. You won't find them.

BRIDEGROOM (*angrily*). Yes, I'll find them.

FIRST YOUTH. I think they've taken another path.

BRIDEGROOM. No. Just a moment ago I felt the galloping.

FIRST YOUTH. It could have been another horse.

BRIDEGROOM (*intensely*). Listen to me. There's only one horse in the whole world, and this one's it. Can't you understand that? If you're going to follow me, follow me without talking.

FIRST YOUTH. It's only that I want to . . .

BRIDEGROOM. Be quiet. I'm sure of meeting them there. Do you see this arm? Well, it's not my arm. It's my brother's arm, and my father's, and that of all the dead ones in my family. And it has so much strength that it can pull this tree up by the roots, if it wants to. And let's move on, because here I feel the clenched teeth of all my people in me so that I can't breathe easily.

BEGGAR WOMAN (*whining*). Ay-y-y!

FIRST YOUTH. Did you hear that?

BRIDEGROOM. You go that way and then circle back.

FIRST YOUTH. This is a hunt.

BRIDEGROOM. A hunt. The greatest hunt there is.

(THE YOUTH *goes off.* THE BRIDEGROOM *goes rapidly to the left and stumbles over* THE BEGGAR WOMAN, *Death.*)

BEGGAR WOMAN. Ay-y-y!

BRIDEGROOM. What do you want?

BEGGAR WOMAN. I'm cold.

BRIDEGROOM. Which way are you going?

BEGGAR WOMAN (*always whining like a beggar*). Over there, far away . . .

BRIDEGROOM. Where are you from?

BEGGAR WOMAN. Over there . . . very far away.

BRIDEGROOM. Have you seen a man and a woman running away on a horse?

BEGGAR WOMAN (*awakening*). Wait a minute . . . (*She*

looks at him.) Handsome young man. (*She rises.*) But you'd be much handsomer sleeping.

BRIDEGROOM. Tell me; answer me. Did you see them?

BEGGAR WOMAN. Wait a minute . . . What broad shoulders! How would you like to be laid out on them and not have to walk on the soles of your feet which are so small?

BRIDEGROOM (*shaking her*). I asked you if you saw them! Have they passed through here?

BEGGAR WOMAN (*energetically*). No. They haven't passed; but they're coming from the hill. Don't you hear them?

BRIDEGROOM. No.

BEGGAR WOMAN. Do you know the road?

BRIDEGROOM. I'll go, whatever it's like!

BEGGAR WOMAN. I'll go along with you. I know this country.

BRIDEGROOM (*impatiently*). Well, let's go! Which way?

BEGGAR WOMAN (*dramatically*). This way!

(*They go rapidly out. Two violins, which represent the forest, are heard distantly. The* WOODCUTTERS *return. They have their axes on their shoulders. They move slowly among the tree trunks.*)

FIRST WOODCUTTER.
    O rising death!
    Death among the great leaves.

SECOND WOODCUTTER.
    Don't open the gush of blood!

FIRST WOODCUTTER.
    O lonely death!
    Death among the dried leaves.

THIRD WOODCUTTER.
    Don't lay flowers over the wedding!

SECOND WOODCUTTER.
    O sad death!
    Leave for their love a green branch.

FIRST WOODCUTTER.
    O evil death!
    Leave for their love a branch of green!

(*They go out while they are talking.* LEONARDO *and* THE BRIDE *appear.*)

LEONARDO.
    Hush!

BRIDE.
    From here I'll go on alone.
    You go now! I want you to turn back.

LEONARDO.

Hush, I said!

BRIDE.

With your teeth, with your hands, anyway
you can,
take from my clean throat
the metal of this chain,
and let me live forgotten
back there in my house in the ground.
And if you don't want to kill me
as you would kill a tiny snake,
set in my hands, a bride's hands,
the barrel of your shotgun.
Oh, what lamenting, what fire,
sweeps upward through my head!
What glass splinters are stuck in my tongue!

LEONARDO.

We've taken the step now; hush!
because they're close behind us,
and I must take you with me.

BRIDE.

Then it must be by force!

LEONARDO.

By force? Who was it first
went down the stairway?

BRIDE.

I went down it.

LEONARDO.

And who was it put
a new bridle on the horse?

BRIDE.

I myself did it. It's true.

LEONARDO.

And whose were the hands
strapped spurs to my boots?

BRIDE.

The same hands, these that are yours,
but which when they see you would like
to break the blue branches
and sunder the purl of your veins.
I love you! I love you! But leave me!
For if I were able to kill you
I'd wrap you 'round in a shroud
with the edges bordered in violets.

Oh, what lamenting, what fire,
sweeps upward through my head!

LEONARDO.

What glass splinters are stuck in my tongue!
Because I tried to forget you
and put a wall of stone
between your house and mine.
It's true. You remember?
And when I saw you in the distance
I threw sand in my eyes.
But I was riding a horse
and the horse went straight to your door.
And the silver pins of your wedding
turned my red blood black.
And in me our dream was choking
my flesh with its poisoned weeds.
Oh, it isn't my fault—
the fault is the earth's—
and this fragrance that you exhale
from your breasts and your braids.

BRIDE.

Oh, how untrue! I want
from you neither bed nor food,
yet there's not a minute each day
that I don't want to be with you,
because you drag me, and I come,
then you tell me to go back
and I follow you,
like chaff blown on the breeze.
I have left a good, honest man,
and all his people,
with the wedding feast half over
and wearing my bridal wreath.
But you are the one will be punished
and that I don't want to happen.
Leave me alone now! You run away!
There is no one who will defend you.

LEONARDO.

The birds of early morning
are calling among the trees.
The night is dying
on the stone's ridge.
Let's go to a hidden corner
where I may love you forever,

for to me the people don't matter,
nor the venom they throw on us.
(*He embraces her strongly.*)

BRIDE.

And I'll sleep at your feet,
to watch over your dreams.
Naked, looking over the fields,
as though I were a bitch.
Because that's what I am! Oh, I look at you
and your beauty sears me.

LEONARDO.

Fire is stirred by fire.
The same tiny flame
will kill two wheat heads together.
Let's go!

BRIDE.

Where are you taking me?

LEONARDO.

Where they cannot come,
these men who surround us.
Where I can look at you!

BRIDE (*sarcastically*).

Carry me with you from fair to fair,
a shame to clean women,
so that people will see me
with my wedding sheets
on the breeze like banners.

LEONARDO.

I, too, would want to leave you
if I thought as men should.
But wherever you go, I go.
You're the same. Take a step. Try.
Nails of moonlight have fused
my waist and your thighs.

(*This whole scene is violent, full of great sensuality.*)

BRIDE.

Listen!

LEONARDO.

They're coming.

BRIDE.

                      Run!

It's fitting that I should die here,
with water over my feet,
with thorns upon my head.

And fitting the leaves should mourn me,
a woman lost and virgin.

LEONARDO.
Be quiet. Now they're appearing.

BRIDE.

Go now!

LEONARDO.
Quiet. Don't let them hear us.
(THE BRIDE *hesitates*.)

BRIDE.
Both of us!

LEONARDO (*embracing her*).

Any way you want!

If they separate us, it will be
because I am dead.

BRIDE.

And I dead too.
(*They go out in each other's arms*.)

(*The* MOON *appears very slowly. The stage takes on a strong blue light. The two violins are heard. Suddenly two long, ear-splitting shrieks are heard, and the music of the two violins is cut short. At the second shriek* THE BEGGAR WOMAN *appears and stands with her back to the audience. She opens her cape and stands in the center of the stage like a great bird with immense wings. The* MOON *halts. The curtain comes down in absolute silence*.)

(*Curtain*.)

SCENE 2: *The Final Scene. A white dwelling with arches and thick walls. To the right and left, are white stairs. At the back, a great arch and a wall of the same color. The floor also should be shining white. This simple dwelling should have the monumental feeling of a church. There should not be a single gray nor any shadow, not even what is necessary for perspective.*

(Two GIRLS *dressed in dark blue are winding a red skein*.)

FIRST GIRL.

> Wool, red wool,
> what would you make?

SECOND GIRL.

> Oh, jasmine for dresses,
> fine wool like glass.
> At four o'clock born,
> at ten o'clock dead.
> A thread from this wool yarn,
> a chain 'round your feet
> a knot that will tighten
> the bitter white wreath.

LITTLE GIRL (*singing*).

> Were you at the wedding?

FIRST GIRL.

> No.

LITTLE GIRL.

> Well, neither was I!
> What could have happened
> 'midst the shoots of the vineyards?
> What could have happened
> 'neath the branch of the olive?
> What really happened
> that no one came back?
> Were you at the wedding?

SECOND GIRL.

> We told you once, no.

LITTLE GIRL (*leaving*).

> Well, neither was I!

SECOND GIRL.

> Wool, red wool,
> what would you sing?

FIRST GIRL.

> Their wounds turning waxen
> balm-myrtle for pain.
> Asleep in the morning,
> and watching at night.

LITTLE GIRL (*in the doorway*).

> And then, the thread stumbled
> on the flinty stones,
> but mountains, blue mountains,
> are letting it pass.
> Running, running, running,

and finally to come
to stick in a knife blade,
to take back the bread.

(She goes out.)

SECOND GIRL.
    Wool, red wool,
    what would you tell?
FIRST GIRL.
    The lover is silent,
    crimson the groom,
    at the still shoreline
    I saw them laid out.
(She stops and looks at the skein.)
LITTLE GIRL *(appearing in the doorway)*.
    Running, running, running,
    the thread runs to here.
    All covered with clay
    I feel them draw near.
    Bodies stretched stiffly
    in ivory sheets!
(The WIFE *and* MOTHER-IN-LAW *of* LEONARDO *appear.
They are anguished.)*
FIRST GIRL. Are they coming yet?
MOTHER-IN-LAW *(harshly)*. We don't know.
SECOND GIRL. What can you tell us about the wedding?
FIRST GIRL. Yes, tell me.
MOTHER-IN-LAW *(curtly)*. Nothing.
LEONARDO'S WIFE. I want to go back and find out all
about it.
MOTHER-IN-LAW *(sternly)*.
    You, back to your house.
    Brave and alone in your house.
    To grow old and to weep.
    But behind closed doors.
    Never again. Neither dead nor alive.
    We'll nail up our windows
    and let rains and nights
    fall on the bitter weeds.
LEONARDO'S WIFE. What could have happened?
MOTHER-IN-LAW.
    It doesn't matter what.
    Put a veil over your face.
    Your children are yours,

that's all. On the bed
put a cross of ashes
where his pillow was.

(They go out.)

BEGGAR WOMAN *(at the door)*. A crust of bread, little
girls.

LITTLE GIRL. Go away!

(The GIRLS huddle close together.)

BEGGAR WOMAN. Why?

LITTLE GIRL. Because you whine; go away!

FIRST GIRL. Child!

BEGGAR WOMAN.

I might have asked for your eyes! A cloud
of birds is following me. Will you have one?

LITTLE GIRL. I want to get away from here!

SECOND GIRL *(to the BEGGAR WOMAN)*. Don't mind her!

FIRST GIRL. Did you come by the road through the
arroyo?

BEGGAR WOMAN. I came that way!

FIRST GIRL *(timidly)*. Can I ask you something?

BEGGAR WOMAN.

I saw them: they'll be here soon; two torrents
still at last, among the great boulders,
two men at the horse's feet.
Two dead men in the night's splendor.
(with pleasure)
Dead, yes, dead.

FIRST GIRL. Hush, old woman, hush!

BEGGAR WOMAN.

Crushed flowers for eyes, and their teeth
two fistfuls of hard-frozen snow.
Both of them fell, and the Bride returns
with bloodstains on her skirt and hair.
And they come covered with two sheets
carried on the shoulders of two tall boys.
That's how it was; nothing more. What was
      fitting.
Over the golden flower, dirty sand.

*(She goes. The GIRLS bow their heads and start going
out rhythmically.)*

FIRST GIRL.

Dirty sand.

SECOND GIRL.

Over the golden flower.

LITTLE GIRL.
>Over the golden flower
>they're bringing the dead from the arroyo.
>Dark the one,
>dark the other.
>What shadowy nightingale flies and weeps
>over the golden flower!

(*She goes. The stage is left empty. The* MOTHER *and a* NEIGHBOR WOMAN *appear. The* NEIGHBOR *is weeping.*)

MOTHER. Hush.

NEIGHBOR. I can't.

MOTHER. Hush, I said. (*at the door*) Is there nobody here? (*She puts her hands to her forehead.*) My son ought to answer me. But now my son is an armful of shriveled flowers. My son is a fading voice beyond the mountains now. (*with rage, to* THE NEIGHBOR) Will you shut up? I want no wailing in this house. Your tears are only tears from your eyes, but when I'm alone mine will come—from the soles of my feet, from my roots—burning more than blood.

NEIGHBOR. You come to my house; don't you stay here.

MOTHER. I want to be here. Here. In peace. They're all dead now: and at midnight I'll sleep, sleep without terror of guns or knives. Other mothers will go to their windows, lashed by rain, to watch for their sons' faces. But not I. And of my dreams I'll make a cold ivory dove that will carry camellias of white frost to the graveyard. But no; not graveyard, not graveyard: the couch of earth, the bed that shelters them and rocks them in the sky.

(*A woman dressed in black enters, goes toward the right, and there kneels. To* THE NEIGHBOR.)

Take your hands from your face. We have terrible days ahead. I want to see no one. The earth and I. My grief and I. And these four walls. Ay-y-y! Ay-y-y!

(*She sits down, overcome.*)

NEIGHBOR. Take pity on yourself!

MOTHER (*pushing back her hair*). I must be calm. (*She sits down.*) Because the neighbor women will come and I don't want them to see me so poor. So poor! A woman without even one son to hold to her lips.

(THE BRIDE *appears. She is without her wreath and wears a black shawl.*)

NEIGHBOR (*with rage, seeing* THE BRIDE). Where are you going?

BRIDE. I'm coming here.

MOTHER (*to* THE NEIGHBOR). Who is it?

NEIGHBOR. Don't you recognize her?

MOTHER. That's why I asked who it was. Because I don't want to recognize her, so I won't sink my teeth in her throat. You snake! (*She moves wrathfully on* THE BRIDE, *then stops. To* THE NEIGHBOR) Look at her! There she is, and she's crying, while I stand here calmly and don't tear her eyes out. I don't understand myself. Can it be I didn't love my son? But, where's his good name? Where is it now? Where is it?

(*She beats* THE BRIDE, *who drops to the floor.*)

NEIGHBOR. For God's sake! (*She tries to separate them.*)

BRIDE (*to* THE NEIGHBOR). Let her; I came here so she'd kill me and they'd take me away with them. (*to* THE MOTHER) But not with her hands; with grappling hooks, with a sickle—and with force—until they break on my bones. Let her! I want her to know I'm clean, that I may be crazy, but that they can bury me without a single man ever having seen himself in the whiteness of my breasts.

MOTHER. Shut up, shut up; what do I care about that?

BRIDE. Because I ran away with the other one; I ran away! (*with anguish*) You would have gone, too. I was a woman burning with desire, full of sores inside and out, and your son was a little bit of water from which I hoped for children, land, health; but the other one was a dark river, choked with brush, that brought near me the under-tone of its rushes and its whispered song. And I went along with your son who was like a little boy of cold water—and the other sent against me hundreds of birds who got in my way and left white frost on my wounds, my wounds of a poor withered woman, of a girl caressed by fire. I didn't want to; remember that! I didn't want to. Your son was my destiny and I have not betrayed him, but the other one's arm dragged me along like the pull of the sea, like the head toss of a mule, and he would have dragged me always, always, always—even if I were an old woman and all your son's sons held me by the hair!

(*A* NEIGHBOR *enters.*)

MOTHER. She is not to blame; nor am I! (*sarcastically*) Who is, then? It's a delicate, lazy, sleepless woman who throws away an orange blossom wreath and goes looking for a piece of bed warmed by another woman!

BRIDE. Be still! Be still! Take your revenge on me; here

I am! See how soft my throat is; it would be less work for you than cutting a dahlia in your garden. But never that! Clean, clean as a new-born little girl. And strong enough to prove it to you. Light the fire. Let's stick our hands in; you, for your son, I, for my body. *You'll* draw yours out first.

(*Another* NEIGHBOR *enters.*)

MOTHER. But what does your good name matter to me? What does your death matter to me? What does anything about anything matter to me? Blessèd be the wheat stalks, because my sons are under them; blessèd be the rain, because it wets the face of the dead. Blessèd be God, who stretches us out together to rest.

(*Another* NEIGHBOR *enters.*)

BRIDE. Let me weep with you.

MOTHER. Weep. But at the door.

(THE GIRL *enters.* THE BRIDE *stays at the door.* THE MOTHER *is at the center of the stage.*)

LEONARDO'S WIFE (*entering and going to the left*).
He was a beautiful horseman,
now he's a heap of snow.
He rode to fairs and mountains
and women's arms.
Now, the night's dark moss
crowns his forehead.

MOTHER.
A sunflower to your mother,
a mirror of the earth.
Let them put on your breast
the cross of bitter rosebay;
and over you a sheet
of shining silk;
between your quiet hands
let water form its lament.

WIFE.
Ay-y-y, four gallant boys
come with tired shoulders!

BRIDE.
Ay-y-y, four gallant boys
carry death on high!

MOTHER.
Neighbors.

LITTLE GIRL (*at the door*).
They're bringing them now.

MOTHER.

It's the same thing.
Always the cross, the cross.
WOMEN.
Sweet nails,
cross adored,
sweet name
of Christ our Lord.
BRIDE. May the cross protect both the quick and the dead.
MOTHER.
Neighbors: with a knife,
with a little knife,
on their appointed day, between two and three,
these two men killed each other for love.
With a knife,
with a tiny knife
that barely fits the hand,
but that slides in clean
through the astonished flesh
and stops at the place
where trembles, enmeshed,
the dark root of a scream.
BRIDE.
And this is a knife,
a tiny knife
that barely fits the hand;
fish without scales, without river,
so that on their appointed day, between two
    and three,
with this knife,
two men are left stiff,
with their lips turning yellow.
MOTHER.
And it barely fits the hand
but it slides in clean
through the astonished flesh
and stops there, at the place
where trembles enmeshed
the dark root of a scream.
(*The* NEIGHBORS, *kneeling on the floor, sob.*)

(*Curtain.*)

BIBLIOGRAPHY

Díaz-Plaja, G. (ed.). *El Teatro. Enciclopedia del arte escénico* (Barcelona: Noguera, 1958).

Leavitt, S. E. "The Popular Appeal of Golden Age Drama in Spain," *University of North Carolina Extension Bulletin*, XXVIII, No. 3 (1948), 7-15.

Parker, A. A. "An Approach to the Spanish Drama of the Golden Age," *Tulane Drama Review* (September, 1959), pp. 42-59.

————. "Reflections on a New Definition of Baroque Drama," *Bulletin of Spanish Studies*, XXX (1953), 142-151.

Reichenberger, A. G. "The Uniqueness of the Comedia," *Hispanic Review*, XXVII (1959), 303-316.

Rennert, H. A. *The Spanish Stage in the Time of Lope de Vega* (New York: 1909).

Roaten, D. H., and Sánchez y Escribano, F. *Wölfflin's Principles in Spanish Drama 1500-1700* (New York: 1952).

Valbuena, A. *Literatura Dramática Española.* (Barcelona: Labor, 1950).

A CATALOG OF SELECTED
DOVER BOOKS
IN ALL FIELDS OF INTEREST

A CATALOG OF SELECTED DOVER
BOOKS IN ALL FIELDS OF INTEREST

CONCERNING THE SPIRITUAL IN ART, Wassily Kandinsky. Pioneering work by father of abstract art. Thoughts on color theory, nature of art. Analysis of earlier masters. 12 illustrations. 80pp. of text. 5⅜ × 8½.   23411-8 Pa. $3.95

ANIMALS: 1,419 Copyright-Free Illustrations of Mammals, Birds, Fish, Insects, etc., Jim Harter (ed.). Clear wood engravings present, in extremely lifelike poses, over 1,000 species of animals. One of the most extensive pictorial sourcebooks of its kind. Captions. Index. 284pp. 9 × 12.   23766-4 Pa. $12.95

CELTIC ART: The Methods of Construction, George Bain. Simple geometric techniques for making Celtic interlacements, spirals, Kells-type initials, animals, humans, etc. Over 500 illustrations. 160pp. 9 × 12. (USO)   22923-8 Pa. $9.95

AN ATLAS OF ANATOMY FOR ARTISTS, Fritz Schider. Most thorough reference work on art anatomy in the world. Hundreds of illustrations, including selections from works by Vesalius, Leonardo, Goya, Ingres, Michelangelo, others. 593 illustrations. 192pp. 7⅛ × 10¼.   20241-0 Pa. $9.95

CELTIC HAND STROKE-BY-STROKE (Irish Half-Uncial from "The Book of Kells"): An Arthur Baker Calligraphy Manual, Arthur Baker. Complete guide to creating each letter of the alphabet in distinctive Celtic manner. Covers hand position, strokes, pens, inks, paper, more. Illustrated. 48pp. 8¼ × 11.
                                                                                                24336-2 Pa. $3.95

EASY ORIGAMI, John Montroll. Charming collection of 32 projects (hat, cup, pelican, piano, swan, many more) specially designed for the novice origami hobbyist. Clearly illustrated easy-to-follow instructions insure that even beginning papercrafters will achieve successful results. 48pp. 8¼ × 11.   27298-2 Pa. $2.95

THE COMPLETE BOOK OF BIRDHOUSE CONSTRUCTION FOR WOOD-WORKERS, Scott D. Campbell. Detailed instructions, illustrations, tables. Also data on bird habitat and instinct patterns. Bibliography. 3 tables. 63 illustrations in 15 figures. 48pp. 5¼ × 8½.   24407-5 Pa. $1.95

BLOOMINGDALE'S ILLUSTRATED 1886 CATALOG: Fashions, Dry Goods and Housewares, Bloomingdale Brothers. Famed merchants' extremely rare catalog depicting about 1,700 products: clothing, housewares, firearms, dry goods, jewelry, more. Invaluable for dating, identifying vintage items. Also, copyright-free graphics for artists, designers. Co-published with Henry Ford Museum & Greenfield Village. 160pp. 8¼ × 11.   25780-0 Pa. $9.95

HISTORIC COSTUME IN PICTURES, Braun & Schneider. Over 1,450 costumed figures in clearly detailed engravings—from dawn of civilization to end of 19th century. Captions. Many folk costumes. 256pp. 8⅜ × 11¾.   23150-X Pa. $11.95

STICKLEY CRAFTSMAN FURNITURE CATALOGS, Gustav Stickley and L. & J. G. Stickley. Beautiful, functional furniture in two authentic catalogs from 1910. 594 illustrations, including 277 photos, show settles, rockers, armchairs, reclining chairs, bookcases, desks, tables. 183pp. 6½ × 9¼. 23838-5 Pa. $9.95

AMERICAN LOCOMOTIVES IN HISTORIC PHOTOGRAPHS: 1858 to 1949, Ron Ziel (ed.). A rare collection of 126 meticulously detailed official photographs, called "builder portraits," of American locomotives that majestically chronicle the rise of steam locomotive power in America. Introduction. Detailed captions. xi + 129pp. 9 × 12. 27393-8 Pa. $12.95

AMERICA'S LIGHTHOUSES: An Illustrated History, Francis Ross Holland, Jr. Delightfully written, profusely illustrated fact-filled survey of over 200 American lighthouses since 1716. History, anecdotes, technological advances, more. 240pp. 8 × 10¾. 25576-X Pa. $11.95

TOWARDS A NEW ARCHITECTURE, Le Corbusier. Pioneering manifesto by founder of "International School." Technical and aesthetic theories, views of industry, economics, relation of form to function, "mass-production split" and much more. Profusely illustrated. 320pp. 6⅛ × 9¼. (USO) 25023-7 Pa. $9.95

HOW THE OTHER HALF LIVES, Jacob Riis. Famous journalistic record, exposing poverty and degradation of New York slums around 1900, by major social reformer. 100 striking and influential photographs. 233pp. 10 × 7⅞. 22012-5 Pa $10.95

FRUIT KEY AND TWIG KEY TO TREES AND SHRUBS, William M. Harlow. One of the handiest and most widely used identification aids. Fruit key covers 120 deciduous and evergreen species; twig key 160 deciduous species. Easily used. Over 300 photographs. 126pp. 5⅜ × 8½. 20511-8 Pa. $3.95

COMMON BIRD SONGS, Dr. Donald J. Borror. Songs of 60 most common U.S. birds: robins, sparrows, cardinals, bluejays, finches, more—arranged in order of increasing complexity. Up to 9 variations of songs of each species. Cassette and manual 99911-4 $8.95

ORCHIDS AS HOUSE PLANTS, Rebecca Tyson Northen. Grow cattleyas and many other kinds of orchids—in a window, in a case, or under artificial light. 63 illustrations. 148pp. 5⅜ × 8½. 23261-1 Pa. $4.95

MONSTER MAZES, Dave Phillips. Masterful mazes at four levels of difficulty. Avoid deadly perils and evil creatures to find magical treasures. Solutions for all 32 exciting illustrated puzzles. 48pp. 8¼ × 11. 26005-4 Pa. $2.95

MOZART'S DON GIOVANNI (DOVER OPERA LIBRETTO SERIES), Wolfgang Amadeus Mozart. Introduced and translated by Ellen H. Bleiler. Standard Italian libretto, with complete English translation. Convenient and thoroughly portable—an ideal companion for reading along with a recording or the performance itself. Introduction. List of characters. Plot summary. 121pp. 5¼ × 8½. 24944-1 Pa. $2.95

TECHNICAL MANUAL AND DICTIONARY OF CLASSICAL BALLET, Gail Grant. Defines, explains, comments on steps, movements, poses and concepts. 15-page pictorial section. Basic book for student, viewer. 127pp. 5⅜ × 8½. 21843-0 Pa. $4.95

BRASS INSTRUMENTS: Their History and Development, Anthony Baines. Authoritative, updated survey of the evolution of trumpets, trombones, bugles, cornets, French horns, tubas and other brass wind instruments. Over 140 illustrations and 48 music examples. Corrected and updated by author. New preface. Bibliography. 320pp. 5⅜ × 8½. 27574-4 Pa. $9.95

HOLLYWOOD GLAMOR PORTRAITS, John Kobal (ed.). 145 photos from 1926–49. Harlow, Gable, Bogart, Bacall; 94 stars in all. Full background on photographers, technical aspects. 160pp. 8⅜ × 11¼. 23352-9 Pa. $11.95

MAX AND MORITZ, Wilhelm Busch. Great humor classic in both German and English. Also 10 other works: "Cat and Mouse," "Plisch and Plumm," etc. 216pp. 5⅜ × 8½. 20181-3 Pa. $5.95

THE RAVEN AND OTHER FAVORITE POEMS, Edgar Allan Poe. Over 40 of the author's most memorable poems: "The Bells," "Ulalume," "Israfel," "To Helen," "The Conqueror Worm," "Eldorado," "Annabel Lee," many more. Alphabetic lists of titles and first lines. 64pp. 5³⁄₁₆ × 8¼. 26685-0 Pa. $1.00

SEVEN SCIENCE FICTION NOVELS, H. G. Wells. The standard collection of the great novels. Complete, unabridged. First Men in the Moon, Island of Dr. Moreau, War of the Worlds, Food of the Gods, Invisible Man, Time Machine, In the Days of the Comet. Total of 1,015pp. 5⅜ × 8½. (USO) 20264-X Clothbd. $29.95

AMULETS AND SUPERSTITIONS, E. A. Wallis Budge. Comprehensive discourse on origin, powers of amulets in many ancient cultures: Arab, Persian, Babylonian, Assyrian, Egyptian, Gnostic, Hebrew, Phoenician, Syriac, etc. Covers cross, swastika, crucifix, seals, rings, stones, etc. 584pp. 5⅜ × 8½. 23573-4 Pa. $12.95

RUSSIAN STORIES/PYCCKNE PACCKA3bl: A Dual-Language Book, edited by Gleb Struve. Twelve tales by such masters as Chekhov, Tolstoy, Dostoevsky, Pushkin, others. Excellent word-for-word English translations on facing pages, plus teaching and study aids, Russian/English vocabulary, biographical/critical introductions, more. 416pp. 5⅜ × 8½. 26244-8 Pa. $8.95

PHILADELPHIA THEN AND NOW: 60 Sites Photographed in the Past and Present, Kenneth Finkel and Susan Oyama. Rare photographs of City Hall, Logan Square, Independence Hall, Betsy Ross House, other landmarks juxtaposed with contemporary views. Captures changing face of historic city. Introduction. Captions. 128pp. 8¼ × 11. 25790-8 Pa. $9.95

AIA ARCHITECTURAL GUIDE TO NASSAU AND SUFFOLK COUNTIES, LONG ISLAND, The American Institute of Architects, Long Island Chapter, and the Society for the Preservation of Long Island Antiquities. Comprehensive, well-researched and generously illustrated volume brings to life over three centuries of Long Island's great architectural heritage. More than 240 photographs with authoritative, extensively detailed captions. 176pp. 8¼ × 11. 26946-9 Pa. $14.95

NORTH AMERICAN INDIAN LIFE: Customs and Traditions of 23 Tribes, Elsie Clews Parsons (ed.). 27 fictionalized essays by noted anthropologists examine religion, customs, government, additional facets of life among the Winnebago, Crow, Zuni, Eskimo, other tribes. 480pp. 6⅛ × 9¼. 27377-6 Pa. $10.95

FRANK LLOYD WRIGHT'S HOLLYHOCK HOUSE, Donald Hoffmann. Lavishly illustrated, carefully documented study of one of Wright's most controversial residential designs. Over 120 photographs, floor plans, elevations, etc. Detailed perceptive text by noted Wright scholar. Index. 128pp. 9¼ × 10¾.
27133-1 Pa. $11.95

THE MALE AND FEMALE FIGURE IN MOTION: 60 Classic Photographic Sequences, Eadweard Muybridge. 60 true-action photographs of men and women walking, running, climbing, bending, turning, etc., reproduced from rare 19th-century masterpiece. vi + 121pp. 9 × 12. 24745-7 Pa. $10.95

1001 QUESTIONS ANSWERED ABOUT THE SEASHORE, N. J. Berrill and Jacquelyn Berrill. Queries answered about dolphins, sea snails, sponges, starfish, fishes, shore birds, many others. Covers appearance, breeding, growth, feeding, much more. 305pp. 5¼ × 8¼. 23366-9 Pa. $7.95

GUIDE TO OWL WATCHING IN NORTH AMERICA, Donald S. Heintzelman. Superb guide offers complete data and descriptions of 19 species: barn owl, screech owl, snowy owl, many more. Expert coverage of owl-watching equipment, conservation, migrations and invasions, etc. Guide to observing sites. 84 illustrations. xiii + 193pp. 5⅜ × 8½. 27344-X Pa. $8.95

MEDICINAL AND OTHER USES OF NORTH AMERICAN PLANTS: A Historical Survey with Special Reference to the Eastern Indian Tribes, Charlotte Erichsen-Brown. Chronological historical citations document 500 years of usage of plants, trees, shrubs native to eastern Canada, northeastern U.S. Also complete identifying information. 343 illustrations. 544pp. 6½ × 9¼. 25951-X Pa. $12.95

STORYBOOK MAZES, Dave Phillips. 23 stories and mazes on two-page spreads: Wizard of Oz, Treasure Island, Robin Hood, etc. Solutions. 64pp. 8¼ × 11.
23628-5 Pa. $2.95

NEGRO FOLK MUSIC, U.S.A., Harold Courlander. Noted folklorist's scholarly yet readable analysis of rich and varied musical tradition. Includes authentic versions of over 40 folk songs. Valuable bibliography and discography. xi + 324pp. 5⅜ × 8½. 27350-4 Pa. $7.95

MOVIE-STAR PORTRAITS OF THE FORTIES, John Kobal (ed.). 163 glamor, studio photos of 106 stars of the 1940s: Rita Hayworth, Ava Gardner, Marlon Brando, Clark Gable, many more. 176pp. 8⅜ × 11¼. 23546-7 Pa. $11.95

BENCHLEY LOST AND FOUND, Robert Benchley. Finest humor from early 30s, about pet peeves, child psychologists, post office and others. Mostly unavailable elsewhere. 73 illustrations by Peter Arno and others. 183pp. 5⅜ × 8½.
22410-4 Pa. $5.95

YEKL and THE IMPORTED BRIDEGROOM AND OTHER STORIES OF YIDDISH NEW YORK, Abraham Cahan. Film Hester Street based on Yekl (1896). Novel, other stories among first about Jewish immigrants on N.Y.'s East Side. 240pp. 5⅜ × 8½. 22427-9 Pa. $6.95

SELECTED POEMS, Walt Whitman. Generous sampling from *Leaves of Grass*. Twenty-four poems include "I Hear America Singing," "Song of the Open Road," "I Sing the Body Electric," "When Lilacs Last in the Dooryard Bloom'd," "O Captain! My Captain!"—all reprinted from an authoritative edition. Lists of titles and first lines. 128pp. 5³⁄₁₆ × 8¼. 26878-0 Pa. $1.00

THE BEST TALES OF HOFFMANN, E. T. A. Hoffmann. 10 of Hoffmann's most important stories: "Nutcracker and the King of Mice," "The Golden Flowerpot," etc. 458pp. 5⅜ × 8½. 21793-0 Pa. $8.95

FROM FETISH TO GOD IN ANCIENT EGYPT, E. A. Wallis Budge. Rich detailed survey of Egyptian conception of "God" and gods, magic, cult of animals, Osiris, more. Also, superb English translations of hymns and legends. 240 illustrations. 545pp. 5⅜ × 8½. 25803-3 Pa. $11.95

FRENCH STORIES/CONTES FRANÇAIS: A Dual-Language Book, Wallace Fowlie. Ten stories by French masters, Voltaire to Camus: "Micromegas" by Voltaire; "The Atheist's Mass" by Balzac; "Minuet" by de Maupassant; "The Guest" by Camus, six more. Excellent English translations on facing pages. Also French-English vocabulary list, exercises, more. 352pp. 5⅜ × 8½. 26443-2 Pa. $8.95

CHICAGO AT THE TURN OF THE CENTURY IN PHOTOGRAPHS: 122 Historic Views from the Collections of the Chicago Historical Society, Larry A. Viskochil. Rare large-format prints offer detailed views of City Hall, State Street, the Loop, Hull House, Union Station, many other landmarks, circa 1904–1913. Introduction. Captions. Maps. 144pp. 9⅜ × 12¼. 24656-6 Pa. $12.95

OLD BROOKLYN IN EARLY PHOTOGRAPHS, 1865–1929, William Lee Younger. Luna Park, Gravesend race track, construction of Grand Army Plaza, moving of Hotel Brighton, etc. 157 previously unpublished photographs. 165pp. 8⅞ × 11¾. 23587-4 Pa. $13.95

THE MYTHS OF THE NORTH AMERICAN INDIANS, Lewis Spence. Rich anthology of the myths and legends of the Algonquins, Iroquois, Pawnees and Sioux, prefaced by an extensive historical and ethnological commentary. 36 illustrations. 480pp. 5⅜ × 8½. 25967-6 Pa. $8.95

AN ENCYCLOPEDIA OF BATTLES: Accounts of Over 1,560 Battles from 1479 B.C. to the Present, David Eggenberger. Essential details of every major battle in recorded history from the first battle of Megiddo in 1479 B.C. to Grenada in 1984. List of Battle Maps. New Appendix covering the years 1967–1984. Index. 99 illustrations. 544pp. 6½ × 9¼. 24913-1 Pa. $14.95

SAILING ALONE AROUND THE WORLD, Captain Joshua Slocum. First man to sail around the world, alone, in small boat. One of great feats of seamanship told in delightful manner. 67 illustrations. 294pp. 5⅜ × 8½. 20326-3 Pa. $5.95

ANARCHISM AND OTHER ESSAYS, Emma Goldman. Powerful, penetrating, prophetic essays on direct action, role of minorities, prison reform, puritan hypocrisy, violence, etc. 271pp. 5⅜ × 8½. 22484-8 Pa. $5.95

MYTHS OF THE HINDUS AND BUDDHISTS, Ananda K. Coomaraswamy and Sister Nivedita. Great stories of the epics; deeds of Krishna, Shiva, taken from puranas, Vedas, folk tales; etc. 32 illustrations. 400pp. 5⅜ × 8½. 21759-0 Pa. $9.95

BEYOND PSYCHOLOGY, Otto Rank. Fear of death, desire of immortality, nature of sexuality, social organization, creativity, according to Rankian system. 291pp. 5⅜ × 8½. 20485-5 Pa. $8.95

A THEOLOGICO-POLITICAL TREATISE, Benedict Spinoza. Also contains unfinished Political Treatise. Great classic on religious liberty, theory of government on common consent. R. Elwes translation. Total of 421pp. 5⅜ × 8½. 20249-6 Pa. $8.95

MY BONDAGE AND MY FREEDOM, Frederick Douglass. Born a slave, Douglass became outspoken force in antislavery movement. The best of Douglass' autobiographies. Graphic description of slave life. 464pp. 5⅜ × 8½. 22457-0 Pa. $8.95

FOLLOWING THE EQUATOR: A Journey Around the World, Mark Twain. Fascinating humorous account of 1897 voyage to Hawaii, Australia, India, New Zealand, etc. Ironic, bemused reports on peoples, customs, climate, flora and fauna, politics, much more. 197 illustrations. 720pp. 5⅜ × 8½. 26113-1 Pa. $15.95

THE PEOPLE CALLED SHAKERS, Edward D. Andrews. Definitive study of Shakers: origins, beliefs, practices, dances, social organization, furniture and crafts, etc. 33 illustrations. 351pp. 5⅜ × 8½. 21081-2 Pa. $8.95

THE MYTHS OF GREECE AND ROME, H. A. Guerber. A classic of mythology, generously illustrated, long prized for its simple, graphic, accurate retelling of the principal myths of Greece and Rome, and for its commentary on their origins and significance. With 64 illustrations by Michelangelo, Raphael, Titian, Rubens, Canova, Bernini and others. 480pp. 5⅜ × 8½. 27584-1 Pa. $9.95

PSYCHOLOGY OF MUSIC, Carl E. Seashore. Classic work discusses music as a medium from psychological viewpoint. Clear treatment of physical acoustics, auditory apparatus, sound perception, development of musical skills, nature of musical feeling, host of other topics. 88 figures. 408pp. 5⅜ × 8½. 21851-1 Pa. $9.95

THE PHILOSOPHY OF HISTORY, Georg W. Hegel. Great classic of Western thought develops concept that history is not chance but rational process, the evolution of freedom. 457pp. 5⅜ × 8½. 20112-0 Pa. $9.95

THE BOOK OF TEA, Kakuzo Okakura. Minor classic of the Orient: entertaining, charming explanation, interpretation of traditional Japanese culture in terms of tea ceremony. 94pp. 5⅜ × 8½. 20070-1 Pa. $3.95

LIFE IN ANCIENT EGYPT, Adolf Erman. Fullest, most thorough, detailed older account with much not in more recent books, domestic life, religion, magic, medicine, commerce, much more. Many illustrations reproduce tomb paintings, carvings, hieroglyphs, etc. 597pp. 5⅜ × 8½. 22632-8 Pa. $10.95

SUNDIALS, Their Theory and Construction, Albert Waugh. Far and away the best, most thorough coverage of ideas, mathematics concerned, types, construction, adjusting anywhere. Simple, nontechnical treatment allows even children to build several of these dials. Over 100 illustrations. 230pp. 5⅜ × 8½. 22947-5 Pa. $7.95

DYNAMICS OF FLUIDS IN POROUS MEDIA, Jacob Bear. For advanced students of ground water hydrology, soil mechanics and physics, drainage and irrigation engineering, and more. 335 illustrations. Exercises, with answers. 784pp. 6⅛ × 9¼. 65675-6 Pa. $19.95

SONGS OF EXPERIENCE: Facsimile Reproduction with 26 Plates in Full Color, William Blake. 26 full-color plates from a rare 1826 edition. Includes "The Tyger," "London," "Holy Thursday," and other poems. Printed text of poems. 48pp. 5¼ × 7. 24636-1 Pa. $4.95

OLD-TIME VIGNETTES IN FULL COLOR, Carol Belanger Grafton (ed.). Over 390 charming, often sentimental illustrations, selected from archives of Victorian graphics—pretty women posing, children playing, food, flowers, kittens and puppies, smiling cherubs, birds and butterflies, much more. All copyright-free. 48pp. 9¼ × 12¼. 27269-9 Pa. $5.95

PERSPECTIVE FOR ARTISTS, Rex Vicat Cole. Depth, perspective of sky and sea, shadows, much more, not usually covered. 391 diagrams, 81 reproductions of drawings and paintings. 279pp. 5⅜ × 8½. 22487-2 Pa. $6.95

DRAWING THE LIVING FIGURE, Joseph Sheppard. Innovative approach to artistic anatomy focuses on specifics of surface anatomy, rather than muscles and bones. Over 170 drawings of live models in front, back and side views, and in widely varying poses. Accompanying diagrams. 177 illustrations. Introduction. Index. 144pp. 8⅜ × 11¼. 26723-7 Pa. $8.95

GOTHIC AND OLD ENGLISH ALPHABETS: 100 Complete Fonts, Dan X. Solo. Add power, elegance to posters, signs, other graphics with 100 stunning copyright-free alphabets: Blackstone, Dolbey, Germania, 97 more—including many lower-case, numerals, punctuation marks. 104pp. 8⅛ × 11. 24695-7 Pa. $8.95

HOW TO DO BEADWORK, Mary White. Fundamental book on craft from simple projects to five-bead chains and woven works. 106 illustrations. 142pp. 5⅜ × 8. 20697-1 Pa. $4.95

THE BOOK OF WOOD CARVING, Charles Marshall Sayers. Finest book for beginners discusses fundamentals and offers 34 designs. "Absolutely first rate . . . well thought out and well executed."—E. J. Tangerman. 118pp. 7¾ × 10⅝. 23654-4 Pa. $5.95

ILLUSTRATED CATALOG OF CIVIL WAR MILITARY GOODS: Union Army Weapons, Insignia, Uniform Accessories, and Other Equipment, Schuyler, Hartley, and Graham. Rare, profusely illustrated 1846 catalog includes Union Army uniform and dress regulations, arms and ammunition, coats, insignia, flags, swords, rifles, etc. 226 illustrations. 160pp. 9 × 12. 24939-5 Pa. $10.95

WOMEN'S FASHIONS OF THE EARLY 1900s: An Unabridged Republication of "New York Fashions, 1909," National Cloak & Suit Co. Rare catalog of mail-order fashions documents women's and children's clothing styles shortly after the turn of the century. Captions offer full descriptions, prices. Invaluable resource for fashion, costume historians. Approximately 725 illustrations. 128pp. 8⅜ × 11¼. 27276-1 Pa. $11.95

THE 1912 AND 1915 GUSTAV STICKLEY FURNITURE CATALOGS, Gustav Stickley. With over 200 detailed illustrations and descriptions, these two catalogs are essential reading and reference materials and identification guides for Stickley furniture. Captions cite materials, dimensions and prices. 112pp. 6½ × 9¼. 26676-1 Pa. $9.95

EARLY AMERICAN LOCOMOTIVES, John H. White, Jr. Finest locomotive engravings from early 19th century: historical (1804–74), main-line (after 1870), special, foreign, etc. 147 plates. 142pp. 11⅜ × 8¼. 22772-3 Pa. $10.95

THE TALL SHIPS OF TODAY IN PHOTOGRAPHS, Frank O. Braynard. Lavishly illustrated tribute to nearly 100 majestic contemporary sailing vessels: Amerigo Vespucci, Clearwater, Constitution, Eagle, Mayflower, Sea Cloud, Victory, many more. Authoritative captions provide statistics, background on each ship. 190 black-and-white photographs and illustrations. Introduction. 128pp. 8⅞ × 11¾. 27163-3 Pa. $13.95

EARLY NINETEENTH-CENTURY CRAFTS AND TRADES, Peter Stockham (ed.). Extremely rare 1807 volume describes to youngsters the crafts and trades of the day: brickmaker, weaver, dressmaker, bookbinder, ropemaker, saddler, many more. Quaint prose, charming illustrations for each craft. 20 black-and-white line illustrations. 192pp. 4⅝ × 6. 27293-1 Pa. $4.95

VICTORIAN FASHIONS AND COSTUMES FROM HARPER'S BAZAR, 1867–1898, Stella Blum (ed.). Day costumes, evening wear, sports clothes, shoes, hats, other accessories in over 1,000 detailed engravings. 320pp. 9⅜ × 12¼. 22990-4 Pa. $13.95

GUSTAV STICKLEY, THE CRAFTSMAN, Mary Ann Smith. Superb study surveys broad scope of Stickley's achievement, especially in architecture. Design philosophy, rise and fall of the Craftsman empire, descriptions and floor plans for many Craftsman houses, more. 86 black-and-white halftones. 31 line illustrations. Introduction. 208pp. 6½ × 9¼. 27210-9 Pa. $9.95

THE LONG ISLAND RAIL ROAD IN EARLY PHOTOGRAPHS, Ron Ziel. Over 220 rare photos, informative text document origin (1844) and development of rail service on Long Island. Vintage views of early trains, locomotives, stations, passengers, crews, much more. Captions. 8⅞ × 11¾. 26301-0 Pa. $13.95

THE BOOK OF OLD SHIPS: From Egyptian Galleys to Clipper Ships, Henry B. Culver. Superb, authoritative history of sailing vessels, with 80 magnificent line illustrations. Galley, bark, caravel, longship, whaler, many more. Detailed, informative text on each vessel by noted naval historian. Introduction. 256pp. 5⅜ × 8½. 27332-6 Pa. $6.95

TEN BOOKS ON ARCHITECTURE, Vitruvius. The most important book ever written on architecture. Early Roman aesthetics, technology, classical orders, site selection, all other aspects. Morgan translation. 331pp. 5⅜ × 8½. 20645-9 Pa. $8.95

THE HUMAN FIGURE IN MOTION, Eadweard Muybridge. More than 4,500 stopped-action photos, in action series, showing undraped men, women, children jumping, lying down, throwing, sitting, wrestling, carrying, etc. 390pp. 7⅞ × 10⅝. 20204-6 Clothbd. $24.95

TREES OF THE EASTERN AND CENTRAL UNITED STATES AND CANADA, William M. Harlow. Best one-volume guide to 140 trees. Full descriptions, woodlore, range, etc. Over 600 illustrations. Handy size. 288pp. 4½ × 6⅜. 20395-6 Pa. $5.95

SONGS OF WESTERN BIRDS, Dr. Donald J. Borror. Complete song and call repertoire of 60 western species, including flycatchers, juncoes, cactus wrens, many more—includes fully illustrated booklet. Cassette and manual 99913-0 $8.95

GROWING AND USING HERBS AND SPICES, Milo Miloradovich. Versatile handbook provides all the information needed for cultivation and use of all the herbs and spices available in North America. 4 illustrations. Index. Glossary. 236pp. 5⅜ × 8½. 25058-X Pa. $6.95

BIG BOOK OF MAZES AND LABYRINTHS, Walter Shepherd. 50 mazes and labyrinths in all—classical, solid, ripple, and more—in one great volume. Perfect inexpensive puzzler for clever youngsters. Full solutions. 112pp. 8⅛ × 11. 22951-3 Pa. $4.95

PIANO TUNING, J. Cree Fischer. Clearest, best book for beginner, amateur. Simple repairs, raising dropped notes, tuning by easy method of flattened fifths. No previous skills needed. 4 illustrations. 201pp. 5⅜ × 8½.   23267-0 Pa. $5.95

A SOURCE BOOK IN THEATRICAL HISTORY, A. M. Nagler. Contemporary observers on acting, directing, make-up, costuming, stage props, machinery, scene design, from Ancient Greece to Chekhov. 611pp. 5⅜ × 8½.   20515-0 Pa. $11.95

THE COMPLETE NONSENSE OF EDWARD LEAR, Edward Lear. All nonsense limericks, zany alphabets, Owl and Pussycat, songs, nonsense botany, etc., illustrated by Lear. Total of 320pp. 5⅜ × 8½. (USO)   20167-8 Pa. $6.95

VICTORIAN PARLOUR POETRY: An Annotated Anthology, Michael R. Turner. 117 gems by Longfellow, Tennyson, Browning, many lesser-known poets. "The Village Blacksmith," "Curfew Must Not Ring Tonight," "Only a Baby Small," dozens more, often difficult to find elsewhere. Index of poets, titles, first lines. xxiii + 325pp. 5⅜ × 8¼.   27044-0 Pa. $8.95

DUBLINERS, James Joyce. Fifteen stories offer vivid, tightly focused observations of the lives of Dublin's poorer classes. At least one, "The Dead," is considered a masterpiece. Reprinted complete and unabridged from standard edition. 160pp. 5³⁄₁₆ × 8¼.   26870-5 Pa. $1.00

THE HAUNTED MONASTERY and THE CHINESE MAZE MURDERS, Robert van Gulik. Two full novels by van Gulik, set in 7th-century China, continue adventures of Judge Dee and his companions. An evil Taoist monastery, seemingly supernatural events; overgrown topiary maze hides strange crimes. 27 illustrations. 328pp. 5⅜ × 8½.   23502-5 Pa. $7.95

THE BOOK OF THE SACRED MAGIC OF ABRAMELIN THE MAGE, translated by S. MacGregor Mathers. Medieval manuscript of ceremonial magic. Basic document in Aleister Crowley, Golden Dawn groups. 268pp. 5⅜ × 8½.
23211-5 Pa. $8.95

NEW RUSSIAN-ENGLISH AND ENGLISH-RUSSIAN DICTIONARY, M. A. O'Brien. This is a remarkably handy Russian dictionary, containing a surprising amount of information, including over 70,000 entries. 366pp. 4½ × 6⅛.
20208-9 Pa. $9.95

HISTORIC HOMES OF THE AMERICAN PRESIDENTS, Second, Revised Edition, Irvin Haas. A traveler's guide to American Presidential homes, most open to the public, depicting and describing homes occupied by every American President from George Washington to George Bush. With visiting hours, admission charges, travel routes. 175 photographs. Index. 160pp. 8¼ × 11. 26751-2 Pa. $10.95

NEW YORK IN THE FORTIES, Andreas Feininger. 162 brilliant photographs by the well-known photographer, formerly with *Life* magazine. Commuters, shoppers, Times Square at night, much else from city at its peak. Captions by John von Hartz. 181pp. 9¼ × 10¾.   23585-8 Pa. $12.95

INDIAN SIGN LANGUAGE, William Tomkins. Over 525 signs developed by Sioux and other tribes. Written instructions and diagrams. Also 290 pictographs. 111pp. 6⅛ × 9¼.   22029-X Pa. $3.50

ANATOMY: A Complete Guide for Artists, Joseph Sheppard. A master of figure drawing shows artists how to render human anatomy convincingly. Over 460 illustrations. 224pp. 8⅜ × 11¼. 27279-6 Pa. $10.95

MEDIEVAL CALLIGRAPHY: Its History and Technique, Marc Drogin. Spirited history, comprehensive instruction manual covers 13 styles (ca. 4th century thru 15th). Excellent photographs; directions for duplicating medieval techniques with modern tools. 224pp. 8⅜ × 11¼. 26142-5 Pa. $11.95

DRIED FLOWERS: How to Prepare Them, Sarah Whitlock and Martha Rankin. Complete instructions on how to use silica gel, meal and borax, perlite aggregate, sand and borax, glycerine and water to create attractive permanent flower arrangements. 12 illustrations. 32pp. 5⅜ × 8½. 21802-3 Pa. $1.00

EASY-TO-MAKE BIRD FEEDERS FOR WOODWORKERS, Scott D. Campbell. Detailed, simple-to-use guide for designing, constructing, caring for and using feeders. Text, illustrations for 12 classic and contemporary designs. 96pp. 5⅜ × 8½. 25847-5 Pa. $2.95

OLD-TIME CRAFTS AND TRADES, Peter Stockham. An 1807 book created to teach children about crafts and trades open to them as future careers. It describes in detailed, nontechnical terms 24 different occupations, among them coachmaker, gardener, hairdresser, lacemaker, shoemaker, wheelwright, copper-plate printer, milliner, trunkmaker, merchant and brewer. Finely detailed engravings illustrate each occupation. 192pp. 4⅝ × 6. 27398-9 Pa. $4.95

THE HISTORY OF UNDERCLOTHES, C. Willett Cunnington and Phyllis Cunnington. Fascinating, well-documented survey covering six centuries of English undergarments, enhanced with over 100 illustrations: 12th-century laced-up bodice, footed long drawers (1795), 19th-century bustles, 19th-century corsets for men, Victorian "bust improvers," much more. 272pp. 5⅜ × 8¼. 27124-2 Pa. $9.95

ARTS AND CRAFTS FURNITURE: The Complete Brooks Catalog of 1912, Brooks Manufacturing Co. Photos and detailed descriptions of more than 150 now very collectible furniture designs from the Arts and Crafts movement depict davenports, settees, buffets, desks, tables, chairs, bedsteads, dressers and more, all built of solid, quarter-sawed oak. Invaluable for students and enthusiasts of antiques, Americana and the decorative arts. 80pp. 6½ × 9¼. 27471-3 Pa. $7.95

HOW WE INVENTED THE AIRPLANE: An Illustrated History, Orville Wright. Fascinating firsthand account covers early experiments, construction of planes and motors, first flights, much more. Introduction and commentary by Fred C. Kelly. 76 photographs. 96pp. 8¼ × 11. 25662-6 Pa. $8.95

THE ARTS OF THE SAILOR: Knotting, Splicing and Ropework, Hervey Garrett Smith. Indispensable shipboard reference covers tools, basic knots and useful hitches; handsewing and canvas work, more. Over 100 illustrations. Delightful reading for sea lovers. 256pp. 5⅜ × 8½. 26440-8 Pa. $7.95

FRANK LLOYD WRIGHT'S FALLINGWATER: The House and Its History, Second, Revised Edition, Donald Hoffmann. A total revision—both in text and illustrations—of the standard document on Fallingwater, the boldest, most personal architectural statement of Wright's mature years, updated with valuable new material from the recently opened Frank Lloyd Wright Archives. "Fascinating"—*The New York Times.* 116 illustrations. 128pp. 9¼ × 10¾. 27430-6 Pa. $10.95

PHOTOGRAPHIC SKETCHBOOK OF THE CIVIL WAR, Alexander Gardner. 100 photos taken on field during the Civil War. Famous shots of Manassas, Harper's Ferry, Lincoln, Richmond, slave pens, etc. 244pp. 10⅝ × 8¼.
22731-6 Pa. $9.95

FIVE ACRES AND INDEPENDENCE, Maurice G. Kains. Great back-to-the-land classic explains basics of self-sufficient farming. The one book to get. 95 illustrations. 397pp. 5⅜ × 8½.
20974-1 Pa. $7.95

SONGS OF EASTERN BIRDS, Dr. Donald J. Borror. Songs and calls of 60 species most common to eastern U.S.: warblers, woodpeckers, flycatchers, thrushes, larks, many more in high-quality recording.
Cassette and manual 99912-2 $8.95

A MODERN HERBAL, Margaret Grieve. Much the fullest, most exact, most useful compilation of herbal material. Gigantic alphabetical encyclopedia, from aconite to zedoary, gives botanical information, medical properties, folklore, economic uses, much else. Indispensable to serious reader. 161 illustrations. 888pp. 6½ × 9¼. 2-vol. set. (USO)
Vol. I: 22798-7 Pa. $9.95
Vol. II: 22799-5 Pa. $9.95

HIDDEN TREASURE MAZE BOOK, Dave Phillips. Solve 34 challenging mazes accompanied by heroic tales of adventure. Evil dragons, people-eating plants, bloodthirsty giants, many more dangerous adversaries lurk at every twist and turn. 34 mazes, stories, solutions. 48pp. 8¼ × 11.
24566-7 Pa. $2.95

LETTERS OF W. A. MOZART, Wolfgang A. Mozart. Remarkable letters show bawdy wit, humor, imagination, musical insights, contemporary musical world; includes some letters from Leopold Mozart. 276pp. 5⅜ × 8½.
22859-2 Pa. $7.95

BASIC PRINCIPLES OF CLASSICAL BALLET, Agrippina Vaganova. Great Russian theoretician, teacher explains methods for teaching classical ballet. 118 illustrations. 175pp. 5⅜ × 8½.
22036-2 Pa. $4.95

THE JUMPING FROG, Mark Twain. Revenge edition. The original story of The Celebrated Jumping Frog of Calaveras County, a hapless French translation, and Twain's hilarious "retranslation" from the French. 12 illustrations. 66pp. 5⅜ × 8½.
22686-7 Pa. $3.95

BEST REMEMBERED POEMS, Martin Gardner (ed.). The 126 poems in this superb collection of 19th- and 20th-century British and American verse range from Shelley's "To a Skylark" to the impassioned "Renascence" of Edna St. Vincent Millay and to Edward Lear's whimsical "The Owl and the Pussycat." 224pp. 5⅜ × 8½.
27165-X Pa. $4.95

COMPLETE SONNETS, William Shakespeare. Over 150 exquisite poems deal with love, friendship, the tyranny of time, beauty's evanescence, death and other themes in language of remarkable power, precision and beauty. Glossary of archaic terms. 80pp. 5³⁄₁₆ × 8¼.
26686-9 Pa. $1.00

BODIES IN A BOOKSHOP, R. T. Campbell. Challenging mystery of blackmail and murder with ingenious plot and superbly drawn characters. In the best tradition of British suspense fiction. 192pp. 5⅜ × 8½.
24720-1 Pa. $5.95

THE WIT AND HUMOR OF OSCAR WILDE, Alvin Redman (ed.). More than 1,000 ripostes, paradoxes, wisecracks: Work is the curse of the drinking classes; I can resist everything except temptation; etc. 258pp. 5⅜ × 8½. 20602-5 Pa. $5.95

SHAKESPEARE LEXICON AND QUOTATION DICTIONARY, Alexander Schmidt. Full definitions, locations, shades of meaning in every word in plays and poems. More than 50,000 exact quotations. 1,485pp. 6½ × 9¼. 2-vol. set.
Vol. I: 22726-X Pa. $16.95
Vol. 2: 22727-8 Pa. $15.95

SELECTED POEMS, Emily Dickinson. Over 100 best-known, best-loved poems by one of America's foremost poets, reprinted from authoritative early editions. No comparable edition at this price. Index of first lines. 64pp. 5³⁄₁₆ × 8¼.
26466-1 Pa. $1.00

CELEBRATED CASES OF JUDGE DEE (DEE GOONG AN), translated by Robert van Gulik. Authentic 18th-century Chinese detective novel; Dee and associates solve three interlocked cases. Led to van Gulik's own stories with same characters. Extensive introduction. 9 illustrations. 237pp. 5⅜ × 8½.
23337-5 Pa. $6.95

THE MALLEUS MALEFICARUM OF KRAMER AND SPRENGER, translated by Montague Summers. Full text of most important witchhunter's "bible," used by both Catholics and Protestants. 278pp. 6⅝ × 10. 22802-9 Pa. $11.95

SPANISH STORIES/CUENTOS ESPAÑOLES: A Dual-Language Book, Angel Flores (ed.). Unique format offers 13 great stories in Spanish by Cervantes, Borges, others. Faithful English translations on facing pages. 352pp. 5⅜ × 8½.
25399-6 Pa. $8.95

THE CHICAGO WORLD'S FAIR OF 1893: A Photographic Record, Stanley Appelbaum (ed.). 128 rare photos show 200 buildings, Beaux-Arts architecture, Midway, original Ferris Wheel, Edison's kinetoscope, more. Architectural emphasis; full text. 116pp. 8¼ × 11. 23990-X Pa. $9.95

OLD QUEENS, N.Y., IN EARLY PHOTOGRAPHS, Vincent F. Seyfried and William Asadorian. Over 160 rare photographs of Maspeth, Jamaica, Jackson Heights, and other areas. Vintage views of DeWitt Clinton mansion, 1939 World's Fair and more. Captions. 192pp. 8⅞ × 11. 26358-4 Pa. $12.95

CAPTURED BY THE INDIANS: 15 Firsthand Accounts, 1750–1870, Frederick Drimmer. Astounding true historical accounts of grisly torture, bloody conflicts, relentless pursuits, miraculous escapes and more, by people who lived to tell the tale. 384pp. 5⅜ × 8½. 24901-8 Pa. $8.95

THE WORLD'S GREAT SPEECHES, Lewis Copeland and Lawrence W. Lamm (eds.). Vast collection of 278 speeches of Greeks to 1970. Powerful and effective models; unique look at history. 842pp. 5⅜ × 8½. 20468-5 Pa. $14.95

THE BOOK OF THE SWORD, Sir Richard F. Burton. Great Victorian scholar/adventurer's eloquent, erudite history of the "queen of weapons"—from prehistory to early Roman Empire. Evolution and development of early swords, variations (sabre, broadsword, cutlass, scimitar, etc.), much more. 336pp. 6⅛ × 9¼. 25434-8 Pa. $8.95

AUTOBIOGRAPHY: The Story of My Experiments with Truth, Mohandas K. Gandhi. Boyhood, legal studies, purification, the growth of the Satyagraha (nonviolent protest) movement. Critical, inspiring work of the man responsible for the freedom of India. 480pp. 5⅜ × 8½. (USO) 24593-4 Pa. $8.95

CELTIC MYTHS AND LEGENDS, T. W. Rolleston. Masterful retelling of Irish and Welsh stories and tales. Cuchulain, King Arthur, Deirdre, the Grail, many more. First paperback edition. 58 full-page illustrations. 512pp. 5⅜ × 8½. 26507-2 Pa. $9.95

THE PRINCIPLES OF PSYCHOLOGY, William James. Famous long course complete, unabridged. Stream of thought, time perception, memory, experimental methods; great work decades ahead of its time. 94 figures. 1,391pp. 5⅜ × 8½. 2-vol. set.
Vol. I: 20381-6 Pa. $12.95
Vol. II: 20382-4 Pa. $12.95

THE WORLD AS WILL AND REPRESENTATION, Arthur Schopenhauer. Definitive English translation of Schopenhauer's life work, correcting more than 1,000 errors, omissions in earlier translations. Translated by E. F. J. Payne. Total of 1,269pp. 5⅜ × 8½. 2-vol. set.
Vol. 1: 21761-2 Pa. $11.95
Vol. 2: 21762-0 Pa. $11.95

MAGIC AND MYSTERY IN TIBET, Madame Alexandra David-Neel. Experiences among lamas, magicians, sages, sorcerers, Bonpa wizards. A true psychic discovery. 32 illustrations. 321pp. 5⅜ × 8½. (USO) 22682-4 Pa. $8.95

THE EGYPTIAN BOOK OF THE DEAD, E. A. Wallis Budge. Complete reproduction of Ani's papyrus, finest ever found. Full hieroglyphic text, interlinear transliteration, word-for-word translation, smooth translation. 533pp. 6½ × 9¼. 21866-X Pa. $9.95

MATHEMATICS FOR THE NONMATHEMATICIAN, Morris Kline. Detailed, college-level treatment of mathematics in cultural and historical context, with numerous exercises. Recommended Reading Lists. Tables. Numerous figures. 641pp. 5⅜ × 8½. 24823-2 Pa. $11.95

THEORY OF WING SECTIONS: Including a Summary of Airfoil Data, Ira H. Abbott and A. E. von Doenhoff. Concise compilation of subsonic aerodynamic characteristics of NACA wing sections, plus description of theory. 350pp. of tables. 693pp. 5⅜ × 8½. 60586-8 Pa. $14.95

THE RIME OF THE ANCIENT MARINER, Gustave Doré, S. T. Coleridge. Doré's finest work; 34 plates capture moods, subtleties of poem. Flawless full-size reproductions printed on facing pages with authoritative text of poem. "Beautiful. Simply beautiful."—*Publisher's Weekly*. 77pp. 9¼ × 12. 22305-1 Pa. $6.95

NORTH AMERICAN INDIAN DESIGNS FOR ARTISTS AND CRAFTSPEOPLE, Eva Wilson. Over 360 authentic copyright-free designs adapted from Navajo blankets, Hopi pottery, Sioux buffalo hides, more. Geometrics, symbolic figures, plant and animal motifs, etc. 128pp. 8⅜ × 11. (EUK) 25341-4 Pa. $7.95

SCULPTURE: Principles and Practice, Louis Slobodkin. Step-by-step approach to clay, plaster, metals, stone; classical and modern. 253 drawings, photos. 255pp. 8⅛ × 11. 22960-2 Pa. $10.95

CATALOG OF DOVER BOOKS

THE INFLUENCE OF SEA POWER UPON HISTORY, 1660–1783, A. T. Mahan. Influential classic of naval history and tactics still used as text in war colleges. First paperback edition. 4 maps. 24 battle plans. 640pp. 5⅜ × 8½.
25509-3 Pa. $12.95

THE STORY OF THE TITANIC AS TOLD BY ITS SURVIVORS, Jack Winocour (ed.). What it was really like. Panic, despair, shocking inefficiency, and a little heroism. More thrilling than any fictional account. 26 illustrations. 320pp. 5⅜ × 8½. 20610-6 Pa. $8.95

FAIRY AND FOLK TALES OF THE IRISH PEASANTRY, William Butler Yeats (ed.). Treasury of 64 tales from the twilight world of Celtic myth and legend: "The Soul Cages," "The Kildare Pooka," "King O'Toole and his Goose," many more. Introduction and Notes by W. B. Yeats. 352pp. 5⅜ × 8½. 26941-8 Pa. $8.95

BUDDHIST MAHAYANA TEXTS, E. B. Cowell and Others (eds.). Superb, accurate translations of basic documents in Mahayana Buddhism, highly important in history of religions. The Buddha-karita of Asvaghosha, Larger Sukhavativyuha, more. 448pp. 5⅜ × 8½. 25552-2 Pa. $9.95

ONE TWO THREE . . . INFINITY: Facts and Speculations of Science, George Gamow. Great physicist's fascinating, readable overview of contemporary science: number theory, relativity, fourth dimension, entropy, genes, atomic structure, much more. 128 illustrations. Index. 352pp. 5⅜ × 8½. 25664-2 Pa. $8.95

ENGINEERING IN HISTORY, Richard Shelton Kirby, et al. Broad, nontechnical survey of history's major technological advances: birth of Greek science, industrial revolution, electricity and applied science, 20th-century automation, much more. 181 illustrations. ". . . excellent . . ."—Isis. Bibliography. vii + 530pp. 5⅜ × 8¼.
26412-2 Pa. $14.95

Prices subject to change without notice.

Available at your book dealer or write for free catalog to Dept. GI, Dover Publications, Inc., 31 East 2nd St., Mineola, N.Y. 11501. Dover publishes more than 500 books each year on science, elementary and advanced mathematics, biology, music, art, literary history, social sciences and other areas.